ISLAM IN
WEST AFRICA

ISLAM IN WEST AFRICA

By

J. SPENCER TRIMINGHAM

OXFORD
AT THE CLARENDON PRESS
1959

Oxford University Press, Amen House, London E.C.4

GLASGOW NEW YORK TORONTO MELBOURNE WELLINGTON
BOMBAY CALCUTTA MADRAS KARACHI KUALA LUMPUR
CAPE TOWN IBADAN NAIROBI ACCRA

PRINTED IN GREAT BRITAIN
AT THE UNIVERSITY PRESS, OXFORD
BY VIVIAN RIDLER
PRINTER TO THE UNIVERSITY

Preface

THIS book, which continues my studies of Islam in Africa, is primarily a phenomenological study of the religious life of West African Muslims. My special aim has been to try to assess what has been the result of the impact of Islam, the way it influences African society, and, conversely, the way the African community moulds the Islam it receives. It is concerned with what is, not what ought to be; with the living beliefs and practices of particular peoples, not with the ideal of Islamic thought and practice. At the same time it embraces more than the actual study of Islam in West Africa since it is concerned with the way Africans have assimilated it, the degree to which it fulfils their religious aspirations, and, where these cannot find expression in Islam, in what directions they are fulfilled.

Though a study of this nature, concerned with the interaction of cultures, is necessarily based on the past, the historical background has not been included since the writer has completed a study of the history of Islam in West Africa. A summary would only duplicate the material and prove inadequate since not all the conclusions accord with commonly accepted ideas of West African Islamic history and could not be clarified in a few lines.

The material upon which this study is primarily based was collected during a year's survey undertaken in 1952 and sponsored by the Church Missionary Society and the Methodist Missionary Society. In addition, it takes into account secondhand information based on the work of others. Such a tour embracing such a vast area, inhabited by so many and contrasting peoples, has severe limitations. I do not claim an exactness of knowledge and insight into the religion of the many peoples the area embraces. That could only have been acquired by close study of one group over a similar period. But to study one community would have been to defeat the aim I had in view. At the same time the material collected was so copious that it actually proved an embarrassment and the exigencies of publication have necessitated my being severely selective.

There are many elements in the treasury of my experience which have not found expression in this book. But the form in which the survey was conceived, carried out, and ultimately embodied in a book was unsuitable for a vertical as contrasted with a horizontal survey. I do not think the material could have been collected without such planning, but other questions arose whilst in Africa and whilst writing it which, given the plan and the framework, could not be pursued. At the same time it must be pointed out that these deeper studies cannot be done except on a firm foundation of historical and empirical research. With that as a background the way is open for a more imaginative approach to the religious survey, that of intuitive understanding and deeper insight. This, however, is not the place to elaborate an approach to religious survey which has not been attempted.

I wish to record my thanks to the two societies which made my tour possible and to the University of Glasgow for providing me with the opportunity to work on the material collected. I must also express an especial debt of gratitude to the Africans with whom I worked, for without their help whatever I have been able to do, however imperfectly, would have been impossible. The second chapter was delivered at the Selly Oak Colleges, Birmingham, in November 1956 as the James Long Lectures.

J. S. T.

University of Glasgow

CONTENTS

MAP

ABBREVIATIONS

A.É.F.	Afrique Équatoriale Française.
Afr. Fr. R.C.	*Bulletin du Comité de l'Afrique Française: Renseignements Coloniaux.*
A.O.F.	Afrique Occidentale Française.
Barth, *Travels*	H. Barth, *Travels and Discoveries in North and Central Africa* (1849–55), 5 vols., 1857.
Bull. Com. Ét. A.O.F.	*Bulletin du Comité d'Études historiques et scientifiques de l'Afrique Occidentale Française.*
Bull. I.F.A.N.	*Bulletin de l'Institut Français de l'Afrique Noire.*
D. Isl.	*Der Islam.*
Delafosse, *H.S.N.*	M. Delafosse, *Haut-Sénégal et Niger*, 3 vols., Paris, 1912.
J.R.A.I.	*Journal of the Royal Anthropological Institute.*
J. Soc. Afr.	*Journal de la Société des Africanistes.*
Marty, *Guinée*	P. Marty, *L'Islam en Guinée: Fouta-Diallon*, Paris, 1921.
Marty, *Soudan*	P. Marty, *Études sur l'Islam et les Tribus du Soudan*, 4 vols., Paris, 1920.
N. Afr.	*Notes Africaines*, Dakar.
R.M.M.	*Revue du Monde Musulman.*
Palmer, *Sud. Mem.*	H. R. Palmer, *Sudanese Memoirs*, 3 vols., Lagos, 1928.

I

Geographical and Social Setting

1. THE LAND

THE deep influence which geography exercises upon man is as evident in West Africa, where there are no outstanding physical characteristics and where climate dominates, as in a country of extreme contrasts like Ethiopia. Its central characteristic is the vast savanna bounded by desert or semi-desert steppe in the north and rain forests in the south. In contrast with these boundary regions it offers a type of environment which lends itself to migrations, culture contact, and the formation of new social and political groupings. It is not, therefore, by chance that this savanna is the main historical region of West Africa and its peoples the most influenced by Islam.

The Arabs called the country south of the Sahara *Bilād as-Sūdān*, 'Land of the Blacks', in opposition to *Bilād al-Bīḍān*, 'Land of the Whites', that is, North Africa and the Sahara. In normal usage it is restricted to a wide band south of the Sahara stretching across Africa from the Atlantic in the west to the Abyssinian plateaux in the east, and from the Sahara in the north to the equatorial forest. East Africa, although also a land of blacks, was known as 'Land of the Zanj'. The Sudan is divided into three main regions: western Sudan, whose waters drain either into the coastal rivers or into the Niger; central Sudan, which is orientated partly towards the Niger and Benue and partly towards the Chad; and eastern Sudan, which belongs to the basin of the Nile. This study is restricted to western and central Sudan.

West Africa is essentially a climatic region, for no physical barriers separate it from the Sahara in the north and equatorial regions in the south. Zones of climate and vegetation depend upon the intensity of the rain and length of the rainy season. During winter months the hot, dry north-easterly wind known as the *harmattan* blows. This then recedes towards the north and its opposite, the south-west monsoon, a warm, humid wind coming from the ocean, appears. In coastal regions the rainy season begins in April and continues to mid-July, then the rains gradually decrease, to be followed in October by another short rainy season. Sudanese regions have only two seasons, a wet and a dry. In this climatic whole parallelism is the dominant trait. A series of bands, differentiated by gradations of rainfall and types of vegetation, mark stages of transition from Sahara to humid forest. The gradualness of transition makes the stages difficult to define, but four main climatic zones are sufficiently clear.

The south Saharan Zone has the usual features of a desert zone: rare localized rain and a ground temperature much hotter than that of the air by day and much colder at night. The Sahilian Zone (Arabic *sāḥil*, 'shore', i.e. 'borderland') is distinguished from the Sahara by having a regular but short rainy season which provides pasture for camels and goats, but is insufficient for cultivation without irrigation. On the Mauritanian and Senegal coasts is a different climatic region known as the Sub-Canarian. The Sudanese Zone, which occupies the greater part of West Africa, is marked by two maxima and two minima of temperature, and especially by the regular alternation of a rainy and dry season. Between the south Sudanese climate and the dense forest stretches a band of transition belonging to the Guinean Zone but more attenuated and covered with savanna. In the Guinean Zone (also called Liberio-Dahomean) temperatures are more equal than in the Sudanese Zone and the humidity excessive. It has one season of rain from April to November with a lull in August–September. Precipitation may reach two metres or even three. Geographers apply the term 'Guinean' to all that is 'equatorial' in West Africa (two seasons of rain or one long rainy season) and 'Sudanese' to what is 'tropical' (one rainy and one dry season).

Vegetable life depends largely upon climate, and botanical zoning coincides approximately with climatical zoning. Variations are due to the nature of the soil and the relief of the country which influence temperature and rains and consequently vegetable life. The following botanical zones are distinguished.

The south Saharan Zone is less desolate than that of the Algerian Sahara. It consists of vast stretches of steppe, covered here and there with a xerophyte vegetation. The soil is not in itself sterile, and where it rains the pasture enables camels and sheep to be bred. It possesses a few oasis regions, of which those of the west (Ḥawḍ) and centre (Azawād) are poor, but those of the east (Air and Bilma) have palm groves and cultivation. It is essentially a zone of white nomads, with black cultivators predominating in the oases.

The Sahilian Zone, which forms a band of transition between the Sahara and Sudan, is a region of grassy plains interspersed with thornbush and acacia where the steppe changes to savanna and bush country. The grass is short but provides good pasturage for the horses and humped cattle of the semi-nomads, whilst agriculture (millet and ground-nuts) enables a sedentary black population, numerically superior to the white or mixed pastorals, to support life. The Sub-Canarian climate zone, which borders the Atlantic, gives rise to a peculiar botanic zone distinguishable from the Sahilian of the same latitude by greater humidity.

The Sudanese Zone provides the most characteristic scenery of West Africa. Its aspect of perennial gramineous plants and trees with caducous leaves changes according to the season. In the dry season the trees shed their leaves and the grass becomes harsh and yellow or disappears altogether. Towards the end of this season, after the bush has been fired, leaving scorched tree-trunks sticking out of the ground, it looks its worst. But then, even before the rains begin, the trees begin to put forth leaves and, with the onset of the rains, grass grows with exceeding rapidity and the country breathes once more.

Although the regularity of the rains give these vast savanna lands a remarkable unity they are not of uniform monotony. The herbaceous savanna, where the rains are sufficiently prolonged and temperatures not too high, is characterized by exceedingly high grasses, especially in humid depressions, though the constancy of the *harmattan* hinders tree development. On the other hand, in forest grassland clumps of great trees stand out of the expanse of grass; in typical bush country grasses mingle with shrubs to form impenetrable thickets; whilst on the laterite plateaux are found open forests characterized by stunted and gnarled trees. From the human point of view the Sudanese Zone is a land of agriculture, where basic food crops of millet, maize, and yam, and export crops such as ground-nuts, cotton, tobacco, and indigo, can be grown. At the same time it is a land where sheep, goats, and cattle find abundant herbage.

These different types of savanna continue up to the edge of the dense forest, through the more humid Guinean Zone. This is still savanna, but more vigorous than that of the Sudanese Zone, with high grass and clumps of trees which here and there form true forests. A new feature is the 'forest galleries', bands of dense forest fringing the courses of the streams. Agriculture changes little in character, but manioc, yam, and banana tend to predominate over millet and maize as basic food crops. Without any noticeable transition this wooded savanna changes into the Forest Zone. This is not continuous. It occupies the southern parts of French Guinée, Sierra Leone, Liberia, the Ivory Coast, and Ghana,[1]

[1] The ancient south-saḥaran state is distinguished in this book as Gāna from Ghana, the former Gold Coast.

and has blocks in Togo, Dahomey, and south Nigeria which link with the equatorial forest of the Congo basin.

In all regions situated north of 17° parallel the valleys are normally dry, only exceptionally filled with water for a few hours, but from the Gulf of Guinea up to 6° lat. N. the rivers are full all the year. In the savanna region between these two extremes only a few rivers have water the whole year round. These are marked by a great increase in volume during the rainy season and in country without relief often cover large tracts of country. The greatest rivers, the Senegal and Niger, which never dry up, are very complex. They are drawn towards the Sahara by the general slope of the land and thus bring to arid country water which has fallen in rainy regions. The Senegal at first heads north-east, then describes a great bend to the north-west before falling into the sea. The Niger has the same significance for the Sudan that the Nile has for Egypt, and its course traverses the most diverse gradations of climate and vegetation. Born in Sierra Leone it flows through forest country in its lower course, then through savanna and steppe, and at the apex of its great bend makes an incursion into the Sahara where its valley forms an oasis in an utterly barren land. Below Timbuktu the river concentrates into one stream, then turns south to fall eventually into the Gulf of Guinea. From the east the Niger receives the waters of one major tributary, the Benue, which has provided another way of migration.

2. MAN AND HIS ENVIRONMENT

A similar parallel zoning is found in the distribution of types of life. In the Saharan and Sahilian steppes, in the mountainous zone of Futa Jalon, and in arid parts of the steppe, the breeding of camels, sheep, goats, and cattle provides the chief means for collective life. Pastoralists, conditioned by the need for water and herbage, are forced to migrate during the rains but remain close to points of water during the dry season. Their herds are their capital upon which they encroach as little as possible. They enable them to practise caravan traffic; milk is a basic element in their diet, and their fleeces and skins an indispensable part of their material life. Their dwellings reflect the need to move easily. The Moors and certain Tuareg have tents of wool or camel hair, the majority of the Tuareg have hemispherical huts of skins and mats, and the Fulbe beehive huts of plaited straw.

Whilst the pastoral life is the natural life of the whites, sedentary agriculture is that of the blacks and is characteristic of the vast savanna.

Every aspect of traditional life is bound up with agriculture, but that has not excluded the adoption of new culture, especially since the Portuguese landed on the west coast. Animal breeding is also characteristic of the northern Sudan, but since this involves transhumance they are cared for by Fulbe. The Negro is tied to his village with its fenced family compounds and nearby plantations where work is collective. The relationship of the Negro cultivator to the land, however, contrasts with that of the Egyptian and European peasant. The Negro's subsistence is derived from a shifting cultivation worked by the family as a unit. In contrast to the peasant on irrigated lands he changes his plot every year. He burns the bush, scratches the soil, and after harvest moves on to work another plot. Consequently his roots in the land are light and land rights have not been individualized. His bonds are to his family, not a plot of earth.

Four main types of agriculture are found according to zoning: that dependent upon artificial irrigation (Saharan oases, Senegal and Niger banks) which, even in the Sahara, is an occupation of blacks; rainy-season agriculture with animal breeding, the last being dependent upon the penetration of Fulbe pastoralists; rainy-season agriculture without cattle, characteristic of the Sudanese savanna and humid steppe; and permanent agriculture with hoe and dibble, practised in the forest region.

Since the culture areas correspond roughly with the ecological areas there is a basic relationship between material culture and environment. Thus leatherwork is characteristic of the northern Sudan where cattle are plenteous, camel-hair weaving of the Sahara, and wood-carving of the Guinean Zone. Similarly, architectural types can be equated with the botanical zones. Like the dwellings of nomads those of cultivators are closely related to the nature of the country and type of material available, but they are permanent constructions. In the Sahil and northern Sudan, where it rains during only three or four months of the year, houses are constructed of earth and mud bricks; in the savanna, where good wood is rare, they are built of thorny wood and gramineous plants; and in the forest region wood, bark, and leaves are used. The most widespread type of house in the zone between the Sahil and forest is the cylindrical hut with clay walls and a conical roof of straw supported by stays of wood, bamboo, or raffia. In the forest regions, owing to the heavy rains and type of material available, houses are rectangular, having gabled, double-pitched roofs made of bark and leaves. Within each zone the *genius loci* moulds the style and individualizes the structures.

Sudanese civilizations, being essentially agricultural, are based on villages. Their siting depends on the type of country. In the past the great valleys, being the routes of invasion currents, were not thickly populated. Weak tribes took refuge in less accessible parts such as mountains and swamps. Along the great rivers the inhabitants are mainly fishers. In the Sudan villages are compact rather than dispersed, except among people like the Fulbe dependent upon animal breeding and the Mossi with a strong system of public security. In the past the forest peoples, being gatherers and hunters, lived in scattered family settlements. But most Sudanese villages are compact, divided into family compounds by narrow winding streets; some are open, others enclosed by a wall or fence, others fortified with a palisade and ditch. In the northern Sudan the mud walls enclosed a true town with markets, industries, and even gardens and fields which enabled them to support a long siege.

3. RELIGION AND SOCIETY

An outline of the relationship of African religion and society is a necessary prelude to the subsequent study of the effect of Islam. So bound up are they that neither can be understood in isolation, for religion animates and regulates every aspect of life.

Africans believe in a Supreme Being who created the whole cosmos. It is regarded, though not necessarily worshipped, as creator and ultimate source of all life, but in contrast to the created worlds of spirits It is impersonal, unknowable, and communion with It is impossible.The Creator is the generator of spirit force which, after animating the various forms of creation, returns to the Creator. The world is created in harmony. The forms of creation, temporary receptacles of divine force, radiate it, and the interaction of radiations may disturb the harmony of the divine cosmos. The purpose of the all-embracing ritual of village life is to maintain or restore the harmony. This basic conception of power pervading the universe, possessed by ancestors, men, animals, and things, makes the world a sphere of dynamic relationship between forces. Religion is primarily ritual, the action of man to maintain power in equilibrium and preserve the harmony of this dynamic cosmos.

Ritual action has a double aspect, the cult of ancestral spirits and the cult of the spirit forces of nature. Man never dies because life force is eternal. Death is caused through disruption of the harmony of forces, but the dead remain integrally associated with their earthly family. The basic cell of life is the family. The harmonizer and restorer is the head of the family. He is the priest of the family cults and earthly steward of the family estates; in other words, he is the trustee to the ancestors for the welfare of the family and its heritage.

Besides the spirits of ancestors men have to reckon with the spirits of all that is living. Hence derive beliefs and ritual surrounding fecundity and the cyclic resurrection of vegetation. The cycle of labour, from the first clearing of the land to the final reaping, cannot be undertaken without contact with all the forces involved. Attunement to and control of forces involves techniques, hence the need for specialists who possess knowledge and power to deal with them; hence rites and divinatory practices.

The Negro world then is a world of spirit forces: of the dead, living, and nature, among which the living form but a small minority. These forces cannot be classified into categories of good and evil, for power is essentially impersonal and neutral. If harmony is maintained all is well, but if broken calamity falls on individual and community. The individual is welded through birth and initiation into a holy community, tied to a sacred rhythm of ritual whose function is to maintain the equilibrium of spirit forces. The consequences of this view of life have been profound. A complex social structure has been formed with attendant restraints and disciplines, and, as a corollary, the diminution of personal initiative and responsibility. Religion and society are one. Each group functions as a religious community.

Such is the basic pattern of African religious society, the foundation upon which complex structures were based. But every possible stage of transition is found from simple family and agrarian animism to the organized polytheistic systems of south Guinean peoples. Generally beyond the family, with its ancestor cult, is a specialized group devoted to the cult of a god and its subordinates. This may consist of a group of families (maximal lineages or clan groups) or groups embracing local age-ranges. Each is a religious as well as a social association, having its rites intended to bind and perpetuate the community, and membership involves initiation at esoteric bush schools. Initiation and communion with the spirits of the group mark the paradox of recognition of the individual and at the same time his depersonalization and subjection to the collective will of the group. High initiates ensure that members are faithful to the spirit world and guide the ritual life of the earthly group. Such spiritual families or secret societies or mystery cults, repositories of the myths which explain man and his world, are characteristic of most spheres of West African society.

These basic elements form the substratum of the hereditary, local, and ethnic religions which govern people's understanding of life, but in practice religion is lineal or local, influenced by the natural environment, the people's peculiar bents and psychological patterns, the integration of outside radiations, and migrational and historical circumstances. In their natural form wider social organizations were extensions of the primary cell, the extended family, in which each clan had its defined place in the organization in the same way as each individual had his or her defined place in the family unit. Superimposed political structures did not disturb this basic organization.

Characteristic of Sudan societies are social hierarchization and developed political organization, all closely bound up with religion. Government is in the hands of an aristocracy sustained by an imperial family cult upon the observance of which the welfare of the state devolves. Agriculture is accorded an honoured place except where the ruling class retains a legacy of nomadism. Crafts such as weaving, dyeing, and smithery are the functions of a caste or a corporation. Slavery, unknown to the basic structure, plays an important role, especially its extension in the serf system, a natural development from the basic conceptions of Negro society.

The village, with its chief assisted by a council of kin-group heads, forms the basic administrative unit. The chief is under a regional head who in turn is under a provincial governor responsible to the king. Two forms of royal authority existed which frequently coalesced. Under the stable climatic conditions which prevail in the Sudan the priest, as rainmaker and controller of spirit forces, merged into the sacred king. In the other, kingship had a foreign origin and the founder-king, although an intruder, appears in the mythology of the clan as a saviour. Historical events led to this structure being imposed upon the foundation described first. Conversely, historical events could eliminate the superstructure without destroying the foundation, for these governments did not fully reflect African political conceptions and could be replaced or break up without upsetting society.

It will be obvious from the foregoing sketch that religions like Islam and Christianity, which evolved under the influence of Semitic and Greek cultures, could only substitute their view of life for a religious inheritance so harmonized to the psychology and mode of life of Africans under conditions of great change. Negro societies absorbed radiations from Mediterranean, Berber, Chadian, or Nilotic civilizations naturally, for only traits which accorded with their mentality could gain acceptance. After North Africa had been won over to Islam the Negro world was first invaded by a civilization based on historical revelation and monotheism. African religions are not historical religions, their beliefs and rituals are founded upon a timeless mythology, but with Islam time entered the African world. The way in which Africans dealt with this is the subject of this book.

A brief reference may be made to the invasion of another civilization. Since the partition of Africa, dating from the eighties of the last century, Africa has been swept into the stream of world activity. This sudden impact of Western civilization has created difficult problems. Decay and disruption threaten ethnic religions as never before. The degrees of this decay vary according to the strength of the forces which are uprooting tribal life and the forces of resistance within the social structure. But the indigenous religions, being primarily local and ethnic, appear to have no future in their organized forms, and the religious future of the African lies between Christianity and Islam, on the one hand, and secularism on the other. The most vital feature of the African's inheritance is his sense of community, and in this situation Christianity and Islam are the two forces that can reintegrate social life on a new basis. Whilst our special concern is with Islam we cannot consider it in the present situation without also taking account of the dynamic forces of Christianity and secularism. The African Muslim's reaction to the secular civilization of the West, quite different from that of the pagan, will be the subject of the last chapter. Yet at the same time the African's own heritage is of vital significance. We see village communities with a new pattern of communal life superimposed upon the old, one in which independence and personal responsibility are struggling with the basic conception of African community life. But the new communal life maintains strong ties with the old. Traditional ideas, institutions, and, above all, psychological attitudes, are preserved; and, to an extent that is difficult to realize under conditions of great change, the new community still draws nourishment from its ancient roots. Yet the new forces are revolutionary, tradition is no longer the prime factor governing life, and new forms of African civilization are being forged because the very government of life is being changed.

4. THE PRINCIPAL MUSLIM PEOPLES

Since geographical and historical factors have led to the Saharan and north Sudan belts being most widely islamized, the following classification of peoples who will be frequently referred to is according to climatic belts. Within the belts the arrangement is by linguistic groups rather than by any theories as to their origins.

(a) *Peoples of the southern Sahara*

The southern Sahara is included in the area of survey because it is impossible to consider the influence of Islam among the peoples of the Sudan without taking into account those of the Sahara. Negroes form an important element in the population of the Sahara for its agricultural economy is dependent upon them, but since they are embraced within the social organization of Moors, Tuareg, and Teda, speak their languages, and culturally belong to the Saharan rather than to the Negro world, they are not treated separately.

(i) *Moors.* The inhabitants of western Sahara are known under the vague term of Moors.[1] They are often referred to as *Bīḍān*, 'Whites', in opposition to *Sūdān*, 'Blacks'. They are not a homogeneous people, though almost all now speak the Ḥassāniyya dialect of Arabic, but consist of Berbers, Arabs, and Blacks, with a predominance of Berbers, given coherence by social relationship and language. From the thirteenth century groups of Maʿqil (Ḥassān) Arabs irrupted into southern Morocco and moved progressively southwards, reaching the Senegal at the beginning of the fifteenth century. They gained political control over the western Berbers who were gradually arabized. Like all Saharans the Moors are stratified in a number of social groups[2] of which the *zwāyā* or clerical clans are most important from the Islamic point of view.

(ii) *Tuareg*[3] speak a common language (Tamāhaqq) belonging to the Berber family and have preserved a Libyco-Berber alphabet (Tifīnagh). They divide into two groupings: unchanged camel nomads living in the mountains of central Sahara (with whom we are not concerned) and Nigerian nomads inhabiting the desert north of the Niger buckle and the Gurma region within it. Through living in a different environment and in contact with Negroes, the Nigerians have changed in physical characteristics, mode of life, and custom. Certain tribes occupy

[1] Under this designation are included: in southern Mauritania, Arab suzerain tribes (Trarza and Brakna) and their vassal Berber tribes and clients (Zanāta and Ḥarrāṭīn); in the Hawd the Awlād Delīm, Rigaibāt, Mashḍūf, Ṭālib Mukhtār, Girganke, and the Shurafā of Tishīt, Walāta, and Nema; north of the Niger buckle and in Azawād are some 30,000, including the Kunta and the Berabish.

[2] On their social organization see pp. 135–6.

[3] Tuareg is the designation employed by Arabs (*Ṭawārīq*, sing. *Ṭarqī*), who probably extended the name of a tribe of the Ṣanhāja (Targa) to the whole of the *mulaththamīn*, 'muffled people'.

temporary villages of huts and have become so dark that they can hardly be distinguished from Songhay and Hausa. They are loosely grouped in federations of tribes under a chief (*amenokāl*) who exercises nominal authority. A system of classes (*aserkam*) divides the tribes into nobles (*imoshar*), pastoralist vassals (*imghad*), clerical clans (*inislimen*), Negro serfs (*iklān*), and an artisan caste. The Tuareg are monogamous, women hold an important position in society, and descent, except among the Ullimmeden and other southern tribes, is matrilineal.

Islam took many centuries to gain their allegiance and even today it has little influenced social life. The way of life of clerical clans (*inislimen*) is similar to that of other Tuareg except that they do not bear arms. This pacifism does not derive from their religious character but from their status as social inferiors who pay dues for their protection.

(iii) *Teda-Daza* or *Tubu*[1] inhabit a vast area of the eastern Sahara from the Libyan desert in the east to Haggar in the west, and from Fezzan in the north to the Chad region in the south. Naturally, in view of the nature of their land, they are not numerous (about 100,000). Their main groups live in the mountainous ranges of Tibesti, Borku, part of Ennedi, the Kawar group of oases, and northern parts of Kanem and Waday. They are a dark-skinned, lean people of short or medium height, with regular and fine features, thin lips, straight nose, and smooth hair. They speak a Sudanese language allied to that of the Kanuri and have cultural affinities with the Tuareg, but are distinct from both. Those of the west are pastoral nomads; eastern tribes have cultivation and tend date-palm groves, and caravan traffic is an important source of income. Authority is vested in a council of notables. The *derde* of Tibesti and chiefs of other tribes nominate war-leaders but otherwise have little authority. The majority of Teda are monogamous and women are independent and respected. The adoption of Islam has not upset their traditional way of life.

(*b*) *Peoples of the northern Sudan*

(i) The *Fulbe*[2] are a class society embracing the most diverse groups whose only common factor is language. They divide themselves into

[1] Tūbū (*Təvo*) is the Kanemi term, the people of Tū or Tibesti. Those of the north call themselves Tēda. The southern call all *Dāza*, a term the northerners apply to those of Kanem. Shuwa Arabs and Wadayans call them *Quraʿān*, Awlād Sulaimān *Karada*, and Tuareg *Ikarada*.

[2] Many names are employed to designate the Fulbe. The French call them *Peuls* or *Peuhls* from the Wolof pronunciation of *Pulɔ*, singular of their own name *Fulḅe* or *Pulḅe*. They are called *Fulāni* by Hausa (sing. *Ba-Felanche*) and Moors, and *Felāta* by Kanuri, Teda, and in eastern Sudan. Tuareg say *A-Fuli* (pl. *I-Fulān*, *I-Fellān*), Mande *Fūla* or *Fila*, and Mossi *Silmise* (sing. *Silmiga*).

red (*woḍēḅe*) and black (*ḅalēḅe*). The characteristic Fulbe are the non-Negro nomadic herdsmen.[1] These immigrants seem to have allied themselves with south Saharan Negro nomads (Lauḅe) and adopted their language.[2] Small groups live in regions no one else wants, like the poor savanna of Ferlo (Senegal), but the majority live among Negro cultivators to whom they either pay some form of tribute or have a mutual agreement whereby they graze cattle on fallow land and exchange milk and butter for grain. The nomads live for their cattle which they only sell to satisfy tax demands. They occupy camps of shelter-type beehive huts and herd their cattle into stockades. Islam has had little cultural and religious effect and Negro-Fulbe regard them as pagans even when they profess Islam.

The black element of sedentary agriculturalists is by far the largest and they are the strongest Muslims in West Africa. The first stage of transition is semi-nomadism. When they become herdsmen to Negroes they loose their freedom of movement, change many customs, and become bilingual. Others acquire serf-cultivators and live in permanent settlements. The process of religious change is seen in the Gambia where the upper class remain pagan, whilst their Pulār-speaking serfs are becoming Muslim. The decisive change comes when they mix with Negroes and adopt Islamic customs. Although poor they have a strong feeling of racial pride and to this Islam adds religious superiority. The day comes when a Negro Pulo cleric proclaims a *jihād*. They rise, overwhelm the pagans, and found a state. This happened in Futas Toro, Bondu and Jalon, Masina, Hausaland, and Adamawa. As a result of this reversal of fortune the leaders of the *jihād* become an aristocracy, and the conquered Negroes fall into various social strata. Settled Fulbe become negroid and acquire new social attitudes and economic values centred on agriculture, though continuing to manifest ethno-religious pride. This third stage marks the completion of the transition to an Islamic Sudan society.

(ii) The *Senegalese group* includes the Wolof (660,000), Tokolor (300,000), Serer (270,000), and Jola (135,000). The Wolof and Tokolor are entirely Muslim, but Serer and Jola are adopting Christianity. All are cultivators of millet and producers of ground-nuts. The Serer ruling class (by material filiation), which is of foreign origin, and

[1] In northern Nigeria nomads (called *Firian Kiriabe* or *Bororo'en* (sing. *Wororbe*), and by the Hausa by the berberized form *Abore*) number 450,000 out of a total Fulbe population of over 3,000,000.

[2] The language, a member of the family which includes Serer-Sin, Wolof, and Tokolor, is called Pulār in Senegal. Fulfulde in Masina and Nigeria, and Pulpule in Futa Jalon.

the warrior class have become Muslim, but the masses (native nobility, free peasants, and various caste and servile people) remain pagan, though Christianity is spreading. The Wolof, the most 'evolved' people of French West Africa, are defined by cultural and social rather than racial characteristics. They once formed a group of five kingdoms, Salum, Kajor, Baol, Walo, and Jolof, covering a large area between the Senegal and Gambia. Although the first penetration of Islam goes back to the fifteenth century the religion did not gain the masses until the nineteenth century when the process of conversion was so rapid that it was completed by its end.

The Tokolor[1] may be distinguished from Fulbe in view of the role they played in the history of Islam. They are a group of mixed Negro stock modified by absorption of Fulbe and, to a lesser extent, Moors, and by a thorough islamization, for their ruling class was converted in the eleventh century. Their main concentration is in Senegalese Futa where they inhabit both banks of the river from Dagana to half-way between Matam and Bakel, but colonies have been formed in the Kayes region (Upper Senegal), Nyoro in the Sahil, Segu on the Niger, eastern Masina, Dingiray east of Futa Jalon, and elsewhere.

(iii) *Northern Mande.* The term Mande is primarily linguistic. The chief divisions of the northern (Mande-Tan group) are Mandinka, Bambara, Dyula, Soninke, Khasonke, and Bozo.

The Soninke[2] (450,000) are differentiated from other Mande since, through living in the Sahil and formerly in the Sahara itself, they are

[1] The term Tokolor (or Tokoror) is used by Wolof for those Negroes with whom they are in contact who speak the same language as the Fulbe. Arab geographers adopted the word under the form *Takrūr* from which they formed the ethnic *Takrūrī* (pl. *Takārīr*), a word which came to designate any west Sudan Negro. They have no name for themselves, for they are not so much a people as a hierarchized class society. When pressed they call themselves *Hal-pulāren*, 'Pular-speakers', or *Fūtankōbē* (sing. *Fūtankē*) from their centre in Senegalese Futa.

[2] The terminology applied to the various groups is confusing, Their own name is *Sōniŋkē.* Moors call them *Aswanik*, and Wolof *Sere-kule* (hence *Sarakole*), 'red man'. The general term in the Niger buckle is *Marka*, which often refers to Mande-speakers who claim a Soninke origin. Those living on the Dya (west Masina), a Soninke dispersion-point, take their name of *Dyakanke* from the locality, and their colonies on the upper Gambia and in Futa Jalon are so called. The *Tubakai*, a colony in the west of Futa Jalon, take their name from the village of Tuba. At Jenne they are called *Nono* from the name of the first immigrant clan. The few groups which still exist in the Sahara are known as *Azēr*. Fulbe, Hausa, and Songhay call them Wangārbē, Wangārāwa, and Wankorē respectively, but these terms are by extension applied to any Mande. The Dyawara of Kingi, though speaking Soninke, are on historical grounds a separate people, and their colonies in Gidimaka, Kayes, Bafulabe, and elsewhere have adopted the language of those among whom they live. Pagan Mandinka in Upper Guinea use the word 'Soninke' as equivalent to 'cleric', which shows the role they played in those parts as representatives of Islam.

interpenetrated by Berber and Fulbe. They are agriculturalists attached to the soil, yet also great travellers and outrival Dyula as traders in west Sudan. As the basic population of the south Saharan kingdom of Gāna they were islamized at an early date and have played a considerable role in the islamization of the Sudan. Islam has deeply influenced their social life, but, like Saharans, the ruling classes and agriculturalists tend to leave practice to clerical clans.

Mandinka,[1] Bambara,[2] and Dyula speak the same language and have the same type of social organization and cultural characteristics but are differentiated by reason of habitat, history, and, in a vague way, by religion, Bambara being regarded as pagan, Mandinka as semi-Muslim, and Dyula as wholly Muslim. For centuries the Mandinka were the dominant people of the region between the Niger and the Atlantic but, though the rulers of Māli and traders adopted Islam, the cultivators remained faithful to ancestral cults. During the last 150 years Islam has been spreading and is professed by over 50 per cent. Though in touch with Islam for centuries only about 20 per cent. of the Bambara have adopted it. The Mande dispersion within the Niger bend and Voltaic region is known as Dyula.[3] Essentially northern Sudanese in social organization and material culture they have formed agricultural colonies around their trading centres in south Sudanese and forest zones. Unlike Soninke traders they have had little Islamic influence upon pagan communities such as Senufo and Kulango among whom they live, yet, through the nature of their occupation and new habitat, Islam is deeply implanted as a social characteristic, and they figure prominently in this survey.

Other northern Mande are the Bozo, Somono, and Khasonke. Bozo (30,000) fishers and agriculturalists occupy the Niger and Bani banks between Segu and Dioila and Niafunke. Islam has been spreading since

[1] They call themselves Mani-ŋka or Mandi-ŋka. The English tend to use the form Mandingo (the Western singular form Manḍiŋkɔ) and the French Malinke (west Guinea, Maliŋke). They number about a million and a quarter, and are divided into groups taking their name from their locality.

[2] They call themselves *Bãmana* (sing. *Bãmanaŋka*). Europeans have adopted the Muslim term Bãmbara (*ban*, 'to refuse', *bař̇a* suffix of agent, cf. *seli-bař̇a*, 'prayer' or Muslim), interpreting it as 'rejector' of Islam instead of rejector of the uterine filiation. Many Bambara, on becoming Muslim, tend to call themselves Dyula. The region they now occupy borders on that of Moorish tribes in the north, with Masina to the east, and Mandinka in the west and south. The majority (850,000) live in French Sudan. Colonies are found in Masina, on the banks of the Bani and Bafing, in French Guinée and Senegal.

[3] *Dyula* means 'trader' in Soninke, Mandinka, and Banmana, and it is difficult to decide whether the Dyula derived their name from this or their name became equivalent to 'trader' in other dialects.

the fourteenth century and all have been Muslim since the nineteenth. They should be distinguished from neighbouring castes of fishers, Sorko of Songhay origin, Subalbe of Fulbe origin, and Somono. The last-named became Muslim *en masse* about 1860 and are now propagandists of Islam on the right bank of the Niger. Islam has been spreading among the Khasonke (Khasoŋgolu, 50,000) of the Kayes, Bafulabe, and Nyoro regions for a long time, but still claims less than half.

(iv) *Northern Voltaics*. For the student of Islam the feature which distinguishes Voltaic peoples (Gur language group) is their insusceptibility to Islam. Although the northern groups have been in contact with Muslims for centuries, Islam has made no significant inroads. Among the Voltaics the Mossi stand out by reason of their complex social and political structure. The term Mossi (correctly *Mosi*, sing. *Moγa*) belongs to the immigrant warrior class who moulded subject peoples into one political organization. In the sixteenth century they split into two kingdoms of Wagadugu and Wahiguya (Yatenga). Under the chaotic conditions of the nineteenth century they were the only stable states. On either side of their territory rose the Fulbe states of Masina and Gwandu but the *jihād* leaders passed them by. The incorporation of many peoples into the Mossi structure had led to great changes, the most obvious being their adoption of the Mole language. Neighbouring groups, such as Gurunsi, Dogon, Bobo, Lobi, and Bussance, have not been subject to this process. But others, such as the Gurma (140,000) living between the Mossi and the Niger, were at one time tributary to the Mossi and influenced by their higher civilization. Islam is said to have about 90,000 adherents in the *cercle* of Wahiguya, the region of strongest penetration, but of this figure Mossi only number about 20,000, the rest being foreign settlers.

(v) *Songhay–Zerma–Dendi*. The people fringing the middle Niger mark a zone of transition between the Mande world and central Sudan. The Songhay (250,000)[1] live along the Niger bend from Mopti through the lacustrine and Timbuktu region to Gao. The Zerma (80,000) live south of Gao (Niamey, Doso, and Tila Beri) and south of them are the Dendi (24,000). All speak dialects of an isolated Nigritic language belonging to the Sudanic family. The Songhay show the same ethnic complexity as other Sudanese. They are Negroes, but urban elements in Jenne, Timbuktu, and Gao have absorbed Tuareg and Moors. These form the aristocratic classes. One class, the *Arma*,

[1] The word Songhay (correctly *Sõŋai*) designates not the people but the country. The people are referred to as Sõŋai Bor'ey and Sõŋoyte, ethnic names of recent formation.

are the descendants of the Andalusian soldiers responsible for the downfall of the Songhay empire. The northern Songhay who have been in continual contact with Saharans are Muslims. The Zerma, who migrated to the middle Niger four centuries ago, were little influenced by Islam until the Fulbe movement began in Nigeria early in the nineteenth century. They and the Dendi have minorities which remain pagan.

(vi) The *Hausa* language, which belongs to the Chado-Hamitic family, gives linguistic unity to a large part of Northern Nigeria. Hausa-speakers number 5,480,000 in British territory and over half a million in French Niger Colony. Although the generic *Hausāwa* (sing. *Ba-Haushe*) is employed they have no name for themselves[1] and employ regional terms. The Hausa are industrious cultivators, skilful artisans in leather and matting work, and enterprising traders found on every Saharan and Sudan trade-route. Although a class religion in the Hausa city-states Islam did not gain a hold upon the cultivators until after the Fulbe conquest (1802–17). When the British took control at the beginning of the present century it was estimated that 50 per cent. of Hausa-speakers were pagan, but so rapidly has Islam spread that today Muslims probably number 75–80 per cent. Large blocks of animists (known collectively as *azna* or *māguzāwa*) still survive between Sokoto and Katsina and in French Niger Territory, but they are coming more and more under Islamic pressure.

(vii) *The Chadian peoples* are composed of diverse elements. In Bornu, Bagirmi, and Waday a large number of Negro peoples have been formed through the intermingling of many groups with Teda, Fulbe, and Arabs. The linguistic confusion, which bears witness to their diverse origins, is extraordinary. Groups given coherence by their geographical habitat and history are the Kanembu, Kanuri, Bagirmians, and Wadayans. All are islamized, although amongst them, especially in the south, many groups of pagans remain.

The Kanembu are sedentary agriculturalists inhabiting Kanem, north-east of the Chad, and a narrow girdle around the western and northern shores of the lake. When the penetration of Islam began in the twelfth century Kanem was the seat of an extensive nomadic chieftaincy. At the beginning of the fourteenth century the dynasty was compelled to move to Bornu where they intermingled with the So to form the Kanuri, today the dominant people of Bornu. The Kanuri

[1] The term *Ausa* applied to the left bank of the Niger was attached to this linguistic group, the eastern region becoming 'the eastern people'. Similarly the Hausa have no general term for the Songhay whom they refer to as *Yammatāwa*, 'westerners'.

(called Beri-Beri by the Hausa) number 1,297,000 in Nigeria (752,680 in Bornu Province) and others live in French Niger and Chad territories. In the strict sense the word Kanuri belongs to the ruling class but it is now a linguistic term applied to all who speak the language. The political development of Bornu and its islamization led to the breakdown of tribal divisions, the diffusion of the language, and the fusion of many peoples.

The peoples of Bagirmi, if their traditions and linguistic affinities are to be accepted, have a common origin. The ruling clans derive from Kenga who conquered the region at the beginning of the seventeenth century and became Muslims. The populations of the Chad Islands (Yedima, called Buduma by the Kanuri, and Kuri) have become Muslim during the last seventy years. South of the Chad in the swampy region of the Shari live Kotoko, Musgu, Mandara, and others, all of whom are influenced by Islam.

The Wadayans proper are derived from Maba and their language has become the *lingua franca* of the region. The principal tribes are the Kodoy or Abu Senun, Awlad Jemma, Malanga, Mandaba, and Mandala. Other groups related to the Maba have been converted to a form of Islam: Karanga, Kashmere, Marfa, Kajanga, Ali, Moyo, and Kajagse. Also Muslim are Zaghāwa cattle-breeders now largely sedentary, Baele or Bedayat (called Anna by Teda and Tarawiya by Arabs), Maṣāliṭ, and Dājo in Dar Sila. Islam extends little south of lat. 11°, apart from Arab and trading groups.

(viii) *Arabs of the Central Sudan.* Arab influence was strong in western Sahara where the Berbers were arabized, but the Tuareg and Teda of the centre were unaffected. In Sudanese regions it was strongest in Nilotic Sudan and from there Arab tribes penetrated into Waday, Bagirmi, and Bornu. The term Shuwa is applied by the people of Bornu[1] to these tribes. They fall into two groups: *abbāla*, camel nomads, and *baqqāra*, cattle nomads. Those who settled in regions suitable for camels were unaffected in their mode of life, but those who gravitated southwards to country where the camel cannot live adopted cattle-rearing from the Negroes. The *baqqāra* have been modified by miscegenation with Negroes and change in mode of life, though the Arab element is clearly recognizable. Most inhabit fixed villages during the rainy season where cultivation is done by Negro serfs and clients.

[1] The word *Shuwa* is not used by the Arabs who retain their tribal names. The suggested derivation from Arabic *shāwīya* (*shāt*, 'ewe'), as meaning by extension 'pastor', seems unlikely. In Bornu they number 98,900 (1952 Census).

The Awlād Sulaimān are distinct from Shuwa. Migrating from Fezzan after 1842 they installed themselves on the borders of Kanem, roaming from Air to Abeshe and from Borku to Ennedi. They live like northern Arabs and speak their dialect. Another type of Arab are Ja'aliyyīn from the Nile who form a merchant class (*jallāba*). The Tunjur are probably a Hamitic people from the Nile region who adopted Arabic and trekked westwards. Most now live in Kanem (30,000) and others are found in Bornu, Waday, and Darfur.

(c) *Peoples of the southern Sudan*

The south Sudanese zone, where the *harmattan* reigns supremely, is a kind of no-man's-land situated between the Sudanese and Guinean regions. The neo-Sudanese civilization has not deeply affected the paleo-nigritic peoples of this belt and consequently Islam, which only began to penetrate during the eighteenth to nineteenth centuries, has had little influence.

Linguistically the belt may be divided into a western zone where Mande prevails, a Voltaic zone in the centre, and a Nigerian zone in the east.

The upper Guineans (Kisi, Loma, Kpelle, Manon in French Guinée; Mende and Temne in Sierra Leone) do not properly belong to the Southern Sudan, but it is convenient to include them here. They inhabit sub-tropical savanna which has no severe dry season.[1] Western Guinea, which has felt the influence of neo-Sudanese civilization, is the area of strong Islamic penetration. The mountainous region of Futa Jalon stands out, not merely from the climatic but also from the Islamic view-point, for the primary factor leading to the diffusion of Islam throughout western Guinea was the formation of a Fulbe theocratic state in these highlands.

Most peoples of the wide estuaries of the coastal region remain pagan, but they are interpenetrated by Muslims. Two in particular, the Nalu (7,000) and Susu (320,000 in Guinée and 50,000 in Sierra Leone) whose original homeland was Futa Jalon, are almost wholly Muslim. Half the Yalunka (Jalonke) of Sierra Leone, a branch of the Susu, remain pagan. Others of the Mande linguistic group, to which the Susu belong, have acquired a Mandinka ruling class and among such Islam has penetrated (40 per cent. of the Mende and all the Vai in Sierra

[1] Western Guinea has four climatic and vegetation zones: (*a*) Lower Guinea, the alluvial coastal plain, (*b*) Middle Guinea, the mountainous regions of Futa Jalon, (*c*) Upper Guinea which has a Sudanese orientation, and (*d*) Forest Guinea orientated towards the sea.

Leone and Liberia). Others of the Mande Fu group are little influenced (Loko, Kpelle or Gerze, Loma, and Busa). Whilst the Temne (500,000) are 50 per cent. Muslim, others belonging to the same linguistic group are little influenced. The extent and degree of Islamic penetration is unequal. Thus the Balante of Portuguese Guinea are animists except for the Mané group who are Muslim. The Tenda, a federation of three unrelated peoples occupying the north-western flank of Futa Jalon, have remained pagan except the Boeni section who were formerly serfs of Fulbe and adopted their language, customs, and religion. Islam has penetrated in varying degrees Mande peoples who are differentiated for regional or historical reasons: Manyanka (Ko-Mende) dispersed between the Vai and Toma in Liberia, Konyanka of Beyla, Dyomande in Mau country around Tuba, Sidyanka in Futa Jalon; and Wasulunka, Toronge, and Futanke in French Guinée.

The mass of Voltaic peoples of this south-Sudanese belt have resisted Islam. In the Ivory Coast there are large blocks of Dyula (100,000) but the majority of the indigenous peoples remain pagan; among the Kulango (40,000), for example, only 1,000 Muslims are found. Penetration of neo-Sudanese influences in the Northern Territories of Ghana and Togo led to the formation of states: Dagomba, Mamprusi, Gonja, and Wala. Islam has gained a hold over the Dagomba ruling classes, it has penetrated some Mamprusi groups, claims all the Wala (26,000), and has influenced Dagati and Lobe. Towns, such as Bobo Dioulasso (Haute Volta) and Bonduku (Ivory Coast), since they are Dyula trading centres, are Muslim. Similarly in the Northern Territories of Ghana where the proportion of Muslims is only about 5 per cent. the chief Islamic centres are the towns of Bawki (Mamprusi), Yendi, Tamale (Dagomba), Salaga (Gonja), Wa (Wala), and Kete Krachi.

The peoples who stretch through the northern regions of Togo, Dahomey, the middle belt of Nigeria, and the Cameroons need not be enumerated. They are predominantly pagan, though everywhere there is some penetration of Islam in the Sudanese mode which does not preclude the practice of pagan rites. Muslims are mainly immigrants such as Hausa traders. In many parts Muslim domination has led to the political ascendancy of Islam, but there has been no mass adoption of the religion. The belt is split by an Islamic current which runs along the west bank of the Niger to the coast. The Nupe and northern Yoruba belong to the belt. Ilorin region became a Fulbe emirate and 60 per cent. of the Yoruba in the northern region are said to be

Muslim. The Nupe as an example of a people in transition from ethnic religion to Islam have an important place in this study. They live in the country situated north and south of that section of the Niger which flows through Niger Province. They number about 350,000 and are an amalgam of many groups of different ethnic and cultural traditions linked together by a common language. The Nupe came within the sphere of the Fulbe revolution at the beginning of the nineteenth century and today two-thirds are Muslim. Other Nupe-speakers (Gbari 155,000 and Igbira 147,000) remain animists though many Muslims are found among them.

The Bauchi and Adamawa plateaux stand out as special regions, not merely on account of their physical features but because they are the homeland of ethnic groups with special characteristics. They are regions where live many small pagan tribes upon many of whom the Fulbe imposed themselves during the early part of the nineteenth century but amongst whom Islam has not made serious inroads. For instance, in the Jos Division of the Bauchi plateau 100,000 of the 132,500 inhabitants are indigenous pagans. Where Islamic penetration is strong it is due to special historical factors. Pagan peoples are not limited to the plateau region but inhabit all the low-lying country around it (Jamaa, Shendan, and the southern divisions). Southern Zaria Province is mainly pagan. The Tiv, the largest people (766,000) in the middle belt who live south of the Benue and escaped Fulbe pressure, remain pagan with strong Christian penetration.

In Adamawa at the beginning of the Fulbe revolution all the inhabitants, including Fulbe nomads who had discovered the land to be especially suitable for their cattle, were pagan, and though a Muslim Fulbe dynasty was founded and was kept in existence by the British, the majority of the tribes (except for former slaves) remain unaffected by Islam.[1]

The Guinean Zone is a region of higher civilization stretching from the Ton of the Ivory Coast to Benin in Nigeria. Islam has made significant penetration only into the Yoruba of south-western Nigeria who are therefore the only people of the zone to come into this survey.

[1] Islam has penetrated into the northern part of French Cameroons. Apart from the peoples who belong to the north Sudan who are wholly Muslim (Shuwa Arabs 25,000, Kotoko 20,000, Bornuans 5,000, and Hausa 4,000), or who are partially islamized (the Fulbe (260,000), Mandara (12,000), and Mbum (5,000)), tribes of Sudanese origin who are partially and superficially islamized are the Bamum (52,000), Tikar (13,000), Vute or Ba-Bute (13,000), and Baya (35,000), and there has been some penetration into the Fali (Mongo, 28,000).

2

The Process of Religious Change

I. CULTURES IN CONTACT

STUDENTS of culture contact in Africa tend to confine their attention to the relationship of Western culture with animist communities, shown graphically in this form:

ANIMIST	animist-WESTERN
western-ANIMIST	WESTERN

But this scheme expresses only partially the interaction of cultures in West Africa since it ignores that of Islam which for centuries has been conditioning many African societies. The student of culture contact is therefore faced with a much more complicated situation for he has to take account of three cultural fields in dynamic relationship:

Animist social, political, economic, and religious culture;[1]
Islamic social-religious culture in the form in which it impinges upon the African;
Western culture in the form in which it affects the African.

Having thus given Islamic culture its place in the situation we find that the resultants of contact are extremely intricate. The animist, Islamic, and Western are 'parent' cultures, ideal types, none of which is found in a pure uncontaminated form. What then are the possible dynamic interactions between them? This may be expressed graphically (see figure overleaf).

[1] The term 'animism' must serve to designate the total system of belief and practice of West African peoples. Animist culture as compared with the universalist culture of Islam seems particularist since it expresses itself in diversified local cultures, yet it may be regarded as a cultural whole since it expresses a unique attitude to life. The thousands of different expressions within this whole are referred to as ethnic or local religions. Similarly the word 'pagan' is as imprecise as 'animist', since in origin it means 'country people' and can be applied to the religion of the majority of Muslim and Christian cultivators, but both terms are loosely employed here for those attached to ethnic religions.

This scheme gives a unified picture of the interrelationships of the three 'parent' cultures which qualify, modify, and condition each other. They have arranged themselves into three pairs and, although it may

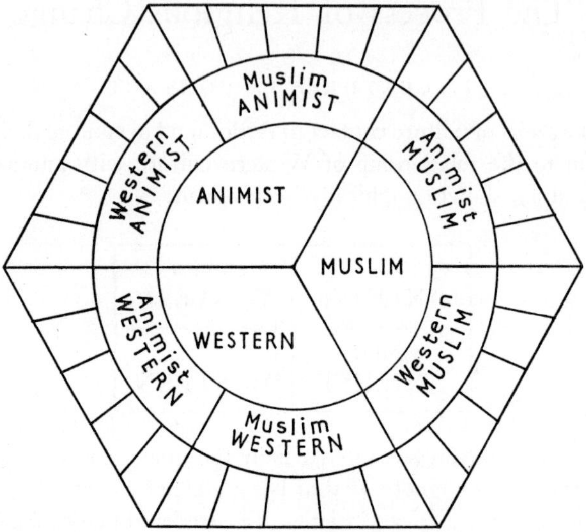

not be strictly correct, it helps to think of each as alternately positive and negative to the other, each in a condition of determinism and freedom. The following are a few selections of the results of contact:

1. a > M. ANIMIST conditioning MUSLIM

The animistic Muslim. Reversion from Islam to animism.

Animistic elements in Islam: dynamism, spiritism, cultism, magico-religious practices; ceremonies associated with Islamic institutions of circumcision, marriage, and death.

Local custom holding its own against the encroachment of Islamic law.

2. m > A. MUSLIM conditioning ANIMIST

Animist reaction to Islamic influence.

Pagan myth and ritual reflecting Islamic myth and ritual.

The process and psychology of conversion to Islam.

The stages from the islamized animist to the Negro Muslim.

The resultant animist-Islamic culture complex.

3. a > W. ANIMIST conditioning WESTERN

The African convert to Western religion, the animistic Christian, animist practices in African Christianity. African separatist sects.

The conditioning of the Western government official, missionary, and trader working in animist areas: *le type du colonial*, social and economic attitude of a ruling minority, European cantonments, influence of African labour upon economic planning, methods of work, recruiting (agriculture, mines, home life).

Application of customary law in courts. The school in the bush.

4. w > A. WESTERN conditioning ANIMIST

Breakdown and decay of African religions. Pathological forms of African religion. Psychology of conversion to Christianity and of westernization. The christianized African and the Western-influenced animist. African Christian sectarianism.

Effect of the secularization of political, economic, social, and religious theory. Money economy degrading the bride-price system. Western-type school. Application of Western legal ideas and procedure in tribal courts. The African official, teacher, mechanic, mine worker. Nationalist movements.

5. m > W. MUSLIM conditioning WESTERN

The conditioning of the Western government official in Muslim areas.

The conditioning of government policy: official recognition of Islam, application of Islamic law, religious neutrality policy involving freedom for Islamic and prohibition of Christian propaganda. Maintenance of the *status quo* in the Fulani feudal system in Northern Nigeria.

6. w > M. WESTERN conditioning MUSLIM

Resistance and reaction to secular civilization.

Economic and social revolution caused by the abolition of slavery.

Effect of Western economy and education. Growth of a Muslim *évolué* class. The Western-influenced Muslim: official, teacher, and mechanic.

Application to Muslims of Western law and legal procedure.

Problems which the French and Portuguese policy of assimilation imposes upon Muslims. Political change and nationalist movements.

This sixfold scheme, based on three ideal cultures, does not account fully for any of the examples, and if we want to arrive at the contemporaneous we have to work out the interactions of these six which gives another thirty squares, shown graphically upon the outer rim of the hexagonal form. The examples given above can then be placed in their full setting. However, we need not complicate matters unduly by working them out, and the following examples will suffice:

m W > a M. Western governments' recognition of Islamic law (No. 5) converting the nominal Muslim (No. 1) into an orthodox Muslim.

a M > w A. The effect of Islam upon the westernized animist. Yoruba influenced by Western ideas adopting Islam as a religion, not as a civilization.

w A > a M. Western rule providing the conditions whereby the animistic Muslim reverts to animism.

The sixfold cycle represents the main fields of interaction that have to be taken into account. The special concern of this book is with the first and last pairs.

2. FACTORS OF RESISTANCE AND ACCEPTANCE

The spread of Islam and resulting distribution of Muslim communities is due to many factors, historical, geographical, and psychological. On the broadest canvas there were two main historical waves of advance. The first was its slow spread from the eleventh to the seventeenth centuries through the agency of traders and clerics (the Berber impulse of the Murābiṭīn in the eleventh century and the work of the first *askiya* of Songhay were of minor importance). The feature of this period is its adoption as a class religion—the imperial cult in the Sudan states and the religion of the trading and clerical classes. The second impulse came with the Negro-Fulbe movements of the nineteenth century which led to the formation of Islamic theocratic states, and was followed by a period of consolidation, especially under the conditions provided by the European occupation.

Since Islam came from the north and the Islamic states of both periods were based in the northern Sudan its peoples were gradually islamized. Geographical factors hindered its southerly progress and account in part for the survival of animist groups in the north. Climatical zoning is latitudinal and change of climate often halted invading peoples. In the south Sudan poor communications and dispersion of population in small communities hindered contact. The forests of the Guinean zone imposed an insuperable barrier to steppe-nurtured peoples. The incidence of yellow fever, malaria, and sleeping sickness, famine and tsetse-fly zones rendered many regions impenetrable. Highlands in the midst of the steppe, like Hombori, Bauchi, and Mandara, and swamps such as fringe the great lakes of the Niger and Chad served as retreats for animist groups.

But more must be taken into consideration than historical and geographical factors. The psychological aspects are equally important. Acceptance or resistance to Islam is determined by innate factors as well as by the circumstances of pressure. Resistance is inherent in integrated animist societies.

The reactions of the different economic categories may be outlined before we proceed to examine these elements in more detail. Islam spreads easily among townspeople. It is a civilization and cannot establish itself solidly without a strong foundation of urban life. Towns in which commerce, industry, and learning concentrate are important meeting-places of contact influences and people engaged in these occupations become Muslim. Islam, therefore, makes immediate appeal to the urban mind, individualistic and wide-visioned, yet limited by the interests of market and workshop. Islam also appeals to the nomad mind. It has no hierarchic priestly system, its method of worship is simple and free, and it makes no far-reaching demands for change of outlook and mode of life. In other words it is a layman's religion. Islamic culture among nomads is, in general, Islam in its most primitive form. Fulbe, Tuareg, and Teda nomads have remained true in essentials to their traditional culture, but west-Sahara arabized Berbers, finding in Islam a compensation for their decline in status, have allowed it to effect great changes in social institutions. Islam appeals to trading peoples on both these grounds, for trade in Africa is a kind of nomadism and yet is bound up with urban culture. On the other hand, its appeal to the rural mind whose centripetal outlook turns essentially upon the tending of life, crops, livestock, and children, is correspondingly weak. The farmer's religion harmonizes exactly with the interests of his daily life. Islam has no natural substitute for this integrated structure and is only adopted voluntarily after a religious vacuum has been created. Although every Hausa trader accepted Islam, agriculturist Hausa resisted its encroachment over their lives even after their rulers adopted the outward apparatus of an Islamic state. ʿUthmān dan Fodio's justifications for the *jihād* in Hausaland were genuine enough, yet even after its success pagan rites were openly practised, whilst today, after a more thorough islamization, they are perpetuated in the *bōri*, and many communities remain pagan.

Islam has not always had the opportunity of following external conquest with the apparatus for deepening the broken surface. Songhay of the middle Niger who became Muslim during the askiya régime discarded their veneer after its collapse, only to be re-islamized during the movement emanating from the *jihād* of ʿUthmān dan Fodio. The Bambara, as they descended the valley of the Niger and occupied the regions of Segu and Karta, came under strong Islamic influence from Soninke. They incorporated Islamic elements into their religion, but did not become Muslims until the Tokolor conquest. Immediately the French occupation freed them from the Tokolor yoke they threw off their Islam and their religious 'associations' gained new vigour. Similarly Shehu Ḥamadu of Masina forced those Dogon who lived on the plain to accept Islam, but this evaporated after the occupation. He did, however, obtain lasting results among groups where the ground had been prepared by the work of Soninke agents.[1] Return to the land in an animist environment has even led to long islamized people adopting the local cults.[2]

The extent of effective Islamic penetration must not be overestimated. Even in the north many peoples (Serer and Jola in Senegal and Bambara and Dogon in the Sudan) have been little influenced. The Khasonke riverains of the Upper Senegal indicate how long it takes Islam to influence people in touch with it for centuries. Only conquest enabled Islam to gain a foothold. When the French took over these territories large numbers who had been forced to pay it nominal allegiance reverted, but an inroad had been made and some, such as the Dyalo (Sero) branch whose chief, Mori-ba, made his submission to al-ḥājj ʿUmar in 1855, remained Muslim. The advance of Islam since the

[1] Mass conversions were not necessarily ephemeral when other factors were involved as is shown in the case of the Somono. These are a group of fishers on the Niger of mixed origins (Bambara, Bozo, and Soninke), formerly subject to the Bambara of Segu and speaking their language. In 1860, when al-ḥājj ʿUmar, after taking the Soninke town of Sansanding, was menacing Segu, Ḥamadu III, ruler of Masina, sent a contingent of troops along the right bank of the Niger with the object of recapturing Sansanding. The army was delayed at Koni and the soldiers of Masina employed themselves proselytizing among the Somono with such success that they burnt their 'idols' and embraced Islam *en masse* (see M. Delafosse, *H.S.N.* ii. 294–5). In the Somono we have a group of mixed origins, subject to Bambara chiefs, who were sufficiently acclimatized to Islamic influences to be ready to reject their old religious safeguards and find in Islam a means towards unity and self-assertion.

[2] M. Delafosse gives an example of the regression of long-islamized Soninke groups to animism in consequence of their loss of slave labour and return to the land (*R.M.M.* xi (1910), 39–40). P. Marty (*Études sur l'Islam en Côte d'Ivoire*, 1922, pp. 150, 456) gives instances of Mande and Fulbe in the Ivory Coast, Fulbe and Bambara in the Sudan (*Soudan*, ii. 160–1), and of freed slaves (*Guinée*, p. 449) who 'buried the Qur'ān'.

French occupation has been largely follow-up. To judge by what he sees along the trade-routes the traveller may conclude that West Africans are mainly Muslim, but if he gets off the high road into the villages of the bush his impressions will be greatly modified. The dispersion of traders has led to the formation of settlements all over animist regions, but they remain distinctive foreign elements. This is especially true of a vast region comprising the Haute Volta, Ivory Coast, and Ghana. All the Voltaic peoples resisted Islam. Some conditions for Islamic penetration were present with regard to the Mossi, their situation in the Sudanese zone and the presence of Muslim minorities engaged in specialized activities, Dyula traders, Hausa shopkeepers, and Fulbe herders. But the most important factors were absent. Their strong feudal system provided peace and prosperity and impressed habits of order and hard work, whilst immigrant Muslim communities were under the control of a minister of state. The historic fact that they were never conquered by the armies of Māli and Songhay, nor by nineteenth-century Muslim adventurers, and their control of their Fulbe pastoralists was such that no local cleric like those of Masina, the Futas, and Gobir was able, by taking advantage of internal troubles, to set up a theocratic state.

Peoples with less-developed political systems, such as the single-celled paleo-nigritic communities who live along the belt 10° lat. N., have been equally resistant. Until the present century southern forest peoples lay outside the range of Islamic radiation. The religious systems of the Yoruba, Dahomean, and Gold Coast regions contrast with the simpler religions of the Sudanese. Only special conditions, such as the conquest of northern Yoruba and the decay of their religion, opened the way to Islam. On the other hand, Islam made no inroads among the Ibo of south-eastern Nigeria for the conditions necessary for its diffusion and assimilation were absent. They were out of the Fulbe range for the climate was unsuitable to invaders. There were no towns and no ruling classes to realize the advantages of Islam.

The real factors of resistance are those institutions, like family and mystery cults, which govern community life. Elements of animist culture, if viewed in isolation, would not appear to offer great obstacles. The ancestor cult could be accommodated in the early stages of transition since belief in immortality is integral to Islam and the family attitude it supports accords with Islamic psychology. Similarly exogamy is not in direct opposition to Islamic law, though Islam tends to favour in-marriage. The real obstacle to conversion is the integration of religion with every aspect of life, and Islam seeks to change the basis of authority.

When we proceed to consider all the factors involved we shall see that group conversion is normally but the highlight of a long process of historical change. Not only does Islam cast a long shadow before it, but also in order to be accepted in a free situation the ground has to be prepared. The decisive point generally results from a combination of external pressure and internal breakdown of religious authority. Historical and psychological factors aiding the spread of Islam will be considered next.

Objective Factors. The main historical factors leading to the spread of Islam have been trading relations or economic proselytization, religious imperialism, and the opening-up of Africa by Western powers.

(*a*) *Trading Relations.* Islam was first introduced into West Africa by traders. Their activities in purveying Islam along with their goods have continued ever since. Muslims, being members of a supra-tribal society with widespread links, tend to get the trade of a region into their hands. Soninke, Dyula, and Hausa have been important Islamic trading peoples, but their influence, being dependent upon other factors, has been unequal. Rarely have they obtained political power. An exception is the Dyula community of Kong who held a monopoly of the weaving industry as well as commerce and used their economic power to obtain political control and even embark on conquests. In modern times the economic-religious movement of the Murīds in Senegal has been a powerful proselytizing force. Through the settlement of traders elements of Islamic civilization become absorbed into the folkways of local culture. Islam is a necessary passport for animist traders working in Muslim areas. They become Muslims less from conviction than as a matter of course, just as they adopt their de-nationalizing dress.

(*b*) *Religious Imperialism.* Islam in power is secularized theocracy and this always leads to forms of religious imperialism (not necessarily by force) and the application of the principle of *cujus regio ejus religio.* This factor became powerful with the formation of theocratic states during the last century, the principal period when Muslims forcibly converted animists. Such conversions were shallow, but when succeeded by an organized and stable government the conquered animists gradually adopted the imposed religion. The conquests of Askiya Muḥammad of Songhay, whose effect on the spread of Islam was ephemeral, may be contrasted with those of Shehu Ḥamadu which led to the permanent conversion of the peoples of Masina. In consequence of the

European conquest the *jihād* proper has had its day and although examples can be given of indirect pressure being put on pagans by Islamic chiefs in Northern Nigeria and fanatical outbursts in Bambara country against Komo and Nama shrines, these are exceptional. In Ivory Coast and Dahomey, for instance, the clergy are concerned primarily about their own communities and make no protest against the idolatry around them because the ethnic religions are in a sense the established religions. The Dyula have scarcely influenced the pagan communities of Senufo and Kulango among whom they have been settled for 300 years, largely because political power, except in Kong and Odienne, remained in the hands of pagans.

Conquest brings a great increase in the number of slaves. This has been more of an aid than a hindrance to the spread of Islam. It might not appear to be in the slave-raider's interests to narrow his field by fostering conversions, but the Fulani of North Nigeria regarded conquered territory, whether the inhabitants were Muslims or pagans, as a reservoir of slaves. Slave-raiding broke up village religion and dispersed tribal groups, and the slaves, when settled in villages to cultivate for their masters, accepted Islam as an integrative factor.[1] What conquest could accomplish in only a limited way was carried through in consequence of the

(*c*) *Opening-up of Africa* by European powers and the policy adopted by colonial governments. New facilities for communication, security along trade-routes and growth of towns gave traders a formerly unheard-of radius of activity. In towns the detribalized and those temporarily isolated from their religious milieu, feeling the need to link themselves with another social group or to regroup, found their common denominator in Islam. Under the system of indirect rule adopted in Nigeria the rulers and their subordinates in the native administration, from district chiefs to doorkeepers, did not hide their contempt for pagans. Sons of local chiefs sent to native authority schools adopted Islam in order to be with the majority and escape the feeling of being despised.

But the most important effect is the way the impact of Western civilization has weakened the foundations of the local religions, set in motion a social revolution, and thus prepared the way for the adoption of a universalist religion. This leads on to the

[1] In Futa Jalon are 300,000 descendants of slaves out of a population of 750,000, in Liptako (Dori), 55,000 out of 80,000, and in Adamawa the Fulbe, numbering only from 50,000 to 100,000, claimed a quarter of a million serfs.

Subjective Factors which derive primarily from Islam as a civilization.

(*a*) *Religious and Social Reintegration.* When communal life was broken through conquest, forcible removals, and slave-raiding, or today is imperilled or disintegrating under new conditions and demands for which the local religious foundation is inadequate, individuals, families, and even ethnic groups, feel the need for a religion which will help to reintegrate their social structure. That Islam has proved such a factor of integration is shown throughout all that follows.

(*b*) *Accommodation and Syncretism.* The way Islam adapts itself to animist peoples and the psychological process of its assimilation will be studied later. This process is simplified by the fact that African Islam is characterized by a series of gradations. Thus the form in which the animist first encounters Islam is little removed from animism so far as the psychological aspects of conversion are concerned. Islam, therefore, does not at first appear to demand a violent break with the past and has many points of contact. It is true that it possesses a body of legal regulations affecting every sphere of life which might be expected to conflict with local custom, yet an examination of social forms shows that many Islamic elements fall within the framework of African customary law and far less points of conflict arise than with Christianity. The most obvious sphere is that of marriage. The traditional marriage system, especially the key institutions of polygamy and bride-price, have proved serious obstacles to the adoption of Christianity. Islam, on the contrary, has not experienced this difficulty since these institutions are part of its marriage system. Conformity to regulations which conflict with customary law is not insisted upon since the clerical mediators of the law are Africans. Islam also makes precise and reasonable ethical demands and such elements as its taboos fall naturally within the sphere of African mentality.

(*c*) *Cultural Prestige.* Through its system of intellectual and material culture Islam opens new horizons. It is the religion of the Book and from that stems the superiority Muslims display when confronted with pagans. Desire for knowledge and pride in the acquisition of letters has been an important factor in the past, but today this desire is mainly directed into other channels.

But we must not think of movement into Islam as primarily a social and cultural phenomenon. Not merely does the religious factor operate in the wider context of these contact influences, but it exercises a definite attraction.

(*d*) *Religious Values.* Christianity has never been able to escape from the dilemma as to whether it is justified in employing material as well as spiritual means for its extension. Islam has never experienced this dilemma. But it has not resolved it by relegating the spiritual to what seems a secondary place. Religion is the vital cohesive element in the Islamic system and, however obscured it may seem, it is in fact omnipresent.

The religious factor gains ground primarily through ritual and customary observances, for it is these rather than difference of belief which first strike people in contact with another religion. Islam's obvious signs are the prayer ritual, the Ramaḍān fast, death ceremonial, and taboos. Its animistic ideas are important, yet Islamic animism is not local and limited like the old, but a universal animism, and the animistic Muslim can take his place in a universal society. The laicization of religious functions adds to its appeal. Clerics form a new class but they are not members of a priestly caste, the profession is open to anyone with the training and gifts. Similarly Islam laicizes the magic it recognizes as part of the religious structure. The cleric is at one and the same time teacher-guide and medicine-man.

Islam has powerful religious assets which, if combined with other forces, exercise a strong influence. It has the utter certainty of being the true faith, and it is this which impresses more than the idea of the one God. Islam offers a heaven of a recognizable, because material, bliss; and the confident assurance the Muslim displays of attaining Paradise exercises a clear attraction. Life's problems are settled because Islam has its answer to those both of this world and the next. If the cost of affirming the unity of God, which means the cost of breaking with former safeguards, is not too great a new world lies wide open. Islam bases its apostolate upon its spiritual authority, the efficacy of its religious practices, and the longing men feel for a religion of certainty. This apostolate is not necessarily exercised consciously, but none the less it works surely within the context of all the other factors.

Contact Agents. The important thing about the agents of Islam is that they are Negroes spreading Negro Islam. The *Bīḍān* (Whites) have not played the great role some have assigned to them. They are too proud, showing only too plainly that they despise the *Sūdān* (Blacks), to be good propagandists.[1] The effective representatives of Islam are

[1] P. Marty (*Soudan*, iv. 193) mentions as exceptional a white Tawātī trader settled at Sansanding in the eighteenth century, whose tomb is honoured because he 'took part in all the prayers of the mosque of his quarter alongside the blacks, which is very unusual for a white Muslim'.

traders and clergy, whose functions are often combined in the same person. The role of traders has already been treated. Like the trader the cleric forms part of animist society. Like the griot or praise-singer he has a position in the chief's entourage as well as in village life. Al-Bakrī reports that Muslims held positions at the court of the pagan king of Gāna. By recognizing the cleric the chief seeks to increase and harness on his people's behalf all resources of cosmic power. Although, like the griot, the cleric is regarded as a social inferior there is this difference, he does not belong to an endogamous caste, but to a class whose members can obtain wives from local society. Tradition and history are full of accounts of how the son of a cleric by the daughter of a pagan chief succeeded his maternal grandfather and raised Islam to the status of the imperial cult. When Muslim overrule is established the cleric in each pagan village establishes a routine of Islamic calendar observance. These clerks consolidated the gains of secular rulers, stabilized the Islam of neophytes, and inculcated the routine of Islamic social practice. Through these agents intermediary communities are formed. Wherever the mediator takes up his residence, though but temporarily or periodically, he marries a local woman and a Muslim family is created within the animist community. The family acquire land for subsistence cultivation and through the mother the children grow up as members of the local group and yet through their father are linked with the wider world.

Muslim chiefs, officials, policemen, soldiers, and servants to Europeans may also act as agents of Islam. The initiative of chiefs as agents has often been stressed but needs analysing more carefully. Provided Islam is 'in the air', only when a chief belongs to a different ethnic group from that of his subjects will he consider joining Islam in order to reinforce his authority, but he does not expect his subjects to follow his example. The settlement of an alien Muslim group amongst animists, leading to the formation of an *imperium in imperio*, has sometimes made it difficult for a chief to maintain his authority unless he adopted Islam. But examples may also be cited of chiefs who joined Islam only at the last ditch after the majority of the subjects had been influenced. If Islam is not 'in the air' ruling classes wearing a cloak of Islam when they imposed themselves on pagan communities may shed it altogether, as, for example the Mbanya kings of the Gonja in Ghana. Chiefs as agents tend to cancel themselves out. It is not so much that they are important as agents as that the chiefship system provides conditions which aid the penetration of Islam. Only rulers of theocratic states attempted to propagate Islam among their subjects. Islam, with its concept of the equality of believers and the right of the clerics to criticize secular rulers, is a potentially anarchic factor. Chiefs may adopt the religion as a link with higher civilization, but they do not necessarily wish to be imitated by their subjects. Thus the chiefs of Māli, Songhay, and Bornu did little to encourage their subjects to adopt Islam. At the same time, when Islam becomes the imperial cult it inevitably exerts a wide influence. Muḥammad Belo wrote: 'It is well known that the government of a country follows that of its chief. If the chief is a Muslim then the country is *dār al-Islām*, if a pagan then it is a pagan country.'[1] In this he is right. If the chief is a Muslim then the country is regarded as *dār al-Islām* although his subjects remain pagan, for Islam receives recognition as the state cult.

Over-simplification and a piecemeal approach must be avoided in assessing the causes of religious change. The impact of Islam is far more complicated than any listing of historical and psychological factors make apparent. In a given situation we are faced with the interaction of objective and subjective forces; also, as has been indicated, religious change is not merely a question of stimulus but of response. When studying a particular community we have to consider all these influences: the intensity and duration of contact and consequent habituation to Islamic elements, and psychological factors such as inherent forces of resistance and the losses sustained or advantages gained from acceptance.

3. THE PROCESS OF RELIGIOUS CHANGE

The difference between Islam as a developed civilization with a body of religious doctrine and the African religio-social systems with which it is in contact is so profound that the psychological shock of conversion would seem as great as with Christianity. It is not so in practice. The reason is that African Islam in contact with animists is characterized by a series of gradations which act as insulators passing Islamic radiation on, diminuendo, to animist societies. Thus the form in which Islam first makes its impact upon the animist seems little removed from animism. This gives Islam the advantage of rarely finding itself in direct contact with animists in a form whose cultural level is too high to render mutual understanding possible. Consequently the psychological shock involved in change of religion is reduced to the minimum. Islam does no violent uprooting but offers immediate value

[1] M. Belo, *Infāq al-Maisūr*, London, 1951, p. 184.

without displacing the old. Further, the agents of Islamic radiation are people who, whilst possessing a supra-tribal outlook and higher cultural background than the animist, are African, who live happily in the village and take to themselves local wives.

Three main stages in the assimilation of Islamic culture are discerned in animist societies subject to Islamic radiation. Discussion of these will help to distinguish apparent changes from real in any particular community. The first stage is preparatory, the infiltration of elements of Islamic culture into animist life. The second is the conversion, characterized more by the break with the old order than the adoption of the new. The third is the gradual process by which Islam changes the life of the community.

The first stage, the preparatory conditioning of people for the acceptance of Islam, is characterized by the breaking down of barriers and the adoption of aspects of the religious and material culture of Muslims. Such elements are the wearing of Islamic amulets, ornaments, and dress, and the acquisition of food and household habits. These elements are not in themselves specifically Islamic, though they are factors which distinguish Muslims from pagans. At the same time, the adoption of a new material trait does not necessarily involve the assimilation of its inner significance. Thus Songhay and Hausa chiefs have adopted the Tuareg muffler, but not the mouth-taboo with which it is associated.[1] Islamic elements also enter into the religious mythology and practices of animist cultures, for they can absorb a good deal without change in inner direction. Through Mandinka the name for God has been applied by forest peoples in western Guinea to their creator-god,[2] but it remains an impersonal spirit who plays no role in communal life, and is not offered prayer or sacrifice.

The pagan Bambara illustrate the way Islamic elements can be assimilated without upsetting the religious system. In addition to the vague belief in Ngala they have adopted the Islamic calendar, the festivals of fast-breaking and the great feast being celebrated as the chief feasts of the ancestors. The orientation of the grave follows Muslim custom. Islamic religious terms and expressions are in daily use. *Ṣadaqa* is employed for offerings to gods, differentiated in the sense of 'alms' from their own terms; whilst the expression *bisimilay* (*bismillāhi*) is

[1] An association noted by Ibn Ḥawqal who travelled among them in A.D. 960: 'They claim that the mouth is shameful and must be concealed like the pudenda because what goes out from it is more tainted than what goes out of the latter' (*Ibn Ḥawqal*, ed. J. H. Kramers, i. 102).

[2] Kpelle (Gerzé) and Kono *yala*, Manon *wala*, Gbanda *ngala*, Toma (or Loma) *gala*, and Kisi *hala*.

used in sacramental invocations and magical incantations. The meaning is not known, it is a phrase of power.[1] Islamic myths, such as the seven heavens and Adam and Eve, have entered their mythology, and a legend attributes the Komo society to its acquisition by Mūsā, *mansa* of Māli, when on pilgrimage to Mecca in A.D. 1324.

At this stage neither religious nor social life is affected. At most they may be called pagans with a veneer of Islam. Many dislike saying they are pagans, especially schoolboys and others brought into touch with a wider life beyond the tribe. Out of 343 children in a Methodist school in Bunumbu circuit of Mendeland only one would admit having a pagan father (or uncle or guardian), whilst 211 said their fathers were Muslim and 131 Christian. So the old religion is weakened through the shame of being despised. All that can be said of people at this stage is they are significant in the negative sense that they are not hostile to Islam. Young men go to towns, plantations, and mines to earn money to marry and are influenced by Islam. On their return they settle down to cultivation with all that means of the farm religious cycle. When traders come to the village they say they are Muslims and perhaps pray with them. The elders tolerate all this provided it is not characterized by separation from communal ritual. Villages acquire praying-places for the convenience of traders. In Temne villages prayer-enclosures (*an bɛsɛ*) delineated by logs or stones may be seen immediately adjacent to an ancestor house (*a-boro məsar*) in which are stones representing the ancestors. These villagers who call themselves *a-Mɔre* (Muslims) use both, they 'make *salli*' on the one and offerings to their ancestors' spirits on the other.

The chief elements of Islamic religious culture which are assimilated are not those belonging to its inner genius but its animistic elements. Their assimilation is facilitated by the animist's consciousness of impersonal power working through persons and things. He is ready to make use of any available magical technique. Consequently the Islamic magician finds him credulous of his alleged powers and ready to buy his charms and amulets. So the characteristic Mende 'medicine' (*to halei*) is associated with texts written on wooden slates and suspended in various ways in houses and on farms. The word *jinn* is employed by everyone in contact with Muslims for spirits of all kinds and it is

[1] Similarly Mende have acquired a vocabulary which merely reflects Islam and has little influence upon their religious ideas as is evident from their practice. Such words are *Aijɛnɛ* (heaven) and *Jahannama* (hell), the idea of a Day of Judgement, *seli* (to pray), *jumbui* (Ar. *dhanb*, sin).

significant that pagan Yoruba say *anjɔnu*, reflecting an earlier adoption, whilst Muslim Yoruba say *alijano*.

There is as yet no break with the old religion, but a stage is reached which is characterized by the assimilation of significant elements of Islam, the consequent parallel existence of two religions in the community, and a weakening of the local religious structure, until a point of crisis is reached. This is the dividing line when the old religious authority is consciously rejected. But we must make it clear that we can rarely talk of an individual and never of a community being converted to Islam in the sense of any sudden reorientation of life around a new centre. There is a long process during which this reorientation is being effected. So far this assimilation has had little to do with Islam as a higher religion, but mainly with Islamic animistic and cultural elements. Nor does the adoption of specific religious elements involve any radical revolution in religious belief because they have not undermined faith in customary religious safeguards. Cult communal rites continue to follow the traditional pattern, though signs of weakening are evident since the attitude of the group to them is no longer uniform, whilst some rites and ceremonies are mutilated or neglected.[1] If the significance of the first germinal stage is the negative one that the people are not hostile to Islam, the significance of the second is that they are Muslims in the sense that they are favourable to it. Although there is no definite point in this process of change where one can state 'Here animism ends and Islam begins', there is a point where one can say of an individual, 'This man is a Muslim, not a pagan'. He is an animistic Muslim undoubtedly, but a change has taken place in his inner consciousness whereby he has crossed a boundary-line and is on the threshold of a new world.

A similar boundary-line is also evident in family or village life which marks the end of the rule of the old order, and this is far more significant than individual changes. Change of religion is as fully a social as an individual matter. The two aspects are interwoven. A pagan who goes to work in town may find it expedient to become a Muslim, but on his return home he assumes his natural place in village life. He is not a rebel against his society. Adoption of Islam by individuals

[1] As has been pointed out objective pressures may weaken spiritual authority. So important are religions like the Komo that anything which weakens the relationship of the community with the supernatural powers these rituals embody, leaves the way open for the adoption of Islam. These cults also follow cycles of flowering, arrest, decline, and revival, and during a period of decline a community may be susceptible to pressure to adopt Islam as a new safeguard and integrative factor.

is significant merely as a factor aiding the conditioning of village mentality in its favour. But when a whole family or village becomes Muslim this is not the result of the cumulation of such individuals as the culmination point of an Islamic movement within it, deriving from the interaction of many influences, a movement which leads the village to make the decision to give up inherited safeguards and to base life around a new centre. What really marks the change is shown by the answer to the question, 'Who or what governs life?' There comes a point when the ritual pattern is disrupted, a point in family life when ancestral conciliation no longer rules, a point in village life when the chief spirit around whom worship was concentrated is rejected for the formerly unworshipped sky-god whose name becomes a synonym for Allah as alone worthy of worship, whilst former gods become subject or evil spirits; a point symbolized by the neglect or destruction of images, masks (*persona*), *boli*, and other material supports of spirit.

Chiefs often find it politically expedient to be accepted as Muslims, but make no fundamental change. They are still pagans who have adopted outward aspects of Islam, but they have not passed the boundary line. The clergy, however, are getting a hold and the one thing to which they are opposed is communal idol worship over which they have no control. The point comes when the chief gets rid of his 'idols'. Europeans in south-west Nigeria exhibit beautifully carved figurines which the then Alãfin of Oyo, supreme head of the Yoruba, who had recently made this break, had dispersed. This is especially significant when chiefs are divine (the Alãfin is the incarnation of Shango, god of lightning and smallpox) whose divinity was transferred to their effigies. Islam seeks to eliminate the forms of former worship and the clergy do not compromise once their position at the chief's court is no longer that of an additional soothsayer and magician but recognized representatives of the supreme God.

Holas, in his study of the function of the mask among the Kono of French Upper Guinea, shows how profound a role it plays in the religious, social, and political life of people uninfluenced by Islam:

> Le Masque, c'est le *code moral* personnifié. Le Masque, c'est l'agent permanent, chargé de sauvegarder le coutumier non écrit. Il est le *Grand Initiateur*, qui fait de l'embryon humain une unité sociale valide; il la guide à travers les vicissitudes de la vie, la protège, et la punit au besoin.[1]

It is obvious why the mask must lose its authority when people step

[1] B. Holas, *Les Masques Kono*, Paris, 1952, p. 147.

over the dividing-line. Islam seeks to be the ruling factor in life and although the mask may continue to operate in islamized societies it has lost its former socio-religious function, and may even degenerate into a form of clowning. More commonly the material symbols of the dying cult are not destroyed but simply neglected. Ancestor houses gradually disintegrate under wind and rain and are not renewed, whilst masks are sold to visiting anthropologists.

Missionaries in the interior of the Gambia stated that a neighbouring Fula village 'became Muslim overnight'. It was not so simple as that. Mandinka and Fula clergy came from French territory to receive courses of injections at the mission dispensary and remained for weeks at a time propagating Islam in the neighbourhood. The process took years before the villagers decided to embrace Islam as a community. Behind this the work of the previous two centuries, whereby 90 per cent. of the people of Gambia became Muslim, should not be forgotten; so that at last the Fula abandoned their defences, made the decisive break, and joined the dominant religious stream. This point, therefore, marks conversion, a real break with the things of the past and a beginning of the process of becoming an Islamic community.

Hausa Māguzāwa villages provide examples of all stages of change. First the process by which aspects of Islamic social practice are assimilated without displacing traditional rites (*tsāfi*). Their ancestral cult has already disappeared independently of Islamic influence, and their most important communal rites are offerings to spirits by family head, village chief, or a priest (*sarikin arna*). But the local cleric becomes more involved in family affairs. He is associated with the naming and marriage ceremonies and funeral rites. Through his mediation the family seek God's blessing and yet maintain traditional rites upon which their religious outlook is still concentrated. But a point is reached when the community makes a definite break with *tsāfi*. Allah is recognized (perhaps through a communal calamity) as a righteous and stern deity who cannot tolerate other gods than He. The great mourning feasts, associated with beer drinking and libations on graves, are discontinued. Adoption of the Islamic lunar calendar has already led to changes in the ritual cycle of the agricultural year and the family rites change to Islamic fertility rites. Communal worship of spirits is not abandoned, but becomes confined to a mediating group of initiates (*'yan bōri*), which means a change in the whole conception of relationship with spirits. Individual offerings, it is true, go on everywhere and *bōkāyē* (medicine men) as well as *'yan bōri* offer sacrifices to conciliate spirits causing illness, but the significant thing is that the communal cults are broken and can never again rule village life.

Hausa say of a Ba-māguje who has made the break: *kwanche māguzanche* 'he has discarded paganism'. *Kwanche* is used for discarding old clothes to put on new. The outward changes are the most important. Islam reaches the soul through these. The inner change is a long process about which no one is consciously concerned. *Māguje* (pl. *māguzāwa*) is derived from Arabic *majūs* (Qur'ān xxii. 17) and *māguzancho* means 'the way of the *majūs*' or 'heathenism'. Its application was an attempt by the jurists of Northern Nigeria to find a formula by which irreconcilable Hausa pagans in their midst could be admitted among those who are allowed to retain their religion upon payment of *jizya*.[1] The pagans of Gobir and Maraḍi in French territory are not known by this term but by the Hausa word for 'pagan', *arne* (*anne*, *asne*).[2]

Among the things which *azna* must discard after adopting Islam are the *fatauchi* or bullroarer associated with pagan ceremonial; fertility rites for which there are Islamic substitutes; and the *kōrāna* (or *jīgo* or *gausami*), a short forked stick of ḳirya wood erected at the doorway of a compound and village gateway, or a sacred tree, at the foot of which fresh milk is poured every Thursday night and sacrifices offered at certain seasons. For the *kōrāna* is substituted a bundle of Islamic charms (*riḳi*), other types (*kafe*) are installed with sacrifice inside the *zaure* (entrance porch). Religious vocabulary changes completely and there is a horror of words associated with pagan worship.[3] The dispossession of the old conception of 'sacrifice' for that of *ṣadaqa* is especially significant. Thus Mende give up the old red rice sacrifice (*mba gboli* made with red palm oil) for the white rice sacrifice (*mba jaa*). 'Red' and beer, associated with pagan sacrifices and libations, come to be abhorred.

The third stage of assimilation, within which are many gradations, marks the definite transition to an islamized society. It is characterized by genuine belief in the efficacy of Islam's religious sanctions, and

[1] See Saḥnūn, *Mudawwana*, ed. Cairo, A.H. 1324–5, i. 406.

[2] The Hausa also say *kwanche kwaraya* for 'he discarded idolatry'. The *kwaraya* (or *shanchi*) is a pagan contest in which the contestants fight with a band of iron having a knife-sharp edge, worn on the right forearm. It is regarded as their national sport, but I do not know what religious significance it possessed in the old life.

[3] *Tsāfi*, pagan worship, comes to mean 'fetishism', and so with its derivatives, *ma-tsāfi*, 'fetish worshipper', *ma-tsāfa*, place of worship, *gidan* (*ḍakin*) *tsāfi*, 'fetish hut', and *gunki*, 'fetish', though this is still employed by the *'yan-bōri* for their rite.

involves actual change in conduct and social custom. In the sphere of religious practice the village prayer rectangle becomes frequented regularly in the evening, and the fast and religious taboos are observed. Children are sent to Qur'ān schools and the religious orders contribute towards providing many with an inner Islamic society. Thus the individual gains a wider outlook, self-assurance and a feeling of belonging to the *umma* of God.

In the sphere of social usage and custom great changes take place. Since Islam is a universal religion with a sacred law its ultimate effect upon tribal culture is a disintegration of specific aspects of the old order (exogamy, widow-inheritance, initiation ceremonies) and the gradual transformation of society. But the process is such that the disintegration and reintegration seem natural. The new culture gives new values without radical displacement of the old, since Islam has been forced to adapt itself to the mentality and mode of life of Africans. In social practice Islamic ceremonial connected with transitional rites is easily adopted, whereas change of elements affecting the actual social structure may take centuries unless accelerated through the influence of Muslim theocratic governments or the recognition of Islamic law by European goverments.

4. THE RESULTS OF CONTACT

(*a*) *Reciprocity in Culture Contact*

Islam has become an African religion. The changes that ensue from the meeting of cultures are dynamic in character. Islam and African cultures have a reciprocal influence. As it spread among Africans Islam was conditioned by their outlook and customs, but Islam in turn changed their outlook and customs. Consequently every Muslim society varies in its understanding and practice of Islam. In adopting it people reject no more of their inheritance than is absolutely necessary. Certain beliefs and practices, it has been shown, have to be rejected because they are incompatible with Islam or too bound up with the old government of life. But people are atavistically resistant to change in psychological attitudes, and their attitude towards nature-spirits and powers of magic may acquire renewed vitality through association or coalescence with their counterparts in Islam, hence the value of its spiritism and magical practices derived from similar elements in the religion of the pagan Arabs, whose incorporation into a universal religion naturally aids its assimilation by animists.

The acceptance of new religious elements involves reinterpretation, and the interpretation is largely, though not wholly, in terms of the old. The impact of Islam is consequently weakened since acquisitions are assimilated to pre-existing standards, as for example when funeral rites are interpreted as a means of eliminating the dangerous contamination of death, releasing the soul and rendering it harmless to the living. Similarly with the interpretation of the *ʿidda* of widowhood.

At the same time, it must be emphasized, this process is reciprocal. Old ideas cling to naming and death rites, yet they are transformed when given an Islamic character. The process has to be seen, not in static terms of addition and subtraction, but in dynamic terms of growing more fully into Islam. What Islamic culture assimilated from animist culture is transformed in the process, for it is assimilated, not adopted, into Islam; at the same time Islam is affected by what it assimilates. The result is not fusion but synthesis.

The process of islamization adopts the way of myth and fable. Circumcision and excision are given Islamic legends of institution based on the Abrahamic myth. The custom thus acquires a new supernatural sanction; no longer is it practised because it was the custom of the ancestors, but because God ordained it. Consequently it is transformed into an Islamic purification rite. Similarly New Year festivals fuse with 10th Muḥarram. In this way the acts of communal life are enveloped in an atmosphere at once Islamic and African.

The adoption of Islam leads in time to a profound reintegration of the cultural life of the people. What must not be forgotten is that throughout this process Islam must remain true to type. Many elements cannot be assimilated, and though the clergy may have to compromise with irreconcilable practices through force of circumstances, they remain illegitimate and await a reformer to mobilize public opinion against them. The given data of Islam, its dogma and rules, its distinctive apprehension and insight into the totality of existence, cannot theoretically be denatured, though understanding and practice may modify the direction. The crisis Islam faces of losing its true identity is averted by the law books in the hands or memories of clerics, and orthodoxy is governed by the degree to which their rules are applied. Islam changes conceptions of life as its practical rules, fortified by legends, gain acceptance. A considerable time-lag elapses before the Islamic conception of life seeps through, but when it does the culture evolves into something new, in harmony with the Islamic ideal, yet truly African. The readjustment of social life to the new ideal proceeds naturally. The Muslim community based, not on blood relationship but on religion, becomes a reality, with its leaders, norms of conduct, and communal rituals.

When a social unit, family, clan, village, or people, is converted *in corpore*, as for example the whole of the Wolof during the nineteenth century, the structure of society is preserved in an islamized form. Islam has succeeded in doing this better than Christianity. Islam in Africa has developed cultural patterns that are at one and the same time African and Islamic. But the Christian community, especially where formed by converting individuals, comes into being in the midst of the animist community in such a way that it is in conscious opposition to it. Islam reduces the opposition of the community to the minimum through its system of gradations, and its penetration has not led to the formation of the conflict personalities or 'marginal men' characteristic of Western influence. In this way Islam transmutes itself into African life.

(*b*) *The Reorientation of Life through Islam*

The way Islam remoulds the life of individual and community is through the acceptance of an inner principle whereby Islamic religious symbols give new context and driving-points to religious life, and through the adoption of patterns of common religious and social practice. Typical of the first is the redirection of petition. A ceremony like the eighth-day naming is retained, but pagan prayers are changed into Muslim prayers and the ceremony acquires a new orientation. When people pray *for* the dead instead of to the dead they are Muslims, however many pagan ceremonies they still retain.

The unifying features provided by Islam which all acquire are:

1. The recognition of Islamic law in theory, and in practice through the acceptance of the clergy as guides of conduct. With them is associated the Qur'ān school as an essential feature of village life.
2. The 'pillars' as evidence of following the Muslim way: confession of faith (the stress being on 'confession'), ritual prayer, fasting, and almsgiving, with pilgrimage as an ideal goal.
3. The observance of common taboos and common calendar rites.
4. Incorporation of a minimum Islamic element into the transitional rites at naming, circumcision, marriage, and death.
5. Acceptance of the efficacy of Islamic supernatural powers: the ability of the cleric to bring power into activity through ritual words and actions.

It is a remarkable testimony to the unity of Islamic practice to travel through the Sudan from the Atlantic coast to the Red Sea and find all Muslim peoples performing the same burial rites. Outward forms and symbols deeply influence inner life and the adoption of Islamic ritual leads eventually to reinterpretation of life by the Islamic values for which those symbols stand.

The adoption of Islamic legal regulations transforms social institutions. Clergy insist as soon as they can upon certain minimum requirements, chiefly connected with family life. Since an institution like the family has its roots in all aspects of life, change from matrilineal to patrilineal family, or from communal to private ownership of property, must affect the basis of social life. Islamic law is often in opposition to customary law and it may be centuries before it assumes predominance.[1] In practice they are reconciled. What clerics require is reverence for the law, although it is ignored. They, therefore, recognize customary law (modified by Islamic law) as basic law just as in the spiritual sphere they acknowledge forms of animistic belief.

The new culture which emerges as a result of this process may be compared to an embroidered textile. The basic fabric is the animist culture. Upon this is embroidered the Islamic pattern. In time this pattern is woven into the very texture of the background. The actual structure of the ground is no longer discernible, but it remains firmly rooted and provides the variation between different ethnic cultures. This reintegration is still in process, yet there is a recognizable West African Islamic culture, different from that of North Africa, formed through the interaction of Islamic law and indigenous cultures.

The fact that this process of integration is rarely complete implies spiritual dualism. Religious life rests on a double foundation, the animistic underlayer and the Islamic superstructure. Baba of Karo, a Hausa woman, revealed through her autobiography transmitted by Mary Smith, shows how the Hausa spirit cult has its function parallel to that of Islam when she says: 'The work of *malams* is one thing, the

[1] Pressure from other factors is needed before certain institutions can change. Islamic law has been powerless to supplant the custom of Tuareg maintaining traditional life in central Sahara, whereas the new environment of the Ullimmeden and others who live around the Niger bend provided the conditions for Islam to break the hard core of custom. In Senegal Islam gained the allegiance of ruling and warrior classes of Serer, but not of the masses. However, those of Niumi chieftaincy in Gandul, when fighting against the Tokolor *mahdī*, Ma Ba, thought it expedient to adopt Islam (*c.* 1860) and their social life has subsequently been changed. They have lost the class system characteristic of Wolof and Serer society and adopted many Islamic civil laws (see F. Lafont, 'Le Gandoul et les Niominkas', *Bull. Com. Ét A.O.F.*, 1938, p. 414). On the other hand, Islam, greatly as it has influenced the Wolof, has not changed their organization in closed groups.

work of *bori* experts is another, each has his own kind of work and they must not be mixed up. There is the work of *malams*, of *bori*, of magicians, of witches; they are all different but at heart everyone loves the spirits.'[1] Old religious attitudes and customs rule in the sphere of village civilization and interwoven with this is the new civilization. But we can never generalize about the extent to which Islam is the supporting foundation of life for it depends upon the stage of integration reached. If we take a particular community, a Hausa or Songhay village, we may find that the main weight of everyday life rests more upon the old religion than the new. On the other hand, if we go to a Tokolor village we may find that Islamic law has had a profounder effect than upon Berbers of North Africa.

Retention of seemingly conflicting loyalties, attitudes, and institutions does not necessarily signify conscious dualism in people's lives. The African Muslim is not torn between two warring forces. In everyday life the two strands of religious inheritance are reconciled, for they are woven together like the warp and weft of different textures into a cloth of complicated pattern. The natural coexistence of old and new is seen in the canalization of clerical functions. Clergy fall into two categories, not of persons since the same person combines both, but of function—that of the clerk and the medicine-man. Islam in West Africa is 'primitive' religion to the extent that the Muslim clerk is at one and the same time representative of sacred law and medicine-man. In other words, religious and magical elements are scarcely differentiated. The foundation of both is belief in the power of the unseen world, and the possibility of establishing contact either by prayers or by forces.

Besides concepts and institutions assimilated by Islam from former cultures and as it were rebaptized into it, are others retained by Muslims from the old background which, even by the incorporation of Islamic elements, cannot be assimilated.[2] Magic practice, spirit invocation, and possession persist because everybody, clergy included, regard them as efficacious. Hence the persistence, not merely of Islamic clerics practising magic, but of pagan medicine-men and spirit cults, condemned in theory but tolerated in practice. Since these peoples belong to two

[1] M. F. Smith, *Baba of Karo*, 1954, p. 222.

[2] The spirit cults of the Hausa cannot be regarded as islamized, but *malams* recognize the necessity of giving *ṣadaqa* to the spirits; as Baba says: 'When we moved here to New Giwa the spirits filled the town, the European spirits began to come too. The *malams* advised that it would be right to give these strangers alms so that they should dwell at peace in the town' M. F. Smith, *Baba of Karo*, p. 209).

religious cultures such ineradicable features have to be taken into account in this study.

The effect of Western civilization has also to be taken into account and the way it has affected Islamic societies will be considered in the last chapter. All that need be said at present is that in an integrated Islamic community the old and the new are kept rigidly apart. An illustration of the relative position and influence of animist, Islamic, and Western cultures in relation to indigenous life is provided by the markets of Nigerian towns. In the market of the old walled city of Zaria, for example, little is offered for sale that would not have been there before the British occupation. On the stalls will be found baskets of millet, guinea corn and maize, tomatoes, onions, sugar-cane, pepper, spices, and the leaves of plants used for seasoning. Manufactured goods found there are substitutes for native products, like large bowls whose functions are the same as the calabashes they make themselves which have not been displaced. In the market the interwoven strands of the religious fabric can also be seen. The trader in Qur'āns and Arabic legal texts squats alongside the *ḍan mai-ganyē*, the trader selling roots, twigs, bones, feathers, and other ingredients for concocting charms. Down a side street a leather merchant will sell us indifferently a case for our Qur'ān or a sachet for our latest charm. Both these strands are in mutual opposition to the modern wares of the *Sābon Garī*, the 'New Town', where we have to go if we wish to buy a printed Hausa book. Thus while Islam and the pagan underlayer have blended the resultant syncretism is in juxtaposition to the new influences from the West.

5. THE MAIN CYCLES OF ISLAMIC CIVILIZATION IN WEST AFRICA

Islam has played a major role in shaping the cultures of North Africa, Sahara, western, central, and eastern Sudan. These regions can be differentiated and contrasted because they had been moulded in distinctive ways before Islam appeared on the scene. In West Africa three cycles can be distinguished: sahil, west and central Sudan. The first, the Saharan-Sahilian, characterizes the Moorish tribes in particular. The Tuareg come within it, but not the Teda who belong to the central Sudan cycle. Islamic features are the North African form of saint cult and *ṭarīqas*, whose peculiar psychological attitudes were not transmitted to Negro Islam except to a limited degree. Another characteristic is the formation of clerical clans. This type of Islam has influenced the Sahilian zone, including towns like Timbuktu, and Negro slaves.

Though Islam came to West Africa through Moors and North Africans Negro peoples have given it their own distinctive stamp. In the Sudanese belt it is convenient to refer to three Islamic culture cycles: west, central, and east. The eastern or Nilotic Sudan culture, distinguished by a profound arabization and widespread influence of *ṭarīqas*, does not come into this survey and is quite distinct from West African Islam. It has only influenced the regions of Baqirmi and Waday. The difference between the western and central cycles, due to pre-existing factors, is apprehensible by direct contact but difficult to formulate.

The west Sudan cycle is represented by the Tokolor and Soninke, the first Sudanese converted to Islam, who established a distinctive type of Islamic observance. Characteristics appear in the pattern of family festivals (e.g. simultaneous naming, pounding, slaughtering, and shaving at the eighth-day rite), spirit practices, after-life beliefs ('crossing the river'), and special Islamic legends. The Songhay of the middle Niger form a transitional zone having characteristics of both cycles.

The central Sudan cycle, subject to Islamic radiation from the Nile as well as the Maghrib, characterizes the Kanuri and Hausa. Kanembu and Kanuri gave Islamic practice a distinct stamp without being active missionaries, regarding Islam as the cult of the aristocracy and a specialized occupation. The city-state with its elaborate hierarchy and class system contrasts with the village-state organization and occupational caste system of the west. The failure of the attempt to found a theocrasy in Hausaland was due to the power of this structure which captured reforming clerics. On the contrary, in the west the reformers did not carry on the previous organization but formed a type of state more closely based on the precepts of Islam.

Other West African culture areas (western Guinea, southern Sudan, Voltaic, and south Guinean) were not influenced by Islam until the nineteenth century. Their Islam is characterized by the type of missionary influence brought to bear on them and the simultaneous penetration of Western civilization.

3

Influence of Islam upon Ideas of the Supernatural and Human Personality

I. ON BEING A MUSLIM

THE sketch of the process of islamization given in the last chapter shows why such contradictory statements are made regarding the ratio of Muslims to pagans in a particular region or within a certain people and also about the depth of their Islam. For instance, one book states that all Songhay are Muslims, due to the fact that the majority would claim to be so before an administrator, whilst in another book one who had studied the beliefs of the Songhay of the middle Niger writes, 'almost half are not islamized and the rest in general have only a thin transparent Islamic veneer'.[1] It also shows why it is generally impossible to state that a people became Muslim at a particular date or even century. Sometimes it is stated that the Bozo became Muslim in the fifteenth century, whilst others say they changed in the nineteenth century. It depends upon the criteria of the student. An anthropologist studying their social institutions may regard them as pagans for they exhibit the characteristics of an animist society influenced superficially by Islam. Yet the Bozo claim to be Muslims. Islam has been infiltrating into their life for centuries and they are an example of the coexistent parallelism of two religious outlooks. The ideal given by Muḥammad Belo in his *Apologia pro Bello Sancto* connot be applied:

> One cannot judge merely by what is professed. The man who bows down to an idol to gain an hundred thousand dirhems, even though he utters the confession of faith, prays, fasts, accomplishes the pilgrimage and does good works, yet by one act of heathenism destroys a thousand acts of faith.[2]

The actual criterion adopted by *jihād* leaders, including Muḥammad Belo, is shown in accounts of their conquests. After the skirmish of Kelem-Bīn, Muḥammad Belo 'set free those prisoners who could recite the Fātiḥa and perform the ablutions correctly; whilst the remainder, that is to say those who could not correctly accomplish these two

[1] J. Boulnois, *Empire de Gao*, p. 68.
[2] Muḥammad Belo, *Infāq al-Maisūr*, p. 10.

requirements, were reduced to slavery'.[1] Apostasy was refusal to pay tribute, similar to Abū Bakr's attitude at the *ridda* which followed the death of the Prophet. In *Ta'rīkh Sokoto* we read over and over again that the ruler and people of X 'apostatized'. Many of these had never accepted even the outward forms of Islam, and all the phrase means is that they had revolted against the overlordship of Sokoto. In Nupe 'he has been converted' is *wuṇ ágba*, literally 'he has submitted', and a 'convert' is *lagba*, 'one who has submitted'. Al-ḥājj 'Umar called those he forced to join Islam *tūburu*, and in all Mande languages *tūbi* (Ar. *tawba* 'repentance') is employed for both 'submission' and 'conversion' (cf. Ar. *aslama*).

The very act of profession means change, for it involves the acceptance of clergy as guides. If in an atmosphere of disintegrating pagan cults there is no function of family or village life from which the cleric is absent and few in which he has not his part to play, then they are Muslims.[2]

In the studies which follow thoroughly islamized peoples, such as Tokolor, Fulbe of Masina and Futa Jalon, Soninke, Dyula, Songhay, Hausa, and Kanuri, will be drawn upon for illustrations, for only thus can we see what basic changes have taken place and what elements of native religious culture have been retained. At the same time, the religious life of peoples in process of change, like Temne and Mende in Sierra Leone and Nupe in Nigeria, are just as important, for they will show what Islamic elements are first adopted and what elements of animist belief and practice they displace.

2. THE IDEA OF THE SUPERNATURAL

(*a*) *Theology and Ritual*

Islam is not taught as a system of belief but as a legal way. It is important to realize that whilst Islamic law, including the legal requirements of religion, is handed on by written tradition and is therefore exact, the specifically religious elements of Islam, conceptions about the nature of God and human personality, man's relationship with God, and traditions concerning the Prophet, are handed on primarily through

[1] Al-ḥājj Sa'īd, *Ta'rīkh Sokoto*, in appendix to *Tadhkīrat an-Nisyān*, p. 194 (313).

[2] It need hardly be pointed out that labels tell little about what a man really believes. Moreover, if one is born into a society that is naturally religious, in the sense that consciousness of the supernatural world pervades life, a vast amount that is attached to the sphere of religion is simply natural secularism. Hence the place materialistic and magical beliefs occupy in religion, since they derive from fear and the desire to exploit the unseen world.

oral tradition. Islamic ideas spread by myth and fable and aphorism. The result is that within the sphere of village life one can find an authority on the minutiæ of ritual ablution and prayer, everything in fact dealt with by the *Risāla* of Ibn Abī Zaid, but no one who knows anything about theology. *'Ilm al-kalām*, or scholastic theology, is unknown even by the learned in the great teaching centres. The reason is obvious if *kalām* is seen in its historical context. *Kalām* arose out of the clash with rationalistic tendencies, the Muʿtazilites, on the one hand, and the Aristotelians, on the other. In other words, the function of *kalām* is essentially defensive apologetic. Ibn Khaldūn wrote: 'This science provides the means of proving by rational arguments the dogmas of the faith and of refuting the innovators who, in matters of belief, deviate from the doctrine followed by the first Muslims.'[1] But African clergy have never needed apologetics since religion has never been a subject for scepticism. Thus it comes about that the village cleric can tell one practically nothing about God except that He is One, and he will recount weird tales about the life of Muḥammad, the doctrine of the resurrection and after-life. The community seizes upon Islamic myth (which often reflects animistic Arab mythology by association with a Biblical figure) because it performs a role similar to their own mythology in explaining and justifying ritual and social custom.[2]

The original source in Islamic tradition can generally be divined; but not always, as in the legend of 'the Prophet and the Pig'.[3] In addition, old taboos are islamized by being given an Islamic legend of sacralization; thus Mandinka say the *sa-nan* (*Daniellia Oliveri*) must not be cut down because the Prophet was accustomed to pray under its shade. Clergy regard theology as impractical and unrelated to life, but by means of these stories Islamic doctrine is accommodated to their mode of thought and Islamic usages gain the Sudanese soul.

The first pillar of Islamic action, the 'profession' of faith, emphasizes the contrast between belief and unbelief which is something new in the world of ethnic religions. Beliefs about spirits, for example, are not the subject of scepticism. Knowledge of the supernatural world is traditional knowledge. A superstructure of cosmological beliefs and supernatural lore is in fact largely built upon religious behaviour, although such knowledge is not clearly formulated and is known fully

[1] *Muqaddima*, transl. de Slane, iii. 40.

[2] Most unlikely people relate these legends. A Nupe who knew little about Islam related how, at the battle of Badr, a defeated Meccan leader, on being asked by the Prophet to repeat the *shahāda*, derided it by whistling (cf. Qur'ān, viii. 35). Consequently anyone who whistles will be in danger of the Fire.

[3] See below, p. 67.

only by a few initiates. When a new spirit is discovered its nature is deduced from its reaction to the diviner-propitiator (Mande *n'ya-tigi*) and that leads on to the adoption of ritual. Such formulation is therefore related to the traditional mode of life and institutions of the local inhabitants, for it arose out of them and gives cohesion to their experience of the supernatural. But Islam brings a fixed system of belief, not subject to change according to circumstances or locality, formulated by advanced literate peoples, and unrelated to the life of any particular people. Islam introduces an ideological dualism, formerly unknown, between God and devil, good and evil spirits, this world and the next, heaven and hell, and new legalistic categories of prohibited and permitted. It brings an individualistic conception of religious adherence, and sets up tension between 'believers' and 'unbelievers'. These contrasts are acquired through the combination of Islamic practice and oral tradition.

In the process of islamization as in the animist world institutions are adopted before significant change in belief. The Prophet is reported to have said: 'Islam is external, faith is of the heart.'[1] Clergy regard the law books as authoritative for what constitutes a Muslim, and since they are primarily concerned with what one does, not what one believes, ritual action became the standard of differentiation between believer and unbeliever. The Hausa says *kana salla?* or *kai masallachine?* 'Do you perform ritual prayer?' for 'Are you a Muslim?'[2] Not common belief but common action is the important thing. Ideas orientate themselves around institutions, and thus change the outlook of the family or village unit, and the social unit changes them through the process of synthetizing old and new. Thus people grasp the myths which spread with Islamic institutions, mould them, and even invent them.

The studies of beliefs which follow are therefore incomplete since the ritual action of which they are the theoretical expression is reserved for subsequent chapters. Here it is only necessary to emphasize that although theology and cult are closely related, like myth and ritual in the pre-Islamic stage, performance of the same rites is more significant than common beliefs. This can be illustrated everywhere by the fact that ideas about God and man are tenuous, vague, and associated with elements of pre-existing cosmology. Islam is primarily a distinctive way of performing religious acts, observing specific taboos and social customs.

[1] Aḥmad b. Ḥanbal, *Musnad*, iii. 134–5. Cf. the clear distinction made between submission and belief in *sūra* xlix. 14.

[2] Cf. Fulfulde *jūldɔ*, pl. *jūlbɛ*, 'Muslim', from *jūlde*, 'to perform ritual prayer'.

(*b*) *The Idea of God*

Although no western Sudanese were monotheistic each had a myth of a source of being or demiurge, from which derive myths of how the realm of spirits and mankind came into existence. Mande peoples believe the source of being created twin children (not separate deities, except for cult practices, but complementary principles) from whom sprang all godkind and mankind. Whilst primal deity could not be directly concerned with human affairs the heavenly twin was closely associated with man. Characteristic of Islamic monotheism is the conception of God as illimitable power, excluding all other except spirit beings He has Himself created like angels and *jinn*, and although the polytheism to which Islam is opposed is plurality of gods, not plurality of spirits, acceptance of Islam involves abandoning worship of all beings other than God. If the twin is associated with earth and sky, Allah is always associated with sky, never earth. The earth-god is often simply a *primus inter pares* within a polytheistic complex from which it could not be separated, and therefore could never be associated with Allah. But that equation was possible with the spirit who was not approached by ritual in the old cult.[1] Nupe gave the impression of having had an original dual deity, Sòkó, sky-god, and Guṇnuṇ, earth-god.[2] Ritual was concentrated on Guṇnuṇ, hence the stress was on the act, Guṇnuṇ ritual, and the personality of Soko was relegated to the liturgical background of other cults. Today belief in Guṇnuṇ has disappeared, but a disintegrated form of Guṇnuṇ ritual persists, whilst Soko has become a synonym for Allah. Similarly Abron (Ivory Coast) in contact with Dyula have identified their sky-god with Allah and relegated their earth-god to a subordinate place. The earth-god is the most important in ritual practice in the old religion, and it is always the name of the god for whom no cult exists which becomes a synonym for Allah. Only in this sense does Islam find a point of contact with the idea of a high-god. A characteristic of Songhay and Hausa is that God has no known name. Hausa *azna* call God *ubañ giji* 'Lord', and Songhay *Iri-koy* or *Yer-koy*, 'our Lord'.[3]

[1] The process appears to be analogous to that adopted by the Prophet who stressed that worship was due to Allah, high-god of the Meccans, alone. He complains that He is treated no better than lesser gods: 'They assign to Allah from the tilth and cattle He has produced a portion, and say: "This is for Allah" (as they assert), "And this is for our associate-gods"' (vi. 137, Bell's translation).

[2] See Appendix II.

[3] Boulnois has suggested that the reason why Songhay have no name for God is because He is conceived as wholly spiritual and has no personality (*byia* or double), or derives from a taboo analogous to that which forbids the pronunciation of a person's name under certain circumstances (J. Boulnois, *L'Empire de Gao*, 1954, p. 81).

Where detailed studies have been made of the cosmology of West Africans, as by Mme Dieterlen of those of the Bambara, it is clear why the conception of Allah does not fit in with previous ideas. The difference of attitude is seen if Mande on two sides of the dividing-line are contrasted. Whilst the Ṅala of the Bambara is very vague, employed it is true liberally in salutations and exclamations, and often means little more than 'god' (e.g. Ṅala Pemba), Ala of the Dyula is omnipotent, unique, creator, Lord of all spirits, and sustainer of the law.[1]

Although belief in Allah is introduced as a radically new element, to some extent it correlates itself to previous conceptions. Allah is not thought of as personal spirit who invites believers into communion. No dialectic tension is involved in the relationship of God and man, Master and slave, as is set up in the relation between ancestral spirits and earth-bound members of their family. Allah is supreme power, utterly removed from men, but giver of magical powers. To the extent that God is thought of in old animist modes of thought it is obvious that comprehension only goes part way. If He takes the place of pure spirit He is impersonal. Where thought of as *the* God who rewards and punishes, He cannot be approached even by clergy. They are interpreters of His revealed word, not intermediaries. Clergy can tell one nothing about God except a string of attributes.[2] This is not surprising since it derives from the nature of Islam. Thought about God can only be speculative and that is forbidden. Since He cannot be conceived as an anthropomorphic being, since there can be no symbol of Him, not even mental, nor of His manifestations, and no ritual involving communion, He cannot be conceived at all. But it is not necessary to know anything about God in order to believe in Him. Belief in God shows itself in action, in readiness to perform the rituals and order life as He has ordained. The crucial question in religious change is that whatever was worshipped before, whatever had validity for authorizing sanctions of conduct, must be rejected. Muslims are not consciously adapting old beliefs and there is no question of changing a high-god into Allah at all. The great step is monolatry. This comes as a new departure with the change in the acquired term Allah to acknowledgement that only He shall be worshipped. Then other spirits become

[1] Although, according to L. Tauxier (*Le Noir de Bondoukou*, pp. 251, 266), Dyula invoke the spirit of the sky and the spirit of the earth at the naming ceremony, they have no cult of these spirits.

[2] Terms for the attributes are both Arabic or formations from their languages; for example, in Hausa *Makaḍaichi*, 'the One', from *ḍaya*, 'one'; *Mahalichchi*, 'Creator', *halitta*, 'to create', from Arabic *khalaqa*.

His servants, though they are of greater practical importance in the affairs of man than God.[1]

The second half of the *shahāda* is not held in much account in West Africa, except in the new mythology. The Prophet is known under various forms of *nabī*, but synonyms have been formed in most languages such as Messenger (Hausa *ma'aikin Alla*). The Messenger was sent to announce the good news to man, that is, to transmit the Qur'ān, the divine word, and teach men obedience. The cult of the Prophet is not observed apart from a few clerical circles in Masina and Futa Jalon. The *ṭarīqas* make him rather more prominent, but among the *murīds* of Senegal, who have the psychological characteristics of the cult, he is eclipsed by reverence for their founder. Clergy recite poems and the *Dalā'il al-khairāt* in his honour at festivals.

The Book transmitted by the Prophet cannot be dismissed as lightly as the transmitter. Its influence is enormous. It is the basis of life, not through direct study, but through the legal treatises of the Mālikī school. All clergy are imbued with the feeling of the superiority of their Book. For centuries they have been dealing with illiterate peoples and in such an environment the influence of a written book is out of all proportion to the number of those who can read it.

(c) *The Spirit World*

The supernatural world as comprehended by village Muslims is an amalgam of African and Islamic beliefs, but whilst the Islamic elements are universal the African elements vary from village to village. No detail will be attempted since the belief of each people is a study in itself, whilst, in order to see the effect of Islam, it is more important to consider this all-prevading aspect of life from the point of view of ritual.[2] Although Islam provides a radically new departure with its

[1] With the idea of God comes that of the devil for whom invariably Islamic terminology is employed (Hausa *Shayḍān*, Mande *Syetāne*) since it is an entirely new conception having nothing in former thought with which to correlate itself. But the devil does not loom large in Muslim thought because of the stress laid upon Allah, leaving no possibility for a dualism of authority, and the words are more commonly used simply for evil spirits.

[2] See Chap. 5, § 2. The identity of spirit agency and ritual shows itself in the polyvalence of terminology which embraces both concrete and abstract. For example, the Mande word *ntana*, 'taboo' also embraces 'totem', the object of the taboo. Similarly the Nupe word *kúti* has the meaning of spiritual activity and the rite in which that activity is actualized. *Kúti* means an impersonal channel of divine activity and might be translated by 'communication'. The rite is *kúti-gba*, 'doing *kúti*'. The fact that the Nupe have not much mythology may be due to the fact that *kútiẓi* do not have distinct personalities. They are emanations of divinity, and since contact with them is exclusively through ritual, the identification of agent and rite is natural. Similarly with the Mande *la-siri*. *Siri* means 'link', and *la-siri* expresses the fact or possibility of linking up with divinity. It means religion (more particularly the cult of the family-founder and

stress upon the unique God, it does not deny the existence of spiritual agencies for this is affirmed by the Qur'ān, and the question is: What is the relationship between God and spirits whereby the Muslim may know what attitude to adopt towards them?

Islam condemns any form of relationship with the supernatural world that would limit the sovereignty of God. The change brought about by Islam shows itself in ritual. Clergy endeavour to persuade people to cease making offerings to spirits as independent guarantors of sanctions of conduct, and their efforts are directed towards undermining the authority of heads of communal cults. When offerings to ancestors, for example, are discontinued without causing calamity they cease to be thought of as governing their earthly families, and this is a tremendous break in the link between man and the spiritual world.[1] On the other hand, Muslims as much as pagans regard a spirit world as surrealist and propitiation of nature spirits continues among poeple who have lost ancestral and mystery cults. Former spirits either help God in the government of the world or join the disbelieving *jinn* whom He has created and allows to exist. The good are regarded as intermediaries, executing God's wishes but having a measure of autonomy within the limits He imposes. The relationship between man and the unseen world, therefore, remains an interaction of forces, but the basis has changed from religion to superstitious practice.

Formerly the basic classification was between spirits of the village who were worshipped and those of the bush, to guard against whom magical measures were taken. But following its practice of ideological antithesis Islam splits them into categories of good and bad. In fact, the distinction is between pagan spirits regarded as inimical to man, and Islamic spirits who are neutral. The attitude of the Hausa *iskōki*[2] depends upon the way they are treated, though Hausa assert in consequence of their adoption of Islam that there are believing and unbelieving spirits, *baḳaḳēn iskōki*, 'black spirits', and *farārēn iskōki*, 'white spirits'.[3]

the spirit of the soil on which the family was founded, not the ancestral cult, *mā-n'ya-ko*) and also has the concrete sense of religious cult. Divinity can localize and concretize itself in an object and in ritual, or more correctly, in a combination of the two, altar and mask being part of ritual.

[1] Among Serer the line of communication is: (*a*) *Rog*, supreme God, (*b*) *Fāgol*, ancestral and nature spirits, (*c*) *Yal Fāgol*, people in direct personal relationship with a spirit, a quality transmitted by heredity, (*d*) the ordinary individual. The displacement of the *Yal Fāgol* breaks the whole line of communication.

[2] Sing. *iska*, lit. 'wind'. They also refer to them as *marau da haki*, 'the wind that ripples the grass'. Songhay also use *hew*, 'wind', as a synonym for the doubles of possessive *holē*.

[3] Similarly in the other languages: Dyula *gyina-berē* (good) and *gyina-dyugu* (bad); Songhay *holē koara* (white) and *holē bi* (black).

Islam brings the word *jinn* as a synonym for spirits in general or depersonalized spirit agencies, without necessarily displacing old terminology. Thus Songhay differentiate between *dyin*, the first inhabitants of the earth who became invisible on the creation of man, and *holē*, created corporeal beings like men but invisible, who play a very important part in human life. Because white *jinn* are admitted, practices connected with them are accepted. The Fulani practice of *surkulle*, casting spells by means of incantation, is justified by claiming that it was revealed by believing *jinn*. Clergy are supposed to enter into relations with these good *jinn* for the purpose of divination and magic.[1]

Islam introduces a new category of supernatural beings in angels. They are of little practical importance in religious life because one has no direct dealings with them. The clergy teach that each individual has two personal angels, but among the Hausa at least they have not ousted personal *iska*. In the western cycle some people regard every living thing as having a guardian angel. This may be a transference of the Islamic term to personal tutelary spirits, or an Islamic baptism of the soul every living thing possesses. Angels are employed in Islamic divination lore, as when western clergy address themselves to the angels of the four cardinal points in finding out lucky or unlucky times or days. Mande have adopted the Arabic singular *malāk* (*malāka*, *melege*), but others use the plural (Songhay *almalāhika*: Hausa *malā'ika*, pl. *maklā'iku*), probably because it appears much oftener than the singular in the Qur'ān. Mandinka sometimes call angels *rūhu* (cf. Qur'ān, 70/4, 78/38, 97/4) and Hausa *rauhānī*. Khasonke do not distinguish between *meleke* and *dyina*.[2] Clergy know the names and functions of the chief angels, and there is general uniformity, because, though spread by oral tradition, there is the fixed body of knowledge in the background.[3]

[1] One Nupe cleric said all *jinn* (*àlijènuẓi*) are unbelieving. Satan is omnipresent and head of all *jinn*. Clergy make use of *jinn* as agents of misfortune in order to get people to desist from sacrificing to spirits. *Jinn* are persons but different from us, invisible to us, though we are visible to them. They do not die, but will die with all living things on the Day of Judgement. He said many clergy consulted *jinn*, though he would never do so himself. He made charms for individuals or houses or farm-plots, and also taught his pupils a protective prayer. Whilst he was talking a man entered the hut who appeared to be afflicted with a nervous disease. After he had gone I inquired what was wrong with the man and was told that one night when approaching his home he saw an *àlijènu* which so frightened him that he became ill and was left permanently afflicted.

[2] According to Ch. Monteil, *Les Khassonkè*, 1915, p. 384.

[3] Nupe clerics, for instance, mentioned *Ẓibililu* (Jibrīl), messenger of God; Minkayila (Mīkā'īl) as powerful as Gabriel whose function is to send rain and fructify; Darayilu ('Azrā'īl) who carries the departed spirit to God; Walakīri (an-Nakīr), a twin angel who tests the faith of

3. THE NATURE OF MAN AND HIS DESTINY

Beliefs concerning the nature of man and his destiny after death play a significant role in people's outlook on life. At the present time these beliefs are in a fluid state, even among the long islamized. The animistic strata in which they are embedded is very tenacious and few Islamic conceptions which might take their place have been introduced, with the exception of beliefs concerning the after-life. The personality of man is a sphere to which West African Islam, in spite of the importance of its belief in the survival of human personality, has little to contribute, though Islamic philosophy, which is utterly unknown, has ideas of the soul having much in common with those of West Africans. Eventually these ideas disintegrate, especially among peoples influenced by Western currents, though lingering on in the lore of dreams and witchcraft, and thereby drain the colour out of religious life. Beliefs held by peoples who have been recently influenced by Islam (Nupe in Western Nigeria; Mende, Temne, and Susu in western Guinea) will be outlined first and then those of the more deeply islamized (Mande, Hausa, Songhay, and Tokolor).

Nupe believe that man consists of three principles united in one body or 'form' (*nakà*): *ráyi* (or *láyi*) eternal soul, *èshè* earth-bound soul, and *fiṇ̣ge* shadow soul. *Ráyi* is translated as 'life' for death occurs when it leaves the body. *Eshè* is personality spirit, closely linked with the body around which it lingers for some time after death and whose form it can take as an apparition.[1] The *fiṇge*, which has no connexion with the visible shadow, also called by the same name, travels during sleep and dreams are its actual experiences. A twin has two *ráyis*, one *èshè*, and two *fiṇges*.[2]

the departed (Munkar was not known); Azarasilu (Isrāfīl), sounder of the trumpet at the Last Judgement, and Māliki, guardian of the fires of hell.

[1] *Eshè* is also used for a familiar spirit (*bagi nana de 'shè*, 'this man has a familiar'), generally in a bad sense, and is equivalent to the *egà* of a witch (see below, p. 118). Only certain people have this *èshè*. The witch catches the *fiṇge*, not the *èshè*.

[2] Nupe believe animals have three souls: *rá*ʷ*i*, *nagbaṇ*, and *fiṇge*. *Ráyi*, as with man, is life which goes to *èku*. *Nagbaṇ* is earth soul, but different from man's *èshè*. When a hunter kills an animal or bird he believes that its *nagbaṇ* enters his heart (*nagbaṇ gábá alo u*, 'the spirit of the lion has entered him'). When he absorbs too much of this spirit power with which animals are charged he begins to rave or is taken ill. To nullify or mitigate the effects hunters are hedged in by taboos and perform special rites. If he shoots ten guinea-fowl he throws two away so that the *nagbaṇs* of the other eight will stay behind. Fishermen do the same after a large catch. Clergy teach that there is nothing to be afraid of from *nagbaṇs* of allowed animals killed in accordance with Islamic rites. This entering of an animal's spirit must not be confused with metamorphosis when the *èshè* of a man and *nagbaṇ* of an animal interchange. The *fiṇge* of an

An account of what Muslim Nupe believe happens after death shows that Islam has not modified traditional ideas on the personality of man but has influenced those on the after-life. The four elements of man function harmoniously until God calls the *rá̧yi* when they are dissociated. 'The *rá̧yi* goes to *èku* (next world) and is afterwards known as *kuchi*, the *èshè* remains around the body,[1] and the *fifiṇge* goes off into the bush.' Immediately after burial God sends *rá̧yi* back into the corpse (*ekúṇ*) and twin angels (*Walakīri*) arrive to test his Islam. They open the grave, examine for forty days, and report to God. If the verdict is favourable they return and illuminate the grave, if unfavourable they compress the corpse, and then take the *rá̧yi* to either the good or bad section of *èku*. The bad section is like a prison where the inmates await sentence, not a place of punishment. The good section is like happy family life on earth. They remain in *èku* until the Day of Judgement, when *rá̧yi* will return once more to its body until allotted to either *Alijena* (Firdausi), or *Emiṇa* (*Jahannama*). These places of final repose are now uninhabited. On reincarnation, in which all Muslim Nupe and Yoruba believe,[3] the *èshè* and *fifiṇge* join together, but God provides a new *rá̧yi*. Consequently at the resurrection a large number of *rá̧yis* will return to the same body, though others said *rá̧yi* is needed simply to revivify.

Most peoples of western Guinea have a tradition of 'crossing the water-place' (Mende *tewenjamɛi*). This has been attributed to Islamic ideas, but the *Ṣirāṭ* is almost completely unknown. Pagan Mende say that when a person dies he goes on a journey for three days carrying a bundle on his head. He reaches a river on the fourth day (third, if a woman) and a ceremony takes place on earth to help him to get across.

animal is like that of a man accounting for its dreams and giving forewarning. In the house where the writer was living in a rather isolated place on the outskirts of Katcha, a dog was very restless and whining throughout the day. That night it was killed by a leopard. Nupe explained that the leopard's *fifiṇge* had caught the dog's *fifiṇge* during the day, whence its distress.

[1] A widow is married to her husband's *èshè* until the 115th day after death. A woman's *èshè* may remain linked with her body for a year. It is to the *èshè* and *fifiṇge* that pagans offer sacrifice whereby the *kuchi* or *ezàtsuchi* (i.e. departed *rá̧yi*) is appeased. Many Muslims do the same. Clergy preach against the practice, yet if a dead man's child becomes ill before the fortieth-day sacrifice has been offered they think that the departed man wants him and instruct the family to offer sacrifices to the father's *fifiṇge*.

[2] The following expressions are used: *efo kiṇna*, Day of Resurrection; *efo shìriya* (Ar. *sharī'a* is used in Nupe for 'judgement' only), *efo kiyioma* or *ali-kiyioma*, the Last Day (Ar. *al-Qiyāma*); *efo zuṇmago*, the Last Day; *efo misuṇ*, the Day of the Brink or Brim.

[3] Yoruba hold the same trinity in unity conception of the personality of man: *emi* (= *rá̧yi*) is the divine element which unites *ara* (body), *ɔkàn* (= *èshè*), and *ojiji* (= *fifiṇge*). But the simultaneous influence of Islam and the West has led to such confusion that no summary of the material collected can be attempted.

If good he is taken over, but if bad no one on the other side will answer his cry. The good go to *ŋanyagole-hu* and the bad to *ngombimɛru*, but these words are now falling into disuse and pagans say *Aijɛnɛ* and *Jahanama*. Inhabitants of both places can visit the living in invisible form. The ideas of islamized Mende are in a fluid state. When a man dies his life (*ndɛvui*, lit. 'breath') goes. After burial an angel comes and asks his *ngafɛi* (spirit) three times to whom he belongs. If he answers 'to Muḥammad' he will be able to get across the river. All said that before being ferried over debts had to be paid, quarrels settled, and charity given. What has been left undone must be rectified by the earthly family and then the way will be opened for the crossing. If they had lived a bad life a fierce storm will arise and capsize the boat when, some said, the soul is for ever lost, or according to others it is held until all wrongs are righted by the survivors. None mentioned the existence of an intermediate state but of direct transit to heaven or hell. Susu and Temne knew of *lāhira* (in Temne also *ro-kərifi*, 'place of spirits') where the spirit[1] reposes until the Day of Judgement when good and bad will be separated and sent to paradise (*ar-yana*) or hell (*Yahannama*, sometimes *sā'iri*, Arab. *sa'īr*, one of the seven hells). A few mentioned going straight to heaven or hell after the questioning, but since most continue to make sacrifices to the dead, belief in an intermediate state is necessary. Others spoke of going to a place called Abraham after the questioning in order to await the Day.

Mme Dieterlen has described Bambara beliefs.[2] Each person has two spiritual principles: *ni*, 'soul' and *dya*, 'double', both inherited from the last deceased member of the family. *Ni* is the breath and *dya* the twin of the person and of the opposite sex, the shadow on the ground and the reflection in water. Man has two other principles: *tere* which is disturbed when a taboo is violated and may then become a dangerous force (*nyama*), and *wanzo*, original impurity, which is expelled by the rite of circumcision. Death has the effect of dissociating these elements. The *dya* goes into the water with Faro, whilst the *ni* is incorporated in the altar by the family head. They are reunited in the new-born.

These ideas have been considerably weakened and confused among

[1] Their ideas of the human being were confusing. All said that life (Temne *aŋŋesəm*, Mende *ndɛvui*) went straight to God when recalled. An old Temne said 'If the *aŋŋesəm* goes out then there is no more *ɔfəm*' (person). None seemed to have a clear distinction between soul and spirit, though they said everyone is born with a *yina*. This goes off to the dream-world (*ro-mərei*) during sleep, and after death remains with the body until the fortieth day when 'the wife cooks food for her husband and after that, his *yina* having departed, she is clean and free to marry again'.

[2] G. Dieterlen, *La Religion Bambara*, 1951, chap. 3.

islamized Mandinka. All said that *ni* is the life given by God, not the ancestors. Some said that at birth ancestors sent the *dya* of continuity, but only God can provide *ni*. Some said the *dya* and others the *ni* left the body during sleep and can be caught by the witch.[1] Muslims who maintained ancestral rites said the *ni* went to God and the *dya* remained associated with the altars of the family until reincarnated. Death is caused by *Ṅala* sending *Darayilu* (ʿAzrāʾīl, also called *ni-mina-māsa*, 'chief catcher of souls') who carries the *ni* to Arafo.[2] The *dya* remains linked with the body until the completion of the ritual sacrifices. Others said it remains until the decomposition of the body, and after that went into water or bush, or joined the *ni*. Most said it had a function to perform on the Day of Resurrection (*Lo-ba*) when it is needed to give form[3] to the body. At the Judgement the *ni* is consigned to heaven (*ardyana*) or hell (*dyahanaba*), whilst the *dya* ceases to exist, which presumably means that it returns to undifferentiated spirit.

Hausa believe that all living things have body, *rāy*, and *kurwa*. *Rāy* (translated by the lettered as *rūḥ* though to the majority this word means the archangel Gabriel) is the vital force which animates the body, which Muslims said is the personal spirit which goes to *lāhira*. The *kurwa* is closely connected with the body during life and remains linked with it after death until disintegration. It never dies, but they do not believe like the Nupe that it is reincarnated. The *kurwa* is the double of a person which travels in dreams and plays an essential role in possession (*bōri*) when the 'soul' of an *iska* enters and dominates a human being but without displacing that of the possessed. *Kurwa* then is life-force incarnated in all living things, man, animals, insects, and vegetation.[4] It may be thought of as a double. It is not the apparition (*fatalwa*) of a dead person, nor is it the shadow (*inuwa*), though it can be caught by a witch from the shadow,[5] nor is it the soul-substance used by the *bōka* in magic. It can be translated 'earth soul' but has nothing to do with the metaphysical abstraction the word 'soul' evokes. Whilst *rāy* is

[1] *Moṙo n'ya nyini*, 'to seek [to capture] the soul of a person', 'to bewitch'. *A dya tege-le mbè*, 'his vital spirit is severed', i.e. he is at the point of death.

[2] *Al-Aʿrāf*, the place between Heaven and Hell; cf. Qur'ān vii. 44.

[3] The human body is 'form' which is not determined by its chemical composition and is not to be equated with matter. The soul of a man is not contained in his body but in his 'form'.

[4] *Chiyawan nan tana da kurwa*, 'this grass is full of vitality', *gonakinsu ba su da kurwa bana*, 'their crops are not looking healthy this year', *tun da aka haife shi ba kurwa*, 'he has been ailing ever since he was born'. The expression, *yaron bashi da kurwa*, 'this boy has no *kurwa*', means that he is weak. 'This boy has no *rāy*' would mean that he was dead.

[5] *Maye ya kama kurwansa*, 'the wizard caught his *kurwa*'; *ba shi da kurwa*, 'his vitality is low', said of someone who is weak, declining, i.e. who is bewitched.

abstract principle which can exist without a body, the *kurwa* has the form of the body it inhabits. It inhabits all of it, not any particular part.

When a person is about to die his *iska*[1] deserts the body and is said to wander about until it finds its way to the city of *Jan Gari*. When God snatches his *rāy* (*Alla ya karḅe ransa*) death ensues. The *kurwa* hangs about the body until burial (or disintegration), when, according to Muslims, it too goes to Allah, or, according to Māguzāwa, to *rijiyan rāy*, 'the well of life'. It does not return and it is not the apparition (*fatalwa*). Anyone who died through a witch catching his *kurwa* will not rise on the day of resurrection (*ran kiyāma*) because body, *rāy*, and *kurwa* cannot be reassociated. The Hausa use *lāhira* (Ar. *al-ākhira*) for the place of the departed spirits, for the future state in a general sense, and for the intermediate state before the Day of Judgement. Clergy speak of *barzahu* (Ar. *'ālam al-barzakh*) as waiting place of departed spirits.

Boulnois has described Songhay beliefs which are similar to those of Hausa.[2] *Hundi* is the vital force animating the body and has nothing personal about it. The *byia* ('shadow', which Boulnois translates *double*) is the spiritual part of man, his true personality. It is not pure spirit since it has form and is therefore intermediary between spirit and matter. It enters the body of the baby at the seventh-day naming when it becomes a person.

Old ideas have not in any way been displaced among the thoroughly islamized Tokolor. The vital force is *fittāndu* (north-western Fulbe *wońki*, Soninke *yońki*) and the shadow-soul *ᵐbēlu*. The *fittāndu* (or *wońki*) which goes to the next world is impersonal and is absorbed into deity. The *ᵐbēlu* enters the body on the eighth day after birth, but about its fate there is diversity of belief. Some believe it suffers the fate

[1] The *kurwa* may be contrasted with the personal tutelary spirit (*iska*). The *kurwa* is the inner motive force of a person or thing, its vital principle, whilst the *iska* is a supernatural principle exterior to the being or thing. At birth one is given a personal *iska* of the same sex which remains with one throughout life and also another of the opposite sex which normally leaves after marriage (not to be confused with the two guardian angels—an ill-integrated Islamic introduction). Their duty is to protect against other *iskōki*. An Islamic introduction is the division of persons according to their *iskas* into fire, wind, earth, and water, and only the clergy can divine to which group one belongs. Thus if fire marries water the result is disastrous, but fire can marry wind, earth with water, and like with like. The permanent *iska* must consent to one's marriage, and a betrothed person is watched for signs that it is unhappy. If the fiancé experiences something unusual he will be afraid that their *iskas* are incompatible, that, as he will say (*kafadanmu bai zama ḍaya ba*), 'our shoulders are not one', and the engagement will be broken off.

[2] See J. Boulnois and Boubou Hama, *Empire de Gao*, pp. 78–89.

of the body and others that it goes either into the sky or wanders about the earth until the resurrection of the body. But all agree that it can leave the body during sleep when it is exposed to seizure by witches (*sukuṇābe*). Fula of Futa Jalon say that it is the *ᵐbēlu* which goes to Paradise or Hell, but this appears to be the same as *fittāndu* and *woñki* farther north.

The ideas of the nature of man help towards understanding the meaning of God for the African. God cannot be conceived in terms of personality since He is pure Spirit. Spirit is not non-material but the uncreated, or, in positive terms, divine and eternal as contrasted with created. The first of creation is the heavenly twin, complementary masculine and feminine principles. A human being is created when spirit (masculine principle) fertilizes a soul. The Nupe *ráyi* is not a personal soul, but participation of the person (given individuality by his *èshè*) in a world of spirit. Death comes when God takes the spirit into Himself, the consequent dissociation of elements means that the person ceases to exist, though the soul remains until it is refertilized by Spirit when it becomes again a 'person'.

The dissociation, but not disappearance, of these beliefs begins with decay of the organized cults, yet they remain tenacious in folklore. Religious parallelism explains their persistence and they play a great role in ideas concerning divination, possessive spirit cults, and witchcraft. Islam never developed in its adherents understanding of a distinction between soul and spirit which is essential for the African view of the world. The legalistic Islam of African clerics has nothing to contribute on the personality of man.[1]

Islamic ideas all acquire relate to the next life. These are examination whether a Muslim or pagan, reckoning-up of good and bad deeds, Day of Judgement, and heaven and hell; all of which were basic in the early teaching of the Prophet. Islam exerts its greatest influence upon belief through after-death ritual and this inevitably makes a great difference. Death comes to be thought of as a break in the continuity of life, whether the soul is thought to be asleep in the grave or in some form of intermediate state before the Day of Resurrection. The continuous

[1] It is interesting to recall that Islamic philosophers have speculated along lines which approach these beliefs. The general belief of Islam is that man has only one soul, but philosophers, noting the two words *nafs* and *rūḥ* used in the Qur'ān which are derived from the animistic strata of the Arabs, have postulated that there are two. Others write of the Spirit of Watchfulness (*rūḥ al-yaqdha*) keeping man awake whilst in the body and causing him to sleep and dream when it goes away, and of the Spirit of Life (*rūḥ al-ḥayāt*), giving life to the body, whose departure causes death.

tradition or eternity of the African family is snapped, for the possibility of rewards and punishments, of members being consigned to different quarters of purgatory and eventually to heaven or hell, means that families may be separated.

Apart from these regular elements of Islamic eschatology a further belief concerning the presages of the Day of Judgement, surrounding the name *Mahdī*, remains to be mentioned. This belief, by throwing up men who claimed to be the Mahdī, has left its mark in history. In the revolutionary atmosphere of the nineteenth century, characterized by the formation of theocratic states, devastating wars, and penetration of Western powers, conditions became favourable for such manifestations, but they were limited in scope and effect and did not gain the masses. For the last forty years active manifestations have been almost completely absent, and though the Mahdī idea has by no means died out it is not an important factor in the Islam of West Africa.[1]

4. THE EFFECT OF ISLAM UPON IDEAS OF MORALITY

The same parallelism between Islam and the old religion is seen in the sanctions for ethical conduct as in other aspects of religious life. The ethical code of the past was built up through the ages and formed part of the communal heritage. Moral standards were sanctioned by the ancestors and gods who ensured their observance. The moral range was relatively limited, being confined to the groups united by kinship and initiation. Conformity to the code of the group was essential for the well-being of society.

The adoption of Islam implies a radical transference of the values upon which the unity and continuity of the group depend from the old authorities to God. Islam introduces a legal morality of universal application whose sanction in practice is the books of the law. In theory it tolerates no authority other than its law in the government of individual and social life. A legalistic morality is characteristic of the old order and the new and the transition does not appear to offer insuperable difficulties. Legalistic morality, as conduct or duty, is essentially social. The African moral consciousness was formed under the influence of the spirit world. The bond of kinship inspires fear (of incest, for example) for the welfare of the community, and punishment was not primarily directed against the individual but was impersonal. The Islamic moral consciousness is also communal, though its range extends to all who acknowledge its law, but in addition its morality, with

[1] See Appendix III on present-day Mahdī expectations.

its doctrine of reward and punishment, is much more personal. The individual can obtain salvation apart from the group.

Collective conversion, whatever the way it comes about, means a change in the psychological outlook of the social group, manifesting itself in readiness to accept new sanctions and changed behaviour. This change cannot be described in simple categories of addition and subtraction. Islam displaces cults of ancestral conciliation and initiatory societies, consequently the sanctions of conduct deriving from the past lose their religious basis. The great change Islam brings lies in its exclusive claim for the supremacy of its system of moral conduct. Kin privileges and taboos, although in only a vague sense do they stand in the way of an Islamic ordering of society and powerful as they remain, are superstitions in the eyes of Islam. Though Islam displaces certain sanctions for which it has substitutes, others connected with social relationship and conventional taboos remain. Yet the attitude towards them may be modified since they no longer have a religious sanction. The important thing is that Islam now provides the sanctions of conduct, the other elements become social custom. Practical ethics, therefore, are coloured by the legal maxims of Islam, but rest upon a double basis: approved local custom and universal Islamic law amalgamated as the ethics of the community.

So far there is little evidence of strain in maintaining two standards. Old and the new are reconciled in everyday life. But in practice a third determinant of conduct makes its appearance—the will of the spirits. Formerly the spirits were an integral part of religion, but after islamization and the decay of cult associations they no longer fulfil a true functional role in community life. Spirit practices are illegitimate, and their influence may be a disturbing factor. The Hausa *iskōki*, for example, influence not merely *bōri* initiates, but all people of the village, and the spirits may indicate a line of conduct which flouts both the ethics of the community and Islam. In practice it is Islam with which they come into conflict, hence it is mainly its upholders who find themselves in difficulty, and clerics and sometimes territorial chiefs are torn by conflict when they recognize the reality of the spirits and are unable to prevent their wives from participating in *bōri* rites from fear of the consequences. Territorial chiefs are confronted with problems when spirits disapprove of new economic measures, or, in Hausaland, because of the close connexion between *bōri* and organized prostitution.

Old mechanical ethics persist within the Islamic framework of life, and genuine Islamic piety combines with gross superstition. Wrong behaviour is thought to be supernaturally punished. Charms placed on crops work the same way, whether they are Muslim or pagan, in bringing calamity upon the thief. Supernatural forces are neutral in essence; whether the result is good or bad depends upon what you do or avoid doing.

Belief in predestination and resignation to one's lot is characteristic of the religious outlook on life, but too much stress should not be placed on this for predestination in Islam does not preclude the exercise of man's will and it is resignation *after* the event which leads to the ejaculation, 'God has written'. Before the event no one knows what has been decreed, therefore enterprise is not necessarily inhibited. This attitude to life does not in practice find itself in conflict with beliefs in divination or the employment of protective charms.

Actual behaviour in relation to the moral sanctions of Islam could only be discussed in relation to particular peoples, or sections of society, as, for example, the contrast between clergy, traders, and cultivators in one village, but a few generalizations may be made. To the clerics it is by keeping the law that man is saved. There are, therefore, different standards for clerics and people. The learned are absorbed in rigid legalism, content with the practical observance of the law, but the generality are not expected to keep it. What the clerics seek is such consistency of character and conduct as will distinguish a Muslim community. Islamic taboos are accepted without difficulty. Here animistic ideas help Islamic law, for it is a realistic conception to the animist that indulgence in certain kinds of food or actions can call down supernatural wrath. They are also an important element in the achievement of Islamic solidarity and religious self-consciousness. You have only to hear Muslims shouting *Kāfir!* at a child who is urinating while standing instead of squatting to realize that such a taboo forms one of the distinguishing marks between a Muslim and a pagan. These sanctions are the same for all Muslims and constitute a bond between peoples. In this connexion one should note that the Islamic restriction of moral obligations to the *umma* does not differ essentially from the former attitude which restricted them to the kin-group or members of a fraternity. Islam extends hers to all Muslims but not to all men.

Islam brings in the question of values. Its morality is fixed, hence it becomes a question of whether existing ideas and actions conflict with the ideal standard. The problem arises as to how infractions are to be dealt with. Under custom they were punished by the exercise of either ritual, moral, or legal sanctions, or a combination of these. If a man transgressed the ethics of the family the ancestral spirits punished him. Islam denies this and asserts that it is God who punishes even though a spirit is the instrument. The old morality was bound up with community life and infractions were dangerous to communal well-being. Islamic law is not bound up in this way to the community, and many elements find difficulty in being accepted into the body of approved custom; thus in practice different standards of value are accorded to different parts of the code.

Islam specifies categories of wrong actions. In the eyes of the clerics omission of the prayers may be more sinful than idol worship:

> In heaven three men will be wanting. . . . The first is the man who gave half his attention to the worship of idols (*tsāfi*). . . . The second is the man who was a bastard, and had no father; his mother followed a crooked path. The third is a man who excelled them all in evil, he refused to pray five times.[1]

In practice the community forms its own attitude. There is universally accepted positive or negative behaviour such as the obligation of almsgiving or the prohibition on eating pig. Then behaviour disapproved by Islam but retained by the people as part of the body of social custom. Although Islamic taboos will generally be observed, any prohibitions or obligations which are opposed by custom will not be accepted. Finally, there is behaviour like prostitution which falls into an indeterminate field which society condemns, but about which it is not prepared to take action. Conflict appears when an Islamic state takes upon itself the duty of order and punishment. In the conflict those instincts which prevent the formation of a new order are called forth. Hence all theocratic states have degenerated and the representatives of Islam have made no attempt to purify the moral law of magical elements.

Idea of the Sacred. A primary idea of religion is the distinction between sacred and profane. The sacred are persons, things, or actions having a special relationship with the supernatural, whilst the profane have no such significance. Everything in any way concerned with religion is regarded as infused to some degree with supernatural power. For the purposes of the comparative study of religion the words *mana* and taboo are now linked with this question of holiness. Holiness is the power (*mana*) attributed to sacred persons, things, or actions that would ordinarily be regarded as natural or profane. The word taboo is used for any prohibition resting on a magical use, anything reserved for a

[1] From a Hausa funeral song in C. H. Robinson, *Specimens of Hausa Literature*, Cambridge, 1896, pp. 10–11.

supernatural being. The one term implies the other. There is no essential relationship between morals and religion in this distinction between sacred and profane, it is simply a question of a man's or a thing's relationship to the supernatural.

Into the world of such ideas of holiness Islam brings something new. The God of Islam is entirely self-contained and beyond all intimate relation with His creation, therefore the idea of holiness has gone in the development of Islam as a higher religion. Islam was ritualized and secularized, sacred and secular are one, subject alike to divine law. This is the teaching brought to Africa, but along with it came the continuance of the old idea in popular Islam. The ordinary Muslim, needing to maintain relationship with the supernatural world, had imbued the term *baraka* with these qualities of a link between God and man. So in theoretical Islam the idea of holiness has completely disappeared, whilst practical Islam has islamized the forces under the term *baraka*. The principle is relationship with the supernatural: the holy man is recognized as one near to God; the formula of the amulet is primarily the word of God, even though magical formulas and symbols irreconcilable with Islam are used. It is surprising that the idea of *baraka* has gained no essential hold upon Negro Islam. It is powerful in the Islam of North Africa, eastern Sudan, and among Moors of the Sahil. Islam was brought to West Africa by people who were saturated in the *baraka* idea, yet the Muslim Negro has not adopted the word for the mysterious forces he recognizes as everywhere present.

Two aspects based on the idea of the holy have therefore to be considered: the introduced Islam conception of legalistic morality, and the persistence of old ideas of the holy. In official Islam the holy has become a negative quality. God is supreme will and power. His authority must not be limited by ethical ideas of His holiness. All that God wills is permitted (*ḥalāl*) and all He does not will is tabooed (*ḥarām*), therefore what is *ḥarām* is no longer the holy. Consequently the Muslim does not need to draw the distinction between good and evil as such, but between what God allows and what He prohibits and this gives a particular cast to moral sanctions. To the Muslim religion means a law which controls and regulates man's whole life. In Islam the 'clean' eclipses the 'holy'. In Islamic ethics, that is the ethics of the divine will, the 'clean' cannot mean the tabooed or forbidden (*ḥarām*) but what God commands, consequently there is no essential difference between ceremonial law and moral law. In practice the distinction has become wider than just the things God allows and those He prohibits though these were the root ideas. Thus the term *ḥarām* is applied to anything of which the community disapproves.

All this came ready-made to the Sudan and these Arabic terms were introduced into African languages. Mande have made a distinction in pronunciation between the two senses: *harāmi*, 'sacred thing, &c.', and *harāmu*, 'forbidden thing'. To Hausa eating pig or worship in a *matsāfa* (heathen temple) is *ḥarām*; ceremonial purity and what is lawful is *ḥalāl*. The terms are extended outside the strictly Islamic sphere as when a Hausa says of his *kun gidā* (family totem), 'the hyaena is *ḥarām* to me'. Native terms for 'clean' and 'unclean' are applied to the old tabooed things. Thus the animal protector of the clan may become an object of impurity and consequently the legend of origin changes. Hausa use *tsarki*, 'purity', almost exclusively for ceremonial cleanliness; *tsarkake* is 'to perform the ritual ablutions', though sometimes it is used for 'purity (cleanliness) of heart'. Normally the phrase *shi mai-tsarki ni*, 'he is a holy man', means he is a good Muslim, he keeps all the rules.

Temne use their old terms: *ra-səm*, 'holiness, *mə-səm*, 'taboo', *dɛr-ɔ-məsəm*, 'sacred place', *wop mə-səm*, 'to hold to ceremonial law'. Pig is *mə-səm*, 'sacred', rather than 'unclean'. The story which accounts for this is characteristic of the whole western cycle. When the Prophet during his *hijra* became thirsty a pig guided him to a place where he could find water, and he decreed that henceforth it should never be killed.[1] There is no evidence that these people once regarded the pig as sacred, though it is found as a family totem. The pig is taken to be the totem of Muslims and a myth has been formed to account for the taboo which follows the normal lines of an African totem respected because of the services it once rendered to an ancestor, in this case, not the ancestor of a kin-unit, but the ancestor of the Muslim community. The deeply islamized, however, regard the pig as unclean. Another story explains that pigs are taboo because the Prophet ʿĪsā turned children into pigs, hence, in order to avoid the rather remote possibility of cannibalism, their flesh is forbidden. Similarly Temne say that monkeys are *məsəm* because they were human beings metamorphosed by the Prophet for violating Friday prayer.

[1] This story has spread into the Northern Territories of Ghana but the writer found no trace of it in the central Sudan though Meek gives a parallel; 'The Bagirmi reverence the wart-hog, because a wart-hog once revealed the presence of water to a Bagirmi chieftain and his army who were dying of thirst' (C. K. Meek, *Northern Nigeria*, i. 177). P. Marty gives another story of the Prophet and the pig which circulates in the Sahil of Nyoro; see his *Soudan*, iv. 273–4.

4

Institutional Islam

I. ORGANIZATION OF THE ISLAMIC CULT

ALTHOUGH Islam does not have a sacerdotal body it has its clergy. Islamic society is a religious society and leaders of the cult and interpreters and teachers of religious law acquired a role analogous with that of European Middle Age clerks. The terms 'clerk' and 'cleric' are employed throughout this book in order to avoid the associations of the French *marabout.* The clerk is primarily a lettered man, but *marabout* has a special meaning through its North African association with the cult of saints, a cult which is exceptional in Negro Islam. It was natural for the French to carry over North African terminology because *maraboutisme* is most apparent among Moors of western Sahara and Sahil, and they employ the word by extension for any cleric, teacher, or devotee. English usage of *mālam*, Hausa term for cleric derived from Arabic *muʿallim*, 'teacher', is better since it simply means 'lettered man', but today it is applied indiscriminately as equivalent to 'mister' and is unsuitable for use over the whole region for a special class.

The cleric stands apart from the laity but only as a lettered man for the profession is open to any free man (except members of certain caste groups) who has received sufficient training to be recognized. He performs specific religious functions, leads in prayer, teaches the young the rudiments of Islam, performs the first sacrifice at the great feasts, names the new-born, conducts the marriage ceremony, washes the dead, and leads the funeral prayers. No function of village life is complete unless he is present.

Clergy fall into three main groups—those appointed for public worship, teachers, and masters of canon law—though the differentiation is only one of function for a village cleric combines all three. The terms for cleric are loosely applied and rarely indicate his degree of learning. *Alfa* is widely used throughout the west and among Songhay as a general term.[1] Mande peoples use *karamoṙo* ('literate', Ar. *qaraʾa*, 'read' and *moṙo*, 'man') and *mōri-ba* (lit. 'great Muslim') indiscriminately for

[1] Many suggestions have been made as to the origin of the term: Arabic *al-faqīh*, *khalīfa*, or *muʾallif*; Mandinka *arfan*, *alfan*, *alfa*, 'chief' or 'master'; and even *alif ba*, a literate.

one who is barely literate and one fully trained in Islamic law. Tokolor and settled Fulbe are more discriminating. They call any cleric *modibbo* (Ar. *mu'addib* ?), the next grade is *tyērno* (pl. *sērenḅē*, *sērnāḅē*), and the highest *fodyo* (= *faqīh*). *Mōdi* is the Soninke term for cleric, but one who has had some training in law is a *fodia*.

The clergy are loosely organized. The chief regional cleric is the *imām* (west *almāmi*, centre *limān*) of the district Friday mosque. In a Muslim area he is appointed by the political chief and in a pagan area by the Muslim community. Each mosque has an *imām* appointed by the community (parish or quarter), who is the chief cleric of the village, and each family has its family cleric. After a death it is the latter who washes the dead, whilst the *imām* conducts the funeral prayers. Once an *imām* has been elected or designated he is there for life. In the Near East an *imām* can be displaced by the *wakīl* or warden of the mosque, but this functionary does not exist in West Africa and once elected it is almost impossible to get rid of an *imām*. When he gets too old to exercise his functions his *nā'ib* officiates for him. In many regions, especially where the Muslim community lives among pagans, the function becomes hereditary in one family, and the *imām* of the Friday mosque becomes the administrative chief of the Muslims, responsible to the political authority. When such a group achieved independence the *imām* became the political chief as in Futas Toro and Jalon.

Among Moors are clerical clans,[1] whose role within the tribal community is that of an hereditary order of clergy. This development was in part a Berber reaction against their inferior status *vis-à-vis* Arab ruling clans, since it gave these sections a special status. Besides Moorish tribes clerical clans are characteristic of Soninke and Tuareg. The latter call them *inislimen* (sing. *aneslem*, Islam-ist) and they are distinguished by wearing the muffler (*taghelmūzt*) with a white forehead bandage. Succession to religious offices such as *imām* and *qāḍī* is also hereditary (in some tribes the son succeeds, in others the mother's brother) even though the heir may be totally ignorant of Islamic law.

Little variation is found in the general pattern in Negro society. Hausa use *mālam*, 'master', for any cleric, but if they want to imply a distinction they will employ any suitable adjective: *ḳaramin mālami*, 'small clerk', *babban mālami*, 'big clerk', *mālamin fāda*, 'royal chaplain', and *mālamin ḳirgi*, 'friar of the cowhide'. The latter will be seen on the roads carrying his undressed goatskin prayer-rug (*būzū*), ablution jug

[1] French *tribus maraboutiques*. Moorish Arabic *zwāya*, sing. *zāwī*. *Mrābiṭ* (pl. *mrābṭīn*) is a general term for cleric.

(*buta*), bookbag (*gafaka*), and pen-case (*kōrami*, *alkurdu*). In Hausaland in connexion with mosques of towns and villages are districts like English parishes within which the position of the *limān* of the Friday mosque is almost like that of a beneficed clergyman. He receives marriage and burial fees, customary gifts and thankofferings at naming ceremonies, recovery from illness or return from a journey, and presents from each family on festival days. Other clergy are under him and have to obtain his permission before performing marriages and burials.

In Nupeland the clerical class is known as *ènà mānẓi* (*māṇ*, 'cleric', from Hausa *mālam*). Each district mosque has one of each of the following: *māṇko* (lit. 'chief cleric') the chief *imām*, his deputy the *náyèmi* (Ar. *nā'ib*), *madiu* (?), and *kitābu* (reciter). These all have functions at the *wázùṇ* or Friday Qur'ānic interpretations. Towns are divided into wards within which one cleric is recognized as ward-head. Village clerics are under the district *māṇko* and pay him a percentage of their fees. In Futa Jalon the parish is called *misidi* and has an *almāmi* at the head. The most important clergy are the *fodié*, legal experts, the local heads of mosques are the *tamsīr* (Ar. *tafsīr* = *mufassir*, 'commentator'), then the *serīm*, and the *tabē* charged with teaching.

A characteristic of Islam is its mobility. The mosque is only exceptionally a building. In villages, nomad camps, and town sections it is simply a rectangle marked out with branches, stones, or low mud wall. In towns every local group has its mosque, though they are not easy to find since they are generally a room in a house or courtyard or raised square in the street. In some villages the square has a fence of reeds and a shelter on one side to provide shade. They are often very small and for congregational prayer only the *imām* enters the square and the rest range themselves behind him. Mosques built of mud and cement are found in towns. From the point of view of construction they fall into groups of local and European styles. The characteristic Sudan architecture reaches its highest perfection in the mosque as the largest single building. It is built in mud with sloping walls, projecting pylons, and crowned with pointed merlons. Beside the building is a quadrilateral tower, diminishing upwards to terminate in a point. The roof is held up with broad pillars which leave narrow dark aisles, allowing only sufficient room to spread out a sheepskin. In front is a large courtyard, surrounded by a wall, where the congregation gather for Friday prayer. This style does not extend into Senegal (except parts of Futa Toro) where today the characteristic mosque is a hut of masonry or wooden boards with a roof of corrugated iron. Western Guinea has two main types, the Fulbe round reed hut, sometimes of great size as at Timbo, and the square, thatched Mandinka type. Besides mosque styles deriving from native techniques European influence has led to a bewildering variety of constructions in which all kinds of modifications and incongruities have been introduced.

Each Friday mosque[1] has its *imām* who leads the Friday prayer and reads the homily standing on a block of wood which takes the place of a pulpit. The muezzin is called *lādan* (Ar. *al-ādhān*, 'the call to prayer') in the centre and often *bilāli* in the west, from Bilāl, the Prophet's negro muezzin.[2] The muezzin's office is voluntary, even in large towns, but he receives alms at festivals. He generally leads the responses after the *imām* in a loud voice so that those at a distance and the women in the *ḥarīm* enclosure can hear. Among the Mende the megaphonist is called *almāmi fangoi*, '*imām* of clear utterance', and the call to prayer is by drumming, big drums being conspicuous objects on verandas of mosques. Only mosques in large towns have minarets and the muezzin calls the prayer from beside the mosque. The office of sacristan is filled by old men and women. They sweep, shake mats, fetch water for ablution, and attend to lamps. They are rewarded for their services by occasional gifts.

In African rites, although there is a cycle of common practice beyond which deviations are not possible, each priest or other master of ceremonies differs in interpretation and procedure. Islam, however, introduces an utter rigidity in its cultic practice. Every detail is laid down for ritual prayer and strict clerics claim that variation renders prayer invalid. In spite of this the average Muslim is content that clergy alone should perform prayer regularly and correctly. Few accomplish the exterior actions without making mistakes and most only observe the Friday prayer. *Ṣallā* and *ṣalāt*, when used without qualifications, normally refer to collective prayer outside the town at the two *'īds*, but they are of course used in their ordinary sense for the five canonical prayers. Ritual prayer is distinguished from informal prayer, e.g. Nupe *jiṇ sála*, 'to perform *ṣalāt*', and *ba àdǔwa*, 'to pray' (Ar. *ad-du'ā*); Hausa *yi salla*

[1] Friday mosques are everywhere known by a corruption of Arabic *jāmi'* or (*masjid al-*) *jum'a*: Mandinka *dyāma*, Wolof *dyuma*, Soninke *missi-dyuma*. The term for roofed mosque is generally derived from *masjid*: Mande *misiro*, *misidi*; Tuareg *temezzid*; Teda, *moshidi*; but for oratories only Hausa has adopted Arabic *muṣallā* under the form *masallachi* and spread it among neighbours. Other peoples formed 'places of prayer' (Mande *sali bolō*) or 'places of prostration'.

[2] But a vast number of other terms have been formed: Futa Jalon *salli*, Songhay *almudyin* (Ar. *al-mu' adhdhin*) and *kati-koy*, 'caller', Dyula *wata-ri-bar̃a*, and Hausa *mai-kiran-salla*, 'he who calls to prayer'.

and *yi addu'a*. Mande Dyula use *syeri*, lit. 'prostration' for 'ritual prayer', and a mosque is *syeri-bolõ*, 'place of prostration', similar to Arabic *masjid*. The five prayers are divided into two cycles, the first consists of the dawn prayer only and the second comprises the other four. Thus when a cleric says 'I have accomplished the second prayer', he means the third. Prayers are known by corruptions of the Arabic names, for example:

	Nupe	*Fulfulde*	*Nupe*	*Hausa*
ṣalāt aṣ-ṣubḥ	àsuba	julde fadyiri (Ar. al-fajr)	dawn	dawn
ṣalāt aẓ-ẓuhr	zúrù or azafari	julde sallifana	1.30	2.00–3.00
ṣalāt al-'aṣr	asàri or lăsàri	julde lassara	3.00	4.00–5.00
ṣalāt al-maghrib	mágarì or magaruba	julde fitiri[1]	7.00	7.00
ṣalāt al-'ishā'	lishia	julde safako (Ar. shafaq)	8–9.00	8.00–9.00

A feature of West African Islam is the Qur'ān interpretation session known by a corruption of Arabic *wa'ẓ*, 'sermon, exhortation' (Mande *wādyu*). These are given in large mosques every Friday (and every day during Ramaḍān) after the *khuṭba* has been delivered.[2] Among the Nupe for the *wazuṇ*, the first reciter (*karātuṇjiṇchi*) who knows the Qur'ān by heart, recites a passage, then a *māṇ* known as *wazuṇjiṇchi*, 'preacher', reads or recites it again and translates roughly into Nupe; and a megaphonist (*goga*, lit. 'interpreter') repeats his translation in a loud voice. Yoruba call the recital *wāsi*. The *alfa* and one or more *ajanāsi* (co-interpreter) read a passage in unison. Then the *alfa* (called *oniwāsi*) translates (interprets) in Yoruba, and the third (*arowāsi* or megaphonist) repeats the translation in a loud voice. The Hausa perform *wa'azi* (or *wa'atsu*) before and after Friday prayer in mosques, public places, or streets. The cleric (*mai-wa'azi*) recites a section and then interprets in Hausa. They say they are forbidden to recite and translate verse by verse. Sudanese Tuareg (e.g. Igellad) meet after Friday prayer for *tiberdyant* when a cleric reads and comments on a passage.

Mosques are little frequented on weekdays except in Ramaḍān, and during the rains prayers are often sandwiched together. Every Friday,

[1] Ar. *fiṭr*, prayer of the breaking of the Ramaḍān fast, the evenings of Ramaḍān, and by extension applied to the sunset prayer.

[2] Ibn Baṭṭūṭa mentions the practice at the *'īd* ceremonial when he was in Māli in A.D. 1352. On the *muṣalla* or praying-place outside the town, 'The *ṣalāt* and *khuṭba* were performed. Then the *khaṭīb* descended from the block and sitting down before the sultan delivered a long discourse which was interpreted into their own tongue by a man holding a spear. It consisted of exhortation (*wa'ẓ*), admonition, and eulogy of the sultan', ed. Defrémery and Sanguinetti, iv. 410.

however, the mosques are packed for *ṣalāt al-jumʿa*. Nomads, who cannot normally fulfil the requirements regarding Friday prayer except in permanent settlements, will come into town if anywhere near. This enthusiasm for Friday prayer is due to the stress placed on this occasion as a symbol of Muslim solidarity and its significance as a state function, whilst the fact that it is based on a direct command in the Qur'ān (lxii. 9) carries weight. In North Nigerian states it is a great ceremonial occasion with processions between the chief's house and the mosque.[1] At the prayer the elaborate hierarchization which characterizes the procession is avoided. In one emirate the leader occupied the *miḥrāb*, behind him in the centre of the first row was the *sarki* (chief) who had the *alkāli* and other clerics on his right and the *magāji* and other officials on his left. The chief *imām* and members of the royal family mingled with commoners in the second row.

In western Sudan after the muezzin has finished calling the prayer the *almāmi* enters and sits on the *mumari* (Ar. *minbar*), a wooden block which serves as seat and pulpit. Three muezzins then mount the tower or other calling-place and call the prayer one after the other. When they have finished the *almāmi* mounts the block leaning on a staff, and reads the homily for the day in two sections. Then he descends, recites the call, and leads the rite of two *rakʿas*. In western Guinea and elsewhere the *khuṭba* is translated into the local language. In Masina region it is recited in Arabic and each phrase translated by the muezzin or an *alfa* into Songhay, Fulfulde, and Soninke.

In the eastern Sudan the English introduced Friday as a day of rest, but the clergy of Northern Nigeria referred to the legal maxim, 'It is blameworthy to abstain from work on Friday in imitation of Christians and Jews', and resisted its introduction. Government offices therefore take Sunday off and their clerks are released on Friday merely in time to spruce themselves up to attend prayer which anyway is held late in the afternoon.

Women, regarded as being in a constant state of ritual impurity, are not allowed to enter mosques. One cleric said, 'They are ignorant and may be unclean'. The Law merely prescribes as blameworthy their attendance at Friday prayer unless 'they are no more women', that is, when menstruation has ceased. In most parts a separate hut or enclosure

[1] In Northern Nigeria the prayer is held very late between 2 and 3 p.m. (a practice H. Barth noticed in 1851, *Travels*, ii. 486). In Bida it takes place after 4, depending on the time the *etsu* elected to arrive. The clergy know the conditions (cf. al-Ghazālī, *Iḥyā*, i. 113–16) but cannot get the rulers to observe them. This practice no doubt derives from that of the Moors who observe the prayer about 3 p.m. when the *zawāl* becomes obvious.

(called *jarirdu* in Futa Jalon) is provided for them where they can hear the megaphonist. Old women are often present at the festival prayers outside the town and among nomads women frequently join in prayers behind the men.

Almsgiving. *Zakāt* formed part of the taxation system of the Islamic states of the Sudan, but under European governments its function as an obligatory state levy has gone and almost everywhere has become confused with *ṣadaqa*, voluntary alms, though a distinction is made in that *zakāt* refers to the voluntary, but socially unavoidable, contribution, levied by the clergy, whilst *ṣadaqa* means 'alms' in a general sense. Payment of *zakāt* at the ʿAshūrā and end of Ramaḍān is regarded as an obligation and when the season approaches the clergy remind their people of the necessity of purifying their sins by offering alms; and it is they who, in default of a regularly constituted Islamic authority, now collect and share out the offerings.[1] Clergy are dependent upon almsgiving, for the institution of *waqf* or *ḥubus* is unknown in West Africa.[2]

The word *ṣadaqa* has spread widely and has played a great role in desacralizing the conception of sacrifice. In animist religion sacrifice is an offering to a divinity to please, propitiate, and sustain its energy, and, when consumed by the worshippers, constitutes a form of communion. Acceptance of Islam leads to a complete desacralizing of such ideas, for Islam has no idea of sacrifice in the African sense. Mande call sacrifice to a divinity *sũ* or *soro* (if a bloody victim). To this all pagans subject to Islamic radiations have added the idea of *ṣadaqa*. This is an offering made in the name of Allah or the ancestors which is not consumed by the offerers but given to poor, children, and clergy. The idea of almsgiving to those in need which can be offered by anyone thus comes alongside direct offerings to a divinity for its own use which can only be sacrificed by a priest. This usage gains ground until, when they cross

[1] In many parts the amount required from each family is announced at the ʿAshūrā but not collected until the end of Ramaḍān when it is handed over to the *imām* of the *jāmiʿ* who announces the contributions from the pulpit block and the general lines of distribution which is made after the prayer. In other places the contribution is still given to the chief since he is responsible for the poor and travellers and supports clergy and teachers.

[2] The Sudanese system of land tenure made the constitution of any *waqf* on landed property impossible, consequently there are no funds from which mosque officials can be paid as in most Islamic countries and they are entirely dependent on fees and alms. The *ta'rīkhs* refer to *awqāf* in urban centres in the past. Askiya Muḥammad 'made a gift to the *jāmiʿ* at Timbuktu, to constitute a *ḥubus*, of a chest designed to hold sixty copies of the Qur'ān'. In Jenne mosques received revenues from property for the support of students, poor, and mosque officials, but today these have all gone, and the institution lingers on only in Timbuktu (cf. P. Marty, *Soudan*, ii. 99, 102–3, 273–4; and for the past, *T. al-Fattāsh*, p. 110/204) where *alhubusi-hu* means house or property left in perpetuity for the use of members of a particular family.

the boundary-line into Islam, *sũ* must cease altogether, since, in the eyes of the clergy, it is idolatry, sacrifice to divinities other than God. The word *sũ-ni-ke-baĝa* ('offerer', 'sacrificer') is used by Muslim Mande with the derogatory sense of 'pagan'. The term *sor̊o* is not transferred to the ram sacrifice at a naming or the Great Feast since there is no sense of communion with God. The old ideas do not go quickly. There is a reaction against beer-libations and 'red' offerings,[1] but offerings (*ṣadaqa*) to ancestors continue for some time. In western Guinea offerings of the staple food during mourning may be regarded as food for the dead, but the actual sacrifice goes to the clerics, whilst the other food, including the animal which is not 'offered', is for feeding the family and visitors. But *ṣadaqa* among Muslims of the Sahil and Sudan means only 'ceremonial almsgiving'. It may be thought to help the dead, though more especially the living, like any other *kaffāra* (expiatory offering), but it is not regarded as food for ancestors. There are two forms of *ṣadaqa* in Islamic societies, the common element being that it is given in the name of God and not consumed by the offerers: that offered at the great Islamic festivals and to sanctify family events at naming, circumcision, and death; and that which seeks to attract divine approval and protection upon man and his activities such as *ṣadaqa* to ask for rain and in connexion with the stages of seed-time and harvest.

2. THE ISLAMIC CALENDAR

Adoption of the Islamic calendar is an important factor in breaking the link with animist cults and in the consolidation of Islam. In agrarian communities the cult cycle is closely geared with the solar year, but the Islamic year of twelve lunar months is an artificial imposition. Townsmen and traders are free to adopt a new cycle, but agriculturists maintain two calendars: the lunar year for the Islamic cult and civil life, and the solar year for all that concerns the agricultural year. The Arabic names of the Islamic months are adopted, though most peoples have an alternative version. This is either translated, or descriptive of the events of the Islamic year, or a mixture,[2] or, as with Mande, the Islamic lunar months are given the names of the solar year months, taking as point of departure the *sunkālo* or hungry period before harvest and the fast

[1] Bambara ritual sacrifices fall into two main groups: *da la sõni*, 'door sacrifice', for the ancestors; and *boli sõni*, 'fetish sacrifice'. The first require 'white' victims, the second 'red' or 'black', and the latter, above all, are regarded by the clergy as incompatible with profession of Islam.

[2] For example, in Songhay Ramaḍān is *haume*, 'shut mouth', Shawwāl is *ferme*, 'open mouth', Dhū 'l-Qa'da is *hinanjem* (Arab. *haniyya*), Dhū 'l-Ḥijja is *tyibsi*, Arab. *kabsh*.

month of Ramaḍān. Consequently they apply the same name to divisions of the year which are entirely different.[1] The week is a division introduced by Islam, and the names of days are everywhere adaptations of the Arabic names.[2] Parts of the day have received new terminology associated with Arabic prayer times, and the day is reckoned from one sunset to another; thus Hausa *daren jumma'a* is our Thursday night.

The first event of the Islamic year is the 10th night of Muḥarram (the 'Ashūrā)[3] to which African practices connected with the New Year have cohered, although, since it is continually moving round the year, it has been disconnected from the agricultural season. The pious fast for from one to three days and most prepare for it by a short fast, ablutions, and a purge to purify the body. Symbolic rites to ensure prosperity during the new year are universal. When the sun has set everyone eats all he possibly can and poor people are invited to participate, for no one must go empty that night so that a prosperous year may be ensured. Hausa have the custom (*jūya bai*) of providing every member of the household with a fowl or goat's head which each must eat with his back turned to the others. Peoples of Senegal, Guinée, and Sierra Leone cook and eat the dried head and feet of the ram slaughtered at the Tabaski feast (an animist survival—linking the new year to the old and drawing the blessing of the sacrifice into the new year?). Susu (and many others) make an offering (*la kayaŋye*) at the time of the last prayer

[1] The following are the Mande solar months applied to the Islamic months (for details see Delafosse, *La Langue Mandingue*, i. 287–9):

1.	*dyõmbende*: mustered slaves (December–January)	Muḥarram
2.	*dõmba ma kono*: waiting for the great day	Ṣafar
3.	*dõmba*: the great day	Rabī' I
4.	*lā siri folo*: commencement of the binding or pregnancy (of the earth)	Rabī' II
5.	*dyibi ni fana*: meal of the bringing-forth	Jumādā I
6.	*la siri lā ba*: end of pregnancy	Jumādā II
7.	*kã mũ dõ*: day of the lightening of the heavens	Rajab
8.	*sunkālo mã kono*: waiting for the *sunkālo*	Sha'bān
9.	*sunkālo*: moon of deprivation	Ramaḍān
10.	*minkālo*: moon of drinking	Shawwāl
11.	*dõnkyi ma kono*: waiting for the *dõnkyi*	Dhū 'l-Qa'da
12.	*dõnkyi*: threshing	Dhū 'l-Ḥijja

[2] For example in Mandinka: *alādi* (or *lahadi*), *tene*, *talāta*, *araba* (*laraba*), *alāmisa*, *aridyuma*, and *sibiti*.

[3] The following are the main terms employed:

Wolof: *Tamḥarit*; Tuareg: *Bianu*;
Fulbe: *Jombente*; Mandinka: *gyõmbende*;
Tokolor: *herran* and *harom*; Soninke: *haranē n'tiale* (10th of the moon of Haranē);
Hausa: *Sallar a-chi-a-koshi* or *chika chiki*, 'festival of full bellies';
Songhay: *dedow*, *dedew dyinger*.

of the year, and on New Year's Day young men and girls immerse themselves in a river seven times. Many believe that on this night God counts all earth-dwellers and designates those who are to die during the year. With the Islamic lustrations is associated a customary ceremony of purification by fire. Songhay, after ablutions, pass and repass over a small fire shouting, '*Yesi hirow*' ('The New Year has entered').[1] After the feast many (Hausa, Nupe, Mandinka, Dyula) have torchlight processions and contests between age-groups.[2] The explanation a Nupe cleric gave was that Nimrod had decided to put Abraham to death. Abraham threatened him with hell-fire, but Nimrod was not turned from his purpose and he was cast into an immense pyre, but survived without a hair being singed.[3] A Mandinka cleric in Sierra Leone carried the custom back to Noah and the flood, saying that the day God evaporated the water and the ark grounded was 10th Muḥarram.

When day comes special prayers are offered in all mosques. In Bida (Nupe) they begin with the ceremony of 'the opening of the book'.[4] This consists of readings from the 'Book of the Years' (*takàda eyaẓe*) which gives prophecies for the year. The days of the week are assigned to prophets in this order, Adamu, Mamadu, Yakubu, Nuhu, Ayubu, Musa, Isa, and the year is known after the prophet on whose day it begins. One *māṇ* reads in Arabic, the *māṇko* (chief *imām*) translates into Hausa or Nupe in a low voice, and the *goga* shouts it out in Nupe. After that the *māṇko* states the amount each one has to pay as *sadaka* (=*zakāt*) each month. Then follows the homily (*hutuba*) and a prayer by the *imām* in Arabic, translated into Nupe, and shouted out by the *goga*. Prayer is made for all departed Muslims from Adam onwards and departed *etsus* of Bida. Then follows prayer for the reigning *etsu* and his people, for rain, deliverance from famine, and so forth. The whole ceremony takes about an hour, after which the *etsu* rides in procession and visits the tombs of his predecessors in the three compounds through which succession to the throne rotates, and at each compound the *māṇko* prays for the dead *etsus*.

1 P. Marty, *Soudan*, ii. 79; A. Dupuis, *La langue Songoi*, p. 129.

2 Nupe, *wōriwò*, 'waving flaming torches', Hausa *jīfan wuta*, 'throwing fire', or *wowo* (*wauwau*). This seems to be falling into disuse among Hausa and the Tuareg of Air, but is celebrated with immense enthusiasm by Nupe, although they claim it was only introduced with Islam. They call Muḥarram *etswa navuǹ*, 'the month of the torches', or *etswa wōriwò*.

3 Cf. Qur'an, xxi. 68–69. Ch. Monteil (*Contes Soudanais*, 1905, p. 177) relates a similar story for 10th Ramaḍān, which is probably a mistake for 10th Muḥarram, in which Nebuchadnezzar is the tyrant.

4 Hausa *būḍe takarda*. In some Hausa states the ceremony is performed by a special court official (*maga-takarda*) at the entrance to the ruler's compound.

The next festival is the Prophet's birthday[1] on 12th Rabīʿ al-Awwal (19th in Hausaland). This is little celebrated by the people except in Bornu, but clergy gather in the mosques and hold recitals of the *ʿIshrīniyyāt* of al-Fazāzī, the *Takhmīs* of the same poem by Abū Bakr Muḥammad Ibn Muhīb, and the *Dalāʾil al-Khairāt*. In Futa Jalon the *karamokos* keep it as a day of fast and prayer and recite poems in Fulfulde in honour of the Prophet.[2] Dyula keep it as a festival day when young men parade with arms and war equipment 'to guard the Prophet from his enemies'. The 26th Rajab, 'when the Prophet accompanied by an angel-guide visited the seven heavens and seven hells', is observed by some clerics and is a recognized school holiday. On the 14th Shaʿbān prayers are recited for deceased kinsfolk but graves are not visited.

Ramaḍān is preceded by two days of festival (cf. Shrove Tuesday). The fast[3] is observed fairly strictly, for African life is so open that it is difficult to conceal the fact that one is not fasting. The daily prayers, neglected throughout most of the year, are more strictly observed. Hausa have a saying (*azumin jemage*) for those who observe the fast but neglect the devotions, which has acquired proverbial significance for half-doing something. Many are assiduous about both because they believe that thereby sins committed during the year are remitted. The 27th day, Lailat al-Qadr, generally confused with the Night of Power, is observed by clergy who say that God spends this night regulating the affairs of the world. Since it is the night the Qur'ān descended, many spend it reading the Qur'ān in relays. In the evening ablutions are performed and incense burned to speed the *jinn* on their way to prison. A Mande feast of the virgins has been attached to this date. In western Guinea children sing for presents, young men and maidens parade the streets, singing and dancing all night.[4] They carry around 'floats' with representations of animals, boats, and the like. In Hausaland during Ramaḍān the commentary of Jalālain is read and translated by two

[1] Mandinka and Dyula *dō-mba ma*, 'day of the great dance', *anabi dō*, 'the Prophet's day'; Moorish Arabic *mūlūd*; Masina region *mūlūd dō-mba*; Soninke *modinu n'tiale*; Tuareg *gāni*; Kanuri-Teda *gāni* and *lebi lowel*; Hausa *sallar gānē* or *sallar tākūtaha*; Wolof *gāmu*; Songhay *almudu dyinger*, *hay dyinger* (birth festival) or *hay tyidyi* (birth night).

[2] P. Marty, *Islam en Guinée*, p. 336.

[3] 'Fast' is generally a corruption of Ar. *ṣawm*: West Mandinka *suñgo*; Dyula *suñ*; Hausa *azumi*; Songhay *haume* and *hamme*. Ramaḍān is 'the month (moon) of the fast', in Dyula *suñgari*; West Mandinka *suñ-karo*; Mende *sungalui*; Hausa *watan azumi*; Nupe *etswa ázun*; Bozo *moriye sun'keu*. But we also get Wolof *kori*; Hausa *watan ḳishirwa* (thirst month).

[4] Temne *mada* (dance of the young) and *watupa*; Dyula *kururi* (one sleeps not).

mālams, disposing of two *ḥizbs* each day,[1] and during the last night the whole Qur'ān is recited (called *tukuri*). In the entrance hut of the chief cleric a group of from five to ten read a *ḥizb* in turn until the sixty are completed. People drop in and leave alms in a calabash placed in the centre of the circle. In Nupeland in 1952 it was performed in three places in the large village of Katcha and at twenty in Bida.

The new moon is anxiously awaited for if it is not seen the clerics will insist on another day of fasting. Its appearance is greeted with bursts of firing, beating of drums, and general rejoicing.[2] About eight o'clock in the morning the festival prayer (*ṣalāt al-ʿīd*, Songhay *sarty-ille*) is held at a special praying-place outside the town (Hausa *masallachi yīdi*) where the men assemble by quarters. The *imām* leads a prayer of two *rakʿas* in a low voice which is shrilled out by another cleric, then mounts the pulpit-block which has been carried from the mosque and recites a two-part *khuṭba*. In Nupeland this is translated from Arabic into Hausa and then into Nupe, for having studied through the medium of Hausa they seem unable to translate directly. In western Guinea they have an unusual practice at both *ʿīds*. The *almāmi* standing on the block is covered with a white cloth (or a number of cloaks) like a canopy, under which he remains for half an hour reading sermons aloud and interpreting. Temne said he was communing with Muḥammad, Gabriel and the spirits of the dead. When the cloth is removed the people press upon him to rub their hands in his sweat and wipe it over their heads and bodies. Mende said there was power (*kpaya*) in the sweat, and when they rubbed it on themselves they got *ngauwanda* ('grace'). Many return home from the prayer by a different route from the one taken when going. This, they say, is in accordance with a tradition that the Prophet ordered the first believers to perform the prayer outside the mosque in order not to be surprised by the infidels, and to return by different routes in order not to seem too large a group of people. Strict clergy disapprove of the drumming and dancing that goes on throughout the night.

[1] In Hausaland any commentary is known as Jalālaini. Recitation of *ḥadīth* was a feature of the religious life of Morocco which penetrated sahilian centres. *Tadhkirat an-Nisyān* (p. 17/26–27) says that in Timbuktu 'the recitation of the *Ṣaḥīḥ* of Bukhārī during Ramaḍān in the *qaṣba* of the pashas was an old custom'.

[2] This festival (Ar. *al-ʿīd aṣ-ṣaghīr* or *al-fiṭr*), like the Great Feast, is known as *salla*; particular terms are: Tamahaqq *tisendar*, *amūd* (Air); Tokolor *korka*; Wolof *kori*; Soninke *suñkaso n'tyale*; Western Mandingo *suñkaro sali*; Dyula *miñgare tulu*, 'feast of the moon of drinking'; Fulbe *julde sumaye*; Songhay *ferme dyinger*, '(mouth-) opening festival'; Hausa *ƙaramar salla* or *sallar azumi*; Nupe *sálagi*, 'little feast'; Yoruba *irun awe*, 'prayer of the fast'.

Before the most important feast of the year, *al-ʿīd al-kabīr*[1] on the 12th of Dhū'l-ḥijja, towns are thronged with sheep. They are particular to ensure that the ram fulfils the legal specifications otherwise the benefit may be lost. Hausa say the best animal is a ram with black rings around the eyes,[2] and when it has not been blessed with these characteristics they anoint its head and feet with henna and put kohl round the eyes. On the festival morning the men process to the *ʿīd* plot outside the town for prayer and homily as at the previous festival. When this is finished the drum sounds and they bring a ram to the *imām* who, reciting 'In the name of God, God is great, O God accept this offering', cuts its throat and the drum sounds again.[3] Then everyone returns home, slaughters his ram before his house, and distributes it among relatives, clerics, and poor. The bones are carefully buried, but head and feet are kept for the *ʿAshūrā*. The skin is often tanned and dressed for use as a prayer-rug. North African beliefs regarding the utility of the sacrificial ram on the Last Day have spread throughout the Sudan. Songhay say they support the bridge Ṣirāṭ on their backs, but the majority believe that all the rams turn into a large horse which carries you over the Ṣirāṭ. Unlike other feasts there is little drumming and dancing, and the three days are spent resting and visiting friends.

3. THE TRAINING OF THE CLERIC

The training of the cleric begins in the Qur'ān schools which are still very numerous.[4] Teaching is not a profession exclusive of other occupations. Teachers are not paid fees, for teaching is regarded as a voluntary pious work,[5] though they receive gifts from the pupils'

[1] Tuareg *tafazkē* and *aramat*, Ullimmeden Tuareg *afasko*, *tafisko*, 'spring' (πάσχα, Heb. *pesaḥ*), adopted under the form *tabaski* by Soninke, Wolof, western Fulbe, and Mandinka, alongside their own terms for 'the Great Festival': Mandinka *sali-ba*, Hausa *babbar salla*, Nupe *sálakó*, Soninke *bano n'tyale*, Khasonke *bana salo*. Corruptions of *ḍaḥīya* also appear: Hausa *sallar layya* or *lāhiya*, Fulfulde *jūlde laiha*, Yoruba *ileya*. Other terms are Songhay *tyibsi* or *tyusi* (*dyinger*) from Arabic *kabsh*, 'ram'; Fulbe (Futa Jalon) *duki* and *jūlde donkiri*, Dyula *dõ-ñgi-ma*, 'day of songs'.

[2] *rāgō mai-kwalli* = Ar. *kuḥl*, or *tōzalī* = Berber *binzūla*.

[3] In the Sudanese states it is always the political chief who gives the order for the first sacrifice.

[4] In Katsina province of Northern Nigeria where the population numbers a million and a half, which means 150,000 children of school age, there were 4,864 Qur'ān schools with 30,340 pupils in 1950. In addition, there were 2,009 schools with 9,896 pupils of a grade beyond pure recitation. In French Northern Cameroons where Muslims number 260,000 there are only 5,000 children in Qur'ān schools.

[5] Shaikh Ḥamad of Masina, however, fixed teachers' fees at 500 cowries per *ḥizb* memorized or 30,000 cowries for the whole Qur'ān. If the parents were unable to pay this amount he defrayed it from state funds (Ch. Monteil, *Djénné*, p. 151).

parents at festivals and specified stages of memorization. Most teachers augment their income by cultivating or following a profession. Some are traders for whom teaching has an economic value in assuring them a clientele, others hold a public office as *imām*, judge, or village chief; whilst amulet-making forms an appreciable part of the income of all clergy.

A characteristic of Islamic education is its individualism. Anyone who can recite the Qur'ān and write Arabic characters is qualified. He begins with a class of his own children and neighbours naturally send theirs along. Most schools are one-man affairs, but the master who teaches beyond the stage of mere recitation hands beginners over to older pupils. Women teachers are found mainly among Moors in Senegal and Mauritania. There are two grades of schools, distinguished in Hausa as *makarantar allo*,[1] 'tablet-school', and *makarantar ilmi*,[2] 'law school'. In the first children are taught to recite the Qur'ān without understanding. The second embraces all further studies. Generally an *ilmi*-school merely teaches details about the performance of *ṣalāt*, prayers for occasional offices like funerals, some exposition of Qur'ānic texts, and perhaps the study of a book of law.

In Futa Jalon four categories of study are distinguished:[3] *dyangugol*, reading; *windugol*, writing; *firugol*, exegesis, explanation of the Qur'ān in Fulfulde; *fennu* (Ar. *fann*), higher studies. *Dyangugol* is divided into three parts, *alifba*, the alphabet; *sigi*, pronunciation and spelling; *fineditugol* or *rindingol*, joining of letters, sounds, and words; and reading. Writing is studied concurrently with reading.[4] The Qur'ān is learnt in six sections. Beginning with the first *sūra*, they turn to the last and work backwards until they reach the second. Higher studies begin after the Qur'ān is learnt by heart. *Firugol* involves *ka'bē* (or *to-bē*, a translation of *tawḥīd*), study of the divine unity, and *tafsīr*, Qur'ānic exegesis in Fulfulde. *Ka'bē* is based on the *Ṣughrā* of Sulaim al-Awjalī; and some teachers include the *Burhān* of As-Suyūṭī. Along with theology goes the study of *tafsīr*. Hausa *'ulamā* are strongly opposed to the trans-

[1] The terms for teacher and school are frequently derived from Ar. *qara'a*, 'to recite'. *Allo* is Ar. *al-lawḥ*, 'slate'; Mandinka *walara*, *walaha*; Fulfulde *hallu-al*, *wallu-al*.

[2] Songhay: *tirahu* ('place of writing') *koran* and *tirahu tyitab* (i.e. *kitāb* = law book) or *tirahu alem* (Ar. *'ilm*).

[3] See P. Marty, *L'Islam en Guinée*, pp. 349–55.

[4] The Sudani script is derived from that of the Maghrib from which, however, it is distinguishable. Adopted in the days when the Maghribī was still less differentiated from Kufic than it is today, it has remained little changed, whereas the Maghribī has become somewhat more elegant. Calligraphy was not cultivated as an art in the Sudan any more than in the Maghrib and the Sudani script is very clumsy, angular, and irregular.

lation of the Qur'ān,[1] but it is translated orally into local languages at the *wa'ẓ* sessions, in which case it is called *tafsīr*. In Futa Jalon, however, manuscript translations of the Qur'ān exist in Fulfulde and with the help of these Fulbe give their pupils more intelligent instruction than in most parts of West Africa. *Firugol* ends with an examination by the principal *karamokos*. One of them reads sections of the Qur'ān and the candidate translates and comments. If successful he is entitled to be called *tyērno*.

Those who succeed in passing *firugol* can proceed to law proper (*fennu*) which includes study of the *Tuḥfat* of Ibn 'Āṣim, Risāla of Ibn Abī Zaid, and the *mukhtaṣars* of Khalīl ibn Isḥāq and al-Akhḍarī, with commentaries on these works. A few study *tawḥīd* in as-Sanūsī's *Umm al-Barāhīn*, Sulaim's *Kubrā*, and other books. Arabic is studied by means of the *Maqāmāt* of al-Ḥarīrī and the *Burda* of al-Būṣīrī, and grammar in *al-Ajurrūmiyya* and sometimes the *Alfiyya* of Ibn Mālik. Tradition is rarely studied as a separate subject. The few who attain this degree are called *alfa*, which is a high title only in Futa Jalon.

It will be seen from the titles of the law books that the prevailing *madhhab* is that of Mālik; the only exceptions being Shuwa Arabs and Indian Aḥmadiyya who are Ḥanafiyya, and some Bornu jurists, said to follow the same school. In the medieval Islam of the Sudan zone reverence for the law assumes an importance out of all proportion to actual observance. Islam is the written law. Hausa clerics so prize the *Mukhtaṣar* of Khalīl that if one mentions *al-Kitāb* they think the reference is to Khalīl's treatise and not the Qur'ān. In Nilotic Sudan reverence for Khalīl is tempered by Ṣūfism, the one not being more important than the other, but in western Sudan, even though all clerics are linked with a *ṭarīqa*, only the Law is reverenced.

From the nature of their training and reading it is not surprising that their religious compositions are stilted, unnatural, couched in legalistic language, and entirely unoriginal in thought. 'Uthmān dan Fodio, his brother 'Abd Allāh, and his son Muḥammad Belo were copious compilers. Thus 'Uthmān dan Fodio's tract[2] on the conditions under which

[1] When a translation into Hausa was suggested they uttered a shocked, 'It will lose all its *baraka*'. Sultan Sa'īd Njoya of the recently converted Bamum, on his return from Mecca in 1947, decided that the law would be better understood and applied if the Qur'ān were translated into Bamum. The following year a passing Moorish cleric forbade the translation. This question divided the Bamum into two camps before its translation was finally decided upon (see Cardaire, *Contribution à l'étude de l'Islam noir*, I.F.A.N. 1949, p. 92). A previous Sultan Njoya at the beginning of the present century invented a script for writing Bamum. This was at first an ideographic alphabet, then became syllabic, and finally quasi-alphabetic.

[2] Entitled Sirāj al-ikhwān fī ahamm yuḥtāj ilaihi fī hadhā 'z-zamān.

the waging of war upon bad Muslims is permissible is based upon the work of al-Majhīlī, which in turn is a compilation of citations from earlier authorities. Among the writings of al-ḥājj 'Umar are a commentary on at-Tijānī's *Rimāḥ al-ḥizb ar-raḥīm* (on the duties of the affiliated Tijānī), written in 1261/1845, *Suyūf as-Sa'īd*, *Safīnat as-Sa'āda*, and a *ta'shīr* of Fazāzī's *al-Qaṣā'id al-'Ishrīniyyāt*. The literary output of Sudan Muslims is impressive on paper but in fact their writings show no originality and slavishly follow the form and terminology of the books they have assimilated. Given the nature of their training, which stresses only the necessity for establishing precedents, this lack of originality, regarded as *bid'a*, is natural.

4. THE INFLUENCE OF ARABIC UPON INDIGENOUS LANGUAGES

A noteworthy aspect of the spread of Islam is the interrelationship between linguistic and religious factors and here as elsewhere its spread has been accompanied by the absorption of an Arabic vocabulary. The mediating factor, however, has not been Arabic-speakers but the law books learnt by the clergy. This means that Arabic has remained an exotic means of expression. Few colloquial and daily-life words seeped into African languages and when talking in Arabic to higher clergy stilted legal terminology has to be employed for them to be able to understand.

This limited literary diffusion may be contrasted with the part played by Arabic in North Africa, Mauritania, and Nilotic Sudan. Throughout Mauritania a vast linguistic revolution led to the substitution of the Ḥassāniyya dialect of Arabic for Berber and Soninke. Apart from Moors Arabic is only spoken by Arab tribes in central Sudan. Even upon people in contact with Arabs spoken Arabic has had little influence except among urban Songhay and in Bornu and Waday. On the other hand, the literary language of the law books has enriched the languages of Muslims with hundreds of religious, political, commercial, and abstract words and expressions. The difference this has made is evident when the means of expression at the disposal of Wolof, Mande, Dyula, Songhay, and Hausa are compared with those of animist tribes speaking related languages. The last two are especially rich in words of Arabic origin. Common vocabulary for anything to do with Islam provides a link between languages that have no linguistic relationship. The need for wider means of expression became felt everywhere after the establishment of European rule. Through the work of Christian missions the main African languages were reduced to writing and enriched with a wider vocabulary, but the effect of European languages upon those of Muslims is restricted to new needs which do not include religion, and that term covers the whole of traditional life.

Another effect of the influence of Arabic has been to stimulate the writing of African languages in Arabic characters, although its lack of vowels makes the script unsuitable.[1] Tokolor and Fulbe in Futas Toro and Jalon, Hausa, Songhay, and even Wolof, often correspond with each other in their own languages. One reason for the depth of Islam in Futa Jalon may be ascribed to the composition of poems in Fulfulde, for which they have formed a special prosody, whose purpose is to mediate the main features of Islam to the illiterate masses. These versified sermons were preserved by the adaptation of Arabic characters to their sounds through the use of special diacritical points. 'Uthmān dan Fodio also composed verse sermons in Hausa[2] but his initiative was followed by few others. Because of their exaggerated reverence for Arabic Hausa clerics set themselves against the practice of reciting vernacular religious poems and thus stifled this means for spreading religious ideas. It is noteworthy that Fulbe adapted their own language for new religious expressions and employ few Arabic words and phrases compared with the vast number Hausa introduced into similar poems.

Arabic borrowings do not disturb the linguistic equilibrium for they are transformed in accordance with phonetic laws governing African languages. Thus double consonants are separated by vowels and final consonants given a vowel ending, sounds *'ain* and *ghain* disappear, *kh* changes to *k* and *sh* to *s* (*seku* for *shaikh*), s, ṣ, d, dh, ḍ, z, ẓ coalesce into one sound. Although words may be considerably transformed (Hausa: *gaskiya* for *ḥaqīqa*, 'truth', and *alḷowa* for *al-wuḍū*, 'ablution') few undergo the phonetic changes characteristic of Bantu languages in forming verbs and plurals (e.g. Fulfulde *soborere*, 'spur', Tunisian Arabic *shābūr*, becomes *t̲oborēd̲e* in the plural), and in general the Arabic original is recognizable.

A new range of ideas has been assimilated through the formation of

[1] The only alphabet in existence in West Africa before Arabic was the Libyco-Berber Tifīnagh of the Tuareg. All others, excepting graphic and symbolic signs (such as are described by S. de Ganay, 'Graphie bambara des nombres', *J. Soc. Afr.* xx (1950), 295 ff.), were invented within relatively recent times.

[2] Vernacular poems by 'Uthmān and others are given in C. H. Robinson, *Specimens of Hausa Literature*, 1896. Hausa employ the term *ajami* (Ar. *'ajamī*, *'ajamiyya*, 'outlandish') for vernacular texts written in Arabic characters. It is also used for bad Arabic, cf. Spanish *aljamiado* in both senses.

calques, words and phrases formed by mechanical translation of Arabic expressions. This is especially evident in languages like Hausa and Songhay which have the instinct of composition: Hausa *Allah yayi masa jinḳai*, Songhay *yer-koy ma hinni ga*, 'May God have mercy on him', said after mentioning someone who is dead. Also vernacular words gain new significance through the influence of Islamic ideas. From Hausa *ḍaya*, 'one', derives *Makaḍaichi*, the One, and *kaḍaita*, to acknowledge the unity of God; similarly *sulmiya*, 'to fall off', is employed for 'to apostatize'.

5. THE INFLUENCE OF THE PILGRIMAGE

The influence of the pilgrimage begins early in the history of Islam in West Africa and Arab chroniclers have left many accounts of pilgrimages made by rulers of Sudan states since that of Baramandana of Māli in the eleventh century A.D. Apart from rulers ordinary pilgrims visited the holy places throughout the centuries.[1] Sudanese with Mecca as their goal were faced with a formidable journey. Practicable routes fell into two groups: northern across the Sahara to the Mediterranean coast and eastwards to the Red Sea. The Sahara crossing offered no great difficulty provided the pilgrim could join a caravan, but it was costly and could not be taken by the poor unless they travelled as servants or slaves of rich pilgrims or traders. The diversity of routes can be seen from a map of Saharan trade-routes. Western Moors travelled to Morocco, especially after the foundation of the Tijāniyya *ṭarīqa*, since this gave them the opportunity of visiting Aḥmad at-Tijānī's tomb at Fez. Others crossed central Sahara from Timbuktu, Gao, north Nigeria, and the Chad. Hausa preferred to take the route to Tripoli through Agadez, Ghat, and Ghadames because it was fairly safe and they could make their way by trading. The only practical way for people travelling on foot was the eastern route, but it was much more arduous and dangerous, and the robbery, enslavement, and massacre of pilgrims was a common event.[2]

[1] Few of these remained for study in Islamic centres. African *riwāqs* in the Azhar do not include one for western Sudan. They comprise: the *Maghāriba* (North Africans), *Barābra* (Nubians), *Sannāriyya* (eastern Sudan), *Jabarta* (Ethiopians), *Barnawiyya* (Kanuri and Hausa), *Ṣulaiḥ* (Dār Sila and Waday), and *Ardofor* (Darfur). The number of West Africans studying at the Azhar never seems to have been great (in 1952 there were 105 from the A.O.F. and about 50 from Northern Nigeria). The full certificate of *'ālim* can only be given to Egyptians, but foreign students receive a certificate testifying that they have attended the requisite lectures. White West Africans were known as *Shanāqṭa* (from Shinqīṭ in Mauritania) and Blacks as *Sūdān*, or, particularly in the eastern Sudan, as *Takārīr* or *Fallāta*.

[2] Bruce gives an account of the massacre in the Nilotic Sudan of a caravan of Takruri

The nineteenth century was a difficult period for pilgrimage because it was the most disturbed in West African history. Apart from internal wars pilgrim-routes were affected by the crisis the whole Islamic world was undergoing through European penetration. No established religious leaders dreamt of facing the perils, but the fact that ordinary people did attempt it, although they might be enslaved or drafted into Mahdist armies on the way, shows that pilgrimage is an urge from which they could not be deflected by the dangers of the way. When Africa settled down under the control of European powers the position changed and the pilgrimage became easier to accomplish than ever before. New ways were opened by sea and the poor-route eastwards became safe after defeat of the khalīfa ʿAbd Allāh in 1898. In the early days the lure of Mecca governed the direction of irreconcilables to the new régimes. Tokolor, fleeing before the French advance, migrated eastwards to Sokoto where they took part in the *jihād* against the British, then moved on to settle eventually in Nilotic Sudan and the Hijaz. But since the first decade of European rule the motive for eastward migration has been religious.

The pilgrimage is costly to the rich and arduous to the poor so naturally the number who go are limited. It is not especially prized in Senegal and Marty wrote that out of 1,385 schoolmasters only twenty had accomplished it.[1] Hausa and negroid Fulbe of Northern Nigeria are keener than any other West Africans, a psychological factor distinguishing them from eastern Sudan Muslims. Hausa, of course, are an enterprising people to whom it provides an outlet for their love of travel and trade. Many feel that it is virtuous to live and die near the holy places. Thus the Tijānī khalīfa Alfa Hāshim (d. 1934) and ʿUmar Gambo (d. 1918) settled in Mecca, where at least 4,000 West Africans are permanently established.

The principal route is through Maiduguri, Fort Lamy, Abeshe, Ginena, Fasher, Nahud, to El-Obeyd from which the train carries them to the Red Sea. This was formerly the route for heavy camel-borne traffic but today the majority travel by lorry. Still the writer has seen many walking, accompanied by women and children, and leading a donkey laden with their possessions. Pilgrimage is undertaken by the

pilgrims led by Muḥammad aṭ-Ṭawāshī ('the Eunuch'), one of the Negro eunuch guardians of the Kaʿba who had been allowed to visit his homeland and was returning via Sennar and Shendi (J. Bruce, *Travels*, 1805, vi. 400–1, 477). M. at-Tunīsī shows that a regular yearly pilgrimage caravan went eastwards from Waday when he mentions that in 1841 it had to proceed by Awjala and Egypt owing to the strained relations which then existed between Waday and Darfur (*Voyage au Ouaday*, p. 236).

[1] *R.M.M.* xxviii. 31.

poor primarily from desire to earn reward in the next world, for not only is the journey arduous but the returned pilgrim does not enjoy an enhanced reputation. Yet they feel that it is worth all the miseries. Some arrive back with new gaudy clothes, but the majority do not wear any distinctive dress. The charm-making power of the pilgrim may be increased (many are found selling relics, generally spurious, from the holy cities), but he does not enjoy greater consideration, and if he is a cleric he must be careful not to incur the jealousy of fellow clerics. He tells stories of the wonders he has seen, but one aspect he is silent about, the hardships of the journey, the slights and contempt to which he has been subjected, and the way he has been rooked by the inhabitants of Mecca.[1] He cannot accomplish it under seven years[2] for he has not only to earn enough to feed himself and his family on the journey, but has to save money to pay for railway fares, the sea-crossing from Suakin to Jidda, entry fees and pilgrim's dues,[3] guides, sacrificial sheep, lodging and keep in the Hijaz. All these are very onerous. The difficulties have led many to settle on the way, particularly on the return journey. Those with money who go by the land-route take a year and quite a number prefer to do this rather than take the easy route by sea or air and be scorned on their return as pseudo-pilgrims.

Although the motives of the poor are primarily religious, those of the rich are mixed. As in the past newly converted chiefs affirmed their adherence to a world faith by heading for Mecca, so today new adherents, from a petty chief in Sierra Leone to the Alãfin of Oyo in Yorubaland, set off soon after conversion with the view of enhancing their standing in the new religion. Air travel has made its accomplishment simple for men with money and they need not be away longer than three weeks.[4] Again, as in the past, it has the effect of stirring in

[1] There are exceptions. When an emir went on pilgrimage in 1934 via Fort Lamy and Khartoum, 'he complained of the rapacity he encountered in the Hedjaz which forced him to obtain an advance of £350 from the Minister at Jeddah', *Nigeria: Annual Report on the Northern Provinces*, 1934, p. 6.

[2] The average time taken by those who follow the eastern route is seven years, and fifteen is not uncommon. The number of pilgrims passing annually is about 8,000 (7,904 West Africans passed through Suakin in 1946). This means that at any one time there are 50,000 to 60,000 actually on the move.

[3] The Hijaz entrance tax (£5) and pilgrim's dues (£25) were abolished in 1952.

[4] The pilgrimages of the well-to-do by sea, land, and air routes are today organized by governments. In 1956, 305 pilgrims from the A.O.F. travelled by sea. Other French routes go across the Sahara and eastwards from the Chad region. A total of 2,483 pilgrims from Northern Nigeria were issued with travelling certificates and passports for the 1956 pilgrimage. Of these 2,420 were travelling by road and 63 by air. Since more than 1,500 Nigerians booked flights the majority must have been neo-Muslims from south-west Nigeria.

them a temporary zeal for enforcing provisions of Islamic law.[1] Thus a Dahomean chief was found hurrying home in order to rectify an inheritance which had not been settled according to Islamic prescriptions. Saʿīd Njoya of the Bamum (Cameroons) wrote on his return from Mecca in 1947:

> The question of amulets particularly engaged my attention. Seeing that Arabs are satisfied with prayer alone I asked one of them if the wearing of amulets is enjoined upon Muslims. 'Never', he replied, and then explained as follows the origin of the desire for them, 'Before the penetration of Islam into the Sudan the Sudanese were so steeped in idolatry that the religion destroyed paganism only imperfectly. When in their turn the Sudanese were ready to spread Islam they preached it with this pagan defect. Thus it is that Hausa and other Africans received only an Islam polluted with amulets.'[2]

The pilgrimage plays an important part in giving African Muslims a conception of Islam as a world religion and of a common religious inheritance. Travelling the whole way entirely through Muslim countries gives them the impression that Islam is the religion of Africa. However difficult the journey and however much they suffer from Meccan extortion, they get a sense of the brotherhood of Islam, transcending tribal divisions. Many pilgrims gain some conception of current political issues in the Middle East and are a factor in the diffusion of eastern political and religious influences in West Africa.

6. THE INFLUENCE OF THE RELIGIOUS ORDERS

(a) *The Cult of Saints*

The first thing the student of Islam notices in West Africa is the absence of a saint cult among Negro peoples. Later as he travels around he finds that it does exist. It is the focal point of the religion of the whites of Sahara and Sahil regions and amongst Negro peoples (Wolof in particular) in the Senegal and borderland regions influenced by Moors. But it can be said definitely that the cult of saints is not an integral part of the religious life of most West African Negroes. This is surprising. The cult is an important factor in the lives of Hamitic peoples from Morocco to Egypt and the eastern Sudan. Arabization

[1] On the reforms which Askiya Muḥammad tried to initiate see *T. al-Fattāsh*, p. 15.

[2] Cardaire, *Contribution à l'étude de l'Islam Noir*, 1949, p. 19. The 16th chief, Idrīs Njoya (1895–1923), after a peculiar religious history, became a Muslim in 1918. Both Islam and Christianity spread rapidly among the Bamum: Christians number 15,000 and Muslims between 20,000 and 30,000 out of a total population of 80,000 (see *The Peoples of the Central Cameroons*, Ethnographic Survey of Africa, Western Africa, part ix, pp. 56–57).

and the depth to which the religious orders took hold may account for this in part and in West Africa arabized Hamites are the most fervent devotees of saints.

In central Sudan spirit cults take its place. Belief in spirits springs from contact with nature, whilst that in saints arises from belief in the *baraka* of a person. Similarities between aspects of the saint cult and Hausa *bōri* spirits may be mentioned. Saints are spirits with links with certain places (tree, hill, tomb). They travel faster than light, visit each other, and are heard talking. They are amoral, do evil as well as good; inflict misfortune, disease, and death upon those who incur their anger, but also cure and restore to life, and respond to their worshippers. Some saints appear as animals and others possess their devotees. Danger is rife at visitation rites (*ziyāra*) when correct procedure and propitiation by gift and sacrifice are necessary. All these are characteristic of *bōri* spirits.

'Maraboutisme' is essentially subjection to a religious personality and his cult when dead. It made its appearance among the Moors through their link with North African Islam, which is saturated with the idea of *baraka*. Moorish clerics became affiliated to *ṭarīqas* and spread their litanies in the Sudan, but the saint cult did not spread with affiliation and is only found in its characteristic form in the Sahil region. The saint is one invested by God with power to work miracles, a quality to be distinguished from the working of magic, but this power is attributed to few holy men in West Africa.[1] Relatively few stories are told of miracle-workers. They are related of *jihād*-leaders like 'Uthmān dan Fodio and especially al-ḥājj 'Umar,[2] and of a few present-day clerics such as Shehu Fanta Mādi Kaba (1878–1955), 'the sharīf of Kankan', who achieved a great reputation in western Guinea. But this is a different thing from the power of *baraka* and on the border-line with magic.

The real test of the existence of the saint cult is the continuity of veneration after death, and although the Moors endow those revered during their lifetime with an enhanced reputation after death, Negroes take no care whatever of the burial-place of their saints. Even when tombs are preserved no cult practices grow up. Marty affirms that at Touba the hut-tombs of the founder and his sons do not attract pilgrims, for 'pious visits to the graves of great marabouts, so much in honour in

[1] Marty writes of Futa Jalon: 'Le don des miracles n'est pas le fait des karamoko foula, et fort peu ont joui de la réputation de thaumaturge. Encore, ces prodiges étaient-ils tout à fait accidentels.' *L'Islam en Guinée*, p. 478.

[2] Aḥmad al-'Adnānī compiled an account of 'Umar's miracles called *'Iqd al-jumān wa 'd-durar li 'l-ba'ḍ min karāmāt ash-shaikh 'Umar* (MS. Biblio. Nat. 5559, 5734).

North Africa, are absolutely unknown in Negro country, among Dyakanké as among other islamized peoples'.[1] The areas where tombs are found and their numbers provide an indication of the strength of the cult and show that it belongs essentially to Moorish regions. The most honoured saints are those who have living representatives to maintain their cult. The most famous in Hawd and Sahil are those of Aḥmad al-Bakkā'ī at Walata and Muḥammad al-Fāḍil on the road from Gumbu to Walata, near the wells of Dār as-Salām. The majority of tombs are only the centre of a clan cult. They are generally unpretentious buildings, conforming to the architecture of the region, in which the actual grave is indicated by a box of wood, as in North Africa, or a mound of mud. Even here tombs are not well kept; that of Muḥammad Fāḍil b. 'Ubaid, second head of the Fāḍiliyya, near the well of al-'Āfiya, is rapidly becoming a ruin. The Soninke and other Negro peoples of the Sahil, although so closely in touch with Moorish devotion, rarely venerate tombs.[2] Timbuktu, in close relationship with the Maghrib for centuries and not a centre for Negro Islam, contains many tombs of religious leaders.[3] The cult is also found in the Masina region (capital Jenne). In Nigeria the only tomb known as a *qubba* is that of 'Uthmān dan Fodio, a gloomy ill-kept building, visited sometimes by those about to set off on pilgrimage. 'Uthmān himself prohibited tomb reverence and offerings at graves. The tomb of Mālam Dendo (d. 1833), founder of the present line of *etsus* of Bida, at Raba, is a small, crumbling mud building with a thatched roof, which no one seems to visit. The real proof of the existence of the saint cult is whether people visit them to make special requests, and this Negro Muslims rarely do. Among Negroes pilgrimages to shrines are only characteristic of the Wolof who visit the tomb of Aḥmad Bamba at Touba (Baol) on 19th and 20th Muḥarram when a vast concourse congregates (40,000 in 1945 and 250,000 in 1956). Wolof members of the Ḥāfiẓiyya Tijāniyya visit the tombs of al-ḥājj Mālik Si (d. 1929) and other leaders at Tivawan in Cayor. But with Negro peoples in general, although public opinion canonizes devotion, learning, or manifestation of power in the living, no account is taken of these same men when dead. This is perhaps related to the fact that pagan Sudanese pay little attention to the graves of

[1] P. Marty, *Guinée*, p. 359. This Touba is the Qādirī Dyakanke settlement in the north of Futa Jalon founded by al-ḥājj Salīm in 1815.

[2] Cf. P. Marty, *Soudan*, iv. 192.

[3] Many of these, such as Sīdī Balqāsim at-Tawātī who gained a reputation as an innovator in the ritual of Friday prayer, are mentioned in *Ta'rīkh as-Sūdān*. Maḥmūd al-Kāti gives a list of thirteen tombs in Timbuktu and Jenne regions at which intercessory prayer is efficacious (*T. al-Fattāsh*, pp. 91–92 (170–4)).

ancestors once the full ceremonies have been accomplished. This is connected with their idea of the personality of man which is severed from the disintegrating corpse, whereas Islamic belief links the soul with the corpse, one day to be resurrected, which it visits and to which honour can therefore be paid.

(*b*) *The Influence of the Ṭarīqas*

Only two *ṭarīqas*, the Qādiriyya and Tijāniyya, are of significance in West Africa. Scattered groups calling themselves Shādhiliyya are found, but they are not interrelated, except in western Guinea, and came into existence through individual clerics receiving initiation whilst in North Africa or on pilgrimage. Sanūsī influence, at one time strong in the Chad region, is of little significance today.[1] The ʿArūsiyya-Salāmiyya[2] was introduced into the Chad region by the Tripolitanian tribe of Awlād Sulaimān, but they changed to the Sanūsiyya,[3] and then became Tijāniyya. Trading relations have led to individuals adopting North African orders. ʿIsāwiyya[4] travel along trade-routes from Zinder to the Upper Volta, but they are chiefly charlatans and jugglers and do not propagate. There are a few Raḥmāniyya in Banjagara.[5] These are of no importance and here we shall seek to assess the influence of the two main orders in the life of Muslims today.

To anyone approaching West African Islam from the eastern Sudan and North Africa the religious influence of the *ṭarīqas* seems very modest indeed. Adherence means little more than an affiliation which adds a few litanies to daily prayer and enjoins mutual obligations between members. French writers have noted the contrast between the role the orders play in the A.O.F. and North Africa. M. Brévié wrote that for the majority of Sudanese Muslims their attachment is merely

> the wearing of a label to which no precise significance is attached: the adding of a formula to one's prayer. It means primarily following the way which one's father or religious initiator followed. You belong to this or that mystical order

[1] Representatives of many *ṭarīqas* are found in the sub-saharan massif of Air which has always been a cross-roads of cultural influences. Besides the Qādiriyya which is the strongest, we find the Tijāniyya, Sanūsiyya (Kel Owey and Kel Igāzer), Madaniyya, Ṭayyibiyya, and ʿArūsiyya.

[2] Founded by Abū 'l-ʿAbbās b. ʿArūs (d. 1460) and reorganized by ʿAbd as-Salām al-Fitrī of Zlīten (d. 1795).

[3] G. Nachtigal, *Sahara et Soudan*, French transl. Paris, 1881, p. 380.

[4] The ʿIsāwiyya, a derivative of the Jazūliyya, was founded by Muḥammad b. ʿIsā (d. 1523/4), patron saint of Meknes.

[5] *Afr. Fr. R.C.*, 1912, p. 19. This *ṭarīqa*, a derivative of the Khalwatiyya-Ḥafnāwiyya, was founded by M. b. ʿAbd ar-Raḥmān al-Jurjurī, *c.* 1715/28–1793/4.

by reason of race. You are born a Tijānī when you are born a Tokolor, because the Tokolor conqueror, al-ḥājj ʿUmar, was a propagator of Tijānism; whilst you are a Qādirī if born a Pulo, since the Fulbe of Shehu Ḥamadu and in general all the old Sudanese races, had for long been Qādirī.[1]

The orders in West Africa became ordinary non-esoteric religious associations. They are important in assessing West African Islam. They were used by leaders like al-ḥājj ʿUmar as a means for binding devotees, through the oath of allegiance, to the cause of the *jihād*, and have been the cause of bitter feuds and rivalry among Muslims. Today few people do not have a vague link through their cleric to ʿAbd al-Qādir or Aḥmad at-Tijānī. But it must be realized that they rarely have anything to do with mysticism. Their leaders were the ordinary clergy leading their ignorant co-religionists in prayer and teaching them their religious duties. Yet account must be taken of the fact that a few are well versed in the doctrine and rules of their order, whilst genuine mystics are not unknown.[2] Further, though the ordinary member knows nothing of the mysticism upon which his order is based, attachment has an important bearing upon his moral life. In Nigerian states injunctions of the clerics have little effect in inducing observance of the moral code of Islam, but admittance to the Tijānī order may change an individual's life. Tijānīs are stricter than Qādirīs, hence their greater influence. They stress observance of positive precepts as well as of prohibitions such as smoking and drinking, lying and corruption, and a Tijānī in Hausaland will have nothing to do with *bōri*. Consequently an initiated member feels that he belongs to a religious élite. The orders have exercised an important missionary and political role, but from the religious point of view they represent the puritan rather than the mystical aspect of West African Islam.

(c) *Doctrine and Practice*

Many Moors and Fulbe of Futa Jalon are acquainted with the teaching and regulations of their 'way',[3] but the majority of clergy are very ignorant and differ greatly in tendencies, practices, and devotions,

1 J. Brévié, *Islamisme contre 'Naturisme' au Soudan Français*, 1923, p. 205.

2 See Th. Monod's account of Tyērno Bokar Ṣāliḥ Tal, a descendant of al-ḥājj ʿUmar, in 'Un poème mystique soudanais', *Le Monde non chrétien*, no. 2, 1947, pp. 217–28; idem, 'Un homme de Dieu: Tierno Bokar', *Présence africaine*, nos. 8–9, 1950, pp. 149–57.

3 The term *ṭarīqa* is little known. Hausa employ *tsarīḳa* rather for 'to perform the *dhikr*', whilst they say *jama'a alkādirāwa* for the local congregation. Often the vernacular word for 'way' is employed (Mande: *Tijāni-sīra*). *Wird* is used in the sense of link or affiliation: Mande *wurudi*.

The tie of unity is no more than the link with one's local cleric. Even a common name is often lacking. Some clergy are both Qādirī and Tijānī. Moors like Muḥammad Fāḍil, his son Sa'd Bu, and Bu Kunta conferred both traditions indifferently, although a Tijānī rule prohibits joining other *ṭarīqas*. But in most cases the rule is observed. In spite of all divergences there is a norm of belief and practice. Ṣūfism is their theoretical foundation. This shows itself in the chain of authority which links the village cleric to the saintly founder, in the language used at the investiture of a *muqaddam* and initiation of a *murīd*, in the litanies, prayers, and manuals of instruction.

At the head of each order is theoretically a *shaikh*. Under him are local agents, generally called *muqaddams* and sometimes *khalīfas*, who enrol, train, and initiate new members, collect dues and organize the collective *dhikrs*. Among Moors the establishment (*zāwiya*) of a *muqaddam* is generally a compound enclosing a group of buildings with sections for the *muqaddam*, his family, disciples (*ṭalaba*), pilgrims (for it generally encloses a tomb), and a mosque and school. Few *zāwiyas* of this kind are found among Negro peoples except in Senegal.

Ritual is centred around *dhikr*, performed alone and in congregation. At initiation the aspirant (*murīd*) swears an oath of allegiance, receives a rosary, and is allocated litany 'tasks' (*awrād*, sing. *wird*) to be recited with its aid.[1] A degree of mystery is attached to the permission to recite *awrād* and the phrase 'to take the *wird* of Shaikh X' means to be initiated into Shaikh X's *ṭarīqa*. Clergy in Northern Nigeria tried to make out that the *ṭarīqas* were secret societies whose liturgies only the initiated should know. *Dhikr* as a method for the cultivation of the divine presence is almost unknown. It is thought of as individual or collective 'praise' of God and the Prophet. At the congregational séance (Ar. *ḥaḍra*)[2] under the leadership of the local *muqaddam*, litanies and invocations are chanted in rhythm. They are supposed to

[1] Songhay *dityir* (Ar. *dhikr*) means 'to tell beads'. The Qādirī rosary has 99 beads divided into three groups, and that of the Tijānīs consists of 100 beads divided 12, 18, 20, 20, 18, 12. These arrangements are in accordance with the requirements of their respective litanies. The term for rosary is a corruption of Arabic *tasbīḥ* or *tasbiḥa*, e.g. Hausa *chasbi* (the various types having their names, e.g. *kub* is a rosary made of wooden beads, *yamsur* one made of black beads decorated with silver), Nupe *tasabi* (repetition of the rosary is *àsàlatù*); Songhay *tesbiha*; Mandinka *tasabiya*. The rosary acquires symbolical importance from its use in initiation and cult practices. It is a symbol of authority. Among Dyula the new family head always inherits his predecessor's rosary even though, as a result of the encroachment of Islamic law, he is entitled to nothing else of his property. An initiating shaikh when about to die designates his successor by handing him his rosary and prayer-mat.

[2] An abridgement of *ḥaḍrat Allāh* (or *an-nabī*), 'the presence of God (*or* the Prophet)'.

concentrate thought, feeling, and action upon God or, more commonly, the Prophet, for they believe that mystical union with God is exceptional and that it is better to seek to attain contact with Muḥammad. Provided the ritual is correctly performed Tijānīs hold that the Prophet comes at the second reading of the prayer, *Jawharat al-Kamāl*.[1] The phenomenon of possession is one of the deepest expressions of religious experience among Sudanese and the experience of *dhikr* normally has analogies with this, yet in West Africa this aspect of *dhikr* has caught on only to a limited degree. The noisy *dhikr* is performed by Qādirīs in the central Sudan, particularly in Bornu and Waday which have been influenced by *ṭarīqas* of the Nilotic Sudan, but Kunta and Moors are opposed to it. Tijānīs prohibit extravagances but the Ḥamālist branch has performed extravagant *dhikrs* since the time of the founder. However, the musical aptitude of the African, characterized by the chant, highly developed rhythm, and antiphony, has found expression in the recital of religious poems in Arabic and vernaculars at *dhikr* gatherings.

(*d*) *Qādiriyya*

Most Qādirī mystical lineages in West Africa go back to al-Mukhtār b. Aḥmad (1729–1811) of the Arab Kunta tribe[2] who founded a *zāwiya* in Azawād, north of Timbuktu, which became the centre of the order. From him derive the affiliations of the two *jihād* leaders, Ḥamadu of Māsina and ʿUthmān dan Fodio.[3] Another famous shaikh he initiated was Sīdyā 'l-Kabīr (1780–1868) of the Awlād Birri. His grandson, Sīdyā Bābā (1869–1924), from his *zāwiya* at Bu-Tilīmīt in the Trarza region, gained great influence over Moorish tribes in Mauritania and Negro peoples (especially Wolof traders) in Senegal.[4] The branch formed by a contemporary of Shaikh Sīdyā, Muḥammad al-Fāḍil (1780–1869) of the Ahl Ṭālib Mukhtār, has become a new order, the Fāḍiliyya.[5] He adapted his teaching to the needs of Negroes.

[1] See the Tijānī manual *As-Sirr al-Abhar*, by M. ʿAlwān al-Jawsqī, p. 3.

[2] Their ancestor Muḥammad al-Kuntī came from Tawāt in the fifteenth century. The *ṭarīqa* is known as Bakkā'iyya after his son, Aḥmad al-Bakkā'ī (d. 1504), but it was Aḥmad's son, ʿUmar ash-Shaikh (*c.* 1460–1553), who spread the *ṭarīqa* among the tribe. He was initiated by the Tawātī reformer, al-Majhīlī, on the latter's return journey from Hausaland. ʿUmar is said to have sent disciples to preach Islam throughout the Sahara, Niger buckle, and Hausaland (according to *Ta'rīkh Kunta*, cf. Marty, *Soudan*, i. 22). He did not have active successors until al-Mukhtār.

[3] M. b. M. b. al-Mukhtār, *Kitāb aṭ-Ṭarā'if* (Marty, *Soudan*, i. 61); ʿAbd Allāh dan Fodio, *Tazyīn al-Waraqāt*, in *D. Isl.* x (1920), 24–25.

[4] This branch is sometimes known as Lesīdiyya.

[5] From one of Muḥammad al-Fāḍil's teachers, Muḥammad al-Aghḍaf (d. 1860), is derived a small tribal *ṭarīqa* which is regarded, without justification, as heretical, chiefly because of

He was succeeded by his nephew, Muḥammad b. ʿUbaid (1823–1901), but his sons, especially Saʿd Bu (1850–1917), had greater influence among Negroes.

Through the propaganda of these Moors and through Negroes studying in their *zāwiyas* the Qādirī *wird* was diffused throughout the Sudan. Negro Qādirīs at any distance from the Sahil, related only to their local clerics, know nothing of the Moorish heads and have little feeling of belonging to a widespread organization. It is otherwise with traders who find affiliation a valuable link.

A famous saint in the Senegal was Aḥmad Bamba b. M. b. Ḥabīb Allāh (d. 1927). Although affiliated to both Qādiriyya and Tijāniyya his way (Murīdiyya) was primarily that of the first, derived from Sh. Sīdyā. His is a genuine Negro *ṭarīqa* orientated for life in the changing Africa. It spread with tremendous rapidity since 1886[1] especially among agriculturist Wolof, but has also proved attractive to pagans, and must be regarded as the most powerful religious force in the Senegal. Its expansion was not arrested by the death of the founder and the great festivals are reported to be occasions of veritable anthropolatry. The mosque of Touba, the spiritual centre, situated on the spot where Aḥmad received the revelation of his mission, is one of the largest in Africa. Great stress is placed on the sanctity of the founder and his successors[2] for this redeems the sins of affiliates, provided they submit themselves, abandon their personal spiritual life, and are ready to undertake the temporal tasks assigned them. A formula forever on their lips is: 'The prayer of the Master obliterates the sins of the *murīd*.' The order has deeply influenced social structure and the relationship of man and land. Agriculture has been sanctified to the service of God and His shaikh and a system of collective farms has been developed.[3]

The Qādiriyya spread from Jenne–Timbuktu region into central Sudan before the Fulbe conquest, but it was only a clerical allegiance. The existing groups on the middle Niger, Zerma, and Northern Nigeria derive from the teaching of ʿUthmān dan Fodio. During the

extravagant *dhikrs* uncharacteristic of Mauritanian Islam. The actual founder was his pupil, Aḥmad b. ʿUmar, known as Bū Ghifāra (d. 1888), but it is known as Ghuḍfiyya after his master. On this order see *Afr. Fr. R.C.*, 1912, p. 16; P. Laforgue, 'Une secte hérésiarque en Mauritanie', *Bull. Com. Ét.A.O.F.* xi (1928), 654–5; A. Leriche, 'L'Islam en Mauritanie', *Bull. I.F.A.N.* xi (1949), 458–60.

1 Murīdiyya membership has increased from 70,000 adherents in 1912 to over 350,000.

2 Aḥmad Bamba was succeeded by his sons: Aḥmad Muṣṭafa Mbake (d. 1945) and Falīlu Mbake (b. 1887).

3 See below, pp. 188–9, and P. Marty, 'Les Mourides d'Amadou Bamba', *R.M.M.* xxv (1913), 3–164.

present century the order has been steadily losing ground and even in the emirates of Sokoto and Gwando the majority of clergy have become Tijānīs within the last twenty-five years. Its role in Bornu and other central Sudan kingdoms was weak. Teachers called themselves Qādirī, but initiation was confined to members of clerical lineages.[1] Most clergy in Bagirmi and Kanem have become Tijānī, though the Qādirī way has held its own in Waday where a type of *dhikr* characteristic of the eastern Sudan is practised.

The *dhikr al-awqāt* is the usual: *al-istighfār*, *as-sabḥala*, *at-tahlīl*, and *ṣalāt ʿalā 'n-nabī*, recited after the set prayers. The guide sets the number of repetitions.[2] The congregational *dhikr* is held mainly by urban groups. Hausa Kādirāwa (s. ba-kādiri) chant it to the rhythm of the *bandiri*, a basin-shaped hide drum beaten with the hands. The use of drums was forbidden by ʿUthmān dan Fodio, but the practice was reintroduced by pilgrims who had acquired it in Falāta settlements in Nilotic Sudan.

(*e*) *Shādhiliyya*

This term applies to the mystical doctrine derived from Abū'l-Ḥasan ʿAlī ash-Shādhilī (1196–1258) rather than to an organized *ṭarīqa*. In Morocco during the second half of the eighteenth century al-ʿArabī b. Aḥmad ad-Darqāwī (d. 1823) initiated a movement back to the primitive teaching and rules of Ash-Shādhilī, and a Pulo cleric from Futa Jalon called ʿAlī aṣ-Ṣūfī when visiting Fez came under its influence, was initiated by ʿAlī aṣ-Ṣūfī al-Fāsī, and returned to his homeland to teach the Shādhilī way. His disciples formed numerous centres of which the best known are the *zāwiyas* at Goumba (founder: Tyērno ʿAlī, 1828–1912), N'dama (founder: Tyērno Dyaw, d. 1865), and Jāwiya (i.e. *zāwiya*, founded, *c.* 1800, by a Mandinka, Tyērno Ismaʿīl, pupil of ʿAlī-aṣ-Ṣūfī). After the French occupation the first two engaged in politics and were suppressed.[3] These groups played an important role in the religious life of Futa Jalon until al-ḥājj ʿUmar's Tijānī propaganda undermined their influence. Many were absorbed into the Ti-

[1] The Kwoyām in Bornu, whom Barth (*Travels*, iv. 14) regarded as an indigenous people of Kanem, seem to have arrived as a *ṭarīqa* group from the eastern Sudan (about 1670?). This is suggested by Landeroin's description of the *dhikr* formerly practised by them (*Documents Scientifiques de la Mission Tilho*, 1911, ii. 397 n.).

[2] Muḥammad Belo, initiated into the *ṭarīqa* of al-Mukhtār al-Kuntī, quotes the *wird* he received in his *Infāq al-Maisūr* (pp. 203–7) and adds, 'Nothing hinders me from persisting with it except its length', which also precludes us from translating it here.

[3] On the history of these groups see P. Marty, *Guinée*, pp. 56–104.

jāniyya, but groups still survive. They have become closed-in communities and do little propaganda. Elsewhere than in Futa Jalon individual clerics ascribe themselves to ash-Shādhilī but there are few organized communities.

Characteristic of the Futa Jalon groups is the emphasis placed on fasting, retreat, and *dhikr*-recitals, called *jarorē* (*jalāla*?) every Thursday night to the accompaniment of hymns. Fasting is observed rigorously, not only in Ramaḍān, but at other periods of the year. Fulbe, in contrast to the gregariousness of Negroes, have a tendency to individualism, and members sometimes take vows never to leave their compound or mosque.

(*f*) *Tijāniyya*

After the death of Aḥmad b. Muḥammad at-Tijānī (1737–1815), ʿAlī ibn ʿĪsā (d. 1844), head of the *zāwiya* at Temasīn (Tamehalt), initiated a period of widespread missionary activity, associated with commercial ventures. Along with his caravans went *muqaddams* and *ikhwān* to Shinqīṭ, western Adrār, Senegalese Futa, Timbuktu, and Segu. *Zāwiyas* were also founded in Kano, Bornu, and Waday.

The first missionary to Mauritania was commissioned by the founder himself. About 1785 he initiated a Shinqīṭī called Muḥammad al-Ḥāfiẓ b. al-Mukhtār b. Ḥabīb al-Baddī, who was passing through Fez, and nominated him *khalīfa* for western Sahara where he preached the Tijānī Way with great vigour. His own tribe, Idaw ʿAlī, was won over to a man and has ever since been the Moorish stronghold of the order. In consequence of the special link with Morocco provided by their affiliation the tribe gained a monopoly over the caravan traffic through Shinqīṭ. The southern Trarza section carried his teaching among Negroes. The Moors in general were too attached to the Qādiriyya-Bakkā'iyya to be susceptible to propaganda, but groups of adherents were formed among Tokolor and Wolof. The Wolof group derive from Mālik Si (1855–1929, whence his branch is called the Mālikiyya as well as Ḥāfiẓiyya) who had his headquarters at Tivawan (Cayor). Although the influence of the Murīds was preponderant among Wolof, his emissaries played an important part in the islamization of Senegal, and, through the Wolof dispersion, many other regions.

The most important event in the history of the Tijāniyya in West Africa was the initiation of ʿUmar Tal (1794/7–1864) by Mawlūd Fal of the Idaw ʿAlī. He is responsible for its vast spread. Whilst on pilgrimage in Mecca ʿUmar met Muḥammad ibn Khalīfa al-Ghālī, *wakīl* of al-ḥājj 'Alī of Temasīn, who appointed him *khalīfa* for the Sudan. Later he broke with the Idaw 'Alī and claimed his authentic initiation to be that derived from Muḥammad al-Ghālī. He maintained no relations with the heads of the order in 'Ain Māḍī and Temasīn, and developed his way for Negroland along independent lines. He strongly opposed the Qādirī clergy, declaring that their Way in relation to his was as iron is to gold, a saying which Tijānīs constantly repeat. He began active propaganda in Dingiray. He first initiated the parish clergy of Futa Jalon where the order superseded the Qādiriyya and Shādhiliyya, and from there it spread throughout middle Guinea. As 'Umar pursued his victorious conquest throughout western Sudan he imposed Tijānī allegiance as the official cult of subjected territories. After his empire broke up, although some returned to old allegiances, many remained permanently attached to Tijānī shaikhs. 'Umar wrote a commentary called *Jawāhir al-Ma'ānī* on the *Rimāḥ* of Aḥmad at-Tijānī which remains still the chief manual of all shaikhs deriving from him.

The order entered Nigeria during the time of Muḥammad Belo, and in greater force when some 10,000 Tokolor and other remnants of the bands of Aḥmadu, son of al-ḥājj 'Umar, driven from Segu and Banjāgara, entered during the reign of 'Abd ar-Raḥmān of Sokoto (1891–1902). Allying themselves with the Sokoto cause they were widely scattered after the British took control in 1902 and formed new groups of adherents even in Sokoto against the wishes of the various Sarākuna Musulmi who were Qādirī. Ever since it has been spreading until (from 1925) it has become the dominant *tarīqa*. Educated youth in Northern Nigeria have adopted it in preference to what they regard as the more vulgar Qādiriyya. It has spread through Nupe and Yoruba Ilorin into the western region. Shaikh Sīdī ibn 'Umar at-Tijānī of the Maghrib, during his grand tour of West Africa (from 1947 to 1950), visited Nigeria and appointed many *muqaddams*. In some parts there have been separatist movements; Tijānīs of Gusau, for instance, built a separate *jāmi'* which caused communal disturbances and was destroyed.

A revival took place in the Sahil towards the end of the century through the work of a number of agents, including Muḥammad al-Mukhtār b. Aḥmad (1860–1930) who received his appointment as *muqaddam* (*c.* 1885) from the *wakīl* of Muḥammad Janūn, *khalīfa* of the Moroccan group and lived at Nyoro. This town, one of the capitals of the Tokolor ('Umarian) empire, is the principal centre in the Sahil and is often visited by shaikhs of Fez and 'Ain Māḍī.

The most significant development since the death of al-ḥājj 'Umar also began in Nyoro. This was the formation of a sect by Ḥamāhu 'llāh b. Muḥammad b. ʿUmar (1886–1943). He derived from Muḥammad b. Aḥmad b. ʿAbd Allāh, a Tawātī linked with the Fez motherhouse, who arrived in Nyoro in 1900 and died in 1909. Tijānī clerics deriving from al-ḥājj ʿUmar (Ba-l-Murtaḍā, d. 1922, brother of ʿUmar and local head, lived in Nyoro) set themselves against him, but he gained adherents among Wolof traders. The controversial element in his *ṭarīqa* was based on a triviality in that Muḥammad b. Aḥmad required his followers to recite the important prayer, *Jawharat al-Kamāl*, after the eleventh bead of the rosary instead of the twelfth. The group adopted other practices, extravagant *dhikrs* with bodily inclinations culminating in nervous crises, which are forbidden to Tijānīs, and the admission of women to some séances. It was his disciple and successor, Ḥamāhu'llāh whose father was a Moor and his mother a black Pulo of servile caste, who developed it as a deviationist sect. He proselytized throughout the Sahil among Moors and Soninke, winning many away from their Tijānī shaikhs. Naturally, since this affected their influence and their pockets, they reacted against the Ḥamālists and the result was a series of disorders in Nyoro (1924), Kaede (1930), and Assaba Nema (1940). The deportations which followed these troubles led to the formation of new nuclei; members exiled in Ansongo gained new adherents not only among Songhay, but in Sokoto Province and Niger Colony. The death of Ḥamāhu 'llāh in exile left members without a grand master and the order has remained dormant, awaiting the appearance of a successor.[1]

Tijānī adherents are more numerous than Qādirīs. In Senegal it was reckoned in 1914 that the proportion of Tijānī clergy was 903 to 483 Qādirī.[2] Members include all Tokolor of Futas Toro and Jalon, a minority of Wolof, Laghlāl of Nema-Walāta, Idaw ʿAli and a section of the Barābish, most of the Soninke, half the Mande Dyula clergy, a minority of the Fulbe (the majority of those in Segu and Futa Jalon), a third to half of Hausa clergy and all those of the Zerma, whilst there are strong centres in Bornu, Kanem, and Bagirmi.

The following are the practices observed in Northern Nigeria. The 'daily office' (*al-wird al-yawmī*) consists of the recital of the *lāzima* morning and evening, and the *waẓīfa* once a day. The *lāzima* consists

[1] On Ḥamālism see P. Marty, *Soudan*, iv. 218–22; P. J. André, *L'Islam noir*, 1922, pp. 67–69; and especially A. Gouilly, *L'Islam dans l'Afrique Occidentale Française*, 1952, pp. 134–61. Another new Tijānī leader who is gaining a widening radius of influence is Ibrāhīm Nyas of Kaolak (Senegal).

[2] *R.M.M.* xxviii. 29.

of each of the following recited 100 times: astaghfir Allāh, ṣalāt ʿalā'n-nabī, and the *tahlīl*. The *waẓīfa* of: astaghfir Allāh al-ʿaẓīm alladhī lā ilāha illā huwa, al-ḥayy al-qayyūm (30 times); ṣalāt al-fātiḥ (50 times); lā ilāha illā 'llāh (100 times); and the prayer, *Jawharat al-Kamāl* (12 times). On Friday afternoon each local group performs the *hailalatu'l-jumʿati*. They squat in a circle with a white 'holy cloth' spread in the centre, 'signifying the presence of Muḥammad'. About 5.0 p.m., at a sign from the *muqaddam*, all recite the *tahlīl* slowly in unison, commencing in a low voice, then faster and louder. When the sun begins to set they recite the word *Allāh* slowly, gradually fading out. They end with the *ṣalāt al-maghrib*. There is no striving after ecstasy. If a Tijānī is unable to join with his fellows on Friday he recites the *tahlīl* 1,000 times and *Allāh* 500 times with the aid of a rosary.

(*g*) *Sanūsiyya* has today little more than historical significance for the central Sudan. After Muḥammad ibn ʿAlī as-Sanūsī (1787–1859) had been forced to leave Mecca he settled in Jabal Akhḍar in the interior of Cyrenaica (1843) where he founded *az-Zāwiyat al-Baiḍā*. This fertile spot in the bleak desert was centrally situated both for influencing nomadic tribes and for contact with caravan traffic from the central Sudan. Although he won over nomadic tribes, his propaganda awakened little response from peasants and urban people attached to older orders, and his missionary outlook turned southwards to the tribes of the Sahara and beyond them to the black Muslim or pagan peoples of the Sudan. In 1856 he moved his headquarters from al-Baiḍā to Jaghbūb, deep in the interior of the Libyan desert, to avoid Turkish interference and strengthen his influence in central Sahara. There he founded a *zāwiya* which, like the ancient *ribāṭ*, was a convent and fort, and became a place of learning and a shrine.

In Mecca as-Sanūsī had won the friendship of a Wadayan noble, Muḥammad ash-Sharīf, who became *kōlak* in 1835. Through him as-Sanūsī succeeded in establishing a great reputation among Wadayans. Such was his influence that when dissensions concerning the succession arose after the death of *Kōlak* ʿAlī ibn Muḥammad in 1874 al-Mahdī was influential enough to settle the dispute. In consequence the new *kōlak* became almost a tributary of the Sanūsī. Under Muḥammad al-Mahdī (1859–1902) the order attained its widest extension and influence. Jaghbūb remained the administrative centre where year by year missionaries were trained and sent out on missions. *Zāwiyas* were set up all over Fezzan, in the Air massif;[1] among Teda and Negroes of

[1] In 1850 Barth (*Travels*, i. 180–1) mentions the fervency of the Tin-ylkum (Ke

Kawār, Tibesti, Borku, and Ennedi; and in the regions of Kanem, Waday, and Bagirmi. The Teda are said to have been converted to Islam in 1855, but this probably means that Sanūsīs regarded them as pagans because of their laxity. At any rate by 1872 they were all Sanūsiyya. *Zāwiyas* were founded in Kawār (Bilma 1860, Chemidour 1879) and Zinder. Propaganda was intensified in Air in 1870 when schools were opened among both Tuareg and Negroes, and in 1897–8 Muḥammad as-Sunnī carried out an extensive mission in Kano, Damagaram, Damergu, and Air. Al-Mahdī had two able propagandists in the south, Muḥammad al-Barrānī who operated from the *zāwiya* of Bīr Alali in Kanem, and Muḥammad as-Sunnī who, with his son al-Mahdī, operated in Bornu, Bagirmi, and Waday. In 1895 al-Mahdī transferred his headquarters to al-Jawf in the Kufra oases group and again in 1899 to Gouro (Qiru) oasis in Dār Gurani between Borku and Tibesti. The French brought an end to Sanūsī domination in central Sahara and Sahil. In 1900 they occupied Bagirmi, then Kanem, and in 1906–7 took Kawar, Bilma, and 'Ain Galakka (Borku). In 1909 Abeshe in Waday was captured and in 1913–14 Tibesti, Borku, Wajanqa, and Ennedi. The Sanūsīs lost all political control over central Sudan and their spiritual influence declined. The 1914–18 war saw a Sanūsī rising in central Sahara, which involved the Ullimmeden, Air Tuareg, and Teda. Order was gradually regained though French operations were not completed until 1923. Today, except in Kanem, Waday, and Air, Sanūsī influence in the central Sudan is negligible.

Tinalkum), who operated the carrying trade between Murzūq and Air, in performing the *dhikr* of the Sanūsiyya. Most Tuareg of Air refused affiliation because it made too great demands for change in their customs.

5

The Background of the Old Religion

I. SCOPE OF THE INQUIRY

HAVING examined the official religion of Muslims we now turn to the unofficial religion. Both are associated in the pattern of Negro Muslim religious life and have to be taken into account in subsequent chapters on social life. Study of the pre-Islamic residue in West Africa is different from that of countries which have been Muslim for centuries. In the latter old customs are fully embedded under the levelling of Islamic civilization, but in West Africa we are confronted by a missionary situation[1] and the process of forming the Islamic pattern of society in which custom is fully embedded is still going on. There are consequently two aspects to examine: the actual process of change in order to see what elements are eliminated and what are retained; and, second, the natural animistic and magical elements of a Muslim community, both those imported with its civilization and those accepted as ineradicable custom. Survivals are firmer among established Muslims since they are part of the general body of custom. In fact, active rooting out belongs to the early stages when people have made the decisive break. A Mandinka missionary in Sierra Leone trying to break the power of the village cultic cycle will fulminate against offerings to spirits, although noticeable in Muslim Mandinka villages are bowls at the foot or branch-fork of a tree whose base is covered with blood and feathers—the remains of offerings to *da-siri*.

The functions of priest and magician should be clarified, for this shows why Islam seeks to supplant the first and interferes so little with the second. The function of the priest, whether family head or grand-

[1] Islam was only a class religion until the nineteenth-century revolutionary movement carried it among cultivators. Pagans survive in every Islamic community. Even among Tokolor there are sub-groups of artisans, labourers, fishers, and agriculturalists, who, though Muslim in name, are pagans in practice. Pagan medicine-men operate in Muslim areas because they are regarded as socially useful. Muslims commonly send their griots, barbers, or blacksmiths to participate in cult ceremonials on their behalf. Women, by maintaining old cults, also ensure that the family makes the best of two worlds. Although we are not concerned with pagan cults as such the existence of practitioners in Islamic communities has to be taken into account in assessing the total impact of Islam, since they modify the outlook and practice of clergy, who must be ready, for example, to employ black magic otherwise they will lose custom.

master of an initiatory cult, is essentially social. As director of cult ceremonies he stands at the central point of the social organization, acting as intermediary between this world and the unseen in the communal interest. The magician, on the other hand, is an isolated practitioner, having little connexion with the cult as an institution. When a community adopts Islam the priest must be displaced from his socio-central position, but the magician (and the diviner too, once his functions are separated from the cult) is allowed to exercise his functions, even though clergy in their analogous role claim to be able to perform them, for people do not trust their powers and want an alternative. But there is a great difference from the former position since they now belong to the realm of superstition, performing practices not recognized by the official religion.

Techniques employed in Muslim communities fall into two groups: personal and communal relations with the supernatural, and manipulation of impersonal magic power. In practice both are often associated. In divinatory practice, for instance, consultation with the spirit world is combined with manipulation of objects, whilst magical power can be conferred and sometimes operated by a supernatural agency.

2. THE CULT OF SPIRITS

Communal cults fall into two groups:

Cults of Social Groups

Family. Cults of ancestral spirits, royal clan, twin cult.

Territorial Group. Communal and village cults of territorial spirits, such as Mande *nyȧna dugu da siri*.

Cults of Mystery Societies

Cults of initiatory associations which transcend natural and territorial groupings: in the western cycle those of the *komo* type, and in the central cycle cults of the *bōri* type.

Islam in its struggle to become the controlling agency in communal life condemns, not belief in, but worship of spirits. This accounts for its variable action upon different elements in animist structure. After it gains ground communal cults are disinherited; ceasing to be family or village cults they become cults of initiated only. Priests of certain communal cults may survive islamization because their functions are important for the well-being of society, as, for example, those of 'master of the water' among fishing peoples. Everywhere offerings to nature spirits and independent practitioners flourish without incurring censure from representatives of Islam.

Islam is strongly opposed to the materialization of the spiritual and where its attack and rooting out is most effective is against 'idol worship', that is, cult of spirits symbolized by fetishes[1] like Yoruba statuettes, Mande *boli* or *dyo*, Temne stones (*a-boro məsar*) symbolizing culture heroes or ancestors, cones of clay, sacred animals symbolizing earth and water, or masks of mystery cults. So in Mande languages *nya-kō*, 'spirit cult' is in opposition to *silāmi ya kō*, Islamic cult; and *nya kō dē*, 'animist' to *silāmi dē*, 'child of Islam'. In attacking what gives the appearance of idolatry, Islam breaks up the cults with which the symbols are associated, but leaves other forms of animism intact. The cultivator can only detach himself in a limited way for he fears the annoyed spirits of nature or the dead will trouble him, the soil will cease to germinate the seed as he sows, and the bush remain hostile. Only the uprooted and townspeople whose link with the land is broken dare do this. But most people are cultivators and every village has its cycle of animistic observance to ensure the falling of the rain and the fertility of the soil. Old functionaries, heads of family or village, rainmakers, masters of the soil or river, continue to perform their rites. No cleric would think of questioning them. They change like everything else, some are discontinued, others survive, some take on Islamic symbols, but propitiation in some form or other continues as before.

(*a*) *Cults of Social Groups*

Nupe illustrate the changes which take place when Islam is adopted. The family cult (*nbà*) of ancestral spirits (*ndakó*) involves visiting graves and offering prayer and libations of beer. Other family cults are those of *bàkómba* (twin spirit) living in the compound,[2] and the *kpanká* (lit. 'truant') who are water-spirits. Sacrifices to spirits with names, like certain *alijenuẓi* or *kpàta tsóẓi* (or *egi nuwoṇ*), 'the master of the watering place', a spirit which women seek to acquire, are generally individual. Nupe territorial rituals are centred on the cult of impersonal

[1] The word 'fetish' may have to be used, since Muslims talk of them in the same way as Christians, for a material symbol which is the abode of supernatural power, to which offerings are made. It is natural to identify the spirit with the symbol which represents it, just as the animistic Christian may identify the saint with his statue or ikon. 'Amulet' refers to the material object which houses impersonal power. Islam sanctifies amulets and condemns fetishes.

[2] The cult of twins is almost universal among Nupe since all families have a twin somewhere in their past and once adopted the cult is continued.

spirit channels *kútịzi*.[1] Formerly each district had a chief priest (*ndăzó*) dedicated to Guṇnuṇ, and every village had its priest (*ẓigi*), messenger of the *ndăzó*, acting as medium between Guṇnuṇ and other *kútịzi* and the people.

With the adoption of Islam the mourning feast (*mba*) on the eighth day after death is islamized by substituting Islamic prayer (*àdŭwa*) for *ebalà* (prayer with libation). Intercession is offered to ancestors in general, for Islam has nothing in common with the family particularism of the ancestor cult, and in time even that disappears. Propitiation of household twin spirits continues since it has characteristics of an individual cult kept up by women, and each house has its place for offerings (*efu*). Communal *kútịzi* take much longer to go than the ancestor cult. Everywhere they are disintegrating, yet although no longer the cult of the whole community everyone likes to feel that their pagan fellows are maintaining the link on their behalf. *Ẓigịzi* are decreasing in number and only two *ndăzó* were mentioned. Guṇnuṇ survives as a fertility cult. Remnants like the Guṇnuṇ stick (*nuṇgbere*), a charm protecting property, become unrelated mechanical magical elements.

Mende religion, though entirely different from that of Nupe, is based on the same groups of ancestral, family, and nature spirits. After the adoption of Islam the old form of sacrifices to ancestors is abandoned and a new form based on the idea of *ṣadaqa* (Mende *saa*) is adopted. Just as they approach a chief through an intermediary so they make use of those who have 'crossed the water' as a body, associated with Prophet and saints, to intercede with God. The ceremony (*lɛɛhinɛi*) takes place every Friday when they are especially accessible. Rice flour is prepared, kept overnight for the *nagfɛi* of the dead who are not named, and then given away. This is a strictly family ceremony into which the cleric does not enter. That probably means that it is doomed to go as Islam gains greater hold. However that may be, neighbouring Temne have a similar ceremony at the two great festivals when the cleric has a part to play. The family head prepares a bowl of rice for recently dead relatives and a general bowl for ancestors in bulk, and individuals prepare special bowls. When the *karamoko* arrives they sit around the bowl touching it as at the seven plates ceremony.[2] They talk in Temne to the dead and the *karamoko* says an Arabic prayer. The

[1] See above, p. 53, n. 2. Different terminology is used for the two categories of communal spirits: (*a*) *ṇbà* (n.), *yiṇbà* (v.), worshipping spirits of ancestors; *mba*, mourning feast held on eighth day; *ebalà* (n.), *làba* (v.), prayer with libation from a sacred calabash (*evo balà*). (*b*) *efu* (n.), *jiṇfu* (v.), offering to *kútịzi*; *enyawo*, sacrifice of fowl or goat to *kútịzi*; *enyawoba*, altar.

[2] See below, p. 181.

dough is kept until morning and then, since 'it has lost its virtue', it is given away. All recently islamized have survivals or transitional rites of this kind.[1] In time prayers *for* the dead are substituted for prayers to or through the dead, and that means real islamization. The cult of the family spirits may be dismissed as playing no real part in the lives of Muslims.

Since no cleric denies the power of nature spirits their cults are more difficult to eliminate. In the early stages Islam sets up conflicts until old and new integrate. Muslim Temne intend to make the best of both worlds and sacrifice to spirits (*kərifi*) is a communal as well as an individual obligation.[2] Temne are at a transitional stage, but when Islam has gained the whole people priests are discredited and survivals become part of accepted custom. Some communal cults like masters of land and water survive islamization. The Bozo *dyi tu*, 'Master of the Water', is an important person in a fishing community. He is the intermediary between the community and Faro, the spirit of the water to whom the river belongs.[3] As hereditary trustee of the rites his function is to transmit the wishes of Faro and indicate what offerings are necessary in order to retain its goodwill. Cults of nature and clan heroes are tenacious for group welfare is felt to be bound up with them. Thus Dyāwara (Kingui and Bakhunu) sacrifice white cocks and young bulls each year at the tomb of their hunter ancestor, Daman Ngille, to ensure his protection.[4] Similarly the Mande *dugu da siri* are essential for the protection of the village and the cleric is afraid to face, not only communal hostility, but the wrath of the spirits by opposing village ritual. He may succeed in substituting himself for the soothsayer and prognosticate what sacrifices are necessary, but he cannot take the place of hereditary priests. Cults of nature spirits exist in some form or other among all Muslims whatever their stage of islamization.

[1] For example, Nupe practice of talking to the dead called *kuchi gaṇgaṇ*, Mandinka sacrificing to ancestors at festivals, or Teda sacrifices of flour and water on graves.

[2] Here is an example of *a-bɛmpa kərifi* from a Muslim village. A chicken is killed before the stone or tree of the *kərifi* which is sprinkled with the blood. Then the *ɔmen* (priest) repeats the connective *loŋtha* (see below, p. 122, n. 2) several times and talks to the *kərifi*. Rice flour is offered and taken back to the house. When cooked the villagers return and offer the sacrifice (*sathka*) by placing a portion of the rice and chicken on the stone or tree, the *ɔmen* pleads on behalf of the people, and they eat the consecrated rice.

Such practices take place in Muslim villages showing all the outward apparatus of Islamic observance and are an example of the conflict going on in society between cleric and *ɔmen*. On one occasion an *ɔmen* seized on a village calamity to recall people to the worship they were neglecting, and the clergy were powerless.

[3] See G. Dieterlen, 'Note sur le génie des eaux chez les Bozo', *J. Soc. Afr.* xii (1942), 149–55; *La Religion Bambara*, 1941, pp. 40–55.

[4] G. Boyer, *Un Peuple de l'Ouest Soudanais: Les Diawara*, Mém. I.F.A.N., no. 29, p. 22.

(*b*) *Cults of Mystery Societies*

The action of these associations crosses the boundaries of natura land territorial unities. They differ from other cults, not only in beliefs, rites, and organization, but in the spirit which binds members together. They tend to weaken the authority of natural groups, and there are instances of conflict in individual lives between the claims of the natural or traditional religious organization, the one into which one is born, and the specifically religious organization into which one is initiated. For our purposes a mystery cult may be defined as one which transcends natural limits, admission to which involves initiation, thus such widely differing cults as Mande *komo* and Hausa *bōri* can be embraced.

During the last millenium the *komo* type of religious organization spread widely in western Sudan parallel to traditional cults. How far this was due to fermentation caused by the appearance of Islam we cannot say, but this religious link, the new 'faith', if we may so put it, does not supersede the old religious grouping, and develops in the more complex structures. Legends associating the introduction of the *komo* with the Māli king, al-ḥājj Mūsā,[1] may have some relationship, whilst Islam demonstrates that religious grouping can transcend natural barriers. A local cult of a spirit has the characteristics of a founded religion. The owner of a spirit altar (Mande *boli-tigi*) admits members (*boli-din*') to the society of which the spirit is protector. From such modest beginnings no doubt arose such widespread cults as Komo, Nama, Kworē, Kono, Nago, and Dyara in Mande country. Though in places they may seem to have an ethnic character, in fact they override such limitations.

As a founded religion the *komo* is characterized by cosmology and myths, elaborate ritual, and the initiates' feeling of unity and solidarity. It is an early stage of the unlocalized religious organization. It prepares the way for Islam, yet stiffens resistance against it. Naturally it is just this type of organization to which Islam is implacably opposed, and which, once Islam is adopted, is proscribed, forced underground, and

[1] The introduction of the *komo* is attributed to a mythical founder, Mūsā (= Orpheus). This is the Māli king, who, when on pilgrimage (A.D. 1324), bartered a magical garment for the spirit of the society. He also brought back a sacred canoe, still preserved under conditions of secrecy in a pool (Kouro, near Narena in Manding), as well as numerous *boli*, some of which fell into the Niger and were transformed into fish (the *n-tigi*, 'master' of the Niger, a sheat fish, is one). Other legends ascribe the introduction to other immigrants or pilgrims. On these legends see J. Henry, *L'Ame d'un peuple africain: les Bambara*, 1910, pp. 130–4; Ch. Monteil, *Les Bambara du Ségou et du Kaarta*, 1924, p. 270. It is probable that al-ḥājj Mūsā sought to gain control of the *komo*, just as Fulani rulers of Nupe sought to gain control of the anti-witchcraft society, *ndakó gboyá* (see S. F. Nadel, *A Black Byzantium*, pp. 141–2).

becomes a *religio illicita*. The function of the *komo* is communal protection: it punishes murderers and thieves, and counteracts the malevolence of witches and other anti-social powers. Its spirits are represented on ritual occasions by masked dancers, incarnating the *komo*. Each local society has its sanctuary, altars (*boli*), masks, members both living (*komo-deu*) and dead, priest (*komo-tigi*) generally of the smith caste, and its taboos; no woman or uncircumcized is allowed to see anything of the rites.

Komo and other societies, wielding great authority over initiates, introduce a dualism into Mande religious life. The spiritual family tends to have more authority than the family or village community. They have played an important political role and in many parts remain powerful supporters of the social organization. Any breakdown in the relationship of individuals or communities to them leads to the adoption of Islam.[1] The effect of Islam has been unequal and breakdown depends upon the help of other factors such as the fermentation caused by the impact of the West. Clergy are opposed to them ostensibly as undisguised heathenism, but especially because of the power they wield. If Islam is to become the ruling factor in community life, that is, if the clergy are to increase their power, it must weaken this bond, and among thoroughly islamized peoples they have either gone underground or fissured into vestigial remnants. They are something the clergy can pillory and preach against, something that does not admit of compromise like the village *da siri* who become spirit servants of God. All the same they remain influential in Mande regions and retain full authority over newly islamized. Sometimes the clergy act openly against them, as when they incited a group to destroy sanctuaries of the *nama* and *komo* cults at Toko near Segu in 1945 and 1947.[2] In Sierra Leone and neighbour-

[1] Mme Dieterlen writes: 'The recruitment of members is variable from region to region on account of the expenses which the initiation ceremony and participation in the rites involve. Certain villages abstain out of poverty, and it even happens that conversions to Islam are provoked by this fact' (*La Religion Bambara*, p. 154). She also shows that the infringement of the central taboo of the *komo*, whereby the people have 'lost their soul' and fear of the vengeance of Faro, leads to the abandonment of the village, and often conversion to Islam (ibid., p. 164).

[2] See M. Griaule, 'Les Religions noires' in *Ency. de l' Empire Français: A.O.F.*, 1949, i. 142. Other instances of open intolerance are mentioned: 'A Konodimini, dans la même région, non contente d'obliger le village à construire une mosquée, une minorité a exercé, inutilement d'ailleurs, les plus dures pressions sur les autres habitants en s'attaquant de préférence aux plus faibles. A Tintam, à Borko, près de Douentza, en 1945, les prêtres totémiques et les chefs de familles sont menacés jusque dans leurs sanctuaires et les lieux sacrés souillés volontairement. Dans la région de Sanga (cercle de Bandiagara), en 1946, un instituteur fait subir de graves sévices aux enfants qui refusent de "prier" et oblige ceux qui appartiennent à certaines castes à souiller les lieux interdits.'

ing parts of French Guinea the adoption of Islam has not yet seriously weakened their influence and the *poro* includes Muslims and Christians as well as pagans. But there are signs of change in their status. Formerly sanctions of behaviour were drawn from them, but after joining Islam they are theoretically derived from a new source, and societies tend to decline, retaining certain functions and losing others. In the Temne village of Masumbo a mosque has replaced the local association 'bush' (sacred grove) of the *Manɛkɛ* society.[1] It is on the actual site, and the mosque derives its holiness from the old as well as the new and is a symbol of Islam's conquest and link with the old. Here the action of Islam has led to the disappearance of the local bush.

But complete disappearance is unusual. All Susu in Sierra Leone, though Muslims, belong to the *Gaŋgama-e* (men) and *Bondo* (women). Clergy have tried to stop Muslims joining the *poro*. An initiated member cannot leave, but he may be persuaded to avoid participation in the rites. Chiefs must belong, for the *poro* has an important political function. Not all Mende Muslim chiefs are members, but the reason turns out to be 'because my father did not belong', that is, he was of Mandinka stock. Among Muslim Yoruba there has been a decline in membership of Ogboni and other burial guilds but '*obas* and other chiefs must join and offer many sacrifices for political reasons'. All the same there has been strong, and sometimes successful, opposition to Ogboni and other guilds burying Muslim chiefs.

The Mande mystery cult organization may be contrasted with that of the Songhay-Hausa cycle. A type of cult Islam is unable to displace is that of possessive spirits (Hausa *bōri*).[2] Like the Komo it is no longer the cult of the community, but a *collegium initiati* and its evolution from folk religion to proscribed mystery cult can be traced:

First stage. It is the religion of the community and still remains the folk religion of Songhay of Dendi and Hausa māguzāwa. It is not specially characterized by possession.

Second stage. With the coming of Islam and its acceptance as the aristocratic religion it continues as the religion of the lower social strata

[1] Temne, a recently islamized people (over half are Muslim) in a transitional stage, have a number of these societies: the *pɔrɔ*, a society with complex trans-tribal ramifications; *Ragbenle* (men and women); *Bondo* (women's society, also widespread); *A-gboki* (women's dancing society); *gbaŋgbani* (men); *Manɛkɛ* (men); and *Kɔfɔ* (men). Some, like the *Tarancis* and *Almania*, are dancing societies, not mystery cults.

[2] It was apparently not characteristic of the So peoples of Chad region, and seems to have been acquired by Kotoko with the decay of their old religion and acquisition of Islam (see Lebeuf and Detourbet, *La Civilisation du Tchad*, 1950, p. 156).

(*talakāwa*, slaves, and women), and induced possession makes its appearance.

Third stage. In states of North Nigeria it is established as a private cult of possession, practised mainly by women. It is considered a *religio non licita*, but must be taken into account in any estimate of religious life.

This type of cult has an elaborate hierarchy of personalized spirits, officiants, initiation ceremonies, and ritual practices. It is strong among Songhay and Zerma of middle Niger,[1] central Fulbe,[2] and Hausa,[3] among whom Islam has been active for centuries.[4] These cults seem to be characteristic of periods of religious breakdown and imperfect assimilation of the new religion, whether Islam or Christianity.[5] Islam's cult of the supernatural is too deficient to satisfy many central Sudanese. Its clergy are powerless when confronted with the phenomena of possession and though they regard these cults as illegitimate and cannot islamize them they have been forced to recognize that they have a function

[1] For an account of the cult of *holē* among eastern Songhay and Zerma see J. Boulnois, *L'Empire de Gao*, 1954.

[2] Fulbe in Hausaland call spirit-possession *hendu* (pl. *keni*) and this word is extended to mean 'spirit' in order to avoid using their names, for 'they follow their names'. It is even practised by some nomads (see F. W. de St. Croix, *The Fulani of Nigeria*, Lagos, 1945, pp. 56–57).

[3] The pioneer study of Hausa *bōri* was by A. J. N. Tremearne, *The Ban of the Bori*, London, 1914, whose material was drawn primarily from Hausa in North Africa. Among more recent studies are: P. G. Harris, 'Notes on Yawri (Sokoto Province) Nigeria', *J.R.A.I.* lx (1930), 326–34; Landeroin in *Mission Tilho*, ii. 529–34; J. Greenberg, *The Influence of Islam upon a Sudanese Religion*, New York, 1946; Mary Smith, *Baba of Karo*, 1954, *passim*; H. Leroux, 'Animisme et Islam dans la Subdivision de Maradi (Niger)', *Bull. I.F.A.N.* x. 604–42; and, for the Algerian variety, E. Dermenghem, 'Les Confréries noires en Algérie', *Revue Africaine*, 1953, pp. 314–68. The few notes which follow are selected from material collected in Zaria.

[4] This type of possession cult has made its appearance elsewhere than central Sudan. During the religious revolution of the last hundred years it was introduced among Khasonke of upper Senegal and spread among northern Mandinka. It is based on the power of a good spirit *dyidē* ('child (*dē*) of the water' *dyē*) to deal with maladies inflicted by possessive spirits. Apart from the chief (*dyidē kuntigi*) there are two groups of members: initiated (*tondē-mi na yelena*, 'mounted members'), married to the spirit; and uninitiated (*tondē-mi ma layēlē*, 'unmounted members'), people healed by being mounted become affiliates. Apart from regular reunions and admissions special sessions are held before and at the end of Ramaḍān and on Tabaski. For an account of this cult see G. Chéron, 'Le Dyidé', *J. Soc. Afr.* i (1931), 285–9.

Other western peoples have acquired possessive spirits since their islamization, but not this type of cult. Wolof *tur* which possesses a woman is regarded as a protective spirit of her family. Serer do not normally have them and where instances of possession occur it is due to the influence of a Wolof or Socē healer (see G. J. Duchemin in *Prem. Conf. Int. Afr. de l'Ouest*, ii. 352; G. Balandier and P. Mercier, *Les Pêcheurs Lebou du Sénégal*, 1952, pp. 114–19).

[5] Dahomean *vodū* in Haiti is an example in a Christian environment of the same type of cult as Hausa *bōri*. A comparison of the *zār* of Abyssinia and Nilotic Sudan shows the same basic elements.

to fill in society by their proved technique of healing. If a Hausa woman thinks that an *iska* is asserting over her claims for recognition she would never dream of consulting a *mālam*, even if wife of one, but consults the local *sarauni*. A brief sketch of the highly elaborate Hausa cult will show the characteristic features. *Bōri* is the cult of *iskōki* which possess humans. Possession is manifested in various ways, especially in forms of hysteria and particular illnesses. Anyone subject to attacks not dispelled by ordinary charms consults a *bōri* priest (*andi*) or priestess (*sarauni*). Forms of treatment vary but the important method is control by initiation of which there are three types. When free *iskōki* are feared, but when mastered they are protectors. The 'raw' or uncontrolled spirit therefore has to be 'cooked' (*girka*). The ceremony lasts for some days and all initiates (*'yan bōri*) attached to that particular *andi* or *sarauni* take part. Afterwards the initiate is a member of a new community, the *bōri jamā'a* or *collegium lymphatici*. Special performances are held on three ritual occasions during the year: just before and just after Ramaḍān[1] and at the *Shān Kabēwa*, 'Pumpkin Festival', as well as on such occasions as initiations or communal calamities. They involve dances of possession executed by mediums called 'horses' or 'mares'.[2] Stimulated by music the mediums dance until the spirit mounts its horse who enters into a trance. From that time he or she is the spirit, is dressed in appropriate garments, and performs its characteristic actions. The spirit is dismounted (*sauka* or *jirge*) by sneezing.

3. MAGICAL BELIEFS AND PRACTICES

The power employed in medicine should be distinguished from supernatural gifted power. The word *baraka* has not been adopted by Negro Muslims in the sense of the 'holiness' given by God to saints

[1] During Ramaḍān the spirits are believed to take their departure into the bowels of the earth and the ceremony of *rakiyar wata*, 'escorting the moon', is to bid them goodbye. The ceremony of welcoming them back (i.e. bringing them once more under control) is called *tāriyan wata*, 'gathering of the moon'. It is performed immediately after the festival *salla*. These ceremonies take place under a *tsāmiya* (tamarind) or a *kāwō* (asclepias) tree and the rite is known as *gunki*.

Similarly, in Latin America, where similar African spirit cults are practised by Christians, spirits take their departure during Lent and invariably for Holy Week. A rite in which the spirits are 'called' and possess their devotees is performed in order to speed them on their way, and another to welcome them back at Easter (see M. J. Herskovitz, *Man and His Works*, 1950, pp. 571–2).

[2] *Doki* (pl. *dawāki*), 'horse', *goḍiya*, 'mare'. This word, under the form *kūdiya*, is applied in eastern Sudan and Egypt to the priestess of the *zār*, a similar possession cult. Songhay call the 'mount' *bari*. In Hausa, initiates assert, the term *bōri* means 'possession', extended to the rite, but not to the spirit.

which can be absorbed by objects and people with whom they are in contact, but merely means 'blessing'. Thus the Mandinka say *bārika* for 'thank you' as an alternative expression to their own *i ni wāle*. Tokolor and clerics trained among Moors are the only people who say that a renowned cleric 'possesses *baraka*' (Tok. *omo dyogi barke*), or 'emanates *baraka*' (*o barkini*).[1] Most Muslims retain their own terminology. A renowned Hausa *mālam* possesses *ḳwāri*. This is not universal force diffused throughout nature, nor the power utilized in 'medicine', but, like *baraka*, is a gift acquired through contact with a supernatural, a transmissible sacred contagion. In Mande, however, it is the force (*nyama*) inherent in and emanating from all men, animals, vegetables, natural objects, and supernatural beings, but in concentrated and dangerous form.[2] Hausa said *ḳwāri* is possessed by certain amulets, animals, and persons (old *mālamai*, hunters, chiefs, and twins). It is associated with spirits called *ḳwanḳwamai*, through whom it is passed to objects, animals, and men. It can be acquired intentionally through medicine (*māgani*) or involuntarily through sleeping under a tree or in a haunted place inhabited by *ḳwanḳwamai*.

The confusion between magic as acquired or inherent power is shown when Hausa clerics assert that it can be learnt, referring primarily to amulet lore, and that its essential force lies in the magician's *kurwā*, that is, he is born, not made. 'Medicine' strictly is impersonal power. Terms employed refer to the power-infused object and so to power itself. Hausa *māgani*, Nupe *chigbè*, Mende *halei*, and Yoruba *õgùn*, mean 'medicine', whether herbal, European drugs, or magical charms, and also power itself.

In practice magic and religion are not clearly separated. Though magic-technique and operation are mechanical, supernatural beings are often responsible for conferring magical powers. When the two elements are combined then priests act as practitioners. Islamic clergy as well as pagan priests add to their proper vocation that of magician, hence *bŏchi*, 'medicine man', is the normal Nupe salutation given to a cleric. Islamic amulets involve prayer to God as well as occult knowledge. To the wearer the amulet is magical in operation, but religious in drawing on the power of the name of God and His angels. The cleric

[1] H. Gaden, *Proverbes et maximes Peuls et Toucouleurs*, 1931, p. 42.

[2] *Nyama* of living things is connected with the soul, though not necessarily localized in either body or soul, nor need these two coexist for it to be associated with them. *Nyama* of inanimate things is independent but when associated with a *boli* can communicate itself to objects consecrated on it. But although *nyama* is universal, it is conceived more commonly in its dangerous and potentially harmful form.

therefore performs his magical functions within the domain of Islam, and his attitude to magic is based, not on the end, but the method employed. He has to decide whether a practice is lawful (*ḥalāl*) or unlawful (*ḥarām*). If a lawful method is employed to cause harm to an enemy the law is not transgressed, but it is if someone is healed by invoking black *jinn*. In their endeavour to dissuade people from sacrificing to spirits clergy offer protection through Islamic magical method as opposed to placating them, though unless conditions such as urban life warrant it, it is almost impossible for them to avoid prescribing such offerings. Islam brings no change in psychological attitudes towards magic. Clergy have introduced new techniques into the general body of magical practice, but it is simply an addition or substitution of written amulets for old, hence the Fulbe saying, 'those who write are no better than magicians'. Pagans are ready to put any new technique to the test. They readily believe that the 'word' possesses power and written amulets captivate them. But they are not prepared to rely on one method. A Temne Muslim house visited had symbols of three religions on the lintel of the doorway: at the top a printed Temne Christian text, underneath a cloth on which was tied a metal symbol, and beneath that a paper printed with Islamic texts, designs, and cabalistic signs.[1]

Muslim clergy make and sell innumerable charms. In central Sudan Hausa traders have made their fabrication their special domain; in Senegal region it is the preserve of Tokolor. Four regional styles (Senegal, western Guinea, Niger bend, and Hausa-Kanuri) are recognizable by their make-up, style of writing, Arabic formulas, spirits invoked, and symbols employed. Relatively few make use of Islamic magic manuals, though in strong Islamic centres clerics employ Aḥmad ibn ʿAlī al-Būnī's *Shams al-Maʿārif al-Kubrā* (and *aṣ-Ṣughrā*), one of the most important works on the subject. Other manuals employed are stated to be *al-Mujarrabāt* by Muḥammad b. Yūsuf as-Sanūsī (d. 1486), *al-Miʾat al-Faiḍāʾ* and *Khazīnat al-Asrār al-Kubrā*. The lore of amulet-making is transmitted primarily by oral tradition and forms part of a cleric's training.[2] Amulets are confined to two forms: written,

[1] Printed amulets have flooded the markets of Dakar and Bathhurst and clergy were waging war against them since they were endangering their livelihood. They alleged that they were useless since the cleric imparts his 'virtue' when concocting an amulet, whilst the ink was profane in that it had not been prepared from gathered ingredients with appropriate incantation.

[2] The commonest Arabic word for magic-making is *dabbāra*, often employed in the sense of spell-binding: Mande *dabāre*, Hausa *dabāra*, Tamahaqq *eddebāra*, Songhay *dabarey* (*-futukoy*, 'masters of magic'). *ʿIlm* is also used. This is correctly knowledge which proceeds from God, technically the law, but it easily gets this secondary meaning of occult knowledge.

worn on the body or placed on animals and objects for protective purposes; and amulets written on a slate, washed off, and either drunk or rubbed on the body. An amulet contains verses from the Qur'ān, names of angels and *jinn*, mysterious formulas, cabalistic table, description of aim, and sometimes the taboos which must be observed if its power is to be retained.[1] The cleric instructs his client how and where they are to be worn. Charms have names according to type and purpose. Some are protective or preventive, designed to ward off a particular evil. Others are causitive or positive, to enable one to obtain wealth, women, children, power, and the like. Others are vindictive, like forms of the Mandinka *siri* ('tie'), to harm an enemy; whilst a fourth category (Mandinka *gbasa* or *gasa*) are counter-active, to render bad magic innocuous or turn it against the agent. It will be sufficient to enumerate categories mentioned by Muslim Mende (distinguished in their charm-writing capacity as *lukɔstɔbla*). The use of written papers and a new terminology is all that distinguishes them from pagan charms.[2]

Personal—all written:

sɛwɛi,[3] large paper amulets, sewn into leather satchets, and always worn around the neck.

lāsmɔi, small paper charms, sheathed and worn on the body.

lisimɔi, worn on the arm only.

Katimɛi (Ar. *khātim*, Pulār *kātumedye*)—all written:

kpakpɛi (Dyula *bontyē*), buried under doorway or in centre of room.

walɛi, written on a board (*lōḥ*), hung on stick at entrance to cultivation to guard against thieves, whom it drives mad.

kafii, to guard rice farm against witches, buried in anthill or suspended from palm branch over anthill (Temne *aŋkaŋtha*, 'locker').

There are many other *katimɛi* for protecting the house or children against witches.

[1] The taboos are not generally written in the amulet, but the recipient is always informed of those he must keep. They vary according to its aim. General taboos are that it must not be opened, left alone, or touch water, and when taken off for bathing must not be placed on the ground. Certain acts diminish its power, sitting on the mortar in which corn is ground, showing the soles of one's feet when seated, walking over a hearth, and standing to urinate. By this means a cleric can get a pagan to whom he sells an amulet to observe Islamic taboos. Similar prescriptions are given with regard to holy water. In Sierra Leone, the bottle of *manasi* must always be hung up, must not get into the sun, and after anointing with it one must bathe only on certain days and must not use soap.

[2] Native methods are often associated with written amulets by adding roots, stones, and other objects possessing power.

[3] Mande *sebe*, *safe*, *sewe* (Ar. *ṣaḥfa*? 'page, sheath?') is the general term throughout the western cycle.

Nɛsi,[1] 'holy water', is the process of washing Qur'ānic texts from wooden slates, bottling the water, and using it as 'medicine', either internally or externally. It has many uses. It is rubbed over the body and drunk to drive out possessive spirits and cure illnesses. Women use it as *falagɛi* to get their husbands to divorce them. Candidates for chieftainships search out renowned practitioners to obtain a special kind for use on election morning. The Mandinka cleric, called in this function *sebe-tu-la*, ingurgitates the washings from the slate and spits on the parts to be healed or the charm he is writing.

Magical specialists abound everywhere and are in rivalry with clerics for the custom of the people. As Islam spreads among Nupe priests are gradually disappearing, but medicine-men are prospering more than ever in consequence of religious insecurity. Practitioners, Muslim or pagan, are called *chigbè-jinchi*, or *bǒchi*, 'medicine-man'. The practice is only one of the functions of a cleric, but the pagan *bǒchiẓi* are loosely organized and have a chief (*majiṇ chigbè*) in every centre.[2] The difference between pagan and Muslim *bochiẓi* is that, 'pagans offer *làba* (prayer with libation) to spirit-channels, whilst clergy invoke God, Prophet, angels and *jinn*, even in bad medicine (*chigbè dèdè*)'.

Hausa practitioners of *māgani* include the following. The *mālam* in this function, when he is called *mai-tsubbu* (or *ḍabu*, Ar. *ṭibb*, 'medicine'). The *bōkā* is a magical herbalist, exorcist, and charm-maker, employing the *sammu* (poison) method. The *mai-māgani*'s treatment involves herbal lore, though it is the spiritual essence of the ingredients which ensures the success of the treatment. *Magōrī* refers rather to the seller of material for charms than to the practitioner. Finally, there are *masū-bōri* whose methods involve communication with spirits. Hausa charms are innumerable, but little would be gained by listing their names, many of which begin with either *māgani*, *ḍauri* (a tying-up), or *lāya* (Ar. *al-Āya*), e.g. *ḍaurin dawa*, a charm to carry the wearer safely through the perils of the bush (*dawa*). The only people, apart from Moors, who use Arabic words for amulet (*ḥirz* or *ḥijāb*) are Fulbe of Futa Jalon and citizens of Timbuktu and Jenne.

Charms may be vocal as well as material and the two forms are often combined. Recital of incomprehensible Arabic formulas is taken to be incantation—their unintelligibility is not important since it is not a

[1] Fulfulde *nasi*, Temne *manasi*, Creole *lasimāmi*. Pagan Temne *ɔ-men* make holy water (*mafoi*) from leaves and bark which is employed in the same way.

[2] There are a hundred or so such chiefs in the Nupe area. In the town of Katcha (population 3,680) there were two *májin* and twenty *chigbè-jinchi*.

question of what they mean but what they do. Hausa use the Yāsīn incantation to bind against theft and find stolen property. This method is regarded as very drastic, not to be employed lightly otherwise it will recoil. It involves, after preparatory ablution and incantation, the repetition of the *sūra Yā Sīn* a specified number of times and the sacrifice of a ram.[1]

4. SORCERY AND WITCHCRAFT

Illness, misfortune, and death are ascribed to many causes: black magic, the action of spirits or people with special powers, metamorphosed sorcerers, witches, or taboo-breaking. The distinction between sorcerer and witch derives from the fact that the first employs his powers for anti-social ends, whilst the witch resembles the vampire in that he has a power lodged within that may be used for evil purposes, often involuntarily. In such a vast field it is only necessary to indicate the extent to which Muslims share the belief in and fear of sorcery and witchcraft and mention a few agents and counter-agents. Examples will be confined mainly to Northern Nigeria.

No essential distinction exists between the employment of magic in sorcery and its use for good purposes. Islam allows magic (*ruqya*), but condemns sorcery (*siḥr*). Clerics in West Africa are confused as to whether it is the method employed, or the intention, or both, that matters. The boundary between black and white magic in Islam is rather vague. Since the powers and methods employed for both are the same, clergy are regarded as practitioners of the one and the other.[2] Many languages have the same distinction as in Arabic between 'praying for' and 'praying against'.[3] In Hausa the employment of magic to work ill is called *aiki* ('deed') which compares with Arabic usage of *'amal*. *Aikin mālam* is a spell to injure. But there are many other terms.

[1] Al-ḥājj Sa'īd writes that the stronghold of Awgh in Kabi 'had been built by the Leader of Believers, al-ḥājj Muḥammad. According to tradition it was the residence of his shepherds. At the time of its construction the *askiya* chose 500 reciters of the Qur'ān to chant 'Yā Sīn' the full circumference of the walls.' So impregnable did this make Awgh that the author adds: 'In his time the Shaikh ('Uthmān dan Fodio) made fifty-one expeditions against the place without succeeding in taking it, and had to make peace with them'; *History of Sokoto* in app. to *Tadhkirat an-Nisyān*, p. 213/348–9.

[2] The lawful utilization by clerics of magic to harm is demonstrated in *T. al-Fattāsh* (cf. pp. 130–1, tr. pp. 237–8) and *T. as-Sūdān* (pp. 98–99, tr. pp. 162–3).

[3] In Nupe *jiṇ aduwa ebó'za* is 'to pray for someone', and *jiṇ aduwa kpe' za*, 'to pray against'. Similarly with Songhay *ṇare*, whilst *addawa* (Ar. *da'wa*) means 'curse', *a dye nda Tyitab di addawa*, 'he has sworn by the curse of the Qur'ān'. Moors use the Fātiḥa as a curse, pronouncing it 'against' someone whilst holding the palms of the hands downwards, instead of upwards. Soninke have acquired the practice.

A *mālam* who practises magic is called *būdēji* (or *ba būdē*) or *masihirchi* (Ar. *siḥr*) and the practice is often called *sammu*.[1] The *yāsīn* method previously mentioned as a protector is used to harm. Clergy regard this as legitimate if the intention is to harm an evil person who could be eliminated in no other way. It is performed by a group of clergy reciting the chapter while a cock is slowly killed 'over the name' of the victim. The Hausa have a vast catalogue of charms to harm and only two will be described. For *harbin kasko* the cleric mixes a powder of ground-up roots and herbs in a small clay basin (*kasko*) of water, and chants incantations until the soul (*kurwa*) of the person can be seen in the water. Then an iron or brass arrow is shot (*harba*) from a bow of similar metal into the reflection, whereupon, if successful, the water turns red, the victim becomes ill, weakens, and dies unless counter-measures are taken. Another method of invocation-shooting is *harbin allūra* (Ar. *al-ibra*, 'needle'). The cleric puts the fat of a black he-goat inside the tip of a duiker horn, inserts needles, each bearing the name of a spirit, and places a cover over the horn. After incantation he removes the cover, calls a spirit, and tells it where to go. The spirit-needle travels any distance provided it does not have to cross running water, and when it reaches the victim pierces his heart. In Nupe *rógóngà* is the name given to a cleric who employs a round stone called *rógógi* to harm people. He writes his spell on a slate, washes it off, then puts into the water the *rógógi* upon which he has written a name together with spells and leaves it until all the water has dried up. Finally he holds the stone before a fire repeating 'prayers against' the victim.

The sphere of sorcery is wider than the craft of magic employed for evil purposes. Some people have acquired or inherent powers like the dangerous Hausa emanations of *ḳwāri* and *ḳofi* and the evil eye (Hausa *kambun baka* or *kandun ido*). Others have the power of metamorphosis. Hausa believe that the *kurwas* of certain men (called *rikiḍaddu*) and animals can interchange and their destinies are therefore intertwined.[2] This power is not the same as that of witches who also turn into animals. There is generally a verbal distinction between the two (Bozo:

[1] *Sammu* (Ar. *simm*, 'poison') means both the practice intended to cause harm, and also, as its derivation implies, 'to poison'.

[2] Nupe believe that metamorphosis (*ẓè*, to change) can be done through medicine: *makuṇ-duṇni ẓechi*, 'people who change into hyenas'. In this case the *èshè* of the man and the *nagbaṇ* of the animal interchange. The only instance of people being born with the power are the *gwayachi*. The *gwaya* is a buffalo which is linked with a particular man (the ordinary word for buffalo is *èya*). If people quarrel with such a man they believe that he will waylay them at night in his buffalo form.

were-animal, *kwerin'-kwerin'*, and witch, *tongo-tu*, 'eater of souls'). In central Sudan witches are born with a special power or type of soul which makes them 'eaters of souls'.[1] In western Sudan (Mande *sū-bar̊a*, 'witch') a special organ or witch-spirit is acquired either through inheritance or medicine. This quality may be active or latent. Temne credit the witch (*ɔ-ser*) with a special 'bag' (*a-kuntha*) in the body and they speak of it working at night, consuming the flesh until the victim wastes away and eventually, when the heart is consumed, dies. They also believe that they turn into animals in order to destroy crops and attack people. The Mende witch (*honamɔi*), however, has a *honei* witch-spirit) living in its body.[2] Islamization is said to have led many to give up the practice of opening-up a deceased person's body in order to examine whether or not he was a witch.

In central Sudan witches catch and imprison or eat a person's soul. The Hausa say, *māyē yā kama kurwansa*, 'the witch seized his soul', and if death ensues they use the expression *māyē yā chi shi*, 'the witch has eaten him'. The *kurwa* can be caught by a witch from a person's shadow or from his reflection in water. A Nupe *èshèchi* catches the *fifiṇge*. Hausa believe there are many *māyū*. The more lettered and those affected by Western education express a certain scepticism, but they are still very uneasy about it. Anti-witchcraft measures are taken by all leading clerical and ruling households and we hear of suspected witches being hauled off to the mosque to swear that they have not employed their power. Deeper islamization in no way diminishes belief in and fear of witchcraft. In Futa Jalon each village has its recognized witch-family, but all children do not inherit (or do not manifest) the property, transmitted exclusively through women. Their witch[3] too has powers of metamorphosis, of spell-casting, and special relations with spirits.

Fear of witchcraft increases greatly as a result of the spiritual insecurity caused by the adoption of Islam or Christianity and counteraction is an important function of priest and medicine-man. In many places when asked what were the functions of the medicine-man the first given was 'to counteract witches', followed by to heal, administer swear-medicine, interpret dreams, and the like. Clerics, however, are

[1] Nupe believe that witches are born with a different kind of *èshè*, hence a male witch is called an *èshèchi*, but a female witch's equivalent soul is called *egà* and a *gachi* is a 'witch'. The phrase, 'this man has an *èshè*' (*bagi nana de 'shè*) can only mean 'this man is a witch'. In the past the chief of the *găchiẓi* (called *lelú*) was appointed by the chief as a counter-agent.

[2] See K. L. Little, *The Mende of Sierra Leone*, pp. 230–1.

[3] Fulfulde (F. Toro): *nyamnēdyo*, *nyamnēḅe*; v.n. of *nyāmde*, 'to eat' (the *ᵐbēlu*); Tokolor *sukunya*, *sukunyābe* (borrowed from Soninke); *tyukunyāgo*, 'witchcraft'.

unable to do this, consequently the medicine-man is a necessity for Muslim society. Witches must be smelt-out before their victims can be cured. The mystery cults are important for this purpose and when they break up through Islamization the dispossessed priests continue to perform these functions. Nupe *ndăkó gboyá* (lit. 'ancestor of the spirit'), a derivative from the Guṇnuṇ cult, is such an anti-witchcraft cult, directed by a chief (*májiṇ dòdŏ*), not now very active among Nupe proper, but stronger among Chekpã.[1] Some Hausa regions still have a *sarikin māyū* (chief of witches) whose function is that of detection.[2] In Futas Jalon and Toro the *bilēdyo* (pl. *vilēḅe*) is the counter-agent. He is the general medicine-man who continues to function, even in these deeply islamized regions, as exorcist, rain-maker, diviner, herbalist, and, if necessary, black magician.

5. DIVINATION

The part played by divination cannot be overestimated. No important decision is made or act undertaken unless the signs are consulted and prove propitious. The *ta'rīkhs* show leaders in the past consulting diviners.[3] A Fulani will say *sa'a he sare hosete*, 'the propitious moment must be chosen before setting forth', or in Hausa, *ya ḍauki sā'a*, 'he ascertained the auspicious day'. Here the Arabic *sā'a*, 'hour, time', shows the influence of Islamic astrological method. This influence penetrates long before islamization and probably none of their methods are completely free from it. Divination is a vast subject and we need only indicate the ease with which Islamic methods penetrate, the persistence of old methods and practitioners, and the cleric in his function as diviner. Some signs anyone can deduce but most need interpretation,

[1] Chekpã are *aẓe Nupe*, people who have adopted Nupe language and culture.

[2] He was a noted witch himself but when appointed is no longer dangerous except to other *māyū* who are expected to support him with gifts. He has many methods for identifying a witch who has stolen a *kurwa* and forcing him to set it free. If it has been caught from the shadow the *māyē* is made to step over the sick person. If the *kurwa* has been imprisoned he is made to indicate where the bird or whatever else is incarnating it is to be found and when set free the sick person recovers. The afflicted is often guided to identify the witch by means of a diagnosis based on a recalling of the names of everyone he has met recently, or by means of incantations which have the effect of making him call out the *māyē*'s name or a characteristic enabling him to be identified.

[3] For example, Mansa Mūsā before setting out on pilgrimage, *T. al-Fattāsh*, p. 33 (57). Similarly references to omens in dreams are frequent. The *Ta'rīkh Sokoto* recounts how 'Abd al-Qādir, son of 'Uthmān dan Fodio, dreamt of meeting the Prophet and 'Abd al-Qādir al-Jīlānī before setting out on the expedition against Zamfara on which he met his death (see *P.E.L.O.V.*, sér. iv, vol. xix, p. 194, xx, p. 314).

and this is an esoteric art dependent upon practitioners. Pagan peoples have professionals who perform this function, some are hereditary, their powers of divination deriving from communication with a deceased relative, but in Sudan communities ordinary village priests and Muslim clergy are practitioners. The cult of the oracular deity Ifa is the most flourishing part of the declining Yoruba religion and the authority and power of *babalāwos* or priests of Ifa is little diminished. Yoruba have little confidence in Muslim methods and refer contemptuously to Hausa diviners playing with sand. They consult Muslim diviners only in connexion with specifically Islamic ceremonies such as the time of the ceremony for the payment of *iso-yigi* (bride-price). African Islam does not have a special class, for divination is a clerical function, but diviners like Hausa *mai-dūba* exist in all Islamic communities. A Hausa cleric diviner is not called *mai-dūba*, though the practice is called *dūba*. The old terminology is not normally transferred but a new one invented, and a Yoruba cleric when divining is called *alafoshe*.

Pagan Nupe have many methods, for example: by throwing strings of shells called *eba* (*sa 'ba*, 'to divine'; *eba-bǒchi* or *ebasachi*, 'diviner');[1] by means of knots on a cord (*gbako*, *ègbangi*); *kpàkogi*, by a board; and *kpiâkpiâ*, by a charm on a cord. These show signs of being usurped by Islamic methods, for the cleric seeks to discredit pagan diviners and secure all custom for himself. Thus at this stage in Nupe transformation conflicts arise as to whether it is best to stick to the old or try the new. Much depends upon the confidence inspired by the local cleric, but old diviners will continue to make a living for they still exist among long-Islamized peoples like Tokolor (*tīmōwo*, 'diviner', *tīmgal*, 'divination'). Islam does not change the psychological attitude to the practice; all the individual is concerned about is whether it works. Nupe clergy employ four mechanical methods: geomancy, called *háti* (Ar. *khātim*),[2] *tùrabi*, or *jikànà*; *yisabi* (Ar. *ḥisāb*), by numerals; *sortes Qur'ānicae*—use of the Qur'ān or an Arabic book of divination (e.g. threads are placed between each leaf, one is chosen at random, and the cleric interprets); and by the rosary (*tàsàbi* or *tàsba*). This is often only a variant of the previous one. For example, the cleric, after spitting on his rosary, places it before him on his prayer-skin, closes his eyes, and picks it up at random one or more times. From the number of the bead he has taken he deduces the chapter and verse of the Qur'ān. Or he asks his client to select a bead at random and then tells the beads

[1] The practice of *eba* is described by S. F. Nadel, *Nupe Religion*, pp. 38–50.

[2] On the practice of *háti* see S. F. Nadel, op. cit., pp. 55–64.

'good, bad' alternately until he comes to one of the large beads dividing the rosary into three sections which gives him the answer.

Other automatic methods employed by Muslims are augury from the movement of animals or birds, haruspicy or deduction from the entrails of animals, and sortilege with kola nuts, cowries, or pebbles. Dr. Meek writes that the election of chiefs in Northern Nigeria 'is often left to the malams to decide by lot. The names of the candidates are written on slips of paper and thrown into ash-water. The name on the piece of paper which bobs up first is considered to be Allah's choice.'[1] The omens and signs of the heavens must be studied and the astrological side is largely Islamic. Adherence to Islam has everywhere influenced popular belief in lucky and unlucky days. Hausa will not shave on Thursday, nor wash on the last day of the month. Natural phenomena like earthquakes and comets though important as signs[2] cannot form part of the lore of the diviner like auguries from the flight of birds.

Apart from the automatic methods mentioned all employ divination proper. Methods fall into four groups: dreams, ordeal, spirit possession, and necromancy. Clerics claim to consult the spirit of Muḥammad. This is a widespread practice in western Guinea and we have given an account of the *almāmi* doing this at festival prayers in Sierra Leone.[3] When consulted on any major project the Tokolor magician-diviner (*sirruyaŋke*) goes into retreat. On its completion he prescribes prayers, alms, and sacrifices and hands over an amulet he has prepared with instructions as to its use and the taboos to be observed. Similarly the

[1] C. K. Meek, *Northern Nigeria*, ii. 72. In independent Katsina during the nineteenth century when the electors failed to agree the *imām* found the new chief by mechanical manipulation, either by the *sibḥa* or the casting ten times of a parallelepiped numbered on four faces, 1, 2, 7, 0 (see *Mission Tilho*, ii. 467).

[2] After a Christian mission began work at the Temne village of Masumbu near Makeni in Sierra Leone where Islam had gained over 50 per cent. of the people, many animistic Muslims began to attend church out of readiness to reverence and appease all spiritual manifestations. But in 1947 an earthquake terrified the villagers and next day an unknown *fode* from French territory made his appearance. He kindled a fire and told them that Allah was angry, let everyone bring an offering and a firebrand to add to the fire. Then he harangued them about their apostasy. Next day he had disappeared with his gains, but no villager dared show his face in church again.

[3] See above, p. 79. Marty writes of Futa Jalon: 'It is generally agreed that the most pious of the marabouts have divine revelations. The *Wali* of Goumba, for example, often had them. In the course of his conversations with the divinity, he disappeared and returned to earth furnished, not only with information about future events, but also with new intellectual and physical powers. These revelations are given more especially during the nights which precede the two great Islamic festivals: *Julde Sumaye* and *Julde Donkiri*. On these there is no *karamoko* who does not claim, under the form of a monkey or other animal, to have had some communication with Allah. They predict rain and fine weather, the state of future harvests, fat kine succeeding lean and vice versa' (P. Marty, *Guinée*, p. 477).

Tokolor who initiated *jihāds* during the last century went into retreat before the announcement of their mission and before undertaking an expedition, consequently followers regard their orders as the oracle of God.

Survivals from the cult of the dead are found only in the early stages of transition. Muslim Temne, for instance, believe the dead can help or harm the living and therefore must be consulted to find out their wishes or the cause of their anger. For this they perform a 'seven plates ceremony' similar to that described under death ceremonies,[1] at which the *karamoko* talks to the dead.[2] The Susu and Temne crystal-gazing method of divination through spirits of the dead is called *ə-yina Mūsa* (the spirit of Moses). A Temne informant said that 'Mūsa was a great magician (*ɔmen*) who lived long ago'. He appears to be al-ḥājj Mūsā, king of Māli. For this method the *alfa* opens the Qur'ān, mutters, pours water into a calabash, and mixes with it ground-up roots and minerals. Then he calls his boy, covers him with a white sheet, and directs him to gaze into the bowl. Telling his beads with incantation, he calls up a departed spirit and asks it questions through the boy. Consultation with spirits of the dead dies out, but not divination through nature spirits.

The ordeal or 'judgement of God' method may be included. In this the suspect or accuser is either subjected to a process, like handling hot iron, that would normally injure him, or is magical with power to bring down supernatural wrath on a guilty or false accuser, but not harm the innocent or truthful. Swear-medicine is characteristic of the peoples of western Guinea. Anyone falsely accused will ask to take swear-medicine even though the Qur'ān is allowed, since those adopting it would be suspect. They have a firm belief that if they swear falsely on the medicine they will die. 'Clerics are not opposed to this', they said, 'because they make money out of it.'

The Islamic method of divination through dreams (*'ilm-at-ta'bīr*) is diffused throughout the Sudan. The commonest manual[3] is *Muntakhab al-kalām fī tafsīr al-aḥlām* attributed to M. ibn Sīrīn (d. 728), but

[1] See below, p. 181.

[2] Temne have a Spirit of Interpretation, *Loŋtha*, whose permission must be asked before calling upon any other spirit. '*Loŋtha*', they said, is a word which connects one with the spirit world, like ringing a number on the telephone. This is only done by the pagan diviner (*ɔ-thupəs*) not the cleric, but all Temne Muslims make use of him for divination through spirits before electing a chief, administering swear-medicine, and the like.

[3] Such books are known as *deftere fitōre koiḍi* (books of dream interpretation) in Fulfulde, and *fisa tyitāb* in Songhay.

Ta'ṭīr al-anām fī ta'bīr al-manām by 'Abd al-Ghanī an-Nābulsī (d. 1731) is common in Bornu and Futa Toro. Though understood by relatively few and confused by oral tradition with local lore, all clerics learn something of the methods. Various beliefs are held as to what happens in dreams. Some say the dreamer's soul experiences the things dreamed, others that the soul visits the spirit-world and gets the information desired, others that this is given by spirits who visit the dreamer. Interpretation is necessary and only trained people can do this.[1] A common form of *istikhara* ('asking favour of heaven') is the following. The cleric advises his client to recite certain Qur'ānic phrases after each *rak'a* of the next ritual prayer, then shielding his mouth with his hand to whisper his request. After that he must lie down to sleep where he will not be disturbed, on the right side, placing his right hand under his ear. He receives the answer in the form of a dream which the cleric interprets. More commonly the cleric does the dreaming on behalf of his client. He prays two *rak'as*, incorporating a *sūra* appropriate to the request, recites a *dhikr* of one of the names of God until he is almost asleep when he makes his request, and continues with the *dhikr* until he falls asleep. A Hausa or Songhay cleric, when called in to prescribe for an illness, often sleeps on his Book of Divination in order to ascertain the cause of the illness and its cure. Similarly, if a new spirit is suspected of having settled in a house he sleeps on his book to discover who it is, and, if it is 'black', performs the rites necessary to drive it away. But it is more common to resort to professional soothsayers.

[1] Classifications of dreams are known in a vague way. The Prophet said: 'There are three kinds of vision, one comes from God, another from angels, and the third from Satan.' That from God is the clear dream eminent clerics claim to receive; others need interpreting by a practitioner to distinguish between those brought by good or bad *jinn*.

6

Influence of Islam upon Social Structure

ISLAM, being a universal religion, spreads the conception of the inhabited world along with that of the universal God and establishes a link between peoples who formerly had little to prepare them to live harmoniously together. This new outlook is achieved through the sharing of common religious practices. Islamic ritual has significance, not only its religious context, but as a manifestation of a common social pattern. The importance of Friday prayer lies in the way it brings together the whole territorial group, often composed of different ethnic stocks, affirming in each individual a feeling of belonging to a unique religion. So with the month of fasting and its culmination in a festival of rejoicing, and the pilgrimage in which participation is not necessary for the *'īd* celebration on that occasion is the festival of Islamic unity. Similarly Islamic prescriptions and prohibitions link believers and differentiate them from unbelievers. Its regulations, such as that no Muslim may be enslaved, lead to the recognition of wide rights and obligations.

The actual effect of this ideal of socio-religious unity should not be over-estimated. The old bases of community based on kinship, culture, and territory come first. Racial antagonism between black and white on the borderlands remains strong. In the Sahil Soninke, Tokolor, Moors, and Fulbe live side by side, devoid of mutual understanding and often separated by deep-seated hatreds and suspicions. Divisions within Islam, such as confessionalist dislike between Tijānīs and Qādirīs, manifest themselves in social life. Muslim conquerors took little account of Islamic unity. Al-ḥājj 'Umar, Samōri, and 'Uthmān dan Fodio were not deterred from attacking Muslims. Yet over and above the differences which separate individuals and generations, social classes and castes, tribes and peoples, the sharing of a common cult is a factor, affirming the existence of the Islamic community as a religious unit, which cannot be ignored.

Like African society Islam stresses the close connexion between religion and the institutions which bind society. The application of its law affects family structure and kinship relations, the organization of the community, the nature of the state, the authority and functions of chiefs, and the administration of the law. Conflict and compromise between the norms of traditional society and the *sharīʿa* are inevitable. Whilst due weight must be given to the influence of the legal code we must be wary of the description often given of its completely revolutionary character. These societies are not static, but they are guaranteed cultural and social stability by the fact that they are essentially agricultural. When Islam is adopted the community does not suddenly change its social pattern but remains a unity distinguished by its own pattern of custom. In time Islam becomes closely intertwined with communal life, yet without disintegrating its basic structure. One fact accounting for the strong resistance custom opposes is that Islamic law is *ad personam*, in opposition to the direction of law in Africa where it is so communalistic. Only when a Muslim family is compared with a pagan family belonging to the same social group can the effect of Islam be seen. New features are superimposed, but basic customs, the composition of the extended family, the authority of its head, and rules of succession are little affected. Peoples do not adopt Islamic law *in toto* when they become Muslim and it is widely applied only in urban centres. All the same no people remain free from its encroachment. We should not approach Muslim society by taking the ideal standard of Islamic law as our basis and thinking of it as corrupted by local custom or how far people fall short of it, but should take ancestral custom and see how it has been modified by Islam. In the West African situation the frontiers of application between custom and the *sharīʿa* are so variable and fluctuating that it is difficult to give a picture of the actual state of things.

To explain how Muslim West Africa as a whole strikes one approaching it from the eastern Sudan and North Africa we may generalize in this way. What gives Muslims of Hamitic Africa their particular character is the unity of their lives submitted over centuries to the influence of Islam. Pre-Islamic survivals are as thoroughly islamized as pagan institutions embedded in European Christianity are christianized; and although at the present day revolutionary influences from the West are affecting life in many spheres, yet so far as personal, family, social, and religious life is concerned Islam remains the dominant factor. On the other hand, in West Africa what is so evident, even after appreciating the very real influence of Islam, is the dualism in Islamic communities. In the preceding chapter we glanced at religious survivals, now we propose to describe the dualism within social life. Islamic religious institutions are regulated with extreme formalism, but social life is ruled primarily by custom, often in contradiction to the absolute laws of Islam. Where the custom of widow-inheritance is in vogue, as with the long islamized Dyula, Islam as represented by the clergy makes no attempt to get rid of the institution. Unless new factors intervene no cleric sees any reason to object to the brother of the family-head succeeding to his position and property. This is due to the fact that these institutions lie at the root of West African society which Islam is not allowed to break up. Where Islamic law has displaced local custom the African influence can be seen in people's attitude towards new acquisitions. For example, a wife's success in obtaining a divorce depends largely upon the support of her kinsfolk. If they are prepared to support her application and accept the financial obligations, the grounds for divorce need not be in accordance with the provisions defined by Islamic law. On the other hand, if they refuse to support her application, the judge is unlikely to grant it, even if the grounds are adequate.

In time Islam succeeds in imprinting its social pattern. This is most evident in towns. Timbuktu, Jenne, Sokoto, and Maiduguri are Muslim towns in the same way as Fez or Tripoli. But the dualism becomes apparent when we move out of these towns into neigbouring villages of Songhay, Bozo, Hausa, and Kanuri agriculturalists. Their social life displays a mosaic of indigenous and Islamic elements associated in complex and often ill-integrated combinations. When, however, an Islamic element is adopted integrally the indigenous elements tend to orientate themselves around it and this freezes the institution. Whence derives that unity characteristic of Islamic society in North Africa and the Near East, but only of urban communities and long islamized peoples like Tokolor in West Africa.

I. THE FAMILY

(*a*) *The Structure of the Family*

The extended family functions over the larger part of society, but Islamic law recognizes only the simple matrimonial family of man, wife or wives, slaves, and their children, and the Mālikite system gives absolute authority to the husband as its head. In general, after its adoption, the tradition of the extended family and the patriarchal system is maintained, but in a modified form, whilst the matrimonial family and the authority of its head receive greater recognition. The process of change begins with the disappearance of the ancestor cult. Since the dead lose their influence over the lives of the living the unity of the old community is breached and its disintegration into smaller units becomes possible. The authority of the family head lessens, that of the father of the elementary family increases, and personal property is divided in accordance with the provisions of Islamic law.

Islam brings the simple family into greater prominence through its inculcation of duties to the actual father and through the division of his personal property among his children. Among pagan Hausa the family may embrace from thirty to a hundred persons, but among islamized Hausa the family unit consists of father and one or two married sons with their dependants. At the same time the extended family continues to function especially in its political, social, and legal aspects. Succession to headship remains the same. In the Dyula family are three stages:[1] the simple family of man, wife or wives, and their children did not formerly count as a separate unit; the *lū* consists of a number of simple families and is the first family unit with a recognized head (*lū-tigi*) and economic function; and the *so*, the total family, which consists of two or more *lū*, under a chief (*so-tigi*). Today the *lū-tigi* has lost the economic powers and other important rights he once held over the *lū* but he still functions. When he dies his eldest surviving brother succeeds to the headship, property, and wives. If he has no brothers the eldest of the sons of all the line of brothers succeeds. But disintegration is taking place. In Bonduku some families follow custom, whilst others follow Islamic law in the division of a man's effects among his own children. The new *lū-tigi*, however, inherits his predecessor's prayer-skin as symbol of authority. It is the same with the *so-tigi*, the eldest brother inherits command, rosary, prayer-skin, ablution jug, and wives. If a married man who is not a *lū-tigi* or *so-tigi* dies his inheritance is invariably divided according to the provisions of Islamic law, except that his prayer-skin and wives go to his eldest brother. This relates, of course, to his personal, not his inherited, property, for they distinguish between communal property transmitted through brothers (old custom) and personal property shared among his children (Islamic custom). The wives being communal property do not get even the small share allotted them under Islamic law. Islam, therefore, has only affected the division of personal property.

Upon Fulbe in Futa Jalon the effect of Islam has been more profound.[2] The simple family is a recognized unit. At the father's death

[1] See L. Tauxier, *Le Noir du Bondoukou*, 1921, pp. 216 ff.

[2] It was mainly in the theocratic states that attempts were made to get the Islamic law of

his sons and unmarried daughters come under the authority of the eldest son who inherits his Arabic books, arms, and horse as symbols of headship. The wives are dispersed to their respective families to remain under paternal authority until remarried, but those with grown-up children who refuse to leave the conjugal compound come under the authority of the eldest son, who may give them, including his own mother, in marriage. The authority and administrative functions of the deceased pass to his eldest surviving brother, and after him to his other brothers, to revert eventually to his eldest son.[1] Survivals belong to the realm of folk-lore. In Futa Toro, though Islam has weakened the relationship between maternal uncle and nephew, Tokolor still teach children that at the Day of Resurrection 'the mother will not recognize her own son, nor the father his own son; only the maternal uncle will find his nephew, his sister's son'.[2] In such Islamic groups the father is the principal holder of the property of the family, and his sons work for him since they know they will inherit. In return the father provides wives for his sons. This contrasts with the old system where the father spends his earnings on wives for himself. His sons are not his concern, his goods devolve upon his brothers, and his sons may have to work for themselves to acquire wives.[3] Islam, therefore, tends to accentuate the paternal, rather than the avuncular, spirit, and filial submission.

The family is integrated by common worship more than any other group, hence allegiance of individuals to Islam and disownment of the family cult may weaken natural ties and lead to the formation of new ones outside the family. The importance of the African family accounts for whole families going over to Islam, and its spiritual unity is therefore reaffirmed under the new religion. Today Western influences

succession recognized. Delafosse writes of the Fulbe of Masina: 'Du temps de la domination des Diallo, le système de succession en usage dans le pays était le système de succession patriarcale; Sékou-Hamadou l'interdit et imposa à ses sujets la succession en ligne directe' (*H.S.N.* ii. 236). This did not endure (except in Jenne where family, and in part political, authority is transmitted from father to son), and the Fulbe of Masina have remained faithful to the patriarchal system (see Marty, *Soudan*, ii. 297).

[1] See P. Marty, *Guinée*, p. 373.

[2] H. Gaden, *Proverbes et maximes Peuls et Toucouleurs*, 1931, p. 19.

[3] Among semi-pagan Soninke (e.g. Dyāwara of the Nyoro region) the first inheritors are not the children but the father and mother who take the whole estate. If the deceased has no ascendants his brothers inherit. With Muslim Soninke, however, there is a complete reversal, the bulk of the property being inherited by the descendants, whilst the ascendants are only entitled to a sixth. Dr. Nadel (*A Black Byzantium*, p. 173) refers to the adoption of the Islamic law of succession by the Nupe in place of the local custom whereby land is inherited by the brother, and the sons have to remain on it working for their uncle as their sociological father.

have to be taken into account, especially young men reacting against family discipline and the obligations of the local cults. In so far as Islam means a new bond uniting the family the change may seem advisable to the elders. Islam in turn lays great stress on the cultic homogeneity of the family group and does not tolerate confessional differences. Only Yoruba, whose family structure has resisted the disintegrative influences both of Islam and the West, allow religious differences because they do not cause any breach in family solidarity.

Under the Sudan system land belonged to the whole family, dead, living, and unborn. Its very existence was bound up with collective ownership, and loss of land might lead to its disintegration. Family heritage included more than land. Among Mande it included the contents of granaries, animals, serfs, bride-wealth of all its members, houses and their furniture. The effect of Islam is unequal. Where it is adopted, in part at least, as a civil as well as a religious law, it changed custom with regard to the ownership of property with the exception of the land. In theory land is the gift of God and not ancestors, but this is not allowed to break the conception of collective ownership. Changes in the customary system have been confined to urban centres and heavily populated rural areas, as in parts of Futa Jalon and Bornu.[1] New economic conditions under Western rule have here and there led to the application of the Islamic code and fragmentation of land holdings, but normally the customary system of land tenure holds, and real estate, being bound up with this, also remains communal property, whilst personally acquired property is divided according to Islamic provisions.

Islamic culture gives preference to the male line in the transmission and exercise of social and political power and in the place of residence, and where other systems are followed the pressure of Islam is towards their adoption. Tuareg are matrilineal,[2] but change of environment has led to southern Tuareg becoming patrilineal. Whereas among the Ihaggāren of central Sahara the uterine nephew succeeds, among the Ullimmeden the eldest son is the heir. Matrilineal succession has practically disappeared among Negro Muslims but it has left survivals. Filiation in the ruling families of the Wolof is maternal, and islamization even in long-islamized Walo has not modified the custom. The

[1] See P. Marty, *Guinée*, pp. 394–5; J. N. D. Anderson, *Islamic Law in Africa*, p. 186.

[2] Muḥammad Belo when dealing with their customs expresses the attitude of one versed in Islamic formalism towards the practice: 'Among their more barbarous customs is that a section of them do not follow the Muslim law of inheritance, but instead the sister's son inherits'; *Infāq al-Maisūr*, p. 17.

transition is rarely due directly to Islam but its adoption reinforces the pressure of other factors.[1]

(*b*) *Wider Kinship Groups*

Beyond the *so*, the basic social unit, Mande like all Sudan peoples have a wider linkage in a more extended lineage or clan organization whose characteristics are the possession of the same clan name (Mande *dyamu*), an inherited taboo (*tana*), and exogamy.[2] The clan is generally a semi-artificial extension of true kinship beyond any recognized relationship which includes heterogeneous elements such as clients and slaves, and may embrace different language groups. In these exogamous groups marriage is permitted only between a man and a woman of different *dyamus*.

However conservative these social institutions, the adoption of a religion with a rigid legal system must affect the structure of kinship relations. The clan and sometimes the extended family, through losing their former religious significance, cease theoretically to fulfil any real function in the Islamic community. The influence of a centralized state may lead to the disintegration or loss of authority of the larger

[1] The Lebu, as described by G. Balandier and P. Mercier (*Les Pêcheurs Lebou*, 1952), are an example of a society in a process of transition under the simultaneous influence of Islamic and Western pressure. They were formerly dependent upon the *damel* of Kajor, but repudiated his authority at the end of the eighteenth century. A cleric (*seriñ*) called Dyal Dyop formed an independent community in 1795 on Cap Vert peninsula and *seriñ* became the title of the head of the state. The attempt to found a clerical state led to the formation of new villages by discontented elements. Islam did not spread among them seriously until the second half of the nineteenth century, but by 1900 the majority were Muslim.

Three main stages of transition are described: 'transition from an organization of matriarchal type to an organization centred on the maternal line; then to a structure of the Islamic type where the man and the paternal line fulfil the essential functions' (ibid., p. 212). The maternal line still retains important functions. This is seen in the coexistence of different systems of inheritance, for, apart from communal village property, land, streams, wells, and trees, which remains undivided and inalienable, they now have three types of property—maternal, paternal, and individual. Maternal property is generally the most important and must be preserved undivided. It remains in the care of the usufructuary who is the maternal uncle even if younger than his nephews, or, failing him, the eldest maternal nephew. Today it is possible, in case of disagreement, to get the maternal-line property divided, and when this is done the shares become the personal property of the inheritors. Paternal property can be left by the father to his children who can dispose of their shares as they wish. It is divided into three parts by a cleric, one-third going to the maternal line of uncles and aunts, a survival of the old order; and the other two-thirds are divided among the children, two parts for each son and one part for each daughter. Of the property inherited by the children one part can be reserved for the wives of the deceased (ibid., pp. 140–2).

[2] Some peoples, like the Teda, have clans which correspond neither to the maximal lineage nor the exogamous clan but which have a real existence and function.

kinship groups.[1] Belief in the common origin of the clan generally survives all changes, but the Arab custom of marrying within a fairly narrow range of kinship is adopted as Islamic institutions gain ground. The tendency towards endogamy is associated with the appearance of the right to personal property since its adoption ensures that property acquired by individuals is concentrated within the family. Such changes gain ground very slowly and Islamized peoples are at all possible stages of transition. This is not neccessarily due to the unequal rate of islamization of different sections of the community, for Soninke, Tokolor, and Songhay still have clans which are rigidly exogamous. Tribes of western Guinea which had a cognate organization have, on becoming Muslims, changed to the agnatic, a change which is as much due to other historical events as to Islam.

A unilateral kinship group has a name and closely associated with it an animal, plant, action, or natural phenomenon, associated with a legend of service to the first ancestor, which is sacred or taboo. The pressure of Islam is not against such beliefs because they are not connected with religion and in only a few instances have they disappeared. Some Muslims repudiate them as superstitions but will avoid breaking their clan taboo. Certain clans, such as the Timite (Dyula of Bonduku region)[2] composed exclusively of Muslims, have lost their taboo; but most retain it, as, for example, strongly islamized peoples of the Sahil of Nyoro.[3] All Hausa have their *kan gida* ('head of the house'), but no trace of totemism is found among the Songhay.[4] Fulbe clans are said to have lost their totem, but it is possible that they never possessed the institution.[5] The relations created by membership of the same clan tend

1 As with the Nupe, see S. F. Nadel, op. cit., pp. 29, 32–33.

2 See L. Tauxier, *Le Noir de Bondoukou*, p. 274.

3 Cf. Marty, *Soudan*, iv. 277. We even find an islamization of the totemic myth by people who have retained it after centuries of Islam, but this means that it has lost its real significance and become a clan taboo with no marriage significance. For instance, a family of Tokolor of Dingiray have a lion as *woḍa*. They claim to be *sharīfs* and say that since ʿAlī was the lion of God and his mother was Fāṭima bint al-Asad (daughter of the lion) their ancestors took the lion as *woḍa* and enjoy special relations with it (Marty, *Guinée*, pp. 469–70).

4 Cf. J. Boulnois, *Empire de Gao*, 1954, pp. 21 n., 159.

5 Fulbe groups in Senegal, Masina, Guinea, and Northern Nigeria do not have a totem and where we find traces it is probably due to Susu, Mandinka, or Hausa influence. The irregular nature of its appearance shows that it is due to marriage with Negro peoples and the caste system. The very name *tana* which is used in Futa Jalon is borrowed. In Northern Nigeria *mboda* (*woḍa*), sometimes translated 'totem', seems from its usage to be no more than 'taboo' in general. On the contrary, Tokolor (who are Negroes with Fulbe admixture) have preserved their clan *woḍa*. Those who migrated to Dingeray (Futa Jalon) have preserved theirs, though belief is gradually losing force through the pressure of Fulbe clergy who, having no totem themselves, have no difficulty in condemning it and advocating closer marriage. The so-called

to lose their former significance and marriage prohibitions cease to be observed, especially among townspeople, but only in rare instances do they reject their clan taboo entirely. Such beliefs become *disjecta membra* whose retention or rejection is no guide towards estimating depth of islamization.

2. SOCIAL DIFFERENTIATION

Even the simplest societies have some form of social hierarchy based upon heredity, age, sex, and division of labour, but the sharpest forms have arisen as a result of historical events which have led to the formation of grades of nobility, slavery, serfdom, and caste. Saharan life has at all times produced a stratified society, and this also distinguishes many Sahilian and north Sudanese peoples. But although the hierarchical structure derives less from ethnic origins than from historical and economic factors, ideas of origins play a great part in the mythical background relating to these distinctions. This is shown in historical traditions, and it is noteworthy that these are so tied up with the ruling class that their people's origins can only be conjectured. There is the tendency to invent legends to defend the existing state of things and this based itself upon Islam in the nineteenth-century states since the *jihād* provided the justification for clerical rule and enslavement of pagans.

The peoples of the Sudan belt have many social grades. Some depend upon legal status: others are class distinctions depending upon wealth, occupation, and position; occupational groups often have characteristics of closed societies or castes; whilst others are linked with associations such as age-group and mystery-cult grades.

(*a*) *Legal Status*

In the Sudan belt distinctions in legal status fall into three main grades: freemen, serfs, and slaves. Within and cutting through these are various class distinctions. We may illustrate from the social strata found within the states of Northern Nigeria. Freemen include the Fulani, divided into a ruling class (Fulānin Zaurē) and ordinary farmers. Members of the former fill the chief offices of state and from the others local officials are chosen. The *talakāwa*[1] or free proletariat includes every-

Fulbe who became the ruling class of Northern Nigeria were Tokolor clans who preserved their totem, but having become Hausa-speaking call it *kan gida*. It has lost its marriage significance and become a mere clan taboo.

[1] Sing. *talaka*, derived, not from Arab. *ṭalq*, 'free', but from Tamāhaqq *latqa*, Ahaggar *taleqqi*, 'the poor'. It is used in this sense in Mandinka.

one who is not a Fulani, serf, or slave. Hausa and other conquered peoples, though theoretically free, were treated as a kind of serf class. They could own land, but their tenure was precarious since it depended upon the whim of the rulers.

The second group were the *chūchenāwa*,[1] domestic slaves or serfs. These were descendants of slaves, but were treated as persons and not chattels, and under the pre-Islamic régime could not be sold. According to Islamic law slaves born in the house were still chattels (unless the owner were the father). In practice, local custom mitigated this attitude, though their inferior status was evident in such matters as concubinage, property rights, and amount of blood-wit. A Muslim is prohibited from marrying his slaves by contract, but could take them as slave-wives and the children were free. If slaves married, the children were not the serfs of the father, even if he were a freeman, but belonged to the owner. *Chūchenāwa* served as servants or retainers, or lived in villages on their master's domain, farming on their own account. Such serfs paid a tax (*murgu*) to their lord. In some places they had to work for him four days a week during which he was responsible for their upkeep, but they could keep the rest of the fruit of their labour for themselves.[2] They were allowed to buy their freedom and the occasion when a *ba-chūcheni* paid over the redemption money and received his freedom-paper, generally in court, was celebrated like the naming-ceremony of a baby. The *mālam* shaved his head, sacrificed a ram, and gave the freedman a Muslim name. It was often the custom for the master to give his freedman a daughter in marriage in order to strengthen the link of clientship. A social distinction existed between a freeman (*ḍa* or *ḍiya*) and a freedman (*'yan tache*), who continued to regard himself as a client of his former master. At the present day, after the abolition of slavery, former slave status still has a social, and in parts even a legal, effect, but the relationship has changed to one of patronage (*walā'*). Descendants of slaves regard themselves as clients of their former masters, they address their patron as *bāba* (father) and pay him *zakāt* at festivals. The patron can still claim their daughters as slave-wives, and in Northern Nigera should they die without heirs inherits their property.

The third category are the captives or slaves proper (*bāyi*, sing.

[1] Sing. *ba-chūcheni*, derived from Arab. *qinn*?

[2] Among the Fulbe of Masina serfs (*rimayḅe*) paid their master two types of taxes: *dyēgom* or *dyagobērē*, one-sixth of the harvest; and *dyamgal*, a personal tax. In addition, the owner had the right to statute labour or the *corvée* (see P. Marty, *Soudan*, ii. 276).

bāwa). The distinction between these two categories of slave status (in Arabic *ʿabd qinn* and *ʿabd mamlūka*),[1] though not in strict accordance with Islamic law,[2] is a natural one since slavery arises either from the capture or purchase of non-Muslims or from the offspring of slaves. The distinction was very marked: *bāyi* could be sold and were treated as articles of exchange, the master could refuse their marriage, and, according to strict legalists, their children were *bāyi* also and could be sold. The majority of *bāyi* worked on their master's farm. They were an essential part of the tribute (*bāwa gandu*) paid to Sokoto by provincial rulers.

The Mālikite code allows for an attitude of paternalism in the relationship between master and slave, and this helped to maintain the traditional attitude, whereas a rigorist outlook might easily have led to a deterioration in their condition. This school of law tends to give him certain rights of a freeman, whereas other schools give him only half rights. He can hold property, like a wife he can claim freedom if treated cruelly, and he can act as *imām aṣ-ṣalāt*. He has rights in arranging his own marriage and may have up to four wives, whilst a slave-wife has equal attention-rights with the free wives. Further, Islam did not freeze slave status since it allowed for the buying of freedom and manumission.

Another form of servile state is the pawning system by which indebted freemen could pawn themselves to a creditor until they paid off their debt. They were provided for in recompense for their work. They had a legal status in local law, but not in Islamic law. They were not slaves, they could not be sold, and had the right of regaining their liberty whenever they could pay off their obligations. This practice existed among Muslim peoples (Soninke, Songhay,[3] and Kanembu), and among Nupe[4] and Yoruba,[5] but was rare among Hausa and Fulbe. Some Islamic clergy condemned the practice, but others justified it by

[1] See R. Brunschvig, art. *ʿAbd* in *Ency. Is.*² i. 25.

[2] All Sudanese peoples make a clear verbal distinction between these two categories: Fulbe of Futa Jalon: *rimayḇe* (sing. *dīmājo*), household slaves, and *sodāḇe* (sing. *sodāḍo*), captives or trade-slaves; Mandinka *woro-so*, 'born in the house', and *gyõ*, slaves.

The social and economic structure of Sudan society in the past cannot be conceived apart from the slavery-to-clientship system. Under this system the lot of slaves ameliorated itself with each generation and the stages from slavery through various grades of serfdom to clientship are shown by the terminology; for example, in Songhay; first generation *horso* (child of a *banya*, male and a *kongo*, female trade-slave); second generation *sule* (child of two *horso*); third generation *sule-hule* (child of *sule*); and after that *ga-bibi*, free clients (cf. A. Dupuis, *La langue Songoï*, 1917, p. 61).

[3] See *Coutumiers juridiques de l'A.O.F.* ii. 225–6, 242, 332.

[4] See S. F. Nadel, *A Black Byzantium*, pp. 311–13.

[5] See S. Johnson, *History of the Yorubas*, Lagos, 1937, pp. 126–30.

regarding it as a permitted system of hiring. The system was abolished by European powers.[1]

(*b*) *Class Distinctions*

It will be seen from the summary of grades in Northern Nigeria that social distinction is not wholly based upon status, but shows itself in less clearly defined classes. Distinctions between freemen and freedmen and between Fulani and Hausa freemen have been mentioned. Besides racial origins and status, class distinctions arose from position and type of occupation, especially wealth in slaves, lands, herds, and articles of exchange. In general, there are three main classes in the Sudan: a noble or ruling class, such as the Fulbe overlords, but also including chiefs of the indigenous population, descendants of former rulers, elected village chiefs, outstanding warriors, and leaders of the clergy. Then there is a class of merchants, freedmen, or slaves holding important positions; and, finally, a proletariat of agriculturalists and artisans, whether free or servile in status.

Society admits of no precise classification, some elements are elastic, others rigidly fixed. Individuals belonging to the lowest legal status grade may attain a high social grade. Slaves joined the ranks of the clergy,[2] many became war-chiefs and held high offices of state. Certain offices like that of *kachela* in Bornu could only be held by slaves. In Nigerian states the hierarchical system is complicated because an individual may belong to a number of categories. For example, a man may be of the Fulbe nobility by reason of birth, ownership of land brings him into the economic hierarchy; he belongs to the political hierarchy by being a member of the emir's council; as a representative in the House of Assembly at Kaduna he is a member of the national hierarchy; and as a trained *faqīh* belongs to the religious hierarchy.

Moorish tribes of western Sahara and Sahil have a complex social organization. At the top are the relatively pure Ḥassān Arabs who form the noble, warrior, and governing class, and live by camel- and cattle-breeding. Then come the *zwāya* or clerical tribes of arabized Berbers who are tributary to Arab clans, tend their flocks and herds and pay them protection dues (*ghafar* for *khafar*).[3] Consequently they

[1] Pawning was abolished in Nigeria in 1933.

[2] Cf. the Tokolor saying *mattyuḍo, so jangi tan, wonti tōrōdo*, 'a slave (first generation), his studies completed, has become a cleric'.

[3] Many have freed themselves from dependence upon Arab tribes, hence arises a further distinction between free tribes, *zwāyat ash-shams*, and subservient, *zwāyat aẓ-ẓall*. In Adrar these terms distinguish nomads from sedentarized clerical groups.

do not bear arms, but their position is that of an aristocratic class. They also provide the educated and religious element who act as itinerant Qur'ān-teachers, healers, and amulet-makers. The *zanāja* (*idnāgen*) are Berber tributaries (*laḥma*) who pay the Arabs feudal dues (*ḥurma*, lit. 'protection', in Mauritania; *mudāra* in Hawd and Sahil). Next come the *ḥarrāṭīn* (sing. *ḥarṭānī*), sedentary black peoples forming tribes of serfs, cultivating fields of millet around villages. Finally come the slaves (*'abīd* or *nānma*) owned by the Ḥassān and the *zwāya* tribes. In addition, there are caste groups of *mu'allimīn* ('skilled', masons and other workmen), *igāwen* (sing. *igīu*, 'bard'),[1] and Nemadi, a caste of hunters.

The other Saharan peoples have equally elaborate social organizations, but not the Sudanese nomads, the red pastoral Fulbe. This seems to show that although settled Fulbe are highly hierarchized this system was not an original element of Fulbe society. Upon the elaborate systems of the Wolof and Tokolor Islam has had no effect.[2]

Colour and racial pride are strong factors in social differentiation. Negroid Tuareg are looked down upon by those of purer race. The Kel Owi of the Air region have so intermarried with Hausa that other Tuareg regard them as Negroes. They in turn despise the Negroes among whom they live, from whom they can scarcely be distinguished physically. In Timbuktu freemen are divided into two main classes of *ga-korē*, 'white bodies', which includes the Arma (descendants of Andalusian soldiers, now Negroes), and *ga-bibi*, 'black bodies'. The irrational distinction found in all Islamic countries between *sharīfs* and other Muslims exists in West Africa.

(*c*) *Castes*

The next division is that social–economic organization which freezes an individual in the group into which he is born, out of which he cannot marry. These caste groups are free and have the rights of freemen. They are characteristic of the western cycle and the Zerma region forms the zone of transition. Zerma have only two castes, *garasa* (smiths and shoe-makers) and *gyesērē* (griots), and even these have lost the rigid characteristics of a caste system. Other craftsmen are ordinary serfs or

[1] It is from this or the terms used in West Atlantic languages (Wolof *gevel*, Tokolor *gawlo*, pl. *awlbe*) that the French 'griot' is probably derived.

[2] The Wolof have the *garmi* or ruling class by pure uterine filiation, *dom-i-būr* ('king's sons'), nobles by masculine filiation; *dyam-būr*, freemen; *seriñ*, clerics; *badolo*, peasants; *dyāmi-būr*, serfs forming the guard of chiefs; freedmen, serfs, slaves, and caste peoples subdivided according to occupation.

foreigners. In Hausa country castes disappear and social classes and occupational guilds take their place.[1]

Hereditary caste divisions arose out of the need of villagers and nomads for specialists, or of noble families for minstrels to preserve and recite sacred legends. Each village is a unity capable of supplying its own wants and includes representatives of castes who ply a particular craft, whilst other workers move about from village to village. Social grading among the western Fulbe and Tokolor is elaborate, but though marriage restrictions exist between the various grades the occupational caste groups are distinct from these and rigidly endogamous. They are known collectively as *nyenyḅe* which expresses the idea of 'skilled', divided into many endogamous groups: smiths (*wailūḅē*), woodworkers (*lauḅē*) regarded as magicians, leather workers (*gargassabē* or *sakēbē*), weavers (*mābubē*), and griots (*wambāḅē*) who are at the same time troubadours, jesters, panegyrists, and annalists.

Caste groups are free and have the rights of freemen except in regard to marriage. A member of the butcher caste devoted wholly to cultivation still remains a butcher and can only marry within his caste.[2] Techniques involve the transmission of hereditary lore and that includes relations with supernatural powers, therefore elements of fear surround caste peoples who provide diviners and medicine-men. Many castes though nominally Muslim are in fact pagan and have specific functions or ritual duties to perform at transitional rites. Some caste members attained high office within the class system which cuts across all these grades. As smiths fulfilled priestly duties in pagan societies, so the chief of the smiths in Hausaland and Waday enjoyed special privileges at court, was well versed in the Qur'ān, and collected taxes. There is nothing in Islam to support this system.[3] Its effect has been negligible, though *qāḍīs*' recognition that this type of differentiation is not recognized in Islamic law meant that the exceptional case might have their support against local custom.

[1] The smith caste (*ḥaddād*) is an exception as in Arabia. The word is applied in the Chad region to a distinct ethnic group who are rigidly endogamous, live in special villages scattered among other peoples, and occupy themselves especially as artisans, hunters, tanners, and smiths.

[2] Among Soninke, a man who changed his name in order to marry a woman of a higher caste was punished with 10 to 50 lashes, or one to six months in chains. If she were a virgin he had to pay the price of blood, lost the bride-price, and was expelled from the neighbourhood (see J. H. Saint-Père, *Les Sarakollé du Guidimakha*, 1925, p. 65).

[3] When *askiya* Muḥammad I went on pilgrimage he consulted 'Abd ar-Raḥmān as-Suyūṭi who explained to him that there should be no differentiation in marriage in regard to caste peoples of free status and he gave him the general outlines of Islamic law with regard to the condition of the children of slaves; Maḥmūd al-Kāti, *T. al-Fattāsh*, pp. 15, 19–22.

(*d*) *Associations*

Admission to privileged groups like age-grades and mystery cults complicates social life still further. Admission is gained by initiation, and initiation is rebirth. Each member has his status in a new social family and relationships with other social families above or below his grade, which involves privileges, duties, and obligations. The mystery cults mentioned in the last chapter are important in assessing social grades only at an early stage of islamization, but to complete the sketch of social hierarchization the place that associations of a more secular character occupy in Muslim society should be mentioned. This is the grouping of individuals of the same generation into age-associations. Adoption of Islam leads to decadence of their initiatory rites and simplification of their social function into that of groupings of young men which later in life do not play a great part in the ordering and organization of society. In no place where Islam gains any real hold do they preserve their traditional role.[1] After islamization they exercise conventional sanctions among their own members, but not beyond them. They are laical aid societies which, though desacralized through the influence of Islam, continue to fill a restricted social function.

3. ISLAM AND THE STATE

(*a*) *Islam as Imperial Cult, State Religion, and Theocracy*

The Sudan states came into existence in various ways. Some were founded by an alien family imposing itself upon uncoordinated peoples as Saharan nomadic Zaghāwa formed the state of Kanem, others by a traditional village or district chief gaining control of wider areas by conquest, or by priests of local cults who combined political and religious authority, others by heads of age-group associations becoming leaders of warrior bands. But, however formed, all manifested certain general features. Their foundation was invested with a myth of origin and a religious aura, even if the rulers were of alien origin. Although the state embraced peoples of varied ethnic origins and social structures, it was a political unity in the sense that all recognized the ruling house.

[1] Mandinka and Bambara have true age-grades which islamization has little affected. The root word is *nto* or *tõ*, a member is a *tõ-de*, 'child of the *tõ*', and associations are called *flã-tõ*. These associations cut across social grades and a *flã-tõ* embraces all persons within a particular age-span, covering about three circumcision classes, and in mixed villages link together people of different ethnic groups. The members of each *flã-tõ* elect a chief (*tõ-tigi*), herald, and other officials; each grade has its rites of initiation, symbols, and festivals, but unlike mystery cults many ceremonies are public.

The core of the state had a centralized system of government and a wider system of vassal states. Rule was authoritarian, based, not on right of conquest, but upon the recognition of the sacred ruler whose existence guaranteed the prosperity of all who paid him allegiance. His position may be contrasted with that of the chief of a Moorish tribe who is merely the representative of the *jamāʿa*.

The concept of the state as an independent political institution is just as alien to Islamic as to African thought. Islam in theory recognizes only the existence of the *umma* (and protected communities) with the *imām* as the leader. The constitutional principle of the state is the unity of the political and religious community. Given the concept of the Sudanese state, the assumptions upon which it is based and upon which authority rests, within which the personal status and the religious integrity of each individual were defined by birth, an Islamic state could not be established without overthrowing the whole structure and providing an entirely new source of authority as was done in the nineteenth-century theocratic states.

Religion in the Sudan states did not offer the authorities any opposition. The first level of authority, the basic foundation of these states, was that of the family or village chiefs whose position was sanctioned by religion, in fact they existed to maintain the integral unity of religion and community. It was the same at higher levels of authority whether priest-kings or divine-rulers or the aristocracy of class-kinship cults. The sacred character of the ruler showed itself in the procedure for his election, sacralization, and investiture, in the state rituals and taboos he must observe, upon which the stability of the kingdom and the welfare of the people depended. The state cult was analogous to that of lineage groups, and the heads of states did not, and could not, impose their religion upon their peoples.

The introduction of Islam did not upset the equilibrium of the Sudan states nor provide them with a new basis of authority. *Mansas* of Māli, *jās* and *sīs* of Songhay, *mais* of Bornu, and chiefs of all lesser states, adopted Islam as the imperial cult without disturbance to the mythic basis of their authority. They did not attempt to spread it among subjects other than state servants, for that would have meant their downfall. Village life followed the same pattern as before. Rulers, though calling themselves Muslims and often reinforcing their authority by going on pilgrimage to the sacred house to acquire power, performed all traditional religious functions their position required for ensuring the welfare of the state. Their people could not have noticed any change.

At the same time the adoption of Islam as the aristocratic cult introduced a new and potentially disturbing element. It meant the existence of a competing cult which could be professed by anyone from king to slave. Before its arrival religion was something into which one was born. There were no competing religions, except in so far as mystery societies disturbed the equilibrium. Rulers recognized all religions within the state. Islamic clergy accepted the situation for they were concerned primarily about their position in the social structure which depended upon the traditional tolerance. They could not urge the ruler to prohibit what they regarded as heathenism because he would not enforce it.

This stage, where Islam is the imperial cult, characterizes those present-day states which include a majority or a significant proportion of pagans but whose chief is a Muslim. In Nigeria chiefs who have joined Islam during the last hundred years naturally keep up the old rites. The chief of Biu, controlling the Pabir and Bura, who belongs to the category of divine-kings, carries out all the rites his position entails. Muslim chiefs in Sierra Leone which is a picture of religious confusion show an all-embracing catholicity. They keep up the ancestral cult and the *poro* for they are part of the body of custom they have to maintain, they support Islam to the extent of becoming adherents, and they encourage Christian missions out of appreciation of their work in education and social welfare, attending church services at festivals as they also honour Islamic festivals. The three religions each fulfil a social function, and, since adherents of all are found in each chieftaincy, all are accorded recognition. But the position is not stable. Islam, as religion of the rulers that anyone can join regardless of status or class, naturally tends to dominate. Although villagers may be uninterested the village chief may think it wise to profess it, whilst continuing, like the state-chief, to exercise his traditional religious functions.

The boundary between the status of Islam as imperial cult and state religion is vague, for in the latter there is still a separation between public and private religion. But when this stage is entered the position of Islam is more positive as under *askiya* Muḥammad of Songhay and *mai* Idrīs Alawma of Bornu. *Askiya* Muḥammad as a usurper needed Islam in order to reinforce his power. But before discussing the state where Islam is needed to bolster up alien rule we should mention the way the adoption of Islam by indigenous rulers leads to the incorporation of Islamic elements within the state structure. In central

Sudan states like those of Bornu, Hausa, and Nupe, a religious hierarchy was incorporated into the traditional structure to give the rulers Islamic support. This is maintained, not only in those states which did not fall to the Fulani (Bornu, Gobir, north Katsina, and Abuja), but also in a modified form in those taken over by them. In Abuja, remnant of the kingdom of Zazzau, the chief cleric is the *limāmin jumma'a* who officiates over the *jāmiʿ* and takes the funeral prayers, the *salanke* officiates at festival prayers and prays at the death-bed of chiefs and high officials; the *magājin mālam* is the representative of the Shehu of Bornu and installs the new chief; and the *maga-takarda*, chief scribe, is the chief's chaplain and 'opener of the Book of the Years'.[1]

When Islam really becomes the state religion a breach is opened between ruler and community as long as large sections remain pagan. The cleavage is especially evident when the chief is the descendant of alien conquerors like the Fulbe rulers of Yoruba Ilorin, Nupe, and other Northern Nigerian states. Nadel refers to this 'disturbance of the balance' in the Nupe state and the role played by Islam as the new binding force of a precarious political equilibrium.[2] Under such conditions clergy were encouraged to denounce idolatry and propagate Islam,[3] all to the end of unifying the various peoples the state embraced. This unification, as Nadel shows, is far from complete. Islam did not, in fact, resolve the deep-seated conflicts in these societies and all the Fulani states were disintegrating when the British took over.

The breach between ruler and community is filled in the theocratic state. Contacts with Islam and through it with the Mediterranean Islamic states had contributed nothing essential to the traditional structure of the Sudan state with its sacred ruler, the hierarchy and etiquette of his court, and territorial, fiscal, judicial, and military organization, until the appearance of clerics proclaiming the *jihād* towards the end of the eighteenth century led to the formation of theocratic states. These owed their inspiration not to outside sources, but solely to their study of books of law. In the states they formed, the theory of national, and not merely ruler or state, polity is based on Islam. They may be distinguished as theocracies in the sense that the theocratic principle is dominant in their foundation whatever they degenerated into. The ruler was the

[1] See *Haḅen Abuja*, Zaria, 1946, p. 34; English transl., Ibadan, 1952, pp. 79–80. These titles varied. On the elaborate range of religious officials in Damagaram (capital Zinder) see Landeroin, in *Documents scientifiques de la Mission Tilho*, 1911, ii. 535–6.

[2] S. F. Nadel, *A Black Byzantium*, 1942, p. 67.

[3] Ibid., pp. 142–3.

imām of the whole community, embracing all peoples of the state, and the community was regarded as resting upon the rule of God. In Futas Toro and Jalon the *imām*, leader of the prayer-community, evolved into a leader of the *jihād* and political chief. He was guardian of the law and court of final appeal, head of the political administration and war-leader, though in practice the existence of an ecclesiastical council tempered his actual exercise of power. Anyone who revolted against the authority of the *imām* was the enemy of God. In this way theocrats were able to justify the prosecution of the *jihād* against Muslims who refused to acknowledge their claims. The theocratic state once again affirms the old integrity of the secular and religious group. The unit, however, is not the lineage but all subjects whatever their race or language. The principle of *cuius regio eius religio* was utterly foreign to the Sudan state, as it is in practice in most Islamic states where the principle of personal status ruled, but the theocrats were faced only with Muslims and *kāfirīn*, and they tended to extend the last term to embrace unsubdued Muslims as well as pagans. There were no 'protected communities', and conversion and submission meant the same.

This revolution was accomplished only in a limited way. The leaders of the *jihād* were rarely capable of effecting the transition from military rule to a stable civil administration. They had no experience of a Muslim state, but had in view an idealistic model gained from reading law books. The loss of the old foundations of authority led to instability and revolt and all degenerated from the theocratic principles on which they were founded to a position in which Islam was the state religion. The empire of 'Uthmān dan Fodio was founded as a theocracy, but through alliance with nomadic Fulbe its expansion was enormous. The theocrat resigned his duties as head of the state to devote himself to religion, and the elements of anarchy were so predominant that within a few years his empire had degenerated into an assemblage of slave-raiding and tax-extorting fiefs in practical independence of the titular overlordship of Sokoto. The governors adopted the systems of the states they overthrew. Their authority was only secondarily based on Islam for there was no community of religion, but primarily on right of conquest and exercise of brute force.

This abortive attempt to found a theocracy contrasts with that of Shehu Ḥamadu of Masina, which was as nearly successful in its short life as any Muslim state is likely to be. He succeeded because his conquests were relatively limited in extent, he made no compromise with the past and he was able to obtain community of religion. Ḥamadu called himself *amīr al-mu'minīn* and, modelling his government upon the prescriptions of Islam, formed a sound civil administration. When he took control most of the Fulbe were pagan, but they, as well as Bambara, Bozo, and other pagans under his rule, were made to join Islam and thoroughly taught their Islamic duties. He found the clergy of Jenne were rent by factionism, but he resolved their differences, destroyed the many Friday mosques which existed in the city, built one simple spacious *jāmi'*, and secured unity of Islamic practice. He divided the state into provinces, appointing to each a *qāḍī* and an *amīr*, established the Islamic systems of taxation, military service, and judicature. Although he himself was the court of final appeal he surrounded himself with *fuqahā'* who formed at the same time a council of state and a higher court which did not hesitate to criticize any deviations from strict Islamic principles.

Islam introduces an anarchic element in that the law of God alone is absolute. Friction is possible between the state and the ecclesiastical body who also claim to know the divine will. Another anarchic element derives from the Islamic system of succession. Under African systems electors had a wide sphere of choice within the limits of a particular lineage and when they followed customary procedure their decision was likely to be accepted. But Islam influenced the theocrats. In Senegalese Futa leaders of the revolt and their descendants formed a fixed elective body which tried to follow early Islamic practice by electing the *imām* from among their own members. Since they also had power of deposition, this system, intended to act as a counterpoise to tyranny, led to rivalry, instability, and often complete anarchy. In Futa Jalon the *imām* alternated between the lineage of the first two leaders, out of which developed a peculiar system by which each lineage provided an *imām* in rotation for two-year periods. These methods divided the people into factions. In the states of Sokoto, Masina, and Segu the leaders of the *jihād*, 'Uthmān dan Fodio, Shehu Ḥamadu, and al-ḥājj 'Umar, broke with custom by nominating their eldest sons, instead of brothers or nephews, as their successors.[1]

[1] This always led to family rivalries. Fratricidal struggles were a feature of the long reign of Amadu Shehu, though it is to be noted that al-ḥājj 'Umar, when he appointed Amadu as his successor, made him swear that he should be succeeded by his brothers and not his sons (see *Bull. Com. Ét. A.O.F.*, 1919, p. 27). Muḥammad Belo, 'Uthmān's son and successor, who had gained recognition as *amīr al mu'minīn* over 'Uthmān's brother 'Abd Allāh, would not subject his own son to the dangers and refused to nominate him, saying that the choice must be left in the hands of the three flags (*rāyāt*) of Kunni, Walarbu, and Saḥsabu (see *Ta'rīkh Sokoto*, p. 198).

(*b*) *The Authority and Election of Chiefs*

In the Sudan state the chief is not chief by virtue of the position he holds but by virtue of the less tangible qualities he acquires through the ceremony of investiture which sanctify him and set him apart from profane life. Dynastic stability was attained through a delicate balance of power between parallel ruling lines, each holding at one time different functions: kingship, heir apparency, or electoral power. When an alien became ruler the old balance of power was upset. This is seen in the *askiya* state of Songhay. The sole foundation, apart from right of conquest, upon which the first *askiya* could base his authority was Islam and he performed the pilgrimage to Mecca to obtain divine approval and acquire new symbols. That this counts for little unless the population is Muslim is shown by the subsequent history of his line. The relationship of chief and people is one of mutual interdependence. The chief has his duties, religious as well as political. In the normal course the superimposition of an alien ruler led to a dualism of functions. The 'master of the land', descendant of the first settler, continued to exercise his religious functions in regard to the land, whilst the new ruler became political chief.[1] This was common in many Muslim states. The political chief has the duty of administering justice and ensuring security against enemies, and consequently the right to demand taxes, levies, and other services.

The introduction of Islam leads to the usual parallelism. As imperial cult it provides no basis for the power of the ruler and the dualism was not normally in evidence in his election and sacralization until the era of the theocratic states when an enturbaning took place. From the nineteenth century this practice was adopted in states where Islam was the state cult, parallel to the normal rites. Authority in such states had a kind of ambivalent character, a transitional stage between sacred and profane authority, the sacerdotal character of the chieftaincy deriving

[1] This dualism of secular and sacred leadership is found in the neo-Sudanese states of the Voltaic region. In Mossi the *tenga-soba*, representing the original inhabitants, is the custodian of the land, whilst the *tenga-naba*, representing the conquering clans of Mossi, is the chief of the village. Similarly in states of the Northern Territories of Ghana the *ten'dana* or *tegatu* is the indigenous priest-chief authority, and the *na* or *naba* the political chief (see R. S. Rattray, *The Tribes of the Ashanti Hinterland*, 1932, pp. xi–xii, 549 ff.). The head of the old ruling lineage may be given special functions, generally of a religious nature, at court. The *durbi*, head of the old Durbāwa line dispossessed in the thirteenth century, is a dignitary at the court of the Hausa Sarkin Katsina. He is one of the four electors of a new *sarki*, has functions at court, and at the nomination of pagan functionaries like the *sarkin bōri* (see *Bull. I.F.A.N.* x. 636, 664; H. R. Palmer, *Bornu Sahara and Sudan*, p. 129).

from the old associations[1] and the profane and unessential from Islam.

In the theocratic state the personality of the chief as the symbol of the integration of community and natural environment weakened in a way not evident in states which merely adopted Islam into their system. In these he remains essentially guardian of the soil, protector of the harvest, and bestower of prosperity.[2] Chiefs who become Muslims for political reasons continue to honour the rites of the local religion.[3] Under the old order a new ruling line formed a new myth of authority, but the Muslim conqueror had to base his upon his divine mission. In theocratic states and their descendants there was a complete reversal of the sacred and profane elements. After the death of the first theocrat a council of hereditary electors makes its appearance and a Muslim enturbaning takes place, and though old elements cohere around the installations they are now sanctioned by profane custom, not by religion. The old symbols could not be taken over,[4] not merely because they had been carried off by the dispossessed rulers, but because authority is derived from God and the chain of electors are guided by God in their choice. The two elements are kept separate. The indigenous involves a seven-day retreat,[5] either before or after the Islamic ceremony of enturbaning, the principal rite in the investiture of chief *imāms* before they become political chiefs.

Marty describes the installation ceremony of the *almāmi* of Futa

[1] The rulers of Waday maintained the old Tunjur rites of seven-day retreat and sacrifice on Mount Pleiades (Jabal Thurayya): 'As regards the ancestral custom of making kings on the rock, they have never broken with it altogether, for when Harut's affair was over, Satan suggested to his brother that if he fulfilled the old rites of the rock as practised by the ancient kings, his kingdom would endure' (see the Wadayan Chronicle in Palmer, *Sud. Mem.* ii. 28).

[2] See the account of the installation of the chief of Gulfeil, a small Kotoko state south of the Chad, in Lebeuf and Detourbet, *La Civilisation du Tchad*, 1950, pp. 160–7. The paramount chief of the Dagomba in the Northern Territories of Ghana is enskinned with the old pagan ritual, the Muslim cleric merely adding his prayers and a sacrifice during the ceremonial (see R. S. Rattray, *The Tribes of the Ashanti Hinterland*, 1932, pp. 559, 586).

[3] Thus the *Moi* of the Bolewa of Fika (Potiskum Division), whose people, though some are nominally Muslim, are in practice pagans, performs all the ceremonies incumbent upon him. See also C. K. Meek, *Northern Nigeria*, ii. 2–3.

[4] The chief symbols of authority of the *mais* of Bornu were the *babu* or sceptre (see plate xiv in H. R. Palmer, *Bornu Sahara*, p. 120) and the *sacra* of the kingdom, but the *Shehus* who dispossessed them had a new basis of authority and new Islamic symbols: investiture with the ring, skull cap, and rosary of Shaikh Amīn. Similarly *Askiya* Muḥammad of Songhay acquired new symbols from Mecca.

[5] Accounts of the seven-day retreat are given by Lebeuf and Detourbet (*La Civilisation du Tchad*, 1950, pp. 162–3) for the So; H. Barth (*Travels*, ii. 271, iv. 63) for the Muniyo, a So people, though their dynasty may have been Saharan; and by M. at-Tūnisī (*Voyage au Darfour*, p. 160) for Darfur.

Jalon.[1] This took place in front of the mosque in the holy village of Fugumba. The elected candidate, holding a black sceptre with a silver head and iron point, was dressed in nine gowns. Then the chief cleric, circling him, bound a turban around his head, making seven circuits, one for each province. Following this the newly-invested *almāmi* repeated the *shahāda* and other formulas, vaunted the exploits of his ancestors and himself, announced his programme, and swore to uphold Islam and the clerical party. After an old cleric had delivered an address of advice and admonition the Islamic ceremony was over. The next stage was the native one. The *almāmi* returned to his house and kept a retreat of silence, fasting, and continence for seven days. To ensure the well-being of the new reign the people had scattered grains of rice, millet, and fonio in the house. By rolling his naked body over these seeds he impregnated them with the fertilizing virtue he had acquired during the ceremonies. Each morning the officiating cleric entered and removed a turn of the turban until the retreat was ended.

(*c*) *Influence of Islam upon Systems of Taxation*

Systems of taxation existed in all advanced Sudan states before they adopted Islam, but its regulations provided a permanent system of direct taxation whose utility was obvious. Islamic terminology was employed in Bornu, Songhay, and certain Hausa states where Islam was the imperial, state, or urban cult, but the system was only in full force in the theocratic states of the nineteenth century. That instituted by Shehu Ḥamadu of Masina[2] came closest to *sharīʿa* regulations. *Dyāka* (Ar. *zakāt*) was levied annually, in principle only on the basic crop; and a tithe from the herds of nomads, also called *dyāka* 'by analogy', but according to a different system. Of the *dyāka* one-tenth went to the collector, a fifth to Ḥamadu, and the remainder was divided into three parts, one part each for the governor, military, and poor of the district. At the beginning of each year a capital levy of one-fortieth on gold, cowries, and salt bars was taken, but only in the main centres and on the rich. *Krādye* (Ar. *kharāj*) was levied on crops (but reckoned in cowries) from which those who had fought with Ḥamadu at the time of his first bid for power were exempt. *Muddu* (Ar. *mudd*, a measure of capacity) was an obligatory contribution levied at the *ʿīd al-fiṭr*, the

[1] See Marty, *Guinée*, pp. 14–15; Saint-Père, 'Création du Royaume du Fouta Djallon', *Bull. Com. Ét. A.O.F.* xii (1929), 516–18. Marty also mentions the taboos which the *almāmi* and other chiefs must observe (op. cit., pp. 470–1).

[2] See Ch. Monteil, *Dyénné*, 1932, pp. 106–10.

head of each family paying a *muddu* of millet for each member of the family old enough to fast. Ḥamadu took his fifth and the rest was distributed among clergy and poor. The *pabe* (Soninke *pabu*, 'aid') was a levy for the support of the local army contingent. Finally, *ushuru* Ar. *'ushr*, 'tithe') was a purchase-tax levied on all merchandise, paid in kind, except for slaves, cattle, and horses, when it was paid in cowries. The collector took a tenth and Ḥamadu divided the rest among provincial chiefs. Spoils of war were divided according to the Islamic code and in this respect Masina contrasts with the Fulani states of Nigeria.[1] In these juridical justification for the exactions of chiefs was provided by the application of Islamic terms. The general principles were: *zakāt* fixed in proportions according to the nature of the 'increase': one-tenth of the harvest when it exceeded 300 *mudds* of grain (termed *ushuru*), one-twentieth of commercial gain, one-thirtieth on cattle, and one-fortieth on sheep. The *kharāj* (Hausa *kuḍin kasa*) or land-tax was imposed on all free non-Fulani peoples, whilst pagans in addition had to pay *jizya* (Hausa *gandu*) or capitation tax. Revenue was derived from the sale of offices and from taxes such as death duties, market dues, and the *jangali*, or tax on cattle and livestock, the only tax paid by nomadic Fulani. Taxation varied greatly in the different states, and, as Meek shows, whilst the general system, based on Islamic law, was justifiable, 'the arbitrary methods of assessment, and extortionate methods of collection, robbed it of its religious sanction, and led to the economic paralysis of the country'.[2]

4. INFLUENCE OF ISLAM IN THE JURIDIC SPHERE

(*a*) *Islam and Customary Law*

Law covers three spheres: the body of customary law, Islamic law, and the regulations of the ruling authority (*siyāsa*). In general, custom has the character of fundamental law and Islamic law is subordinate since custom decides what elements shall be adopted or rejected. Thus Mandinka use *lāda* (Arabic *al-'āda*, 'custom') for law, distinguishing the different types: *gyõ lāda*, customary law regulating slaves; *si-ra lāda*, as regulating free men; *silāmī-ya lāda*, as relating to Muslims, that

[1] Muḥammad Belo made an attempt to get the rules of the *jihād* observed. Al-ḥājj Sa'īd writes (*History of Sokoto*, in *Tadhkirat an-Nisyān*, p. 191/308) that in the year he destroyed Dakara and killed Sarkin Gobir, Belo 'distributed the booty in accordance with *sharī'a* provisions for *it had never before been so divided*', but the troops objected and refused to fight unless he returned to former practice, and he was forced to comply with their demands.

[2] C. K. Meek, *Northern Nigeria*, i. 298–90.

is, Islamic law.[1] A feature of West African Islam is its flexibility in practice in regard to African custom, and its immobility and rigid opposition to change when subject to pressure from outside. The Mālikī school which prevails in West Africa allows for the application of customary law, but prohibits any interpretation of Islamic law to adapt it to modern conditions.[2] In other words, it allows for the operation of a wide range of autonomous secular law, not based on the *sharīʿa*, which can be utilized by the *qāḍī*, if necessary exclusively, as the basis for his decisions. It is, therefore, a question of the flexibility of the *qāḍī*, not of the law. In theory, the legal position is the dominance of the *sharīʿa* modified by local custom where this is not in conflict with the *sharīʿa*. In fact, the foundation is local custom modified by the addition of Islamic regulations. It is, therefore, not so anomalous as might appear to find that in Northern Nigeria Islamic law is applied under 'Native Law and Custom'.

In matters relating to the cult Islamic regulations naturally encounter no opposition, but in the sphere of inheritance and family law clergy only partially succeed in getting uniformity, and custom is everywhere applied in matters of civil law. Islamic law can function in towns but cannot gain much hold over cultivators in whom land and life, food and society, are essentially intertwined. Even in a Muslim state, as well as those under European rule, rulers generally recognize the *sharīʿa* as governing only the sphere of personal and social relations. Only in theocratic states was its application extended to criminal offences.

Qāḍīs are guided by social reality, and in practice base their decisions upon custom, even in opposition to the *sharīʿa* where custom is too strong for them to resist. That in practice they are bound to interpret does not constitute a precedent since only their decisions are recorded, not the process by which those decisions are reached. Thus

[1] Where the word *sharīʿa* has been adopted it means 'judgement' (Arab. *ḥukm*); Mandinka *sariya*; Hausa *an yanke sharīʾa*, 'Judgement has been passed.' The distinction between the two codes of law is shown in Nupe: *gàmi nyá Momodu*, Islamic law; *gàmi nyá kin*, customary law (lit. 'the law of the country'). The word *sharīʾa* is ousting Nupe *eboda* for 'judgement'; *sharīʾa (eboda) gboró*, 'direct judgement' (for pagans), *sharīʾa nya koranu* (for Muslims).

[2] *Ijmā*, having fixed the legal texts, is no longer applicable; whilst *ijtihād*, which allows for adaptability to changes, is not recognized. In Islamic countries the study of *fatāwā* is important for tracing the development of Islamic law, for thereby *ʿāda* is assimilated. But in West Africa *muftīs* have never been an institution. Hausa employ the term *mufuti* for a 'judicia assessor' (*faqīh mushāwar*). Each *alkāli* sits with a number of these, whose function is to record the evidence. They may be consulted on legal questions which arise, but do not have to decide whether a certain practice is or is not contrary to the spirit of Islamic law. Their advices are not preserved. The *alkālai* are largely recruited from their ranks. Wolof call these assessors *tamsīr* (*tafsīr*?).

custom is not officially accommodated within Islam, and under changing conditions can gradually be eliminated. On the other hand, anything new, such as Western secular education, is condemned. Modern Islamic governments have made great adaptations of Islamic law to suit new conditions, but in West Africa legalists have strongly resisted innovations. This was due, partly to their isolation from countries of evolving Islamic jurisprudence, and partly to the fact that adherence to the law constituted a form of reaction against Western rule. Today the situation is in a state of transformation. The foundation of legal institutions is ancestral custom, formerly sacred law, but by the adoption of Islam transformed into secular law. To this has been added aspects of Islamic law, often leading to the displacement of the corresponding sections of custom. A third factor is the regulations imposed by the French or British. The situation, therefore, is not a question of the fusion of *sharīʿa* and custom, nor of islamized local custom, nor of law, but of jurisprudence, and it is to the decisions of native courts that help must be sought in the interpretation of Islamic law.

(*b*) *Judicial Organization and Procedure*

In Sudan communities the judicial authority is the local assembly of elders with the village head presiding. The adoption of Islam did not normally lead to any change in this procedure, but problems arose. What elements of the *sharīʿa* shall be recognized, and who is to adjudicate? Islamic law requires skilled interpretation which village assemblies do not possess, consequently customary authorities resist its encroachment. At most, when eventually certain provisions are recognized, the chief and council will consult the local clerics, but only in theocratic states were clerics raised to the status of *qāḍīs* in country districts.

In pagan societies the executive and judiciary spheres are undifferentiated, but when Islam is recognized as state religion there is a tendency towards their partial separation since interpretation of the law could theoretically be entrusted only to trained men. In practice the state made only slight concessions. It was natural that *qāḍīs* should be appointed in towns because they were outside the application of local custom, but their sphere was limited. Only difficult disputes, in which contending parties invoked both customary and Islamic law, or when an award was disputed, would be carried to the *qāḍī's* court. The first trouble provoked by the adoption of Islam generally arises when, after a death, one member of a family, in order to secure a larger share of the property, invokes its law of succession, and endless are the disputes that have arisen in consequence. In the past when this happened the clergy would be consulted but adjudication remained the function of traditional authority.

Independent communities, such as Dyula living among pagan Senufo, sometimes appointed *qāḍīs*. They were elected, like *imāms*, by the council of elders. In the Sudan states they were nominated by the ruler, and in this case were less free since the head of the state as supreme authority could receive appeals, reverse their decisions, and dispossess them. Rulers of theocratic states multiplied the number of *qāḍīs*. Shehu Ḥamadu appointed one for each of the seven wards of Ḥamdallāhi, capital of Masina, and for each country district. Judiciary organization in the state of Futa Jalon is of special interest.[1] The primary courts were those of the *misidis* (parishes), beyond them each province had a court of appeal and a court of criminal jurisdiction; and beyond these was the supreme court of the *almāmi*. Each court was made up of the territorial chief assisted by two or three notables as assessors for customary law, and two or more clerics as assessors for Islamic law. In the early days the administration of penal law belonged to the *almāmi* alone, but his powers were gradually decentralized. The territorial chief judged criminal cases in person; civil litigation was dealt with by his *qāḍī*, or he would call together the *tiku*, assembly of elders, whose judiciary role was considerable.

The *qāḍī* received a salary from the treasury and justice was theoretically free. He was required to hold regular court or audience. Sometimes a courthouse was provided by the ruler or the courtyard of the mosque was used, but more commonly he dispensed justice in his own compound. A *qāḍī* generally carries out notarial functions. He deals with the inventory and subdivision of inheritances and draws up deeds and contracts. For such services he is entitled to a fee. Formerly in Timbuktu he received a tenth of each estate he liquidated and a marriage contract cost a measure of corn and ten kolas.[2] Each judge varied in regard to procedure, and even today 'Northern Nigeria is the only territory under British control or tutelage where the Muhammedan Law of Evidence is still in force in its entirety.'[3] A litigant must produce at least one witness and confirm his disposition by his own oath, but if he can produce a number he need not swear. The Islamic oath is taken on the Qur'ān.[4] Swearing on the tomb of a saint is almost unknown

[1] See Marty, *Guinée*, pp. 364–6.

[2] Marty, *Soudan*, ii. 112.

[3] S. Vesey-Fitzgerald, *Muhammadan Law*, 1931, p. 27.

[4] European officials have not always realized that one does not actually swear on the Qur'ān, but on the word of God, and clergy would therefore advise their clients that no harm would

except at places like Timbuktu where the North African attitude to saints prevails. Trial by ordeal is forbidden by Islam, but the attitude appears where an oath on the Qur'ān is regarded as bringing punishment automatically upon the perjurer.[1] Sometimes a particular verse (v. 91 or the whole *sūra*) is recited to the one being sworn and he is made to eat a kola transfixed by a needle with which the cleric has traced the sacred text during the recitation. Swear-medicine is still resorted to in Sierra Leone and French Guinée by Muslims who wish to ensure that their oath is accepted.

Today great changes have taken place and the actual relationship of Islamic law and custom varies in the different territories.[2] The local assembly can decide only minor cases of civil justice, the more important must go before a recognized court such as the *Tribunal Coutumier* in the A.O.F. presided over by a *qāḍī* and two assessors of each 'custom'.

(*c*) *Criminal Law*

This sphere of law has never formed an important part of the studies of the higher clergy. It is ruled out in modern legislation except in Northern Nigeria which in this respect is almost unique in the modern Islamic world.[3] Penal institutions were little influenced until the advent of theocratic states, and even in them jurisdiction was not vested in the *qāḍīs*' courts but was the prerogative of the ruler or provincial governors.

Islamic criminal law is primarily concerned with the redress of wrongs by means of restitution, fines, damages, and punishments. Arrest and imprisonment was rare because under tribal law the family or village assumed responsibility for the conduct of its members. Islam brings the sense of individual responsibility into greater prominence,

arise from swearing upon the Qur'ān because the formula was incorrect. In Northern Nigeria they are said to have made use of a Qur'ān with one leaf removed to render an oath invalid.

1 As-Sa'dī recounts how *askiya* Ismā'īl (1537–9), having been afflicted with an illness, attributed it to the breaking of his oath of allegiance to the *askiya* he had deposed; 'This is no other than the work of the Qur'ān upon which I swore allegiance to *askiya* Muḥammad Benkan. It is that (Book) which has afflicted me and executed its judgement upon me. I shall not long retain my authority' (*T. as-Sūdān*, p. 94/155). C. K. Meek (*Northern Nigeria*, i. 269) writes: 'I have known of a comparatively highly educated court Malam advising a British magistrate to purchase for his court a fresh copy of the Koran, on the ground that the old one had lost its punishing power!' *Baba of Karo* (p. 181) gives an account of a man who went mad because 'he had sworn a lie' on the Qur'ān.

2 For the position in Nigeria, Ghana, Sierra Leone, and Gambia see J. N. D. Anderson, *Islamic Law in Africa*, 1954.

3 On this question and procedure in regard to criminal offences in Northern Nigeria, see J. N. D. Anderson, op. cit., pp. 195–204.

but in practice Islamic states recognized personal, family, and collective responsibility for crimes. Amputation of the limb of one convicted of theft would be regarded as tyrannical, and generally only kinless or unprotected thieves were so mutilated, but the practice was common in the theocratic and Northern Nigerian states[1] which applied the principle of personal responsibility whenever the guilty one was known and reparation by him was possible, and collective responsibility when the person was unknown or group participation was recognized. Change in attitude towards responsibility was little apparent (since Islam recognizes the responsibility of the *ʿāqila*) until the application of Western codes strengthened the tendency, and even in the Tokolor and Masina states it was customary for the whole village to accept responsibility. This question like all legal matters depended upon local custom, thus a Soninke family was responsible for the price of blood, but not necessarily for other crimes or debts.

The theoretical amount of the blood-wit (in Futa Jalon 33 oxen, but in most places 100 since Mālikī law stipulates 100 camels or 1,000 *dīnārs*) and the amount actually levied varied considerably. In Kanem 50 animals were paid by the chief, the *alifa* of Mao, and 50 by the family of the murderer, but since the *alifa*, as the reconciler, was paid back his own 50, the *dabbu* (Ar. *diya*) received by the victim's family was actually only 50.[2] Again, a slave might be reckoned as half the value of a freeman or, as in Futa Jalon, there was no fixed value and the amount was reckoned, as in the case of animals, according to such factors as age, strength, and value of services lost. In Nigeria the amount of blood-wit has become fixed in cash terms varying in different localities.[3] Adultery was too prevalent and practically impossible to prove for Islamic law to be applied. Cases would not normally come before a *qāḍī's* court, but when they did *qāḍīs* imposed a *taʿzīr* penalty, generally either flogging or a fine. Soninke, for example, imposed a fine on the man (he might also have to reimburse the bride-price) and flogging on the woman. Breaches of religious taboos (drinking intoxicants, gambling, and so forth) would not be brought to court except in

[1] The Fulani–Hausa states levied a wide range of penalties for theft: amputation, slavery fines, or payment of compensation, according to what was stolen, whether negligence was involved, and the thief's status. The position was confusing because members of professional, thief guilds were accorded special treatment.

[2] R. Bouillié, *Les Coutumes familiales au Kanem*, Paris, 1937, p. 211. Among many Moorish tribes compensation for homicide consists of two parts: *diya*, individual settlement paid to the injured party, and *tiwanin*, social reparation for having disturbed the public order, paid to the *amīr*.

[3] See J. N. D. Anderson, op. cit., p. 200.

theocratic states.[1] Under other forms of government, Muslim or European, the secular arm would not act in cases of a breach of religious law in the narrow sense. Drinking was too common to be regarded as an offence, but where notice was taken a fine was imposed. It was more important from the point of view of interpretation. In some cases drinking was regarded as aggravating an offence, in others it lessened responsibility. Islamic law does not recognize witchcraft, gravest of all crimes in African eyes, and village elders settled such questions. Some *qāḍīs* are said to have refused to try cases, whilst others applied local custom.

Execution of the decisions of the *qāḍī's* court rested with secular authority. A murderer's fate might be left to the victim's heirs (this is in accordance with the *sharīʿa*) who were free to choose retaliation, compensation, or remission. In this case the family would decide as a unit. The ruler might add his own additional penalties (sequestration, confiscation of property, or banishment) to any decision of the *sharīʿa* court.

[1] Ḥamadu of Masina appointed a *muḥtasib* in each important centre to watch over the moral conduct of the people and bring offenders before the *qāḍī*. He also had powers of summary punishment. One of his duties was to stop young men in the streets and make them perform ritual prayer, fining them for any mistakes (see Ch. Monteil, *Djénné*, p. 151).

7

The Life Cycle

SUCH events as name-giving, initiation at puberty, marriage, and death are not merely stages in the life of an individual, but affect the pattern of social life, causing the community to take special precautions in the form of transitional rites in order to safeguard its equilibrium. Though Islam is slow to influence the structure and functions of family and kinship relationships it gives these events a decisive imprint, and its practices relating to them are essentials of what Hausa call *musulumchi*, 'the Muslim way of life', as distinguished from *māguzanchi* or *jāhilchi*, 'the pagan way'. The blending of Islamic usage with local practice produces the usual parallelism. For instance, Songhay give a child its true name, in addition to the Islamic name, on the eighth day after birth when the *biya* of a paternal ancestor enters and it becomes a person. This name is kept secret until the day of circumcision.[1]

These rites vary in details, not only between each ethnic group but between classes and localities within them, therefore we shall illustrate by means of a few examples the distinctive Islamic pattern. This framework is also utilized to show how Islamic law has influenced other aspects, like marriage regulations, related to these changes of life.

1. NAMING

The mother and child remain indoors for the first seven days after birth, for the child, being unshaven and unnamed, must not be exposed to harmful influences, and the mother's fate at this stage is bound up with that of her child. The eighth day is the great festival when the child is named. The law says that it is a commendable custom (*sunna mustaḥabba*) to give the child a name, shave the hair off its head, give alms to the poor, and offer a victim as an expiatory sacrifice (*'aqīqa*). The adoption of Islam does not involve any change in respect of the day since most pagans already name on that day, but it influences the chooser or conferer of the name if this is not the father. For instance, among Khasonke, Soninke, and Songhay (Tillaberi) the father's sister and with pagan Hausa the father's younger brother chooses the name.

[1] See J. Boulnois, *Empire de Gao*, pp. 81, 84, 166.

In such cases the right changes to the father or the Muslim cleric, though often the customary person chooses the hidden name.[1] The west Sudan pattern is more elaborate than that of the centre and over a wide area is characterized by the simultaneous naming, shaving, slaughtering, and, in western Guinea, pounding of grain. In western Guinea offering of the staple food is primary, that of an animal *ʿaqīqa* being additional and secondary.

The ceremony performed by Soninke,[2] who were among the first West Africans to become Muslim, will be described first. When the sun has set the *nyamakhala* (female *griotte*) announces the ceremony to both families with the formula, 'X will go out tomorrow', and the father invites the *imām* and village notables. In the morning about eight o'clock the father arrives with his party at his mother-in-law's house. When all are gathered the cleric makes his entry and after greetings the father tells him the name of the child. The cleric then announces the name of the Muslim saint for that day who will be the child's protective saint. The women of the two families now arrive carrying presents. They enter the house, view the child, congratulate the mother, and go out to congratulate the father. Everything now being ready for the ceremony the cleric writes two amulets for protection against *jinn* and witches, which will later be sewn up and hung around the child's neck and waist. A servant brings forward the sheep and lays it down facing east, the cleric prepares his knife and the *griotte* her razor. Then the father calls out the child's name, the cleric the saint's name, the mother her special name, and at the same moment the cleric cuts the animal's throat and the *griotte* shaves.[3] In some places the *griotte* repeats the name in the child's ear, three times for a boy and four for a girl, and then carries it out to receive the blessings of clergy and elders. The shaven hair is placed in a fan along with millet, rice, and ground-nuts and presented to the cleric, who, facing east, places it before him, per-

[1] Considerable variations exist within the same people. Thus with most Songhay the mother still chooses the name and the father is not even present at the naming, but some (Woro of Tillaberi) have changed recently to the father or *alfa*.

[2] See J. H. Saint-Père, *Les Sarakollé du Guidimakha*, 1925, pp. 66–68; B. Niakaté, 'Naissance et baptême chez les Sarracolés de Bakhounou', *N. Afr.* no. 24, pp. 22–23.

[3] Khasonke (cf. C. Monteil, *Les Khassonké*, p. 398) and some northern Mandinka practise the simultaneous naming and sacrificing, but Mandinka of Kankan sacrifice the *ʿaqīqa* at a ceremony in front of the father's house whilst the women remain in the mother's compound. After this the father calls a relative or a *griot* who takes a large kola and cries as he separates it, 'A child is born to A, his father is A, his mother is B, his name is C.' All respond with formulas of blessing. Then a cleric prays and songs in honour of the Prophet are sung. Whilst this is in progress an announcer goes to the women's compound to inform the women of the name. Afterwards comes the distribution of the sacrificial ram, feasting, singing, and dancing.

forms the ritual prayers, and says prayers on behalf of the child and family. Both families must share in the communion of the sacrifice which is divided in traditional fashion.

Throughout western Guinea, by diffusion from the Fulbe of Futa Jalon, grain is pounded[1] simultaneously with the other forms. The *karamoko* places his knife on the animal's throat, recites the ritual formula, and at the same moment as he calls out the name and cuts, the pestles pound and the grandmother shaves. When the pounded rice has been soaked and moulded into balls the cleric 'makes *sadaka*' by placing his hand on it and praying. After consecration it is shared among all entitled to receive a portion. In Futa Jalon the child is carried round the house three times by the mother followed by women carrying swords, knives, and the like if a boy, and women's utensils and ornaments if a girl. The animal sacrifice is often omitted by poorer people but the rice communion is essential.[2]

Dyula of Bonduku celebrate the naming in a special place reserved for such ceremonies.[3] The *almāmi* says: 'May all Muslims present bear witness. May the Spirit of the Sky bear witness. May the Spirit of the Earth bear witness. God has given a boy to A. His father has given him such a name. The name he has given is a Muslim name. We who are present bear witness. It is Muḥammad who orders us all.' He repeats this thrice, then prays that all present may be blessed with children, that ancestors may be granted Paradise, and the child richly blessed. Kola is distributed and a messenger sent with a white and red nut to the women of the husband's *lu* to announce the child's name.[4] The barber shaves and circumcizes the child. The sheep has been killed during the proceedings and the feast proceeds. After it the women hold their own naming ceremony when the grandmother repeats the same formula as the *almāmi*.

Among Songhay of Gao region the father is not present at the

[1] The ritual sacrificial *tyobbal* or *kodde* of the Fulbe consists of little cakes made of crushed millet, maize, or rice, with fresh milk, and sweetened with sugar or honey. This is essential in all these family ceremonies. The sacrificial animal is called in Fulbe *sunna hindē*; *sunna* = Islamic custom, *hindē* = the Islamic name; the ethnic name is called *yettodē*.

[2] With recently islamized Mende the father invites the cleric to 'take the child out of doors'. He carries it a little distance mumbling prayers, names it silently, returns and hands it to the mother saying: 'His (her) name is X.' This name is still often kept secret. There is no shaving or sacrifice, but Mandinka living among them perform the full rite and this is being copied by more affluent Mende.

[3] See L. Tauxier, *Le Noir du Bondoukou*, p. 251.

[4] Kola nuts have an important ceremonial function in West African Islamic life. They are associated with all these transition rites as on other ceremonial occasions.

ceremony (*bongo kyebu*, 'shaving the head') but sends representatives. Two rosaries (formerly rings) are given to the *alfa* who attributes a name to each, one from the father's and the other from the mother's ancestors. The rosaries are taken to the mother to choose one which will be the child's name. The *alfa* pronounces the name and prays, the animal is sacrificed and women shave the child. Others (Goundam region) perform the shaving first, then the hair is carried to the *alfa* who pronounces a blessing with spitting (*sumburku*), the sheep is brought, the cleric asks the father for the name, and his assistant pronounces it and cuts simultaneously.[1]

The Hausa ceremony (*ran suna*, 'naming-day') is held in the *zaure* (entrance hut), usually at the father's house. The women remain secluded in the compound. An old woman brings out the child, the *naibi* kills the sheep (female for a girl, male for a boy), and whispers the *ādhān* and name (chosen by the parents) in the ear of the child.[2] Then he tells it to the *limān* who says, 'let us offer prayers for the Prophet ten times'. He prays in Arabic, repeats the Fātiḥa three times and says, 'we name this child A. May God prolong his life . . .', followed by prayer in Hausa. After the name has been conferred it is customary for beggars to shout it out for the women to hear. The shaving is done the next day when the barber also cuts out the child's uvula (customary among Hausa and Kanuri) and makes the tribal markings.[3] Kanuri do not produce the child at the naming ceremony, but after it the muezzin enters the house and repeats the *ādhān* and name in the child's ear. When the presiding

[1] See *Bull. I.F.A.N.* xvi (1954), 200–1, 204.

[2] Many Hausa still distinguish between a person's real (and secret) name (*sunan fito* or *sunan yanka*) given on the eighth day, and the known name (*sunan wāsā*). This is inherited from pagan custom for *azna* give a child a secret name known only to its parents and itself later, and another chosen according to the season at which it was born. Similarly among other peoples the Islamic name, where it is the personality name, may not always be pronounced, and consequently each Islamic name has its synonym. In Mande languages Gafurē is a synonym for Ḥawā', Binti or Dyāti for Fāṭima, Sad'ya ('resurrection') for ʿAlī, Basaru for Abū Bakr, Bāru or Demba for ʿUmar, and Kutubu for Ibrāhīm. It was reported that the Islamic naming is adopted by pagan Bambara in order to provide a known name.

[3] The ceremony of peoples influenced by Hausa (Nupe, Yoruba, Dagomba) follows the same general lines and is called by the same name, *suna*. Dagomba rarely sacrifice a sheep and their ceremonies, like those of the western cycle, are characterized by the use of sacrificial grain called *gumba*, used at namings, funerals, and expiatory almsgivings, but never at marriages. It consists of millet (sometimes rice) pounded with sugar or honey, and made into balls which must not be cooked. Nupe send a delegate with a gift of kolas to the cleric the day before the ceremony (*tu suna* or *tu kaye*) to ask him to officiate. Before daybreak the father and mother whisper the name in the ear of the sleeping child. In the morning the cleric arrives and first kills the ram, then sits in the entrance hut where the company have assembled, and the father brings 40 kolas and money and whispers to him the name. The cleric names the child and prays, and a barber shaves, circumcises, and makes the tribal markings.

cleric proclaims the Qur'ānic name he places his hand upon a dish-cover made of plaited strips of palm leaves filled with millet.[1]

After the birth of a child the mother is ritually impure. Her period of seclusion varies. Among some people she is freed after the naming, but there is a strong pull to adopt the Islamic forty-day period during which she is not permitted to perform the prayers.

2. ISLAMIC EDUCATION

As the child participates in the life of his family and village he is being trained unconsciously towards full participation. In addition to this natural atmospheric training there are the narrower, consciously-directed Qur'ānic and circumcision schools. The place the Qur'ān school occupies in the structure of West African Islam has been treated under the heading of the training of the cleric. Here we are concerned with it from pupil's aspect.

The object of the school is not primarily the initiation of the child into community life but simply memorization of the Qur'ān by which power is gained in this world and reward in the next. This is accompanied by instruction in the formal duties of Islam. Few villages or nomad encampments are without such a school. In many places both boys and girls attend from about the age of six, the girls being withdrawn after one or two years and not later than the age of ten when they have learnt the mechanism of prayer and one or two short *sūras*.[2] Parents who wish their sons to go to a Western-type school generally send them to the Qur'ān school for a year first. Although most families like to have one or two attending, the majority of the farming folk do not want too many children engaged in memorization. Farm work comes first and during the seasons of intense agricultural activity many schools close down since parents are not prepared to provide the cleric with the unpaid labour which they need themselves. During the season of growth the children often live permanently on the cultivation, engaged in such tasks as scaring birds and marauding monkeys from growing crops. Qur'ān schools are consequently difficult to find, they rarely function except very early in the morning and after nightfall, whilst they have many holidays.

Children are taught in the open air in front of the master's house or

[1] R. E. Ellison, 'Marriage and Child-birth among the Kanuri', *Africa*, ix (1936), 534.

[2] Where women hold an important place in society as among Moors the mother will insist on her daughters carrying their slates along with boys. Among Negroes girls are most evident in schools in Bornu and Futa Jalon.

under a tree. During the rains, if pupils are not out on the master's cultivation, classes are held in a hut or veranda, but rarely in the mosque (following a pronouncement of Mālik ibn Anas) contrary to the practice in eastern countries. The numbers are generally small, about ten or under. Ages may vary from six to eighteen, consequently they are not arranged in classes since each is at a different stage. There are usually two sessions, in the early morning and evening, though at certain seasons they may be increased to three. Times and periods vary between town and country. In towns periods are generally from 7 to 10 a.m. and 2 to 5 p.m. In villages children living at home are more tied to the rhythm of village life. In Futa Jalon the pupil goes to the teacher's house very early, finds his slate and begins to chant his lesson without disturbing the master who sleeps on until seven. From eight until midday pupils work in the master's fields or help his women in their household tasks. From 2 to 4 p.m. they have a second session and then go into the bush to collect wood for the evening fires. The third session is after nightfall from 6.30 to 8.00. Children studying by the light of the fires has struck the imagination of the Mende whose expression for Qur'ān-students is *kandama lopoisia*, 'children around the fire'. Pupils are left much to themselves and work intermittently, playing and chatting together, whilst the master carries on with other occupations, entertains visitors, and sleeps.

The Moorish custom of taking a holiday from midday Wednesday until after the Friday prayer has been universally adopted. Some clergy say one must not teach during this period because *jinn* are learning the Qur'ān. Those in western Guinea say the Thursday holiday is in commemoration of that given by the Prophet to children of Medina upon his son-in-law 'Alī's return from a successful expedition, whilst the Friday holiday is for the master's benefit. There are also other calendar holidays. In Futa Jalon they keep the month of Shawwāl, ten days at 'Ashūrā, the two great feasts, and 26–27 Rajab, 'the day the Prophet visited the seven heavens and seven hells'. In addition, when a pupil attains certain stages in the recitation of the Qur'ān, a holiday is given to the whole school. In some parts these are four, at the end of each 15 *aḥzāb*;[1] in Futa Jalon six, after each section of 10 *aḥzāb*. Generally there are two major individual festivals, one midway and the other on

[1] The Qur'ān is divided into 60 *aḥzāb*, sing. *ḥizb*. Each *ḥizb* is divided into eighths (Ar. *thumn*) and the average pupil learns half a *thumn* a day. Taking holidays into account a minimum of four years is needed to learn the Qur'ān by heart. The second period of primary teaching, which few undertake unless intending to become teachers, consists of going through the Qur'ān again to learn its meaning. This likewise takes a minimum of four years.

completing the Qur'ān.[1] Children are often confided to a master and work for him until they get married. Sometimes he takes his pupils[2] on begging tours during the dry season. In Hausaland they last about three to four months. The length of stay in each village is determined by the generosity of the villagers and the liveliness of trade in amulets.

The master's recompense takes various forms. It is the convention that the Qur'ān must not be taught for money, but the teacher may accept gifts. The pupil takes one when he is first sent to school. He is expected to bring something, a handful of millet, maize, or kola, every Wednesday. Substantial presents of sheep or cattle are made at individual festival stages. But the most important remuneration is the farm work the master gets out of his pupils. The rainy season falls heavily on them. If the fields are any distance from the village they live there for five days, returning home from midday Wednesday until Friday. Classes, if they continue, are confined to one evening session. A Hausa who has been through the mill writes upon this side of the pupil's life:

I want to explain our relation with our teacher during the years of Koran schooling. The teacher's treatment of us is often so harsh that it causes us to take no interest in our lessons. Besides learning, we are forced to perform hard tasks which are so burdensome that they make us stupid with tiredness. We sometimes do simple domestic work: the teacher making us spin his wife's cotton, grind corn, fetch drinking water, bring bundles of grass from the bush, etc. His wife becomes too proud to do any work besides cooking.

In the rainy season many teachers treat us as harshly at working as slaves. Any idea of learning is put aside and we are led to the bush and made to cut a farm of a great extent for us to work. As the rainy season approaches, he drives us daily to the bush in order to prepare the vast farm. Then we start tilling the soil for growing crops.

We continue doing the same thing up to the time of harvest. So at the middle of this season the only possible time for learning is during the night when we want to rest after the labours of the day. On account of tiredness you find some of us falling asleep and knowing nothing of the work. We even forget some of our old lessons during this season.[3]

[1] The boy in festival dress accompanied by his father and family-head proceeds to the cleric's house where the notables have assembled. The cleric has prepared a slate with a verse and decorations, the boy reads the verse, the family-head presents money and kola to the cleric and company, and the former prays aloud for the boy. The next day the boy and his friends promenade the village, visiting each family, reciting his verse, and receives a gift. All the gifts are taken to the master. This ceremony is almost identical everywhere in West Africa.

[2] Hausa *almāgirī* (Ar. *al-muhājir*), itinerant pupil. See the account of Malam Maigari's teaching expeditions in M. Smith, *Baba of Karo*, pp. 131–4.

[3] J. Bala Abuja, 'Koranic and Moslem Law Teaching in Hausaland', *Nigeria*, no. 37 (1951), pp. 27–28.

Corporal punishment is a feature of Hausa schools. Pupils who run away are severely punished. Recalcitrant boys are sometimes tied to a tree and left for several days with little to eat until cowed and submissive. Others are not so harsh as Hausa. Fulbe *karamokos* of Futa Jalon and Masina, for instance, treat their pupils with great kindness.

Marty gives a description of the method of teaching in Futa Jalon.[1] It comprises two sections: *dyangugol*, 'reading' and *windugol*, 'writing'. Reading is divided into three parts. The first is *ba* or the alphabet. The teacher writes the first word of the Qur'ān, *bismi*, on the slate and teaches him to chant it, and so on throughout the Fātiḥa; then starting with the last *sūra* (CXIV) works in reverse order to CIV (10 *aḥzāb*). That ends *ba*, all the letters in their various positions having been covered. Next they return to the Fātiḥa for pronunciation and cover the same section. After that it is gone over a third time for *fineditugol* or *rindingol*, reading proper. When this is completed they celebrate the first festival. *Windugol* or writing[2] is begun at some stage during reading and the two are taught concurrently. Fulbe of Futa Jalon are unique in that after the pupil has learnt to write he is given a copy of the Qur'ān from which he transcribes a section every day. Memorization of the whole Qur'ān is not common except among Moorish clerical tribes. Those Negroes who complete it generally become teachers. Only Moors, Tokolor, Kanuri, and Fulbe of Futa Jalon conduct an examination, the latter requiring a complete recitation before two clerics.

3. CIRCUMCISION

The customs of circumcision and excision are anterior to the introduction of Islam, both being practised by the majority of peoples in the Sudan belt. Where performed at puberty circumcision formed part of the rites of initiation whose purpose was to bring to birth the complete social individual. Islam seeks to destroy former religious associations with which the rite was closely bound up, but clerics are not so opposed to age-group societies, contenting themselves with eliminating their religious functions whereby, though retreats and age-grades continue, they lose their former place in the life of the community.

These rites were never supernaturalized in Islam. They are not mentioned in the Qur'ān and jurists regard the *ḥadīth* material as very

[1] P. Marty, *Guinée*, pp. 349–51.

[2] Pupils make their own reed pens and ink. European ink is unacceptable for writing the Qur'ān and above all must not be used for amulets. Tablets are known by a corruption of Ar. *al-lawḥ*, Hausa *allo*, W. Guinea *allua*, Fulfulde *hallu-al* or *wallu-al*, Soninke *walakha*, Mandinka *walar̃a*.

weak. The *Risāla* of Ibn Abī Zaid followed by West Africans says that circumcision is obligatory (*wājiba*) and excision (*khifāḍ*) 'commendable'. The effect of Islam is to desacralize circumcision, it is simply *sunna* or islamized custom.[1] Clerics relate stories of how Abraham circumcised himself after receiving a command from God, and how one of his wives excised a Negro concubine of whom he was too fond. Through such stories clergy represent the rites as ordained by God, not practised merely because the ancestors did them. The custom is therefore transformed into an Islamic purification rite. Usually the cleric is not involved, though in certain regions he performs the operation, accompanying it with prayer incantation which brings Islam into the former transition rite.

The school in the sacred grove has a deep psychological effect upon the young. Its destruction by Islam without the substitution of an equivalent institution may leave youth without guidance and training as to their place and function in society. But although Islam has no real equivalent it has the rite of circumcision, initiation into manhood, and the neo-Muslim is not subject to the taunt of 'uncircumcised'. Where performed at puberty circumcision embraces two aspects in that it opens the way for both the sexual and social life. It is the rite of circumcision-initiation in that it confers upon the youth adult Muslim status as is shown by the fact that he can join in ritual prayer and keep the fast;[2] and, although impoverished of essential ritual, the ceremony retains adjuncts surrounding a transition rite, including some form of withdrawal.[3] Circumcision is now initiation into the community of Islam,[4] not merely recognition of change of status in the local community.

West African jurists are disagreed about the age at which circumcision should be performed. Some assert that the Prophet selected the seventh day after birth, failing that the fortieth day, and failing that the seventh year. All these are followed, whether practised in infancy or at puberty depending upon former custom or economic circumstances. Yoruba, Nupe, Dagomba, Wala, and the majority of Dyula circumcise either at the naming or fortieth day, though this is blameworthy

[1] Hence the Pular name *sunnigol* or *sugol*. It is significant that no Islamic terminology has been adopted by other peoples whose terms are descriptive or euphemistic.

[2] Hence the Mande term *bolo-ku*, 'washing of the hand', for circumcision, and *sali-de*, 'child of prayer' for 'newly-circumcised'.

[3] The nature of the initiation bush among Muslim Mandinka of Kouroussa is shown in Camera Laye's account of his early life in *The Dark Child*, English tr. 1955, chs. 7 and 8.

[4] It is therefore adopted by those who do not have the practice. Thus the few islamized Kulango follow the custom of the Dyula from whom their Islam came in circumcising on the eighth day and in not excising girls.

according to Khalīl. When performed on the eighth day it naturally has a different character since conferring the name is to become a human being. When performed at a later age, and this is the general rule in the Sudan,[1] it is regarded as a transition rite from infancy to virility. In general, a group of the village community, often connected with the system of age-groups, is circumcised at the same time. When practised on infants it is a family ceremony only, as with Wolof clergy who circumcise on the eighth day and also Moors who do it at a later age. That is the general tendency of Islam to concentrate the rite within the family group and thus weaken it as a cohesive element of the local group. The degree to which it is bound up with the system of age-grades hinders this change.

Among long-islamized the boys simply keep a retreat of two or three weeks in a special hut or under a tree on the outskirts of the village. Magical elements are involved. Among Songhay[2] the village *alfa* finds the propitious day and hour for the collective circumcision (*bangu sola*) and performs magical rites to charm away harmful influences. The candidates are fed on special gruel for the three preceding days and traditional songs chanted to a cadence provided by 'striking the ground' (*dyabu*) with a special stick. The operation is done by the local barber and the boys live in a shelter (*sola*) during the period of healing. They choose a chief (*falanga*) who is the first to be operated on and is expected to show the others an example of stoicism. After the retreat is over the village belongs to them and they parade in men's clothing, red cap and amulets, visiting friends and relations who allow them considerable licence in pocketing what they fancy and in slaughtering any chickens they meet.

4. MARRIAGE AND ITS DISSOLUTION

Whilst all West Africans admit polygamy its practice is restricted by such factors as wealth and woman's role in family and economic life.

[1] Circumcision: Moors and Tuareg *c.* 7th year; Wolof 9–14 (pagan Serer 22–25); Songhay 10–12 (some circumcise at an early age 1–2, 5–6); Masina region *c.* 7; Fulbe, Soninke, Tokolor, Bozo, some Dyula, Mandinka, Hausa 8–15; Teda 12–13. Excision: Moors and some Soninke 7th day, Songhay of Dori *c.* 2, Masina 2–7, Tokolor 4–8, Hausa 7–9, some Soninke and most others at puberty 10–12, or at time of marriage (e.g. northern Dyula). Excision is not performed by nomadic Fulbe, Teda, Arma, and Shurafā' of Jenne and Timbuktu, Wolof, most Songhay, Tuareg, Dagomba, and southern Dyula. Kanembu women have only adopted the practice during the last fifty years. Settled Fulbe conform to the practice of the Negroes among whom they live.

[2] On circumcision and excision among Songhay see Dupuis-Yakouba, *La Langue Songhaï*, art. *bangu*, p. 118; Marty, *Soudan*, ii. 114–17, 286–90; H. Miner, *The Primitive City of Timbuktu*, pp. 158–64; J. Boulnois, *Empire de Gao*, pp. 164–9.

Pastoral nomadic life, with its poverty, woman's independence and modest economic role, does not necessitate the institution so much as agricultural life with its need for many hands to work on the farm and in the home. Islam stresses a husband's duty to support his wife and its tendency is to free women from agricultural work, consequently where it has had this effect polygamy is largely a luxury, depending on wealth and prestige. Customary taboos also tended to justify polygamy. Sexual relations are often forbidden during pregnancy and suckling, and the latter may last from two to three years. Custom seeks to avoid adultery and prostitution by providing legitimate alternatives.

Islam allows unlimited polygamy, but regulates it by introducing two categories of wives, usually referred to as legal wives and concubines, more correctly 'slave-wives'. Both are legitimate and are so regulated by Islamic law. If 'marriage is a union between a man and a woman such that children born to the woman are the recognized legitimate off-spring of both partners',[1] then Islamic 'concubinage' is a form of marriage, although slave-wives do not have the status of consorts. Islam limits the number of free women taken as wives at any one time to four, but the number of secondary wives of slave origin who may be possessed is unlimited. Only men, therefore, in higher status groups have this unlimited freedom of choice.

Regulations relating to marriage vary considerably among different peoples according to the tenacity of custom and the strength of Islamic pressure towards change. In some cases a *modus vivendi* is arrived at. For example, the girl's consent is required before the conclusion of the marriage contract, but because of the ramifications of marriage as a system of alliances and the practice of child betrothal, custom may not recognize this, and in consequence many apply the Islamic right of matrimonial constraint (*jabr*) with the utmost rigour. This right be-longs to the father or, in default of him, his eldest son, or testamentary guardian.[2] Custom may modify these regulations; thus among Soninke after the father's death his brother, not his eldest son, has the right of *jabr*. According to Islamic law the future of the divorcée or widow is in her own hands, but in practice may be decided by the family of her deceased husband. Among Hausa, who rigidly exercise the right of

[1] *Notes and Queries on Anthropology*, 1951, p. 110.

[2] The right of *jabr*, much severer in the Mālikī than in other schools, may be modified by enactments of colonial governments. The *Décret Mandel* (1939), which applies to the A.O.F. and A.É.F., decrees (art. 2) that 'le consentement des futurs époux est indispensable à la validité du mariage'; and fixes the minimum ages for contracting marriage at fourteen for a girl and sixteen for a boy.

jabr, women seek divorce because they are then free to follow their own inclinations.

The main difference between custom and Islamic law is found in the categories of permitted and prohibited. Long-islamized (Tokolor, Soninke, Kanembu, and Kanuri) observe strictly the Islamic categories of prohibited persons and even *kafā'a* (marriage equality) regulations,[1] but difficulties arise with newly islamized over questions of affinity. Many consider first cousin marriage to be incestuous, for cousins are regarded as brothers and sisters, but Islam encourages marriage with both cross and parallel cousins[2] and this practice is frequent among the long-islamized. When Islam begins to affect the system of inheritance such marriages become more frequent by way of compensation, since they help to keep property within the same family and reinforce the disintegrating extended family. Islam thus affects rules on exogamous marriage by its preference for in-marriage. Little notice is taken of Islamic regulations on religious endogamy. Muslims everywhere marry pagan women for 'the intention is that they should become Muslims'. The law enacts that no Muslim woman may marry a non-Muslim, but many[3] not infrequently give their daughters to pagans.

The Islamic Marriage Contract. African marriage is primarily an arrangement between two families, not between two individuals. It is characterized by the payment of a bride-price as guarantee of stability and compensation to the wife's family for the loss of one of its members. Islamic practice, on the contrary, involves two individuals, whilst the purpose of marriage-money is entirely different. Khalīl writes, '*Ṣadāq* is analogous to sale-price',[4] and the conditions are similar to those attached to a sale, for when a woman marries she sells part of her person. The form is the same as for any other contract, with offer and acceptance before witnesses. *Ṣadāq* is legally the property of the wife and there would appear to be grounds for conflict here since its adoption

[1] The *kafā'a* regulations are useful in justifying African prohibited grades. Thus Moors like Sudanese, will not give their daughters to a caste-man, nor will clerical tribes give their daughters to an Arab warrior, though a cleric can marry a warrior girl.

[2] Hausa *auren zumunta*, Kanuri *nyiga durbe*, 'kinship marriage'.

[3] Even Tokolor, cf. *Coutumiers juridiques*, ii. 262. Marty mentions the 'many Fula nobles including certain Almāmis of Timbo, Alfas of Labe, and important Tokolor, who have married heathen wives and have never made them do salam. 'Ajību, almāmi of Dingiray [1876–92], married a *kāfira* who continued to practise fetishist rites in the conjugal *gallé* (compound). Moreover, he married his daughter Kadijatu to a Malinké chief of Sigirinde (Sigiri), and she soon gave up prayer and ate and drank like her husband. Such examples are frequent in Futa, and, if one believes public rumour, tend today to increase' (Marty, *Guinée*, pp. 382–3).

[4] Khalīl, *Mukhtaṣar*, tr. Santillana, ii. 41.

to the exclusion of custom would undermine the social purpose of marriage-money. However, the difficulty has been circumvented. The *ṣadāq*[1] is introduced into the indigenous bride-price system of payment by the bridegroom to the bride's kin. Two aspects are underlined—transference of the woman to another family and a payment to her for the loss of her virginity. It is not necessary to pay all the bride-price at once but the amount must be announced and a minimum sum (in addition to the legal *ṣadāq*) paid, the remainder being paid at intervals or only at the dissolution of the marriage. In addition, the indigenous system generally involves provision of a dowry, and there is a difference here between the western and central cycles. In the west the dowry is remitted by the future husband to his fiancée, in the centre it is property brought by the wife to the marriage.[2]

In the west the following is the general pattern. When a man wishes to contract a consort marriage (Mandinka *furu ba*, 'big marriage') he transfers animals, goods, and money to the bride's family. This 'bride-price' (Mand. *furu sara* or *furu sõngo*) is handed over in two parts, the first when the contract is definitely concluded (*furu loṙo la*, the Islamic ceremony) and the rest, either when the husband takes possession of the wife, or, more commonly, only if he divorces her. Besides the bride-price the husband provides his wife with a dowry (*furu fe*), the principal portion of which (chiefly materials) is sent during the day preceding the consummation; and the rest (toilet articles and food for the feast) during the following week. The dowry is the wife's personal property. If she obtains a divorce the 'bride-price' must be returned, but she retains the dowry. When the husband repudiates the wife the bride-price is generally retained or acquired by the wife's family, though sometimes the unpaid part is not claimed.

Whilst among Mandinka the bride-price is very high, goes to the bride's family, and is paid over a long period, among Dyula it is small (the *ṣadāq*), goes to the bride, and is paid immediately. The bridegroom, of course, has to provide customary presents to bride and family. With Soninke the bride-price belongs to the bride's family,[3] but pre-nuptial

[1] Mālik fixed the minimum *ṣadāq* very low at 3 dirhems and West African jurists are much exercised at estimating this in terms of modern money.

[2] Arab. *niḥla*. There are many exceptions. The latter is the practice of Tokolor and Fulbe in Futa Jalon (*futtē*, bride-price; *soggē* dowry), cf. Marty, *Guinée*, pp. 383, 421. Among Tokolor of Senegalese Futa the whole (including the *ṣadāq* called *teŋe*) is known as *nafore* (Ar. *nafūʿ*), and guarantees the stability of the union. Part of this is turned over to the bride as her dowry. If she seeks divorce the *nafore*, with the exception of the *teŋe*, is restored to the husband.

[3] See *Coutumiers juridiques de l' A.O.F.*, 1939, ii. 218. Soninke of Gidimaka have been

presents, consisting of clothing and household utensils, all go to form her trousseau. Tokolor correctly turn the announced price over to the bride as her nuptial money, but there are always obligatory 'gifts' of animals or money which must be made to the bride's family.

To turn to the central Sudan. At the Hausa marriage (*auran sunna*) the 'marriage money' (*kuḍin aure*) provided by the man consists of:

kuḍin sallama, money for calling (or *kuḍin gaisuwa*).
kuḍin baiwa, acceptance of which signifies that the parents consent to the betrothal (*tashi*).
kuḍin ada'a, thanks-money to the parents.
kuḍin sa rana, money for fixing the day.
kuḍin sadāki (Ar. *ṣadāq*) or *kuḍin sunna*, the essential Islamic payment.[1]

In addition there is *gāra*, the bride's dowry, provided by her kinsfolk, consisting of food, clothing, mats, and cooking utensils. Engagement has a juridical value in custom (though not in Islamic law) in that certain gifts to the bride's parents are recoverable if the girl repudiates the man before marriage (*tāda kangara*), but if she gets a divorce after its consummation the husband could only recover the *sadāki* (less the actual *ṣadāq*) in the past, though now they claim many of the gifts. If the husband repudiates the wife after marriage he can claim nothing and has to pay over any unpaid portion of the marriage money.

Kanuri have three main payments:[2] *kororam*, asking money, only paid if the bride is a virgin; *lugaliram*, the protector's (*lugali*) money, when the date is fixed; and *sadagə*, bride-price, traditionally the value of a slave. When not paid in full the bridegroom must pay *marbi*, regarded

more influenced by Islamic law in that the bride-price is paid by the husband to the wife and belongs to her; cf. J. H. Saint-Père, op. cit., p. 107.

[1] Variations in categories and terminology exist even in the same district, but this gives the general outline. The following are the Nupe terms with the average sums paid in 1952:

Ewó yàwo, bride-price, consists of:
ewó ejiṇda, greeting gift (10*s*.–£3), to seal the betrothal.
godiwagi, 'small thanks' (£1).
godiwako, 'great thanks' (£2).
sàdeki, bride-price proper (average £10), combined with *ṣadāq* (legal minimum said to be 1*s*. 6*d*. or 10*s*.). If the wife gains a divorce this alone is returned.
ewó dangiži, kinship money (£2).
ewó gwada, help money (for the girl's mother, £1).
Money for henna, hair plaiting, bridesmaids, &c.

Yiji yàwo, dowry. This may balance or exceed the bride-price, and consists of clothes, household utensils, food, and the like.

[2] See R. E. Ellison, 'Marriage and Child-birth among the Kanuri', *Africa*, ix (1936), 527–8.

as a token payment but actually the Islamic minimum *ṣadāq*. After the contract ceremony the bride's parents send the bridegroom presents (*fafərai*) of money and clothes which may exceed all the pre-marriage payments made by him; and in addition have to provide the bride with a dowry of household utensils and clothing.

Diversity of practice is found among Songhay. Those in Gao region never omit the bride's *ṣadāq*, whilst others do. The *idyey alman* ('marriage wealth'), traditionally two to four cattle, is paid to the bride's parents, but her family build and furnish a house for her, whilst many give her a dowry (*noyandi*) of cattle. The *imghaden* (vassal pastoral tribes of the Tuareg) pay *tāggult* of two camels to the bride's parents, but they in turn give her a dowry which often exceeds the *tāggalt*. At the Yoruba Islamic marriage (*iso yigi*) there are three principal elements. Traditional bride-wealth paid to the bride's family (called *owo-idano*, 'betrothal money'); the essential Islamic payment, *yigi*, from which Muslim marriage derives its name, divorce being termed *itu yigi* 'untying the *yigi* contract;' and finally, *sadak*, dowry given by husband to wife.

Secondary Marriages. (*a*) *Slave-wives*. According to Islamic law a free woman may not be taken as a concubine, nor may an owner marry his own slave. Strictly speaking, slave-marriage should have ceased with the elimination of slavery, but jurists do not recognize the suppression of slave status by colonial governments, therefore a Muslim may take concubines from descendants of former slaves. Nor is the limitation to the descendants of slaves always followed. Fulani of Northern Nigeria regard the *talakāwa* class as a field of exploitation. If any *talaka* sends a girl to a chief and she is accepted she becomes a *sāḍaka*[1] in that house. Others are obtained by the payment of what is called *ṣadāq* but which the parents keep. The cleric is supposed to be told of these arrangements so that the children will be reckoned as legitimate. In the past the slave who gave birth to a child was no longer a *jāriya* but *umm walad*, and became free after the death of her master. The position and rights of a slave-wife vary considerably, for the jurists are not in agreement. Thus the Dyula slave-wife shares her husband's bed three days instead of six, but strict Mālikīs give her equal bed-rights. After the death of her master her period of *'idda* is two months five days, half that of a free woman.

(*b*) *Nikāḥ Mut'a*, translated 'marriage for pleasure' by Hausa (*auran jin dāḍī*), is a marriage contracted for a previously stipulated period and

[1] *Sāḍaka* = *jāriya*; *sā*, place in, *ḍaka*, house.

is illegal in Sunnī law. If a trader already has four wives, but does not wish to take any one of them with him on his travels for fear of inciting jealousy or because they are strictly *kullē* (secluded), he will arrange a temporary marriage with a fifth. He informs a cleric that none of his wives can travel with him and he wishes to take a temporary wife. He arranges for the cleric to be in the *zaurē* or entrance hut[1] of his compound at the time he leaves it to commence his journey and is married for the period of the journey. The clerics connive at the practice for, they say, 'he has renounced his wives for that period', interpreting liberally the ambiguous Qur'ānic passage in Sūrat an-Nisā', verse 28. On his return the divorce is automatic when, at the *zaurē*, he hands her the previously stipulated *mut'a* (consolatory gift), though it is always called *sadāki*.

Such travellers' marriages (Hausa *auran matafi*) are frequent in towns like Timbuktu,[2] Jenne,[3] and Kano. It is the practice in Hausa towns for prostitutes to contract a *mut'a* marriage for the month of Ramaḍān, the divorce being automatic once the new moon appears. In Kano city, during the two days' licence on the eve of Ramaḍān, thousands of such marriages are contracted. Similarly in Nupeland, 'a man living with a married woman[4] must marry her in Ramaḍān because the law says adultery is wrong during that month'. Although she is already married a cleric performs a conditional marriage for that month only.

(*c*) *Widow Inheritance*. Many peoples do not regard marriage as being dissolved by death, consequently conflict may arise between custom and Islamic law when the future of the widow comes to be decided. Islam rules that widows are free to marry whom they please, but custom may rule that at marriage the wife has broken with her own family and joined that of her husband, the bride-price being the compensation for her loss to the clan. When her husband dies she continues to belong to his group and return to her family would involve restitution of the bride-price. The brother of the deceased is responsible for her protection and has the duty of raising up progeny to him, therefore he does not need to marry her. Islamic pressure is against this custom,[5] but

[1] Whence this kind of temporary marriage is also called *auran zaurē*. It seems to be distinct from *aurən fālo*, 'veranda marriage'.

[2] H. Miner, *The Primitive City of Timbuktu*, pp. 197–8.

[3] C. Monteil, *Djénné*, 1932, pp. 126–7. Ibn Baṭṭūṭa refers to this custom being practised at Walāta.

[4] A common practice among Nupe trading women (cf. Nadel, op. cit., p. 152). Usually the husbands do not divorce them, either because they are dependent upon their earnings or cannot repay the marriage-price.

[5] Cf. Qur'ān, iv. 23 and 26. But marriage with a brother's widow, provided she agrees, is

many islamized peoples retain it; among Mandinka it is obligatory. Western rule has strengthened Islamic law in respect of such questions, for the widow's right of refusal is upheld in modern legislation as in Islamic law.

Little breach with custom is found among more recently islamized. Muslim Yoruba simply accept the widow into the brother's household. This is legal according to Yoruba custom, but illegal according to Islam since there is no fresh contract and no *ṣadāq*. Inheritance follows customary rules and no complications arise on that score. A cleric who already has four wives will waive his claim to the widow in favour of another brother, or he may divorce one of his wives and have a contract ceremony performed with a token *ṣadāq*. But this is rare since it is Yoruba custom that the marriage ceremony can never be repeated. Among Nupe divorce was formerly impossible and if the husband died a member of his family inherited his wife. When a Muslim Nupe dies the family chief sometimes settles the widow's future in traditional fashion, but many now assert their freedom to marry. Among Bozo the future of the widow depends upon who is her husband's heir. If it is a younger brother then the marriage is not dissolved and the family retain the bride-price, but if an elder brother then the marriage is automatically dissolved and the bride-price is returned. The custom persists even among some long islamized, such as Fulbe in Futa Jalon and Dyula. Marty writes:

> The levirate is normally practised in Fula country, as it is also in Dingiray and in the Malinké colonies of Futa Jalon. Tokolor, however, being more faithful observers of the Qur'ān, do not regard the levirate, like the Fula, as an almost obligatory institution. Practically every Fula who has not yet four wives, admits among the number of his legitimate wives the widow of his elder or younger brother.[1]

(*d*) *Marriage by Gift* is found among Khasonke,[2] Songhay,[3] Kanuri,[4] and Hausa,[5] who have introduced it among Nupe and Yoruba.[6] A man

not forbidden in Islamic law. It is common among Moors where the proportional distribution of the estate follows the Islamic rules, for thereby the brother secures control of the widow's share, minute though it is, as controller of her and her children.

[1] P. Marty, *Guinée*, p. 373. See also H. Gaden, *Proverbes et maximes peuls et toucouleurs*, 1931, p. 20. [2] *Allāh manyo*, 'Allah's bride'; see C. Monteil, *Les Khassonké*, pp. 400–1.

[3] See *Coutumiers juridiques de l'A.O.F.* ii. 318.

[4] Kanuri *nyiga maləmla*, 'malam marriage'; R. E. Ellison, 'Marriage and Child-birth among the Kanuri', *Africa*, ix (1936), 526–7.

[5] Hausa *Auren sadaka*. See J. N. D. Anderson, *Islamic Law in Africa*, p. 208; Mary Smith, *Baba of Karo*, pp. 99–100, 151–4.

[6] See S. Johnson, *History of the Yorubas*, Lagos, 1937, pp. 116–17. This custom has suffered a relapse in Yorubaland since a *cause célèbre* in Lagos when an educated girl was sent in

wishing to honour a cleric or seek an alliance with an influential person or even get rid of an unmarriageable daughter, orders his daughter to be prepared and then announces before witnesses the name of the man to whom she is gifted, or simply names him Muḥammad whatever his real name. Then he sends her over to the man as a form of alms (*ṣadaqa*), together with *ṣadāq*. Since it is the bridegroom who should pay the *ṣadāq* this form of marriage is not correct unless he turns it over to his unexpected bride as her dowry.

(*e*) *Local Custom Marriages.* Those peoples who have been islamized within the last hundred years are little influenced by Islamic marriage regulations. Chiefs of western Guinea and many other places do not observe the maximum of four wives. Custom wholly regulates their marriages, even the Islamic ceremony of offer and acceptance being often omitted, and their legality depends upon the correctness of customary observances which would be upheld in court.

Marriage Ceremonies. Marriage falls into three main sections: engagement, the contract ceremony, and the ceremonial surrounding the transference of the bride, her transition from one state to another. The adoption of Islam affects marriage in its legal and social aspects more than as a transition rite. Marriage is generally preceded by engagement (*khiṭba*), though if necessary it can be concluded without this. The times of the contract ceremony and the consummation are distinct. Often the contract is concluded when the bride is a child. Even when she is grown up there may be some months' interval before the celebrations around which the indigenous elements revolve. But the Islamic tendency is towards fusion of the contract with the indigenous rites.

In parts of the western cycle marriages are celebrated only once or twice a year, as was the custom in parts of Hausaland before the Fulani conquest. These marriage festivals (Mande *furu ba dõ*) take place in Shawwāl, 'the month the Prophet married 'Ā'isha', three weeks after Ramaḍān ends, and at the end of Dhū 'l-ḥijja. Marriages at other periods are for special reasons. This practice means that all marriages in a particular district are celebrated at the same time, making it a special event in the Islamic year. Fulbe of Futa Jalon have no specially propitious seasons, but Tokolor of the same region have preferential periods and days. The majority of peoples prefer Friday for a virgin and Monday for a divorcée or widow.

this way to a cleric. The marriage was eventually annulled because it was contracted without her consent; she was twenty-two and the court accepted plea of majority, thus denying the father the right of *jabr*.

The general pattern is as follows. For the contract ceremony the male relations of both families (with the exception of the two fathers and bride and bridegroom)[1] assemble at the bride's house. The fathers are each represented by a *walī*. In the presence of two witnesses and the assembly the bride's *walī* announces the amount of the bride-price (stating the delay agreed upon for its completion), the presents and (rarely) the dowry, and witnesses payment of the *ṣadāq*. The contract is concluded by a handclasp and exchange of kola, both essential elements in sealing business transactions. The cleric is generally present to announce acceptance of the settlement and transference of bride to groom, and to lead the recital of the Fātiḥa and Ṣalāt ʿalā 'n-nabī.

This Islamic ceremony may be performed before the customary rites commence, or inserted in the middle where, as in the central cycle, the rites are in two parts, marking the transference of the bride to the bridegroom's house.[2] Islamic elements in the rites are the henna ceremony, bathing of the bride, her veiling, and the *walīma* feast[3] after she is taken to the husband's house. These are only mentioned as Islamic elements because they are traditional in the Islamic *ʿurs* in most lands, not that they are necessarily introduced by Islam; henna usage, for instance, reached the Sudan long before Islam.

The festivities generally last seven days for a virgin and from one to three for a widow or divorcée. The Hausa rite (*kwanakin anganchi*) in Zaria district consists of three days' festival at the bride's home, then four days' at the bridegroom's home. Three days before the actual contract ceremony (*ḍaurin aure*) the bride (*amariya*) is prepared by having her hands and feet stained with henna and is bathed in the evening. During this period the women are trilling, drumming, singing, and dancing.[4] Then the bride is veiled. The next day the contract ceremony is performed, at which the *mālam* announces the terms in the correct Islamic form and leads the recitation of the Fātiḥa, for which he receives

[1] Exceptions will be found. Aḥmadīs perform the ceremony in the presence of bride and bridegroom, and so apparently did Muslim Khasonke of Medina (see Ch. Monteil, *Les Khassonké*, p. 399).

[2] For example, the Nupe (Katcha) marriage (*Yàwǒjin*): (*a*) *efogo nya yàwǒ*, 'day of the bride's reception', which lasts ten days; (*b*) *emilo*, the day she enters (*lo*) her husband's compound (*emi*); (*c*) *efo yàwǒ wa dzun*, 'day of the bride's appearance'. Six days after the *emilo* the bride shows herself for two hours, then the bridegroom goes to her for the first time.

[3] The word *walīma* has been adopted by many peoples for the feasts involving sacrificial *ṣadaqa* at naming, marriage, and upon completion of a recitation of the Qur'ān.

[4] Clerics were exercised over the question of whether drums and other musical instruments were allowed for their authorities were disagreed (cf. Khalīl, *Mukhtaṣar*, ii. 64), but naturally that makes no difference to the celebrations.

a fee (*kuḍin ḍaure*). That night old women conduct the bride secretly to the house of the bridegroom (*ango*). Meanwhile the bridegroom, if it is his first marriage, is sitting veiled in an *alkyabba* (Ar. *al-qabā'*) in his friend's house. The bride's friend (*ḳawa*), swathed in an *alkyabba*, is set on a mare, and accompanied by girls dancing is conducted openly (Friday morning) to the bridegroom's house. This custom is presumably a means of avoiding dangerous influences attendant on a transition period. It is invariable in villages, but sometimes omitted today in towns. The dancers on reaching the house are met by the bridegroom's friends and refuse to enter until given a gift. After this the mock bride (*amariyan boko*) is escorted within, reveals herself by throwing off her robe, and joins the revellers. The bride's friends remain with her for these four days (called *tururushi*), and the bridegroom stays in his friend's house. On the *kwanan tsīwa*, the night preceding the consummation, the bridegroom and friends are allowed special licence. On the fourth night the marriage feast is held. The formal ceremony (*buḍar kai*), 'unveiling' of the bride by her friend, takes place before the bridegroom is introduced. The couple are in a dangerous state during this period of *angwanche* and protective rites follow custom. Neither must be left alone and the cleric provides protective 'medicine'. Many tribes allow pre-marital sexual relations after puberty rites have been performed, but Islam stresses virginity and most islamized include defloration as part of the rite, and exhibit the 'signs of virginity'. These marriage customs are observed only when a woman marries for the first time. If it is the bridegroom's first marriage he also is subject to special ceremonial. If the bride is a widow or divorcée the ceremonies are simplified, involving little more than the contract ceremony and the legal *walīma* in the bride's house immediately afterwards.

Dissolution of Marriage. In many African societies marriage was undertaken on the assumption that the union would be permanent and divorce was a last resort when all means of reconciliation had failed. Others, however, did not adopt so rigid an attitude. Islam does not regard marriage as a necessarily permanent relationship, and its adoption often leads to a relaxation of the marriage bond. Its facility for divorce breaches more than anything else the old idea of marriage as a contract between two groups. It stresses that marriage is a contract between two individuals who can legally break the contract. A husband can repudiate his wife simply by the repetition of a formula, though the wife has to seek a divorce by judicial process. This attitude may have considerable effect upon former practice. Nupe said that before Islam came divorce after the birth of the first child was practically impossible, but now even pagans admit it, though nothing like to the extent of Muslim Nupe. Bozo, though Muslims in name, are said to know nothing of either repudiation or divorce, except for a few more influenced by Islamic clergy.

Divorce is the dissolution of marriage invoked by one of the partners and pronounced by legal means. The *qāḍī* fixes the blame and award. Its effect, and this is the reason for men seeking it and avoiding repudiation, is to enable the successful party to obtain the benefit of the marriage settlement. If the husband gains it on adequate grounds the court may order repayment of the settlement, a privilege he would forfeit if he simply repudiated his wife. The *ṣadāq* and presents to the bride are not recoverable since these were payments for her virginity, and for this reason they are often careful to keep the bride-price separate even if it belongs to the wife. If the woman seeks and obtains a divorce she may be awarded the settlement as well as her presents. That is why it is women who so often demand divorce, more than men who are interested in keeping their wives because of the capital they represent (sums paid or promised), their domestic and agricultural help, and the expense of a new marriage. Repudiation, therefore, is not indulged in lightly, is almost unknown among some peoples (Songhay), and is utilized only for special reasons or by rich men who can afford to lose the settlement and contract frequent marriages. People differ greatly in recourse to divorce. It is common among Hausa but rare among Fulbe in Futa Jalon. Some forms recognized by Islamic law may be completely unknown or not utilized.

The Soninke recognize two forms of repudiation (*warande*) and two forms of divorce.[1] The *dagga ndangara* (revocable repudiation) is the ordinary Islamic *aṭ-ṭalāq al-aḥsan* when the husband who repudiates his wife with a single sentence may take her back any time during the period of retreat (*'idda*); but if the *'idda* is exceeded the repudiation is definite and he cannot take her back without remarriage. The husband can pronounce the repudiation twice and revoke, but the third time is irrevocable. The other type of repudiation (the *ẓihār* form, saying 'you are *ḥarām* to me') is definitive if said in the presence of two witnesses. The repudiated woman keeps her settlement, or, if not paid, the husband is liable for the amount. The first type of divorce, *dungahi muriē*, by mutual consent (Ar. *mubāra'a*), is not very common. Generally the woman proposes to her husband that he free her if she

[1] See J. H. Saint-Père, *Les Sarakollé du Guidimakha*, 1925, pp. 150–2.

repays the settlement (correctly it is *khulʿ* by means of a compensation, *mutʿa*, paid to the husband). The acceptance by the husband must be made before two witnesses, and the settlement repaid before the woman can marry again. The other (*fatahē*, Ar. *faskh*, normally called *taṭlīq* by Mālikīs) is the normal divorce. Soninke men rarely resort to it, but women have no other means if the husband refuses to release them.[1] If the husband seeks and gains it the woman must repay him all the pre-nuptial presents and any instalments received on the settlement. When the woman gains a divorce she has nothing to pay back, and the husband must pay up any unpaid part of the settlement.

At the present day in Nigeria a woman who has been repudiated generally applies to the *alkāli*'s court for a certificate of divorce. It is, however, felt that the 'correct' procedure[2] is for the husband to send a message or write a letter to the wife's uncle to say he has repudiated his wife. Relations come to find out the reasons and seek a reconciliation. If they fail they take the letter to the *alkāli* who tells the father or representative to bring his daughter. The husband is also called and the *alkāli* tries to reconcile them. If this fails he declares the marriage broken and takes one-tenth of the *sadāki* for the *Bait al-Māl*. The *ʿidda* begins the day the *alkāli* grants the divorce, which is not definitive until its expiration.[3] The other forms are accepted, including the triple divorce after which they cannot remarry until she has married and divorced another man.[4] The woman's right to seek dissolution of her marriage by judicial procedure is recognized and the grounds for granting it are interpreted with considerable liberality by the judges.[5]

[1] Though Islamic law makes it difficult for a woman to obtain a divorce, African custom tempers the interpretation and application of the law, and it is not difficult for a woman supported by her kindred to claim a divorce on grounds not allowed by the Mālikī code (impotence, default in maintenance, and undue cruelty). It is rather the possibility of the award involving restitution of the bride-price which makes it difficult for a woman to seek divorce, not the rigorous application of Islamic law.

[2] Hausa *shikan ragai* (Ar. *rajʿa*), revocable repudiation, also called *shikan sunna*.

[3] Hausa often repudiate pregnant wives and apparently many *alkālis* do not bother about the legality of this, or at least do not inquire if the wife is pregnant. All the *ʿidda* means in practice is that the woman cannot contract a new marriage if she is pregnant.

[4] Hausa *shikan batta*, triple divorce. The arranged temporary marriage of a woman (Ar. *taḥlīl*; disapproved of by most Malikites) to enable her to remarry her former husband is called in Hausa *auran kisan wuta*. Remarriage to a former wife after the triple divorce is called *auran kōme*.

[5] 'An analysis made by Smith of 764 divorce cases dealt with in a year by the native court of a northern district of Zaria Province shows that 49 of these concerned applications by women whose husbands had divorced them; the remainder, therefore, were appeals by women for divorce. In 287 cases the court effected a reconciliation'; A. Phillips (ed.), *Survey of African Marriage and Family Life*, 1953, p. 144.

The Islamic facility for wife repudiation has little effect upon family structure where the unilateral kin group holds, nor is it detrimental to the care of children. But where the reduced Islamic family has emerged the disintegration of the household often leads to the neglect of young children. Some Hausa women avoid having children since their production is no insurance against divorce, and for the same reason try to acquire as much wealth as possible by home occupations and trading. The custody of children (*ḥaḍāna*) after divorce or the father's death belongs to the mother until puberty if a boy and until marriage if a girl, the father being responsible for their maintenance. But there are considerable variations, for in local custom their care so often devolves upon the paternal or maternal uncle. In some areas the boy may be claimed by the father or other guardian at any age, in others the father cannot claim him before the age of seven. Among Tokolor and Moors he remains with his mother until seven and a girl until marriage, but with Fulbe in Futa Jalon and Dyula the father takes over all the children immediately.

Married Life and the Position of Women. The amount of freedom women enjoy depends upon custom and economic circumstances more than Islam. Among Saharan nomads their position is high and that extends to many Negroes such as Songhay of Gao.[1] Many Muslim women enjoy almost as much freedom as do pagan women. The Islamic pull towards wife seclusion is apparent among privileged classes and in towns. It is strict among Fulbe of Northern Nigeria and Masina but those of Futa Jalon have any amount of freedom. Complete immurement is rare and only rigidly enforced in the households of chiefs and townspeople. In villages compound seclusion is found only where women do not work in the fields (Kanuri, Hausa, Nupe, and Songhay), but in many communities women do a great deal of work. The tendency to excuse women from farming is due as much to economic and social factors as to pressure from Islam. As M. G. Smith has shown[2] in former slave-states free women did not need to work since this was done by slaves. When slavery was abolished liberated slave women also tended to give up farming. Islam, as interpreted by Hausa clerics, served to rationalize the practice and has led to the gradual extension of seclusion (*kulle*) from urban to rural areas.[3]

[1] Northern Songhay women, like Tuareg with whom they have intermarried, refuse to accept a polygamous marriage. In the canton of Bamba (15,000) only thirty men had two wives (cf. *Bull. I.F.A.N.* xvi (1954), 198).

[2] M. Smith, *Baba of Karo*, pp. 22, 24.

[3] 'In Zaria there are different degrees of seclusion, and the type to be accepted by a woman is agreed upon at the time of her marriage. Marriage with complete seclusion has the highest

Islam affects marriage in regard to such questions as cohabitation, maintenance, wife's duty to work for her husband, and reciprocal fidelity. Obligations that the long-islamized insist upon are those regarding the conjugal abode and the husband's maintenance of the wife. The Islamic regulation that the husband has absolute authority to decide what shall be the conjugal home may lead to conflict where matrilocal customs occur. A universal custom is that a wife need not follow the husband when he moves to another village or goes on travels. The husband is responsible for the upkeep of his wives and children, but again local custom may modify this rule; for example, Hausa women are generally responsible for their own children and engage in home occupations to enable them to do this. The husband must provide a separate house for each wife,[1] during his absence he is responsible for her maintenance and failure to do this often leads to divorce. The length of absence required before a divorce can be granted was the subject of controversy among some *qāḍīs*. The husband's right to punish his wife is recognized, but its exercise varies, for immoderate indulgence is regarded as providing the wife with grounds for divorce and consequent necessity for the husband to restore the bride-price. The husband's attentions to each of his wives, free and slave, are carefully regulated and this type of Islamic custom is adopted quickly, even, as among Bambara, before definitive islamization. A woman's right to own personal possessions is recognized in Islamic law and islamization has often made a difference to women in this way. A Pulo woman in traditional society does not have complete disposal of her fortune, but those of Futa Jalon and Masina have full rights, though generally the consent of the husband is required.[2]

The practice of polygamy in some areas inflicts individual hardship, for poor men are unable to marry. Among the Fulbe of Futa Jalon polygamous households are more common than monogamous, and in addition they have slave-wives. This means that those who belong to the

prestige, but is rarely found except in the households of nobles and wealthy men. . . . A less strict form of seclusion allows the wife to go out at dark to draw water and collect firewood; at the same time she may greet her near kin and close women friends. The freest type allows women to "wander where they will in the locality, help in the harvest, and even cultivate plots of their own". Marriages of this type, characteristic of the poorer peasants, are usually contracted between people whose homes are not far apart, and in them the wife can visit her family whenever she likes' (A. Phillips, *Survey of African Marriage*, p. 137).

[1] With Songhay of Gao, as with Tuareg, the wife's family build her a house and provide its furnishing at the time of marriage. This remains her property and is dismantled and removed at divorce.

[2] Under the Mālikī code a husband has considerable control over his wife's property.

non-privileged classes have to do without wives. Islam encourages markets and towns in which the practice of prostitution is a recognized feature. Sometimes this has reached such proportions that it has caused clergy to react. In towns like Kano they have undertaken crusades against brothels, attempting to move public opinion by predicting calamities, drought, and cattle plagues. In towns and villages in Northern Nigeria chiefs have ordered all women to provide themselves with husbands or be expelled, but in a few months the position was back to normal, for prostitution is closely linked with the *bōri* cult. Prostitutes are the freest, most versatile, and often best educated women in Islamic West Africa. They attend the women's prayer annex, not necessarily in order to find clients, and they will be found attending Qur'ān schools.

5. DEATH RITES AND MOURNING CUSTOM

The influence of Islam in after-death ritual is very marked, its practices are adopted easily, some even before islamization, and there is less variation from its pattern than in any other sphere. The distinctive elements are: ritual washing with prayer, incensing, specified types of graveclothes, and use of a stretcher; separation of the sexes; speed between death and burial; graves of specific form and orientation; ritual funeral prayer; mourners' participation in carrying corpses, repetition of phrases, throwing earth on grave; widow's ritual mourning, washing, seclusion period, and purification; and ceremonial gathering, offering and feasting on first, third, seventh, and fortieth days after death.

When death seems imminent the dying person is orientated so that he faces the direction of the *qibla*. He is encouraged to say the *shahāda*, or it may be said for him, though some clerics are opposed to this, saying that it is beneficial only if said by the dying person. If the family cleric is present he often recites the sūra *Yā Sīn*. In the Sahil the room is fumigated with incense 'to keep the spirits at bay'. Immediately after death the family cleric performs the ritual washing[1] which follows Islamic ritual as closely as his training permits. There is generally a washing corresponding to the ordinary ablutions (sometimes done by a relative), followed by the ritual washing. The water for the final washing is perfumed with herbs and roots (manufactured perfumes are forbidden). In Timbuktu the *dyongolo* is performed simultaneously with the washing. For this a woman pounds myrrh and cotton seed in a

[1] In Futa Jalon it is done by the muezzin, and with the Tokolor of Kayes, E. Fulbe and Tuareg, by women. If the deceased is a woman it is done by the cleric's wife.

metal mortar in a crosswise fashion to avoid the normal method.[1] After the washing the corpse is clothed. Incensed cotton is placed in all the orifices of the body. The grave clothes should consist of not more than five pieces, or one piece wound tightly round the body, but the Moroccan practice of seven is frequently observed in the Sahil. The shroud must be of local material and incensed. The body is placed on a mat.

The time between death and burial will be a minimum of three hours and rarely longer than five to six hours unless death occurs at night or in the case of an important chief. That is why one sees mourners carrying the corpse through the streets at such a rapid pace. In villages the place of burial is normally in the hut or compound, following former custom. In the Sahil we find cemeteries. European occupation has led to them being provided for towns, but villagers still bury in the compound.

The burial is conducted with the simplicity characteristic of Muslims in every land. The men have been sitting outside silently whilst the preparations were going on, some perhaps hurriedly stitching the grave clothes. The body is brought out head first[2] on the mat and placed on a stretcher roughly made of branches which is generally left on the grave. Town mosques provide better-made biers for the purpose. The mourners perform the ablutions before the procession begins if the prayers are said *en route*, or on arrival at the grave when recited there. Only the men accompany the body to the grave.[3] The *imām* precedes the stretcher, often accompanied by the family head, and the mourners are on both sides and behind. The bearers are continually changed for it is a meritorious act to assist. If the burial is in a cemetery the prayers are generally recited *en route* on the outskirts of the village or in front of the mosque square (in which case the *imām* returns), sometimes beside the grave. Where the burial takes place in the compound they are recited on the spot. The prayers are normal with four repetitions of the *takbīr* said without prostration, led by the *imām* of the village or quarter mosque, not by the family cleric who performed the washing. He faces the *qibla* with the corpse before him in such a position as to hide the abdomen if a man and the breasts if a woman, and the congregation

[1] Cf. Miner, op. cit., p. 223; Marty, *Soudan*, ii, 119. The *dyongolo* is the 'petit mortier et pilon en fer que l'on frappe l'un contre l'autre pendant le lavage d'un cadavre afin que le défunt n'entende pas les conversations des assistants'; A. Dupuis, *La Langue Songoï*, 1917, p. 140.

[2] Except Songhay, who carry it to the cemetery feet first.

[3] Dyula women follow burials of women. Soninke women accompany the procession to the outskirts of the village, but must not be present at the prayer.

range themselves in three rows behind him. The megaphonist shouts out the phrases after him and the congregation repeat. The body is then placed in the grave and each throws a handful of earth into it.

The grave is always very shallow, never more than three feet deep. This, they usually explain, is to enable the body to get out at the Resurrection. It has a narrower trench at the bottom which will just take the body lying on its side, and provides ledges to support sticks and straw so that the earth does not touch the body. It is orientated north–south and the body placed on the right side with its face turned towards the *qibla*. This practice has been adopted by many pagans. Clergy differ as to whether the grave should be marked or not, and the general opinion is opposed to this, but sometimes in the Sahil sticks or stones will be seen at the head and foot of the mound. After a short time nothing indicates the place of the graves in the compound or village burial ground. Even with newly-islamized the remnants of the ancestor cult have no connexion with graves. Contrary to Muslims in other parts of the world there is no visiting of graves:

> They wash their hands thus and their feet, they salute one another.
> They scatter in silence, and leave thee in the grave.[1]

After the interment it is the Sudanese rule as in Morocco that participants return to the village in silence by a different route from that by which they came, as after the *ʿīd* prayers. In parts of the Sahil (Kayes, Jenne, Songhay) the mourners return to the house of the deceased for further ablutions, prayers, and readings. All insist that ablutions are necessary after the funeral for all participants in order to remove the contamination of death.

After-death ceremonial consists of the offering of *ṣadaqa* to God on specified days. Fulfilment of the prescribed rites and other obligations of the survivors, such as almsgiving and payment of debts, is regarded as obligatory, not merely in order to eliminate the contamination of death, but for the repose of the soul of the deceased.[2] Muslims have every confidence in the efficacy of their rites and once completed on'

[1] From a poem by ʿUthmān dan Fodio in C. H. Robinson, *Specimens of Hausa Literature* 1896, pp. 80–81.

[2] H. Gaden writes (*Proverbes et maximes peuls et toucouleurs*, p. 61): 'It is believed that he who has left debts is not at peace in the grave as long as they remain unsettled. If the creditor dies unpaid the *ᵐbēlu*, or shadow soul, of the debtor follows the *ᵐbēlu* of the creditor beseeching it to accept payment of his debt, the burden of which oppresses him. But the *ᵐbēlu* of the creditor refuses because it can only be settled on the day of Resurrection. The *ᵐbēlu* of the debtor, therefore, knows no repose, but had the son paid his father's debt before the death of the creditor, the *ᵐbēlu* of his father would have peacefully awaited the Resurrection and Last Judgement.'

the fortieth day there are no offerings of such a nature as would constitute a cult of ancestors.

With Soninke[1] the *imām* on returning to the house calls in a loud voice for the dinner of the dead. A calabash of unpounded millet is placed before him, the others group themselves around, he prays and hands the calabash to the family cleric who washed the body. On the third day the white cloth which covered the body is removed from the roof where it has been displayed since the funeral and washed. They prepare an alms of millet which, after being blessed by the cleric, is ground and mixed with milk to make *sōssē*. In the afternoon the *imām* arrives and puts the *sōssē* into five calabashes. The grave-cloth and clothes of the deceased are brought. He blesses all with prayer, shares the *sōssē* with the other clergy, and gives the family cleric the clothes. All the family remain within the compound for eight days, and during this time the whole village observes mourning; no festivals, drumming, and dancing are allowed.

Susu, Temne, Mende, and other peoples of western Guinea offer ceremonial rice 'sacrifice' on the first, third, seventh, and fortieth days after death, the last being the day the spirit departs, after which the widow is free to marry. Mende practice is as follows. Rice-sacrifice (*safanda jaa*) is offered after returning from the funeral. Three chickens are killed, three calabashes of white rice,[2] with three kolas in each, are prepared. Other rice is prepared for eating, together with a bowl of uncooked rice into which each one puts money. The *fodie* is asked to 'offer the sacrifice'. He and the others place a hand on the three bowls, those unable to reach place a hand on those in front. The *fodie* recites a prayer in Arabic asking Muḥammad and other prophets to intercede with God on behalf of the new arrival; no direct prayer to God being offered. Then the maternal uncle prays in Mende asking the prophets and *ndebla woveisia* (ancestors) to look after the deceased and the family. The money collected is given to the *fodie* as 'passport money' and he divides the rice according to custom. The sacrifices on the third, seventh, and fortieth days are similar but on a larger scale, including if possible the offering of a sheep or goat. Seven bowls are offered on the seventh day, and after the ceremony a relative pours a libation of water on the ground. Susu and Temne practices are similar.[3] Temne have one general bowl for ancestors (*afəm afi*), but special bowls are

[1] See J. H. Saint-Père, op. cit., pp. 159–62.

[2] *Mba lɛwie*, rice dough mixed with honey or sugar. Red rice (*mba bɔi*) is abhorred as associated with pagan practice.

[3] Susu *thamdɔgɔ*, Temne *təmər kabo*, 'to set bread'.

prepared for recently departed persons. These are kept until morning and then, their virtue having departed, given to children. The cleric is always called in to pray in Arabic, whilst the family head talks to the ancestors.

A sacrifical *ṣadaqa* of the staple food is offered nearly everywhere on these days (this apart from the slaughtering of a sheep and preparation of food necessary for the visiting mourners) when clerics offer prayer. Islam is against the heavy feasting and drinking which characterizes the mourning feast of pagans. The Dagomba *ṣadaqa* consists of *gumba*, 'sacrificial grain'.[1] Nupe after the burial return to the house to eat *ṣadaqa*. They say this is the first food the deceased (*kuchi*) eats in *èku*. Relatives give money and kola to the cleric. On the third, eighth, and fortieth day *ṣadaqa* is offered, the last being the day his *ráyi* goes to *èku* to remain until the Day of Judgement. Most Songhay observe only the seventh-day feast when they provide a bull, if they can afford it, for the whole village as *ṣadaqa*, but only the affluent make an offering on the fortieth day when they collect the village clerics for a Qur'ān recital and give them a feast at its conclusion.

Widow's Ritual Mourning. According to Islamic law the widow should observe *'idda* for three periods of legal purity (*qur'*), or four months ten days, during which she may not remarry. A slave-wife observes half this period. If the widow is pregnant the period extends until her delivery. In the Sudan the *'idda* of widowhood is far more strictly observed than that of divorce because of the persistence of old ideas of the soul. Custom varies the period slightly. In some places it is four moons; in Hausaland some said five months, others 130 days, and others 122 days. Nupe said 115 days. In the Timbuktu region it lasts five months fifteen days.[2] South of the Sudan, especially in western Guinea and even among Fulbe of Futa Jalon, the widow is free to remarry after the fortieth-day sacrifice. The heir cannot turn widows out of the house during the *'idda* but owes them neither food nor raiment, custom overriding the *sharī'a* in this respect. At the expiration of the *'idda* the wives are free and can claim the payment of the bride-price if entitled

[1] The word *gumba* has been adopted from Hausa. Among the Māguzāwa it consists of a preparation of bulrush millet mixed with water. In their rite it is 'hung up overnight in a calabash. In the morning it is taken down, milk added to some of it, and this portion is drunk by members of the household and distributed to the neighbours as *sadaka*. The remaining part, without milk, is scattered on the floor of all the huts, in the corn storehouses and on the *jīgō* of *dāšī* wood sacred to Kure and the model hut sacred to 'Inna'; J. Greenberg, *The Influence of Islam on a Sudanese Religion*, 1946, p. 45.

[2] Songhay call the *'idda* period *handu gu serti*, 'five-months stipulation'. In Gao it is the normal four months ten days.

to it. The Songhay woman, however, returns to her own family for the *'idda*, but the heir is supposed to maintain her during this period.

The death of her husband involves the woman in a state of taboo.[1] She is divested of all her clothes and ornaments, bathed and dressed in old or poor garments, black or white according to custom, her hair is let down, disordered, and bound in a kerchief. No jewellery may be worn, nor cosmetics applied. She may wash neither herself nor her clothes. She is provided with Qur'ānic charms to protect her against her husband's spirit, as well as local counterparts (knife, cowries) against attacks of witches. She may not leave her home for a prescribed period (Tokolor: fifteen days) or attend feasts. Among many (e.g. Songhay) she may not leave the house during the whole *'idda*, unless at night when no one is about the village. With some she may not speak to anyone except near relations, and above all not to any man.

The ritual for ending the mourning period varies. The procedure with the recently islamized Mende is as follows. For three days before the seventh-day sacrifice the widows who were virgins when the deceased married them are secluded in a screened part of the veranda. They are looked after by old women and not allowed to go out unaccompanied for fear of the husband's spirit which is around and jealous. They can only eat plantain and no rice. Their heads are shaved and remain so from the seventh to the fortieth day. On the thirty-ninth day they are returned to the screened veranda. Then comes the fortieth day sacrifice after which they are taken out into the fields and washed. On their return each is asked to choose a husband among the right degrees of the family. Similarly with other peoples of Sierra Leone. The Susu widow cooks food for her husband on the fortieth day (*labirañ*) and relatives eat it: 'She is washed like a corpse and then his *bari* (spirit) leaves.'

With Hausa of Zaria the widow's mourning period (*takaba='idda*) begins on the Friday following the death. She must wear 'white charms' wrapped up in white material, not leather, and worn around the neck. If circumstances allow she remains secluded the whole period. The freeing ceremony at the end (*fitar takaba*) is a great festival when all women relatives and friends (*ḳāwāyē*) bring food after nightfall. A small calabash, placed upside down inside a large one which contains water, is beaten all through the night (*kiḍan ruwa*, 'beating water'). Special songs are sung by hired women, all the mourning clothes are given away, and she is washed. In the morning she appears in new clothes, the clergy recite prayers, and the feast is held.

[1] On the taboos Hausa women must observe, see Mary Smith, *Baba of Karo*, p. 212.

8

Influence of Islam in the Economic Sphere and upon Material Culture

I. ISLAM AND ECONOMIC ACTIVITIES

A GLANCE at Islamic economic theory will show in what way a religious culture might be expected to influence economic life. Islamic law never formulated any system of economics, for such ideas belong to the modern Western way of thinking. It was not interested in abstractions like economic theory, but about the conduct of persons. Thus it was less concerned about the way or means by which a man earns his living or acquires his wealth, than with the way he dealt with his gains. It has its rules governing the conduct of traders, but not of markets. It is concerned with the welfare of the community, hence self-interest such as would endanger that is condemned. Since God has decreed one's status in the world, resignation to one's lot is a virtue, whilst avarice, usury, and gambling are vices. Islam recognizes private property, but disapproves of hoarding; consequently it not merely urges one to be charitable (*ṣadaqa*), but has made charitableness a matter of legislation (*zakāt*), whilst Qur'ānic injunctions lay special stress upon the duty of caring for orphans, widows, and destitute. Trade occupies an important place in Islamic tradition, and it has built up a large body of regulations governing contracts, exchange, and loans. Its system of taxation and religious obligations make it necessary to budget for an economic surplus. Its social and labour ethics and legislation influence economic life. Regulations regarding the *jihād* and slavery justified both slave-raiding and the system of economic inequality. The husband's obligation to provide for his wife affects the sex division of labour; its regulations regarding ownership and inheritance could, if adopted, revolutionize traditional economic life by the fragmentation of landholdings and individualization of real property, and disrupt the family as an economic unit.

The converse aspect needs noticing in what is primarily a religious study. This is the way each occupational sphere affects understanding and practice of Islam and the extent to which old religious attitudes are bound up with economic activities; for example, ritual magic with animal productivity, the agricultural cycle and craftsmanship.

West African societies had already achieved fully developed techniques and economic organization before Islam made its appearance. Its influence is most evident in the commercial sphere which in the Sudan belt was wholly taken over by Muslims. Its direct influence in other spheres has been weak. Changes are due primarily to other factors, but once set in motion, Islam, with its body of legal institutions, governs the direction of change in accordance with its own pattern. The main forms of Sudanese economy fall into the groups of pastoralism, agriculture, hunting and fishing, industry and craftsmanship, trade, and clerical occupations. These categories are to a great extent interdependent. There is no closed system of economic differentiation except in regard to certain crafts. Pastoralists, craftsmen, and traders practise agriculture; agriculturalists keep livestock, hunt and fish, whilst their wives and daughters engage in home crafts and petty trading; all village clergy supplement their income from performing clerical duties, teaching, and amulet-making, by cultivating or trading.

2. NOMADS

Nomads have filled an important economic role in the Sudan primarily in breeding camels, cattle, and sheep, but also in organizing or disrupting trade-routes, and in encroaching upon or co-operating with cultivators. They need not, however, occupy us long for Islam scarcely influences their economic life, though it may help to rationalize changes due to other factors. Nigerian Tuareg and southern Arab Kunta lead a semi-sedentary life resembling that of riverain Negroes in many respects. In this case, change of habitat and mode of life provided the conditions by which Islam could gain greater influence. The arabized Berbers whom we call Moors have been considerably modified in their social institutions and this has affected aspects of economic life. In the Sudan belt the only nomads encamped in the midst of Negro agriculturalists, other than southern Tuareg, are the Fulbe, scattered over the whole region, and the Baqqāra, cattle-breeding Arab tribes in Lake Chad region. Fulbe nomads fill an important function in the economy of the Sudan, but Islam has exercised little influence upon them. On the other hand, many have been modified by their Negro environment which has led to settlement and intermarriage, but it is the act of settling which has enabled Islam to change their institutions. With nomadic Fulbe cattle-keeping is a way of life, for cattle are not a commercial but a social asset, representing wealth and capital rather than a source of income. Mixed Fulbe groups, however, have found in settlement the practical utilization of their cattle as a means of exchange.[1] Upon many Baqqāra of Chad region the same Negro influences have been working as upon Fulbe.

Islam suits nomads, but being an urban religion does not revolutionize their social and economic life. The prosperity of herds is dependent upon natural conditions and that involves the continuation of non-Islamic magical ritual. Their social institutions are closely adapted to their needs, consequently they react against any attempt to enforce Islamic law upon them. *Qāḍī's* courts are unacceptable in a society where customary law rules and justice is decided by tribal elders. A feature of nomadic Islam referred to frequently has been the formation of clerical sections to perform religious duties on behalf of warrior clans.

The nomad is more concerned with rights in animals than in land. Pasture-grounds and watering-places remain the concern of the social unit, but Islam, by allowing for individual ownership and through its inheritance regulations, may bring about changes in animal ownership. As with Negro peoples both tribal and individual property rights are recognized. Islam has no influence upon the first but affects the second, though only rarely do women appear to accumulate animal wealth, chiefly through bride-price and inheritance. Islamic contractual law has gained little ground. It has not had any effect upon such aspects as livestock-lease, the agreement by which an owner confides animals to the care of a lessee who receives as recompense milk and a proportion of the increase.

The most successful attempt to regulate nomads before the European era was made by Shaikh Ḥamadu of Masina. He amassed large herds scattered all over the country as property of the state, and appointed an *amīru māgal* as state herd-chief who nominated subordinates to the provinces. These officials also exercised authority over Fulbe tribes in such a way that the state could regulate the use of pasturages, cycles of transhumance, prices of animals and their products, and take precautions against diseases.[2] Western control has had a more profound influence than Islam mainly through the suppression of raiding, the regulariza-

[1] The nomadic Fulbe who emigrated into Futa Jalon became completely sedentarized, chiefly through exploitation of slave labour, and having acquired a taste for the products of the land are forced to some extent to occupy themselves with cultivation. But cattle still ally with Islam as symbols of superiority, a sign of nobility, which they refuse to exploit. Both are the first things to which the new-born child is introduced since it is made to drink milk and the magical water called *nasi*.

[2] See Ch. Monteil, *Djénné*, p. 221.

tion of migrations and caravan traffic, and in fostering the change from nomadism to transhumance.

3. AGRICULTURALISTS

Islam has taken little interest in agriculture which has no essential place in legal texts, and the effect of Muslims upon agricultural economy cannot be compared with that of the Portuguese, who, through their introductions from the new world, revolutionized the economic life of many peoples. Indigenous to the Sudan were *durra* (small millet or Pennisetum) and *dukhn* (sorghum), the basic cereals, rice, fonio, and yam; all except yam being referred to frequently by the Arabic writers. Trade relations after the rise of Islam do not appear to have introduced new basic cultures or methods of cultivation. Traffic across the Sahara, so influential in many spheres, was relatively unproductive in the agricultural sphere, though previous traffic, mainly from the Nilotic region, had brought new cultures.[1] It is true that names for wheat, melon, turnip, cloves, dates, sugar-cane, fig, pomegranate, onion, and the like, in Sudanese languages are derived from Arabic but their cultivation did not spread widely. They were grown in various parts of the north, but primarily as luxuries for foreigners in sahilian ports. Rice, propagated in the Mediterranean world since the eighth century A.D. and spreading into the Sudan, may be an exception, but if so it spread rapidly for it is mentioned by many Arab geographers. No doubt the imported replaced an indigenous variety. The clothing requirements of Islam, however, encouraged the cultivation of cotton.[2]

The economically-exploited system of slavery probably derives from the Saharan system. The freeing of masters from manual labour had led to economic differentiation and the growth of a social hierarchy long before the introduction of Islam. It enabled an Islamic clerical class to be supported, but this was simply a substitution for the priestly class. Workers on the land were scarcely islamized. A kind of antinomy prevailed over vast areas, especially in Fulbe states, between agriculturalists, slaves of the land, who remained practically pagan, and

[1] Trade relations influenced the economy of farmers in so far as they led them to work for an economic surplus to buy things they could not produce.

[2] Al-Bakrī mentions that in Toronka on the Senegal whose people weave the cotton strips called *shakkiyyāt*, 'though there is not a great deal of cotton in their country yet you can scarcely find a single compound which does not have a cotton shrub' (al-Bakrī, p. 173; cf. Ibn Sa'īd for Barīsa, in Abū'l Fidā, *Taqwīn*, p. 157). Al-'Umarī (*Masālik*, p. 66) reports that it was cultivated in Māli. Ad-Dimishqī (p. 240) mentions the (silk?) cotton tree in the Kawkaw region. The word for cotton in the majority of Sudan languages is a corruption of *quṭun*.

Fulbe, slaves of God, who were fervent Muslims. It is obvious, therefore, that the economic revolution caused by the abolition of slavery would affect Fulbe religious life, since it compelled many to abandon their leisured life lounging around mosques and work for their daily bread.

Islam influences traditional economy in so far as its regulations regarding ownership and inheritance gain ground. It has been shown that in general these have not been adopted in regard to land tenure and real property. Change in this sphere came about, in the last century, through the influence of theocratic governments and their successors; and, in the present century, less from Islamic pressure (except where supported by European governments as in Northern Nigeria) than from such factors as scarcity and pressure on land and a heightened individualism encouraged by the conditions of a new age. Nadel has shown that the size of the collective farming groups among Nupe is declining. Formerly they consisted of from ten to fifteen members, today they have often declined to two or three, for sons after marriage tend to claim their personal plots.[1]

Since the family normally forms a working unit Islamic contractual law has not led to the formation of agricultural associations. Labour is still based either on clientship[2] or the collective work of family and neighbours. A notable exception is found in the collective farm settlements formed by the *murīdīn* of Senegal.[3] Under the inspiration of Aḥmad Bamba an Islamic saint cult has given an impulse for the exploitation of uncultivated land, the greater productivity of land owned by members, and price-control of products. Upon joining the *ṭarīqa* the neophyte agrees to surrender himself body and soul to the shaikh. If he possesses land it is for the service of the community; if landless he is allotted a plot, provided with seed and loaned implements and animals. The shaikh's deputies take control of the harvest, which being a cash crop (especially ground-nuts) is assured a more remunerative sale than would be obtained by the isolated cultivator. The system also embraces craftsmen and traders. Revenues are distributed among members either in kind or goods. It is, therefore, a system of collective security in which the shaikh, as trustee of the land and controller of capital and labour, is responsible for the welfare of all affiliated. The system has widened the idea of agricultural co-operation from the traditional one between

[1] S. F. Nadel, *A Black Byzantium*, pp. 242–3.

[2] The *métayage* system of land tenure, under which the proprietor receives a proportion of the crops or cash or labour, is widespread, especially since the abolition of slavery, but is not the direct effect of Islam.

[3] See P. Marty, 'Les Mourides d'Amadou Bamba', *R.M.M.* xxv (1913), 106–12.

members of natural groups to members of the new Murīd society, and, in contrast to the traditional Islamic attitude, sanctified labour under the aegis of Islam.[1]

The adoption of Islamic regulations concerning women may affect agricultural economy. The husband's obligations, women's right to own capital resources, and the tendency towards their seclusion, has in some parts led to new divisions of labour and their economic independence. Hausa have been strongly influenced in this respect. Whilst pagan Hausa women work on the land, among Muslims farm work is the exclusive province of men, the wife's obligations being confined to domestic work. These changes are due to the former system of slave labour rather than to Islam, the attitude of the privileged class spreading to free and serf Hausa.[2] In other regions where women's share in the work of the farm is important Islam has had little effect.

The economic demands that religion makes upon farming communities include offerings to clerics as formerly to cult priests, in addition to other forms of *ṣadaqa* to propitiate the spirits governing fertility and increase. These offerings involve providing for a surplus above mere subsistence requirements. Since the farmer's need to achieve harmony with the spiritual world is as vital as physical labour, the religion of the agricultural cycle follows the old pattern. Cultivation rites vary,[3] but the general outline is much the same and only one or two illustrations need be provided so that our estimate of the relative demands of Islam and of the spirit world may be balanced. The following are the principal rites among islamized Temne. Before clearing the ground they consult the seer, ask permission of the *kərifi*, prepare rice flour dough and make *sadika* at the entrance to the plot. Before burning they make another *sadika*. Before hoeing they build a small hut on piles, place stones in it, chew kola, and spit on them. When the rice is almost ready for harvesting a little is cut, sieved, and placed on a pole at the

[1] More recently the leaders have realized that mechanized agriculture could multiply their production. In 1949 a beginning was made on lands originally sanctified by the manual labour of the founder, on a system of triennial rotation: millet, ground-nuts, and fallow (see P. Pelissier, 'L'Archide au Sénégal', *Les Cahiers d'Outre-Mer*, iv (1951), 222–5). It will be interesting to see what effect this will have upon the original sanctification of land and labour.

[2] Cf. the Hausa saying: 'Farm work is not becoming for a wife. She is free, you may not put her to hoe grass (like a slave).'

[3] Cultivation rites are almost non-existent among Nupe, whether pagan or Muslim. When rains are late the Islamic rain-prayer (*istisqā'*) is performed in the bush (but no fasting), the village head calls upon the *ẓigi* (priest) to do his part, but there are no rainmakers as with their Yoruba neighbours. If danger threatens the farmer asks a cleric to sacrifice a ram on the farm, but these are individual and not communal rites See also S. F. Nadel, *A Black Byzantium*, p. 237.

entrance of the farm as protection against the ɔ-*ser* (witch). This serves to show that the spirits have been paid to protect. The first cutting is beaten, cooked, and eaten on the farm, a little being offered at the spirit-hut as thankoffering to the spirits. The Temne, islamized during the last 200 years, have been too recently influenced for Islam to have changed farm ritual, but there is a gradual addition of Islamic magic ritual. Thus some Temne and Mende, at stage three, after burning but before hoeing, make a *ṣadaqa* of a white kola and remnant of white cloth. These are placed on the earth and hands are laid on them whilst a cleric recites a passage from the Qur'ān. The kola nut is buried and the cloth tied to a pole in the centre of the cultivation.

Similarly with long-islamized cultivators Islam has little influence upon practices vital to the fertility of land and the protection of crops. Marty writes of agricultural rituals among the people of Futa Jalon: 'They are undoubtedly anterior [to Islam], and it is certain that it is by the compliance of the *karamoko* who, being powerless to suppress these popular customs or maybe little desirous of so doing, have set themselves to eliminate all that was too obviously pagan and render them orthodox by islamizing them.'[1] The direct influence of Islam is seen in the addition and then substitution of Islamic magic ritual in place of sacrifice to spirits. Some islamized Hausa have discontinued sacrifice to the *uwar gwōna* (farm-mother), or Magiro or other *iskōki*. Instead they seek the protection of God by making in His name offerings to poor and clergy, and call in the cleric to protect their fields and crops against spirits, witches, thieves, monkeys, and other marauders. He reads the Qur'ān, recites prayers, spits on the earth, and provides an amulet to be tied on a pole or tree. In this way Islam sanctifies the felt need to propitiate the forces which govern fertility.

4. URBAN LIFE AND TRADING

A subsistence economy characterizes the major proportion of men's activities, but this was inadequate for the needs of the inhabitants of the Sudan states who had to pay taxes in one form or another to their rulers, as well as satisfy the economic requirements of religion. In addition, the trading economy introduced villagers to a wide variety of articles they could not grow (such as kola) or make for themselves (clothes and trinkets). Farmers, therefore, had to produce an economic surplus which tax-collectors and traders transported to the markets and trading towns.

[1] P. Marty, *Guinée*, p. 493.

The consequent exchange economy took two forms: one internal, embracing both small-scale trading within the local community and a wider commerce, carried on mainly by individual traders; and an external exchange with North Africa through the sahilian 'ports', whose organization involved large-scale operations and organized caravans. The Saharan routes have been likened to sea-routes in that they are defined tracks between two lines of ports in North Africa and the southern borderland, with along them various oasis ports-of-call. The southern ports were founded by Berbers and other northern organizers of Saharan transport, not by Negroes. In them slaves, gold, ivory, pepper, and other local products were exchanged for Saharan salt and North African goods. Through the trans-Saharan routes Islam was introduced into the Sahil and Sudan, a native Muslim trading element was soon formed and took over the whole internal commercial sphere.

South of the Sahil ports few large towns developed in western Sudan.[1] Towns were mainly residences of rulers and had the characteristics of agglomerations of villages. A considerable proportion of their population engaged in agriculture. They were organized in villages in which members of the same ethnic group congregated, with their own organization, chiefs, councils of elders, and mosques, and following their distinctive customs. Consequently they lacked all municipal feeling and disappeared without leaving a trace. As market centres foreign traders operated in them, but they also were segregated into their own suburb. Ruler towns were unstable, the continual changes in their sites showing that they were centres of village civilization. The various capitals of Māli, though they had a large trading community, were simply collections of villages. Timbuktu and Jenne had different characteristics, since they were founded by members of the Mediterranean civilization for the purpose of trade, and remained stable throughout the centuries. Other trading centres, like Nyamina, Sansanding, and Bamako, were not normally ruling towns. Kano and Jenne were unusual in that they were both capitals and centres of internal trade. None of the founded capitals of the theocrasies of the nineteenth century, such as Sokoto and Ḥamdallāhi, became commercial centres. But the true markets of the Sudan region were traditional centres on trade-routes or outside a village, held on fixed days of the week. Markets were, therefore, not tied to towns whose instability did not upset economic life.

Islam as an urban religion cannot exist in its distinctive form without

[1] The peculiarities of towns in central Sudan are dealt with in the writer's forthcoming *History of Islam in West Africa*.

towns and only townspeople can conscientiously follow its principles. The farmer instinctively resists it as a disintegrative factor. On the other hand, in the town, where life and personal relationships are more secularized, Islam is an integrative factor. Town life and trading involve abandoning local religion, Islamic law can operate over a wider field of social relations, *qāḍī's* courts can function, and teachers attract pupils from a wide area. In the townsman class there are three occupational groups; clergy living on offerings and fees; men of business such as merchants and traders, craftsmen, shopkeepers, and street vendors, for if profit is meagre so is the expense of setting up; and, finally, artisans and manual labourers. The heterogeneity characteristic of towns, however, derives from differences of ethnic origins rather than from divisions of labour. Islam, with its power to call to the one *jāmiʿ* for Friday prayer, is the only integrative factor.

Islam and contacts with North Africa had little direct influence upon means of exchange. Coinage was not adopted in the Sudan states,[1] though shells were in use before they imported cowries. Exchange was the normal practice and in transactions the price was stipulated in mediums of exchange: rings, nuggets or *mithqāls* of gold, strings of cowries (an unconsumable means of exchange), strips or bolts of cloth, bars of salt, measures of grain, slaves or animals. Al-Bakrī says that 'the means of exchange of the inhabitants of Silla are millet, salt, brass rings, and fine cotton strips called *shakkiyyāt*'.[2] Al-ʿUmarī wrote that in Kanem cotton material was the monetary standard: 'they use as money a cloth called *dendi* which is woven in their country. Each piece of material is 10 cubits or more in length.... They also use shells (*wadaʿ*), beads, pieces of copper, and coined money (imported?), but the standard upon which value is based is cloth.'[3] In western Sudan cloth formed the standard (*tamma* = 10 cubits), though for large-scale operations merchants used the *mithqāl* of gold, a term employed later as a fictitious measure. Strings of cowries were used throughout the Niger region, but were less widespread in central Sudan.[4]

Internal commerce was carried on by individual itinerant traders.

[1] Imported coinage was used by merchants but regarded as pieces of precious metal. The *douro espagnol* (Arab. *abū madfaʿ*) was used for a short time in Bornu but was supplanted by the Maria Theresa dollar.

[2] Al-Bakrī, p. 173.

[3] *Masālik*, p. 44; *Ṣubḥ*, v. 280.

[4] Cowries first appeared in Kano in the reign of Muḥammad Sharaf (1703–31); cf. Palmer, *Sud. Mem.* iii. 123. They were imported chiefly through the port of Badagari, spread but slowly, and appeared in Bornu only in Barth's time. They were not strung as in western Sudan and counting was quite a problem.

Few caravans went south of the sahilian ports, but individuals or small groups of traders could traverse the country without difficulty because their function was an economic necessity. In central Sudan the Hausa made trading their speciality, their activities extending throughout what is now Nigeria, across Dahomey and Togo into the Gold Coast where they met the Mande Dyula, the dominant traders of the Voltaic region. Throughout the west the word *dyula* has become synonymous with 'trader'. The traders of western Guinea are Mandinka, Soninke, and Susu. These traders acted as agents for Islamic culture, establishing themselves in villages along the routes, where they remained sometimes for years before returning home. Some settled permanently and thus created new Islamic nuclei. Villages along trade-routes tended to acquire Islamic characteristics, whilst the people of the bush remained pagan. Even where least effective they created favourable milieux for the ultimate spread of Islam.

The chief influences of Islam upon economic life derive from its universalism. In this Arabic helped. Its utility as a written language and its value as a link between scattered traders need not be stressed, and the schools which flourished in trading towns perhaps owed something to the commercial as well as to the religious value of Arabic. Traders introduced large numbers of Arabic commercial terms, such as weights and measures, into Sudanese languages.[1] But although the Islamic element took over the commercial field it brought little that was new. The same exports and the same methods continued when Berbers became Muslims. In the exploitation of Saharan salt-mines and Sudanese gold extraction (a pagan monopoly) there was no improvement. Handicrafts like leather work benefited from northern influences, but owed little to the direct influence of Islamic civilization.

In practice the action of Islamic law is not very effective. In towns trading practices, being based upon economic expediency, are little influenced. In village life the ethic of the individual only partially displaces the collective ethic of the cultivator. Islamic regulations affect the trader most in the sphere of personal and social relations. He regards the duty of almsgiving as important both for the welfare of his soul and the prosperity of his business. Contracts follow customary procedure but have been influenced by Islam and it is difficult to tell in the Sudan

[1] For example, the Arabic *mudd* was adopted throughout the Sudan for a measure of millet. It was an important exchange standard since millet formed the basis of economic life. In some villages the chief kept a standard measure mainly for the convenience of itinerant traders. Similarly with measures of length: Arab. *shibr*, 'span', Mande *sibira*, Songhay *silbi*, Fulfulde *sibre*.

zone which elements are indigenous and which due to Islam. The *qāḍī* will normally allow customary law except in the negative sense that he would not recognize a contract which was directly opposed to Islamic law, such as one concerning the sharing of the profits of a brothel or a self-pawning contract. Though the written contract has been introduced contracts are normally verbal, sealed by a handclasp and the recitation of the Fātiḥa.[1] Estimation of the correct day and even hour is important in drawing up a contract, and a plea before a *qāḍī* that one had been enacted on an unlucky day would have a reasonable chance of being accepted as evidence of its invalidity.

Traders are well acquainted with the devices by which the prohibition of usury may be circumvented. In the modern Islamic world these have ceased to be of interest, but in West Africa they are still prevalent. The prohibition is interpreted as applying only to interest on loans of money.[2] Consequently the legally-minded get around it by loaning goods, the debtor promising to repay double after a year; in other words, he acknowledges that he has received more than the actual amount of the loan. *Qāḍīs* recognize this type of transaction for it has received the sanction of the schools and the creditor can apply to the court to enforce restoration or the equivalent in money,[3] but claims for interest on money lent would not be recognized. The normal small trader needs to borrow very little, but those who wish to make bulk purchases operate with a sleeping partner who receives a proportion of the profit by way of interest. Farmers frequently borrow grain or mortgage their harvest to tide over the 'hungry season' before the harvest, agreeing to repay 1½ measures for each measure borrowed, but these are generally short-term loans. The Islamic prohibition has been beneficial to the farmer and small-scale trader for, in spite of the devices adopted to circumvent the letter of the law, a borrower cannot get heavily into debt since the

[1] Mande: *fatiha dõ*, 'to conclude a contract'.

[2] A successful Hausa business man, al-ḥājj al-Ḥasan, who died in 1955, 'used to find an outlet for surplus capital by advancing money to any promising young men who put up to him a likely sounding trading scheme, asking them to repay half their profits (in some cases less; in some cases none) if they made any. The size of his bank balance can be judged from the fact that he was one of those gilded men of Kano who stipulate for religious reasons that their deposit accounts shall be non-interest-bearing, but who receive instead a substantial "dash" each year' (*West Africa*, 29 Oct. 1955, p. 1020).

[3] Professor Daryll Forde writes: 'In Zaria province, for example, the judges who administer the Koranic law, admit as a valid transaction the sale on credit by a money lender of an article such as a gown, actually obtainable for say 7*s*. cash, for 10*s*. This the buyer proceeds to sell for 7*s*. in order to secure that amount of cash and eventually repays the "seller" the agreed price of 10*s*.' (*The Native Economics of Nigeria*, 1946, p. 165). H. Minor (*The Primitive City of Timbuktu*, 1953, pp. 69–70) reports the same practice in Timbuktu.

interest remains fixed, however many years elapse before repayment, and the creditor has no legal means of enforcing repayment of illegal loans.

Islam exercised little influence upon the industrial sphere, primarily because of the hierarchization of society into craft classes and castes. In central Sudan craftsmen were organized into guilds or trade corporations, bound together by common professional interests, mutual help, and recognition of the authority of the guild-head. The latter, equivalent to the *amīn* of the Arab *sūq*, acted as intermediary between members and central authority, fixed prices for their commodities, and regulated differences. Craftsmen in towns are invariably Muslims, but the Islam of members of the professional castes is superficial. The technique of crafts and the organization of markets involve ritual, therefore Muslim craftsmen cannot abandon old practices. In North Africa craftsmen have a patron saint, but those of West Africa are under the protection of a patron spirit, considered as inventor of the craft. No Hausa smith would neglect to offer sacrifice to Maḳērā, their chief spirit, nor a hunter to Gajērē and other hunter or forest spirits. Similarly with markets. M. G. Smith remarks: 'Despite the long centuries of Islamic proselytization in Hausaland, the market derives its mystical charter and its economic vitality from the traditional pre-Islamic spirits.'[1]

5. INFLUENCE OF ISLAM UPON MATERIAL CULTURE

Sudanese peoples had attained stable forms of cultural organization long before a specifically Islamic culture began to penetrate. Influences from the Mediterranean and Nilotic regions had been so absorbed as to seem wholly indigenous. When Berber traders introduced Islam into the southern Sahil they forged a much closer link than had existed before between the North African and Sudan civilizations and it was naturally this belt, the zone of transition between Sahara and Sudan, Berbers and Negroes, which was most influenced. Islam penetrates most deeply where a strong urban culture is already in existence, but in West Africa, a sphere of village civilizations, it had to create its own urban milieu and cultural characteristics.

The native religious assembly is characterized not by a building but by the sacred grove such as is mentioned in the first account of Gāna.

[1] Mary Smith, *Baba of Karo*, p. 281.

Urban Islam required the large building for worship. For this purpose the type of architecture associated with the Sahil lent itself, and this style became associated with Islamic culture simply because Islam first gained the people of the Sahil. It is not characteristic of Mandinka village civilization, in spite of the inclusion of Jenne and Timbuktu within the sphere of the state of Māli, but is found in the urban civilization of the Sahil and Sudan from Futa Toro to Lake Chad. It is rarely found outside this region with the exception of the Dyula dispersion. The Dyula, deriving from the urban civilization of Jenne, have taken this style wherever they have founded settlements, not only at Bobo Dioulasso in the savanna, but even in the forest country of the Ivory Coast where they continue to maintain it in spite of the different, and seemingly unsuitable, climatical conditions. Their villages have the characteristic Sudanese aspect of straight alleys, running between flat-roofed mud houses, with their pinnacles and water spouts, surrounding an inner courtyard upon which the rooms open. Pylons stand on each side of the heavily-worked entrance door with its carved lock, identical with those of North Africa. But this style of architecture remains exotic since it has not been adopted by the natives of the region.

Islamic contacts modified the economic life of West Africans chiefly in so far as Muslims became agents of economic exchange; consequently they played a pivotal role in the diffusion of Islamic material culture. This is most evident in regard to personal habits and clothing. Islam enjoins personal taboos, forms of hygiene and manners which have inculcated habits of cleanliness, courtesy, and propriety. Here the effect of Islamic legal morality is more evident than in economic life. Though its effect in this sphere varies among different peoples certain elements always go along with islamization and are evident in the village as well as in the town. A Muslim village, even though but superficially islamized, is never quite the same as a pagan village, and the first stage is the adoption of elements of material culture, many of which, though not in themselves specifically Islamic, are associated with its civilization in the eyes of pagans. Material culture is closely allied with religious differentiation. If a man is naked or semi-naked he is a Pagan, if he wears a robe or gown he is a Muslim, if he puts on shorts or trousers he is a Christian. If he urinates squatting he is a Muslim, if standing a Pagan or a Christian. Some cultural elements are adopted in dissociation from Islam as a religious culture, whilst under different circumstances they are adopted because people want to be thought of as Muslims. In this category of material traits actual religious elements must be included. A Pagan in a Muslim environment imitates the external postures of ritual prayer as part of his attempt to assimilate himself, even though temporarily, into his new environment. In the sphere of village civilization the different traits coexist on a basis of religious differentiation,[1] and many elements of material culture will not be assimilated until people have crossed the dividing line.

Traders' importations were naturally governed by demand. New material goods which fit in with established cultural patterns are easily adopted, any which might upset the pattern of life are rejected. But Islam, by modifying habits of mind, opens the way for new acquisitions. In any case they are africanized and become part of African Islamic culture. The stress Islam places upon clothing encourages the art of weaving, but styles of the turban or gown are not the same as those of North Africa. The most important cultural introduction of Islam was the alphabet, but even here, though it has no relation to anything in former life and is wholly associated with Islam, a Sudanese style distinctive from that of North Africa made its appearance.

The distinction between things directly due to Islam and those associated with Islamic culture by no logical process is seen more clearly in the sphere of personal habits. Islamic culture carries with it a deep sensitivity to nakedness and has led to the adoption of clothing and to a general uniformity of type and style, though with local variations and with the usual differences in style and quality between rulers, clergy, peasant, and nomad. The universal type of Sudan Muslim dress consists of short pants and a little smock with short sleeves for men and a wrapper round the waist for women. A long full gown is worn over this on special occasions and by men of rank, together with a cotton cap and a turban; and women add a blouse or voluminous wrapper. Chiefs wear varied types of head-dress; in the west a round or conical headgear, in the centre an adaptation of the Tuareg mouth-veil.[2] These

[1] This may be illustrated by the Mande higher numeral *keme*, which is apparently an ancient assimilation: ancient Egyptian *khemen* (value 80), Berber *temeḍ*, Fulfulde *ḥīmere*, pl. *kēme*. In Māli and among Mandinka pagans today its value is 60, with Bambara it is 80, but wherever Islam has been adopted its value is 100. Three systems of enumeration, therefore, exist in the same language group based on the same word. Traders have had to distinguish them: *mali-ňkeme*, *bămana-ňkeme*, and *silămi-ya-keme* (or *faradye-la-keme*), the Islamic *keme* (see M. Delafosse, *La Langue Mandingue*, i. 274–5; S. de Ganay, 'Graphie bambara des nombres', *J. Soc. Afr.* xx (1950), 296 n. 1).

[2] The peoples of north-central Sudan have adopted many Tuareg characteristics. The visage muffler (but not the mouth taboo with which it is associated) has been adopted in a simpler form, merely hiding the lower part of the face, by northern Songhay, Zerma, Hausa, and settled Fulani chiefs. Many have also adopted the Tuareg sword, arm dagger, and bracelet. Hausa and Zerma chiefs use the Arab saddle, mount from the right, and do not use adjustable

head-dresses are worn by the commons only on special occasions. In general, neither blacks nor whites of the Sudan mind praying with the head bare, contrary to the attitude prevailing in most parts of the Islamic world. Muslims have maintained the custom, universal among pagans, of shaving the head when in mourning. Henna usage[1] is a characteristic of Islamic civilization which has spread widely because of a prophetical recommendation. It purifies, it is known to mollify *jinn* and neutralize their urge to harm. Its application characterizes all Islamic festivities and transitional rites. The night of the great henna (*lailat al-ḥinnā' al-kabīra*), a feature of marriage ceremonial in Morocco and the eastern Sudan, has been adopted by Songhay and Hausa.

Islam inculcates habits of personal cleanliness and refinement of manners, the first being due to its ritual regulations, and its adoption leads to demands for soap and perfumes. The effect of Islamic taboos such as drinking intoxicants and eating carrion has been mentioned elsewhere. The slaughtering of animals according to the Islamic rite is an early acquisition, important in that it makes flesh licit. Islam prohibits mutilations, tattooing, and incisions, except circumcision and excision, and the disappearance of deformation customs is an index to depth of islamization. Tattooed Muslims are generally those, like Dyula, living among pagans whose wives conform to custom in having their children done. Taboos form a common element linking Muslims. Those that run counter to more important things will not be accepted. The taboo on contact with a dog is effective where people have no use for it, but ineffective with people who engage in hunting. Islamization normally leads to the abandonment of the practice, common among many pagans, of eating dogs.

Fermented drink is closely linked with the sacred and plays a great role in religious and social life. Islam naturally seeks to break this link and the prohibition of alcohol is closely associated with the ban on offerings to communal cult deities. This prohibition has had considerable effect even though everywhere Muslims will be found who ignore it. Public opinion can be mobilized against fermented drinks on account of the role they play in pagan life. Here an Islamic taboo has been beneficial and Western influence harmful. Beer, of course, is part of the natural diet of many Africans, and it is not this which is the problem today, but

stirrups. Al-'Umarī says (*Masālik*, pp. 68–69) that the people of Māli used the Arab saddle and method of riding except that they mounted from the left.

[1] Its diffusion in the Sahil is no doubt pre-Islamic. Al-Bakrī says that henna was cultivated at Awdaghast (pp. 157, 168). The Arabic word has been adopted by the Songhay (*alhinna*). Hausa *lalle* may come from Tamahaqq *anella* which itself is probably derived from *ḥinnā'*.

imported or local factory stuff. Clergy do not find this question easy to deal with and almost everywhere one finds controversy. In general, they argue that the prohibition mentioned in their law books only applies to palm wine and spirits but not to beer which has but a small percentage of alcohol. Nupe clergy asserted that God had prohibited *muge* (palm wine), but not *ege* (beer made from guinea corn), nor, surprisingly, *barasa* (trade gin). A few said that beer is prohibited, probably because of its local association with libations, but not palm wine. A great role is played by the kola nut in supplying the place of beer in Islamic rituals. It is an essential element in all ritual surrounding the great events of social life, and consecrates contracts and oaths. Since the law books do not mention it, chewing could be retained, but with an essential change from red to white kolas in Islamic ceremonial in western Guinea, parallel to the change from red to white rice offerings.

Another prohibition concerns representational art. Islam affects symbolic art associated with house decoration largely through the dissociation of idea and symbol. It has a withering effect upon other aspects of the imaginative life. It destroys representational art, less as a result of the actual prohibition, as through its rooting out of pagan symbols, like masks of mystery cults and representations of ancestors.[1] This is the same process as operated in early Islam, for the prohibition is not due to the Prophet's express legislation. We have to remember that under the old régime art was a vehicle of religion, decorative arts were not related to aesthetic appreciation but to the old spiritual world of associated ideas; hence when the symbols are displaced there is no aesthetic need to be satisfied which might be diverted to other channels of art. Islam, however, has not had a negative effect upon music[2] and dancing, the African's natural means of expressing his feelings. Whilst music is the speciality of the griot caste, the dance is the pastime of all classes, young and old, men and women, Muslims and pagans; only clergy and chiefs do not take part out of concern for their dignity.

[1] Lebeuf and Masson Detourbet (*La Civilisation du Tchad*, p. 141), after describing the art of the So peoples, write: 'L'islamisme a tué cet art des représentations et, partant, la technique de la céramique qui, depuis lors, n'a cessé de régresser jusqu'à ne plus pouvoir produire que les grossiers ustensiles contemporains.'

[2] The folk-music of the Sudan was little influenced by borrowings after the rise of Islam, but rulers who adopted aspects of the ceremonial of eastern courts certainly imported some musical instruments; see H. G. Farmer, 'Early References to Music in the Western Sūdān', *J.R.A.S.*, 1939, pp. 569–79.

9

The Influence of Westernism

I. THE IMPACT OF WESTERN CIVILIZATION

IN considering the impact of Western civilization some comparison will be necessary between its influence upon pagan as well as Muslim regions. Nor can modern administrative divisions any longer be ignored since there are differences, not only on broad lines between the colonial policies adopted by British and French, but also by each power at different times, in different regions, and towards Muslim and pagan populations. Also, although boundaries cut across climatical bands and bring most diverse peoples into one political unit, their present political and economic organization is important for assessing the contemporary situation for it has given each division a definite individuality and has governed the direction and speed of the infiltration of Western ideas, the intensity of the resultant changes, the forms of economic and social evolution, and posed problems peculiar to each political region. Thus different forms of political evolution are in progress in French and British Africa. At the same time, Western ideas, working through the new institutions, are causing ethnic groups to differentiate themselves in a quite new form of consciousness from any in earlier African life.

We may recall the scheme of culture contact presented in the second chapter, in which Western civilization is given its place in the contemporary scene of contact, reaction, and adaptation. The culture fields with which we are confronted are:

Local African Cultures: that is, the regional cultures, the inherited traditions and customs of the local folk culture;

West African Islamic Culture: the main theme of this book has been an analysis of the impact of Islam upon African culture and the resulting socio-cultural organization. But further, as a result of the European occupation, has come the challenge of

Western Culture, and it is necessary to see what has been the response of Muslims to its disruptive tendencies leading towards the secularization of life.

This impact, leading to the adoption of elements of material culture (such as technology and cash-crop cultivation) and of its secular ideology, has been unequal in its effect upon different types of societies, such as those of town and village, and upon pagan and Muslim communities, but we may generalize in broad lines as to the contemporary results.

In the sphere of Sudanese village culture the local culture field remains the dominant element, modified in varied degrees, according to region, people, or class, by the Islamic culture, and to a much lesser degree by the infiltration of Western elements. In the sphere of Sudanese urban life the three patterns operate with quite different emphases from those within that of village culture. The Islamic is the dominant culture pattern, Western influence affects certain spheres of life, and the old culture, originally the village civilization, is weakest, for it consists of disparate elements of old social patterns together with remnants of cults and practitioners, which, divorced from their natural setting, become non-functional in the life of society. When we turn to the coastal urban centres once again the emphases are different. In this sphere the Western is the dominant element, the local culture (in Senegalese towns this is the local-Islamic amalgam) comes second, and the Islamic is a semi-integrated intrusion, even in Lagos where the population is 50 per cent. Muslim.[1]

The various cultural agents and forces which lead to the modification of traditional life by the West are:

1. *Political forces*: colonial officials and the policies of the governments they represent.
2. *Economic forces*: European officials of agricultural departments, merchants and the like, acting as agents of world economic forces.
3. *Educational, welfare, and religious forces*: educationists, missionaries, health and sanitary authorities, and the policies lying behind their activities.

It will be noted that these agents are all Westerners and that their personal impact is limited, only the missionaries being closely in touch with African life. It is rather through the *impersonal* action of these Western agents that changes are effected. The really effective agents of transmission are Africans, so we get:

[1] Coastal towns divide into three groups corresponding to the main littoral climates: the sub-Canarian (towns like St. Louis and Bathurst which have a long European history); Guinean (Bissao, Conakry, Freetown, and Monrovia, to name only capitals); and the Beninian (towns of the Ivory Coast, Ghana, Togo, Dahomey, and Nigeria). In this last group the quantitative penetration of Islam varies considerably, but it is represented mainly by immigrants from the interior who are distinct and recognizable in dress and deportment, professions, customs and religion, and remain relatively untouched by the Western ferment in which they are living.

4. *Social forces*: Western-influenced Africans of various types: Creoles in their role as intermediary communities, teachers, government officials, trade unionists, the politically conscious, and the advanced and *évolués* who have studied in Western schools or in Europe. The lead in modification comes from the urban centres which influence the countryside through the links that exist between town and country, urban relatives, villagers working in towns, on agricultural schemes, in mines, and the like.

The forces set in motion as a result of the impact are unparalleled in any previous phase of African history. Formerly outside influences, including Islam, came unhurriedly and naturally, and were assimilated by Negro peoples into their own cultural heritage without radical displacement or resulting in an essentially new point of departure. This was true even of European influence until the present century, for since the Portuguese first landed it has been continuous in a narrow coastal strip and many aspects were absorbed naturally. But the present century has been characterized by the abrupt nature of the impact and the revolutionary type and rate of change that has been set in motion, especially in littoral regions. For example, in the economic sphere stress is placed on industrial crops like cocoa and ground-nuts whose cultivation brings about changes in traditional agriculture which in turn modify social and cultural patterns. People can no longer live in a closed economy in which each social group produces purely for its own needs, but their economy is geared to world needs. Similarly in other spheres, new forms of political and social consciousness and organization are being forged in the process of readjustment. No village remains completely untouched by some aspect of Western influence. So revolutionary are the changes that are taking place that African cultures in their traditional form are unable to cope with the forces and are succumbing to them, for they could not assimilate Western civilization in the same way they assimilated fugitive radiations from earlier civilizations.

At the same time, owing to the impossibility of acquiring a true historical perspective, we need to be cautious in trying to estimate what is actually happening. Anyone viewing the changing scene of Africa today is more likely to over-emphasize the shock of the impact and the rate and depth of change than the reverse. This is because the outward signs of change are so predominantly before our eyes, whereas often they are being assimilated more naturally than we suppose and village people's inner life remains substantially what it was before. This is especially true of those West Africans who were islamized before the impact made itself felt.

The difference between the reaction of pagan and Muslim societies derives primarily from the nature of their socio-religious systems. Islam protected Muslims against the main impact through having provided them with a universalist religion, a social and cultural pattern common to diverse groups, and an attitude of cultural and religious superiority. Other insulating factors derived from the situation of the main Muslim communities in the interior far removed from the main impact, the unsuitability of much of their region for rapid economic development, and the difference in policy adopted by colonial governments towards Muslims and pagans.

Muslims, confronting local African cultures, had been imbued with an attitude of cultural and religious superiority. When faced with conquest by European powers demonstrating a technical superiority they responded by a self-protective withdrawal. The fact that Islam came to Negroes as a civilization gave them greater resistance to Western civilization. No statement could be wider of the mark than that of Dr. C. K. Meek who, after mentioning that Islam has raised 'barbaric tribes to a higher level of civilization and welded them together into one homogeneous whole', goes on, 'thus Muhammadanism, or Semitic culture, has made the way easy for the reception of Western civilization'.[1] In fact, the exact opposite would be nearer the mark; the new order, based on the secularization of the theory behind these influences, is a direct challenge to the fundamental principles upon which Islamic civilization is based.

The powers of resistance inherent in Islamic societies have ensured that the process of change has been gradual, restricted in operation, and allowed to influence only limited spheres of life. Gradually they are giving way, for no people in Africa can completely immunize themselves against the penetration of these forces, especially now that they are finding themselves lagging behind the more open societies of the coastal regions in material, economic, educational, and political development. Youth are realizing that it is necessary to understand the new world into which they are being drawn and therefore coming into opposition to the traditionalists and privileged who seek to retard. All the same, though the impact of the West has created many problems its effect upon Muslims contrasts strikingly with its effect upon pagan societies. This helps us to understand the change Islam has wrought in the lives of Africans who assimilated its culture.

[1] Meek, Macmillan, and Hussey, *Europe and West Africa*, 1940, p. 13.

On the other hand, there is a great difference between the attitude adopted towards Western civilization by long-established Muslims and that displayed by those who have entered the Islamic fold during the last hundred years and have not acquired the conservative mentality characteristic of the first. These have shown themselves ready to come to terms with present realities, have proved more adaptable, and have acquired a more secular attitude towards religion.

One further aspect should be mentioned. Since culture contact has a reciprocal character the other face, the conditioning of the European, should not be ignored. They are just as much in the triple culture situation as African new men. The Islamic environment modifies colonial policy and the administrator, missionary policy and the missionary, economic planning and the expert. This aspect is important since it explains regional differences and the vacillations and modifications of official policy. Similarly the missionary, when allowed to work in Muslim regions, had to adopt a different policy in regions of consolidated Islam from that he adopted in pagan regions. This is one of the factors to be taken into account in explaining, for example, why Christianity in Hausaland is a foreign religion, represented mainly by Yoruba and Ibo but not by Hausa Christians.

2. POLITICAL CHANGE

The contrast between British and French policy towards Muslims is marked. We will look first at British policy in Northern Nigeria. The British entered upon the conquest of the Fulani-Hausa states in the spirit of slave-liberators of the nineteenth century. But once in control they perpetuated the system of rule whose tyranny they had ostensibly set out to end. Their aim was little more than one of expediency, the maintenance of public security as cheaply and as effectively as possible. They accordingly bolstered up the disintegrating states, interfered as little as possible with established institutions, and kept out all 'progressive' influences. They promised the emirs that there would be no interference in religious matters and interpreted this to mean that Islam would be upheld as the religion of any state whose ruler called himself a Muslim and its people insulated against other religious influences.

In adopting his policy of indirect rule Lugard thought that he was following the normal principles of the Sudan state, the virtue of which lay in the way it allowed traditional forms of rule to operate within the general framework. There was, however, this primary difference. The

British conquest followed upon a relatively recent Fulani conquest, in full dissolution when they took over, and they confirmed and stabilized this alien authority which proved unadaptable to changing conditions. The French, on the contrary, by changing the superstructure were building upon sounder principles for this interfered less with primary institutions.

This policy, besides assisting the spread of Islam, enabled Islamic law to gain greater influence. In fact, before they came under British administration rulers and their courts accorded greater recognition to custom than today. Nadel shows how in the Nupe state under British rule Islamic law has been gradually overriding customary law. Through the operation of the principle that a stronger law drives out the weaker, Muslim law becomes predominant. *Qāḍīs* are ignorant of the unwritten code, they make pagans swear on the Qur'ān, and they in consequence feel themselves free from the obligation to tell the truth.[1] Clerics in Northern Nigeria tried to push the application of the *sharīʿa* as far as they could. Generally Muslims take the line of least resistance and allow an award to follow Islamic rather than customary law, but open clashes were not infrequent.[2]

The policy of indirect rule as interpreted in Nigeria shackled its peoples with the existing ruling class, tied down both Muslims and pagans to the *status quo*, and isolated them from the rest of the world; and although this policy failed since it did not take into account the inevitable encroachments of new forces, it succeeded in so retarding the northern emirates that they remained stagnant and undeveloped until recent years.

Yet in spite of this policy political change was unavoidable from the very outset of British rule. Although the administration reinforced the political apparatus, real power was taken away from the chiefs, political boundaries were rearranged, and chiefs' powers were limited since they

[1] See S. F. Nadel, *A Black Byzantium*, pp. 165–74.

[2] See Lord Hailey, *Native Administration in the British African Territories*, 1951, part iii, p. 95. As we have seen, colonial powers were confronted by customary law among Muslims as well as pagans. The extent to which Islamic law was applied depended upon custom (in Northern Nigeria Islamic law came under the provisions of 'native law and custom') and varied considerably in different localities. Colonial powers therefore recognized the application of Islamic law in certain spheres, but had to add to their ordinances the clause, 'excepting those points where customary law applies'. Only in the Gambia is there a definite enactment recognizing Islamic law (Mohammedan Law Recognition Ordinance of 1905). This grants to *sharīʿa* courts jurisdiction in cases between Muslims relating to status, marriage, succession, donations, testaments, and guardianship; but not to civil contracts and criminal matters. In predominantly pagan areas in all territories Islamic law was applied, as exceptional to the prevailing customary law, to Muslims who cared to invoke it.

were subject to the legislative and administrative control of the Protectorate government. The law was that of the colonial authority, for even though Islamic law was recognized the spheres in which it could operate were determined and a western criminal code imposed.[1] Through the secularization of political theory a breach was opened between religious tradition and political life and the former could not have its full effect.

Eventually the government realized the limitations of its policy,[2] mainly through the rise of nationalist movements in the south. Yet long before the policy of isolation had failed, for it had proved impossible to insulate the inhabitants of the north completely. Then the necessity of transforming an artificial creation like Nigeria into a freely-associated self-governing state forced the government to realize that their northern policy must inevitably lead to the formation of another Pakistan, and a belated attempt was made to develop the northern regions. Once they introduced innovations to improve conditions of living, dispensaries and hospitals, schools and agricultural schemes, the influx of new ideas was accelerated.

British policy in Nigeria cannot be compared with that in their other West African territories for in these there were no comparable Islamic states, but rather with French policy in the Muslim regions of the A.O.F. The French, with their twin aims of direct rule and assimilation, showed indecisiveness in their policy towards Islam. Two parallel strands run through it, one pro-Muslim and the other, not so much pro-animist, as an attempt to hold the balance. Certain governors (Faidherbe, Grodet, and de Coppet) adopted a policy of fostering Islam. Like the British they regarded it as a stage towards civilization, and considered as Muslim any village which had a mosque. By reason of their experience in North Africa they felt themselves on familiar ground when confronted by Muslims, whereas the Negro world was strange and unaccountable. In the early days when there was a shortage of administrators Muslims were a useful resource and former N.C.O.s or interpreters were made local chiefs. Similarly they seized upon Islamic law to govern the personal and social life of anyone who could possibly be called Muslim. As elsewhere there was the usual legal dualism

[1] In Northern Nigeria the Muslim courts were given wide powers of criminal jurisdiction, but nowhere else. In the A.O.F. a decree of 17 Feb. 1941 provided a Native Penal Code modelled on the French code.

[2] Sir Donald Cameron was the first governor to criticize the extreme way in which the policy of indirect rule was conceived and operated in Northern Nigeria in a speech to the Legislative Council in March 1933.

between the Code Français as the penal code and Qur'ānic law as the civil code. To smooth their path the French at first recognized Islamic education, although they realized that it was no help towards the civilizing ends they had in view. In the earlier period they tried to regulate it, but afterwards concentrated upon education in French and limited recognition of Islamic education to the maintenance of a few establishments for special purposes such as training of *qāḍīs*.[1]

But the French, as a result of their experience in conquering the Muslim adventurers and dealing with outbreaks of *soi-disant* Mahdīs, also regarded Islam as a menace and this thread runs through their attitude. Islam appeared to them, first as the strongest force opposed to their penetration[2] and then to internal security. The wars of al-ḥājj ʿUmar, Samōri, Rābiḥ, and a host of smaller chiefs had led to political disintegration and anarchy. As in Northern Nigeria their conquests had fragmentated and no powerful states remained. Hence the French encountered no great opposition in their conquest. But once in control, the administrators, however favourable they were to Islam, followed a different policy from that of the British. They had no use for the system of indirect rule and proceeded to eliminate the important Muslim chiefs.[3] A few were retained, though without real authority, in order to smooth the path of transition to a new political order. But whenever expedient, generally immediately they showed signs of disaffection, they were dispossessed. The *almāmi* of Futa Jalon was kept

[1] The British administration also made some provision for the teaching of Islamic law. In 1934 the Kano Native Administration founded a law school with three teachers from the Anglo-Egyptian Sudan. This was taken over by the government in 1947 as the School of Arabic Studies. Although it has produced graduates with an advanced knowledge of Arabic and *fiqh*, they do not compare with those of the past for many of the existing *qāḍīs* trained under the old system of seeking-masters display a most impressive knowledge of the *sharīʿa*. The inclusion of a more liberal range of subjects has, on the other hand, given graduates of the Kano school a wider outlook.

[2] All Muslims were by no means opposed, certainly not the non-privileged and dispossessed who aided the French to eliminate tyrants like the Tokolor and Samōri and heaved a sigh of relief when they were destroyed, yet after a generation or two of peace many of the younger generation tend to look upon these conquerors as champions of Sudanese independence. Islam nourished their opposition to alien rulers and was the strongest obstacle towards the policy of assimilation.

R. Delavignette (*Freedom and Authority in French West Africa*, English transl. 1950, p. 75) shows that French policy 'did not encroach on custom as much as has been supposed. For most of the great chiefs who were displaced by our nominees were themselves feudatories who held their fiefs from the slave-trader for whom they rounded up the game, or they were the soldiers of a Moslem war lord who handed over the pagan cultivators to them as serfs. They did not express, they rather oppressed the old Africa of the land and the villages. And in replacing them by our chiefs of cantons, we have most often merely substituted for a usurper a sort of functionary.'

on for a time but his rule was finally abolished in 1912. After conquering Masina in 1893 they appointed ʿAjīb, *almāmi* of Dingiray and brother of Amadu Seku, as ruler, but in 1902 he was put on pension and the region brought under direct administration. In Futa Toro the authority of the chiefs of the old régime declined considerably to the advantage of the *chefs de canton* appointed by the administration. Minor chiefs were replaced by men of the same stock as the people they administered or by nominees from the army. Where a great indigenous chief such as the Moro Nāba of the Mossi accepted French control peacefully he was allowed to retain his symbolical, moral, social, and religious authority, but his political authority was reduced almost to nothing. Chiefs in general became subordinate officials of the administration.

Shortly before the First World War many administrators, realizing that Islam was in opposition to their civilizing ideals, felt that its spread, accelerated under the conditions provided by their rule, might endanger French hegemony. The result was a number of books with the title theme of L. G. Binger's *Le Péril de l'Islam* (Paris, 1906), culminating in J. Brévié's *L'Islamisme contre 'Naturisme' au Soudan Français* (1923) which set out to show that Islam, on the wane when they took over, had been given new life and unprecedented opportunities for expansion under the occupation; that it was disruptive of the religio-social order of Africans; and that pagan communities which had resisted its encroachments were in danger of social disintegration. A circular drafted in 1911 explained the new slant in policy and affirmed that every effort was to be made to arrest the decline of African religion and consequent disruption of the old society. Restrictions were to be placed on the movements of itinerant alms-collecting and proselytizing clerics, whilst permits to perform the pilgrimage and open new mosques and schools were to be granted only by provincial governors.[1]

Two things strike one immediately regarding the territories formed by Western powers: the artificiality of the frontiers hastily drawn during the closing years of the nineteenth century and the disunities, political, economic, and religious, which exist within these artificial boundaries. The organizations set up by Western administrators could override natural loyalties, but once transition towards a new political order brings out new aspirations the disunities begin to show themselves.

[1] It was this policy which led to official encouragement of the work of P. Marty on regional Islam, an important feature of which from the point of view of the administration was the listing of Islamic clerics and estimates of their influence.

An inevitable result of the occupation has been the awakening of nationalism. There are enormous variations in the degree and extent in which different regions have been affected by Western influence. It has been strongest in coastal areas, including predominantly Muslim Senegal, but away from these areas it has been relatively slow and has had a milder impact. Political activity has been most intense in the areas where Western penetration has gone deepest. The ever-changing political scene is outside the sphere of this inquiry and we are only concerned to point out the influence Islamic allegiance can play in the political scene. This is most evident in Northern Nigeria where religion continually made its appearance in discussions with the Muslim *évolué* class about their political aspirations. Muslims, unlike pagans, had never expected a millennium from the West, but a form of nationalism has appeared which in varying degrees is animated and reinforced by Islam. When pressure from southern politicians forced the British to make progressive moves towards granting self-government a deep cleavage in political ideals showed itself between north and south. Islam as the established religion gave an appearance of solidarity to the north although only two-thirds of the people are Muslim. Southerners had been evolving rapidly whilst northerners had not been affected in any radical way. The ruling authorities desired no change and viewed the aspirations of the southerners with suspicion. Regionalism was inevitable. Nationalist ideas brought out these deep-rooted prejudices and led to the formation of three regions with a central legislature.

A number of groups may be distinguished in Northern Nigeria from the political point of view. There are the ruling classes whose primary concern is the maintenance of the *status quo*. Political parties in the south, as in Ghana, realize that a modern party must have its roots in the rural population as well as the new men, but the authorities in the north sought to preserve politics as the prerogative of an aristocracy. This group finds its political organ in the Northern Peoples Congress. The leaders of the masses, the clergy class, whose ideal is that of a Muslim church-state, perhaps need distinguishing although they do not exert any obvious political influence. Then there are those who favour a modern state based on Islamic constitutional principles but adapted to modern conditions. Relatively small in numbers and confused in aim they favour a democratic pattern of political authority with Islam as religion of the state, and were keen to discuss the character of modern Islamic states. Among them is a minority more deeply secularized by Western education. They react strongly against medieval Islam and the superstitions of everyday life. Islam is scarcely vital to their thought and in the social and political fields they recognize its implications only in so far as allegiance tends to demarcate. Next come non-Muslims who are most self-conscious in the pagan 'middle belt'. Finally, there are southerners born in the north who draw their political biases from their southern brethren. These last two groups find their political organ in the Northern Elements' Progressive Union,[1] which seeks reform of the present autocratic system. The last four, who stand to benefit by change, are critical of local administrations controlled by the old ruling authorities. The formation of new legislatures has not satisfied their political aspirations since only nominees of the emirs can secure election. They feel that local government reform is impossible under the present system and that the emirs cannot provide a foundation upon which to build a modern state.

Except in Northern Nigeria and the Senegal the influence of Islamic allegiance upon political life is negligible. The secularist outlook of administrators of colonial territories led them to maintain an impartial attitude with regard to the various religions practised by the peoples they administered. This attitude has been acquired by politicians of Southern Nigeria and Ghana. Hence they have no patience with Islamic political theory. The formation of the Muslim Association Party in Ghana provoked a strong reaction from Dr. Nkrumah and the radical Convention Peoples Party as bringing religion into politics.[2] Similarly the South Nigerian politicians have no use for the Islamic bias of the northerners.

French policy with regard to the political development of her colonial territories has followed quite different lines from that of the British.

[1] For some time they could not secure representation in the Northern House of Assembly, but have now (1957) seven members.

[2] The Muslim Association was founded in 1932 as a cultural organization to foster Muslim unity and seek for reforms giving greater recognition to Islam in the legal and educational system. It made its first entry into politics in 1939 when it sponsored candidates for the Accra municipal elections. At the 1954 general election the M.A.P. claimed the support of Muslims in the Colony and Ashanti, and of its sixteen candidates only one was elected. Following this the C.P.P. made efforts to secure the support of the M.A.P. members by setting up a Muslim Council, sympathetically considering proposals for establishing Qur'ān schools or introducing the Qur'ān into government schools for Muslim pupils, and by sponsoring a C.P.P. *imām* in Accra. At the 1956 election the M.A.P. put forward only three candidates and won one seat.

In the Northern Territories Muslims are not organized as a separate party but support the Northern Peoples Party which contested each of the twenty-six northern seats. Of the 104 members of the 1954 Assembly fifteen were Muslims (including two Aḥmadīs), that is 7 per cent., which is roughly representative of the strength of Muslims throughout Ghana as a whole (see *West Africa*, 26 May 1956, pp. 324–5).

Direct administration was the rule with the tendency towards closer integration with the metropolitan government. In 1944 a conference at Brazzaville drew up recommendations for the political, economic, and social development of these territories. The preamble to the recommendations states that, 'The goals of the work of civilization being accomplished by France in her colonies does away with any idea of autonomy and all possibility of evolution outside the unit of the French Empire; the constitution of self-government, even in the distant future, is not to be considered.' The colonies were, therefore, to be regarded as parts of greater France and the policy contemplated the assimilation of peoples of different cultures into French civilization. French is the official language, whence vernacular schools were not encouraged and vernaculars not taught in official schools.

The 1946 Constitution abolished the *indigénat* (a special régime applying to all French subjects who were not citizens), formed elective assemblies, and granted manhood suffrage in the sense that those qualified had the right to send representatives to the National Assembly. The proportion of voters to representatives was very high. The Soudan with 900,000 voters elected four deputies and Senegal with 600,000 voters elected two. Their number was increased in 1955 but this did not satisfy the hopes of Africans, for the A.O.F. like other territories had formed its political parties. An important change from the point of view of Muslims introduced under the 1946 constitution was that citizenship was obtainable without the acceptance of French personal law.[1] Formerly the adoption of French citizenship had been practically impossible unless they discarded their Islamic heritage.[2] Since the abolition of the *indigénat* the hereditary chiefs of the religious orders in Senegal have become of increasing political importance for by their support of candidates they can sway the votes of all their adherents.

In March 1956 the National Assembly carried the aims of the Brazzaville Conference a stage farther when it passed an enabling bill giving authority to introduce a wide range of reforms. The general aim was to associate overseas peoples more closely with the management of their own affairs. Apart from the introduction of universal adult suffrage and a single electoral college it makes provision for enlarging the powers

[1] The only exceptions had been the *communes* of St. Louis, Rufisque, and Dakar, the old colonial towns, which were regarded as part of France and organized like French municipalities. Those born in these *communes* have had the right to vote since 1848, but with this unique distinction, that they were the only Africans who could do so and retain their *statut personnel.*

[2] Similarly in Portuguese Guinea the legal status of the *assimilados* was that of *não indígenas* (non-natives).

of Territorial Assemblies by the transfer of powers hitherto reserved to the French Parliament, the setting up of Executive Councils (part elected, part official) alongside these Territorial Assemblies, and of organs of local government, and, on the long-term view, the africanization of the local administrations. It is clear that the closing stages of colonial relationship will be more protracted in French than in British territories.

3. THE INFLUENCE OF ECONOMIC CHANGE UPON SOCIETY

Economic change will be discussed only in so far as it is bound up with social change. The first great revolution was effected through the abolition of slavery. A society not based upon slavery was scarcely conceivable to West Africans and its abolition, however graduated in accomplishment, could not help modifying both economic and social life. At first only traffic in slaves and slave status were abolished. Slaves could remain in a state of servitude but the occupying authorities would not recognize the existence of the slave when individual cases came before them. Some slaves freed themselves but others retained their ties with their masters. Thus harsh treatment was lightened and other abuses prevented but the economy was not radically upset. The serf system was allowed to continue for some time. In French territory measures were taken to abolish the system of *captifs de case* in 1901 for the Soudan and extended to the whole of the A.O.F. in 1909. Resistance came chiefly from Fulbe ruling classes and clergy since it affected both their economic life and prestige, but as a result 'captivity' disappeared more quickly in the A.O.F. than in Northern Nigeria.[1] In Futa Jalon abolition caused an inner *malaise* and was at the root of the troubles experienced in that region during the early decades of the present century. But after a time the people adjusted themselves. Ex-slaves and serfs who retained their link with their masters became tenant-clients (Fulfulde *wallobē*, sing. *wallo*). In general, the master remained owner of the land and received a proportion of the harvest; or, alternatively, the *wallo* was allotted a plot to cultivate on his own account whilst continuing to work his patron's land. Much the same happened in British territories and former slaves became independent farmers.[2] Serfdom still shows

[1] The British abolished the legal status of slavery in Nigeria in 1916. In the Protectorate of Sierra Leone it was not abolished until 1 Jan. 1928.

[2] 'In Northern Nigeria the estate system has, for the most part, disappeared, but some royal estates are still largely worked by ex-slaves, whose position has become assimilated to that of "clients", paying an annual tithe'; C. K. Meek, *Land Law and Custom in the Colonies*, 1946, p. 22.

itself in social and even legal discrimination. Former serfs cannot normally marry outside their own grade and the masters draw upon them for slave-wives. Yet the social set-up is changing, in many areas rapidly, and the descendant of a slave betters himself by acquiring cows and marrying into his patron's family or going to school and emerging among the ranks of the *évolués*. The Western impact has not led to any fusion of classes, but the very possibility of individual changes means a breach in the rigidity of custom. The social effect of slavery survives, not only in the prestige accorded to the former master class, but also in their attitude towards manual work. Settled Fulbe still despise work formerly done by slaves, and this has hindered them from acquiring a new economic outlook. In many parts, notably in Northern Nigeria, they established a monopoly over offices in the native administration.

The reorientation of trade brought about the second immediate revolution. In the past Sudanese looked northwards towards the countries of the Mediterranean for trade and communications with the outside world. The occupation changed the economic outlook from the desert to the sea, from sahilian ports to maritime ports through which flowed the products of the West. A network of roads and railways directed themselves towards the coast. The old Saharan routes became almost lifeless so far as traditional traffic was concerned, whilst at the same time the significance of the Sahara and the role of nomads was transformed through motor and air transport and the radio. This reorientation of trade led to the decay of old towns and the foundation of new ones. River-borne traffic on the Niger was diverted to new ports and old emporiums like Timbuktu were left high and dry. The annual *azalay* or salt-caravan of 6,000 camels which still sets out from this city only serves to point the contrast between its former activity and present decay. Jenne has been deserted for Mopti, and commerce between Tripolitania and Zinder withered when Kano was linked by railway to the coast. But Kano was not killed because it was not wholly dependent upon desert-routes but a meeting-place of traffic from many directions. It changed its commercial outlook, gained a place in the new economy, became a centre for the ground-nut industry, and grew into a great metropolis.

Social and economic factors are closely linked. The difficulty Islam encounters in gaining recognition for its legal regulations has been stressed. Unaided it is not strong enough to change deeply-rooted social habits. This is the reason why such great changes in the way of displacement of custom by Islamic institutions (inheritance regulations, personal property, and wife-seclusion) have been proceeding since the European occupation.

The main influence of the West upon Muslim regions has been in material progress. European demand for export commodities stimulated new economic developments. Although the most important demands have been for the products of the Guinean lands, such as palm oil and cocoa, the demand for ground-nuts in particular (Senegal, Gambia, and Northern Nigeria), for cotton, rubber, and rice (West Guinea), have increased the prosperity of Muslim regions. Schemes undertaken by agricultural departments have transformed the economy of many regions, mixed farming has been encouraged, and the area of arable land enlarged and cultivated on new lines on a basis of individual holdings. Naturally these economic changes have influenced social life, more particularly in parts where Western influence and Islam penetrated at the same time. New economic crops bring in ready money and the effects can be seen in a higher standard of living, increasing cost of funeral expenses, marriage-payments, and wedding celebrations among *évolués*. Among cultivators these payments have not in general risen in terms of real values, for if the traditional marriage-payment is four oxen, it remains four oxen even if paid in cash. Conversely, economic factors explain why some Muslim regions have been so little changed by the impact of the West. Regions like the Chad Territory of the A.E.F. have proved unsuitable for development projects because of the problem of communications. In essentials the economic life of many parts of the Sahil and Sudan is not greatly affected by the European occupation.

Changes have taken place in the character of Sudanese towns.[1] Formerly they did not contrast strongly with the countryside. Now they are turning from collections of villages into urban aggregates,

[1] Among changes in material life are styles of mosque architecture. Mosque building, even in the Sudanese zone, tends to adopt European or pseudo-oriental styles, taking the form of halls of bricks, stones, or concrete, and provided with eastern-type minarets. Since the only examples of large buildings for worship in new materials upon which local or European builders could derive inspiration were Christian churches, the exteriors of many new mosques resemble churches and the minaret a church tower, although the interior gives a dominant Islamic note. These mosques are of every conceivable style. The *jāmiʿ* in Porto Novo which shows Portuguese influence may be contrasted with the mosque built (1943–9) in Kano in an imitation oriental style, incongruous in the sun-baked mud city and replacing a mosque (built originally by ʿAbd Allāh dan Fodio) in the Sudanese style such as exists at Zaria in natural harmony with its environment. With the encouragement of the administrations these imitations are replacing natural mosque architecture.

changes are in progress in their constitution and some forms of municipal organization are emerging. Even in conservative Muslim regions urban society contrasts with the countryside. In Northern Nigeria reaction against the West put Muslims at an economic as well as educational disadvantage and there was an influx of southerners to fill posts as accountants, clerks, foremen, and mechanics. Traditional authority segregated them into suburbs (*sābon garīs*), but their influx posed problems because they were extraneous to the traditional structure.

The effects of new means of communication upon social life have taken vast numbers out of their former isolation. Others periodically leave village life behind to live in towns. This leads to some loosening of old ties, and disintegration of the patriarchal family, already begun by Islam, is accelerated. Industries, commerce, and the increase in possibilities for money-making make the individual more independent of his community. New professions have been created and the administrator, teacher, doctor, and engineer, in this aspect of their life, are outside the old order. They gain increasing influence in the community and consequently reduce that of the old authorities. A real change comes when they assume positive functions.

But the tenacious social structure survives all change. Islamic migrants retain their local and family ties, yet at the same time are socially and spiritually at home in any Muslim group. When Muslims, therefore, come under such disintegrative influences as life in mining centres they are not detribalized. It is noteworthy that settlement in the new towns scarcely changes long-established Muslims. On the contrary, they are the most traditional and conservative of all their inhabitants. Life in towns often accentuates tribal differences. Hausa communities settled in special quarters form ethnic and cultural colonies. Most are geared to the traditional type of trading economy and none of the new openings to youth are open to their sons because of their opposition to modern education. The new urban milieux hardly touch such colonies, and the atmosphere in which their children grow up is little removed from that of a village. They do not tolerate marriage outside their own ethnic group, their youth do not frequent cinemas, bars, and dance halls. In a new town like Cotonou (Dahomey) it is the Muslims (numbering 6 per cent. out of a population of 35,000) 'who represent the traditional element, little touched by Western civilization' and 'refractory to scholastic education'.[1]

[1] J. Lombard, 'Cotonou, ville africaine', *Bull. I.F.A.N.* xvi (1954), 352–3.

4. SOCIAL AND CULTURAL CHANGE

Education is the gateway to the benefits of the Western world. But Muslims had a different scale of values and both political and religious authorities in regions of consolidated Islam set themselves against Western education. So strong was the opposition in Northern Nigeria that they succeeded in insulating themselves for the first fifty years of British rule.[1] Recently changes have taken place in their attitude for the demand for modern educational facilities is increasing.[2] Girls' education has begun but it will be long before the effects will be seen.[3] 'Fundamental education' schemes have been started and are increasing the demand for reading material, but, as Mahatma Gandhi stressed, literacy as such is not education.

As Islam in its penetration into Africa produced a new clerical class so Westernism led to the formation of a class of 'new men', those the French call *évolués*, who have assimilated aspects of Western culture and act as culture-agents between it and the masses. It is largely through them that change in native institutions takes place. The depth and degree of this cultural assimilation demonstrate the difference in the former background of pure African or Islamic culture.

Among Muslims the most profound social and cultural revolution is taking place in those societies upon which currents of both the Islamic and Western civilizations converged simultaneously, that is communities islamized during the last 150 years. Thus in Senegal alongside peoples like Tokolor and Soninke, resistant to cultural currents from the West, are the Wolof who adopted Islam during the second half of the nineteenth century at a time when French influence was penetrating. N. Leca shows that a social revolution is proceeding among the Wolof of Get N'dar (St. Louis) so strong that the former absolute character of caste prohibitions is being relaxed. He ascribes this to

[1] At one time it was hoped to use the Qur'ān schools as a basis for educational development (see the *Nigerian Handbook*, 1933, pp. 177–8), but the scheme was not well received by the clerics and the Director of Education had to report, 'Religious prejudices have, up to the present, prevented any considerable expansion of this scheme' (*Report of the Education Department*, 1932, p. 6).

[2] In 1956 applications for admission to schools in Northern Nigeria were greater than the places available since the administration had not hurried to found schools for which there were insufficient pupils.

[3] The French established a federal *école normale* (teacher training college) for girls at Rufisque in 1939, but it drew most of its trainees from non-Muslim areas, especially Dahomey. Even in 1948 the Senegal, although it has had boys' schools for over a century, was unable to provide its complement of pupils for the Rufisque school (see J. Capelle, 'Education in French West Africa', *Oversea Education*, xxi (1949), 960–1).

The aggregation of the old social framework consequent upon the abolition of native political authorities, the birth and growth of a local *petite bourgeoisie*, with as immediate corollary the enhancement of material values to the detriment of the old customary primacies; and, finally, the diffusion of democratic ideas. . . . These factors work together to create an individualism which is further strengthened by the possibilities for action contained in the receipt of a regular salary.[1]

M. Leca adds that in this society in transformation many traits of the former structure, such as the high position accorded to women in Wolof society, pierce through the Islamic façade. The attitude of such people to girls' education is entirely different from that of people embedded in the old Islamic civilization. Whenever we hear that a West African Muslim woman has become a medical doctor or barrister or is the first to go to Europe to study agriculture we find that she is not from traditional society but is a Creole or Yoruba or Wolof.[2]

Traditional Muslims are being drawn, primarily by material interests, into a new world and are beginning the withdrawal from isolation, but this new outlook is strictly limited in its range. Economic and political change rather increased the domination of Islam over their lives than aided the penetration of Western attitudes. They are little influenced by those aspects of Western culture which reflect new social and cultural attitudes. All the same the old unity is being breached through the appearance of the new men. The French policy of cultural assimilation has not succeeded. It has simply made the *assimilés* men of two worlds. French has made great progress as a code language, far greater than English in British territories, and this has tended to create a wider gulf between the *évolué* and tribal life than has education upon similar people in British territories where the vernacular is encouraged.

In their search for a wider outlook the new men are beginning to look towards other Islamic lands to see how they are faring in the new

[1] N. Leca, 'Les pêcheurs de Guet N'dar', *Bull. Com. Ét. A.O.F.* xvii (1934), 315–16.

[2] The wider cultural associations that have been formed are by neo-Muslims. A Muslim Congress of Nigeria was formed in 1948 'to unite solidly the Muslims of Nigeria, to cooperate in spreading Islam, to accelerate its progress as the religion of humanity, and to maintain close relations with related societies in Mecca, Cairo, Khartoum and England'. In spite of its name it is limited to the western region and does not, so far as I know, operate in the northern provinces. At the third congress held in Benin City in December 1951, attended by delegates from similar congresses in Sierra Leone, Ghana, and Gambia, it was decided to form a West African Muslim League embracing the four countries. At this congress arrangements were made for an assembly of chief *imāms* to meet at Oyo to fix the dates for the two *'īds* which had been a source of conflict. This is symptomatic of the difference in mentality between Muslims of the south and north.

world, and what they learn increases their resentment against the old order of Islamic society and against Western powers. They have little first-hand knowledge of these countries. For those in French territories it is Paris to which the *évolué* looks for the means to reaffirm and renovate his Islamic heritage. There students and parliamentarians meet fellow-students or colleagues from other Islamic lands.[1] Similarly with Northern Nigeria. The British have tried to prevent Nigerian Muslims, especially the few educated, from having contacts with Egypt and other Muslim lands. These have been dissuaded from accepting offers of bursaries to study at the Azhar or modern Egyptian universities. All the same they have not been able to prevent a minority from gaining wider contacts in ever-increasing ways. These factors are operating to draw West African Muslims out of their isolation—an isolation, however, which is still very real.

Since traditional education proved unadaptable to modern standards all government schools treat Qur'ānic teaching simply as a subject, included to satisfy Islamic prejudice. This is the Western attitude towards religion and inevitably leads pupils to adopt a more secularist outlook. They remain uncompromising Muslims in their social-political outlook, but for some Islam as a religious law comes to stand for what retards and its influence on life is weakened. They are assuming greater importance and are often brought into opposition to traditional authority and all it stands for. Some learn to see aspects of the traditional life and outlook through the eyes of westerners and come to regard the religious practices of their family and village as superstitions, yet cannot free themselves from them.

5. RELIGIOUS CHANGE

Although religion is inseparable from the previous discussion of change, certain points need bringing out. The events of the nineteenth century upset the historical equilibrium established between Islam and African religions, and loaded the scales against the latter more effectively than at any previous stage of history. Village religion is serviceable only within the circumscribed bounds of village life. When horizons were widened its limitations were felt, and this led many to adopt either Islam or Christianity parallel to those aspects of the old religion

[1] Certain events closer to Africa now have wider repercussions than just upon *évolués*. African deputies in the Assembly have been attacked in the A.O.F. for supporting French policy in Algeria. West African soldiers in the French army are influenced. The Army of Liberation in Algeria has gained much sympathy, but has had more effect in Mauritania, so closely linked culturally with Morocco.

which are still serviceable. Mystery cults, the equivalent in some respects to the universal religions, lay no claim to exclusiveness, but Islam and Christianity both claim to be exclusive and conflict with the old appeared inevitable. But, as we have shown, Muslims circumvented the problem of any acute clash, and the animist in his Islamic garb can make the best of both worlds and find a place within the new society. Western control has not only aided the consolidation of Islam over regions where its hold was precarious but has also aided its spread over the whole of West Africa. It follows from this that in any study of religious change account must be taken of the fact that we have in many areas the conditions of an Islam engaged in proselytization.

Whilst the coastal regions have been a zone of contact between the Western and animist cultures, with Islam well behind as a third factor except in Senegal, western Guinea, and Western Nigeria, the north Sudan regions tried to insulate themselves against Western culture. The south Sudanese regions resisted both Western and Islamic influences, though not uniformly, for in some parts the one, in others the other, are disrupting religious life. Wherever a spiritual vacuum is created the way opens for new religions, including new African cults. Under the new conditions the most important distinction to bear in mind is that already referred to between Muslims islamized before the occupation and those islamized after it.

Given the unity which characterized society before the European occupation, such changes as lead towards the secularization of political, economic, and social life cannot but have repercussions upon religious understanding and outlook. Westerners pride themselves upon mastering life without reference to anyone beyond man, the very opposite of the old view of life. This attitude also challenges the principles of Islam, hence the instinctive, half-comprehending, reaction of the clergy and authorities against Western cultural offerings such as education. But whereas its impact upon many pagan societies has been such as to breach the old bases of life and cause them to search for a new centre, established Muslim communities erected a wall which is only now being breached as youth is being won to adopt western attitudes.

The established Islam of both the black and white world of West Africa is not the Islam of the twentieth-century Near East, influenced in so many ways by the currents of Western civilization, which is adapting itself to the demands of the modern world, but the Islam of the Middle Ages. The isolationism of Muslim clergy is a very real one. Their contact with the Muslim world of North Africa and the Near

East is very tenuous.[1] The majority of those who travel for study live and work in the restricted mental environment of mosque and *madrasa*, insulated against any revivifying currents. The people affected by travel are the *évolués* who come to disdain the clergy and traditional Islam as out of gear with the spirit of the age. Their interests are not in religion as such, their Islam shows itself in relation to such issues as Muslim solidarity, and of late Muslims in the A.O.F. have been taking a much greater interest in what is happening in North Africa. But, in general, it is true to say that very few signs of the destructive changes evident in the pagan regions can be seen operating, not only on the superstructure of legalistic Islam, but even in the underlayer of popular religion. In fact Islam has acted as a cement for this underlayer and very few have adopted the Western attitude towards it as superstitious practices. Thus clerics are equally opposed to any undermining of the sphere covered by the *sharī'a* and to the introduction of modern methods of treatment and prevention of disease, both of which menaced their double function as clergy and medicine-men. There are signs that their conservatism is being undermined. Although their attitude to the offerings of the West is negative, it proved impossible to exclude everything, and those elements which had to be accommodated were as far as possible segregated as contaminating. When segregation failed they were adopted without ousting the old but running parallel with it. This is what has happened with the treatment of disease. Everywhere the dissimilar and incompatible methods of modern medicine and old magical-religious methods are juxtaposed. The new is being accepted without displacing the old, for thereby an alternative or double safeguard is gained.

As long as worship of the law continues Islamic institutions will adhere to the values of the past, yet religious change of some sort is inevitable through the gradual secularization of life by the appearance of the new men. Of the longer-established Muslims those of Senegal, in

[1] Clergy with a thorough knowledge of the Arabic of their law books when confronted with an Egyptian newspaper or journal were quite unable to understand modern Arabic and showed no inclination to undertake a new discipline. Attempts to reform religious education have had little success. Notice the fate of the *École Coranique Supérieure* founded at Bamako in 1950 by a group of four radical Azhar graduates. They emphasized understanding the Qur'ān as opposed to mere memorization, and included some modern subjects. Numbers quickly rose to 400. But their activities fell under the censure of both secular and religious authority and the administration closed down the school in December 1951, for in French Africa as well as British the administration tends to support conservatives against reformers. A milder attempt in French Sudan is being undertaken by a group called *Jam'iyyat al-Murshidīn* who have opened a number of schools marked by a more liberal use of the vernacular. Similarly a school (*Makarantar Ilmin Musulumchi*) in Zaria, whilst stressing a sound knowledge of Arabic, gives religious instruction in Hausa.

close touch with French culture, are being influenced by currents from modern Islam. Young Hausa, interested in the question of translating the Qur'ān into their language and encountering the opposition of the clergy, were outspoken in branding them as obscurantist. Upon these Islam is losing its power as a spiritual force, whilst retaining its social domination over their life in society. But though new currents weaken its spiritual dominion over the lives of the few, they have not and are not likely to influence much the religious outlook of the masses.

The appearance of Christianity has complicated the religious scene even in areas of consolidated Islam, for although the administrations co-operated with Islamic authority to keep Christian missions out of Muslim areas yet they drew on southerners, a large number of whom were Christians, to fill those posts their activities had created which were boycotted by Muslims. And, though they were segregated, all the same the balance of the old Muslim-pagan equilibrium was upset. Hence the formation of southern element parties and the disturbances in Kano in May 1953. Nominal Ibo Christians make use of Christianity as part of their nationalism over against Hausa-Muslim nationalism. Pagans in the border regions, such as the Middle Belt of Nigeria, where missions were allowed, are adopting Christianity, and these have to be allowed for in political calculations for a unified north.

The reaction of established Islamic societies to the secular civilization of the West has been shown to be largely negative. When, however, we turn to areas of recent islamization we find much greater religious change taking place in consequence of the penetration of currents from two civilizations at the same time. Neo-Muslims involved in two universalist systems are influenced by the individualistic secular attitudes of the West and a different attitude to religion has made its appearance, the most striking aspect being religion as personal religious allegiance. Many have adopted Islam as a personal religion rather than as a civilization. They are absorbing the specifically religious elements of Islam first and the civilization, which seems to some to be backward and retarding, only to a limited degree. In regions of consolidated Islam religion is a question permanently closed by birth, but to neo-Muslims it is an open question about which the individual may hold any opinion and form any allegiance he pleases. Where Western secular influences are strong, as among Yoruba, individual changes of allegiance can take place without causing any outcry from the community, for it is not thought to menace family solidarity or undermine the fabric of society. Many Yoruba families have Muslim, Christian, and pagan members and all join happily in each other's religious festivals, for they are merely acts of social custom like the observance of Christmas in the Western world. Since customary law rules family life, membership of three religions has so far caused few problems in regard to inheritance and the like, though it may do so in the future. Similarly in wider community life religious allegiance does not determine the way men vote at elections or choose representatives. Among the Yoruba religion has been secularized. Their old religion has been so breached that it can never again be the foundation of life (at least in its organized form though one cannot rule out the possibility of the development of a new type of national Christianity or Islam). Both Islam and Christianity have gained large numbers of adherents, especially Islam, yet neither of these religions hold together the social edifice, they are simply the religious department of life. Thus the act of joining the one or the other does not undermine the social structure, and the family remains the real cement of Yoruba society. Although the majority of Muslim Yoruba belong to the poorer class of society, the influence of the new men is determining the direction and values of religion, and the sphere in which religious leaders can operate is circumscribed. Hence, on the one hand, the strength of custom over against Islamic law, and, on the other, the tendency to form Islamic 'societies'.

This attitude towards religious allegiance is also characteristic of neo-Muslims elsewhere, especially in towns. It exists among urban Wolof influenced by French liberalism though to a lesser degree than with the Yoruba because most of the Wolof are Muslim and Roman Catholics are numerous only in towns (Dakar, Gorée, and St. Louis). Similarly with Creole families in coastal settlements (Dakar, Bathurst, Conakry, Sierra Leone Colony, Porto Novo), among whom the difference of attitude was showing itself at the end of the last century as may be seen from the work and writings of the Sierra Leonian Muslim, Edward Blyden, author of *Christianity, Islam and the Negro Race* (1888). Marty writes of the Creoles of Dahomey, that 'Within the same family we find Catholic and Muslim branches; and within the same family we observe that, without any apparent reason, the children change sometimes to the one, sometimes to the other of these religions'.[1] Yet this attitude is not confined to urban communities. Even among newly Islamized cultivators (for example, in Sierra Leone) religion is often regarded more as a family affair and change of allegiance does not excite community feeling as in the Sudan zone. At most, unless stimu-

[1] *R.M.M.* lx (1925), 126.

lated by immigrant clerics, there will only be family opposition. In such a state of flux with Islam and Christianity contending for people's allegiance, religion is ancillary to other claims of life—politics, money-making, and above all the family. A riot over a religious issue would be surprising; people riot over more serious communal matters.

All these neo-Muslims are considerably more influenced by Western ideas than long-established Muslims. In contrast to the Sudanese they are more self-reliant in face of modern conditions, more insistent upon material and intellectual progress. They display great enthusiasm for education and have formed a number of societies for the purpose of opening and maintaining schools.[1] This is the reason why the Aḥmadiyya, a maritime-introduced Indian Islamic sect, has gained a foothold in coastal regions of British territories, but has had little success, and, indeed, has been strongly opposed, in regions of consolidated Islam, for the Aḥmadiyya is itself a Western-influenced Islam.[2]

But though Islam is not allowed to restrict individualistic attitudes and other new gains acquired through the impact of the West, many secularized Africans find it congenial, and it is often joined by those who react against Christianity. Frequently one hears it being advocated as 'the religion of the Blacks' as opposed to Christianity, 'the religion of the Whites'. We have shown that the change from village religion to Islam has been primarily a social phenomenon. Individual villagers did not become Muslims, only immigrants to towns, traders and slaves who had lost tribal ties. But in the new West Africa conversions of individual pagans to Islam are quite common, even in the sphere of the agricultural civilization, though not so common as in towns. The result is that the Islam of these neo-Muslims, even after it consolidates itself, is not the same as in the Sudan. This does not necessarily mean that it will not have an anti-Western tendency, but it is only partial and not wholehearted, for the material aspects of Western civilization are fully appreciated.

[1] The Aḥmadiyya has promoted the setting up of Western-type schools, where the Qur'ān is taught as a subject, and various Islamic societies like the Anṣār ad-Dīn and Nawair ad-Dīn in Yorubaland. These societies have begun to operate in the northern region and may in time influence some of the younger generation. Among neo-Muslims elsewhere all kinds of new societies have made their appearance. Mende have formed *Malodi* (Ar. *mawlid*), mutual-help clubs, which have become widespread. They have a great feast on the birthday of the Prophet, they help the family with funeral expenses, as much as £10 being provided, and wear small black badges with an Arabic inscription. Each member has to pay regular subscriptions, and if a member dies in default they will not help at funeral rites—the kind of discrimination characteristic of Creole Christians. Insurance societies of this kind are characteristic of the whole of the Guinean region from Sierra Leone to the Yoruba.

[2] On the Aḥmadiyya see Appendix IV.

These considerations have a bearing upon the future. The proportions of religious allegiance in West Africa are roughly: Christians 4·4 per cent., Muslims 36·3 per cent., and pagans 59·3 per cent. The number of people who are not yet attached to one or other of the universal religions is still very large, but the ethnic religions are doomed in their old organized forms. It seems unlikely that any of them could develop into universal religions. Undoubtedly new cults will arise, as they are doing today, but they stagnate and decay quickly. Old cults will now and again develop new tendencies and temporary vigour, but there seems little chance of their spreading widely. Those which have appeared are the preserve of initiated and, though they attract many to make use of their powers, they are not religions. Nationalistic cults with racialist tendencies may also make their appearance. But the majority will have the choice between Islam or Christianity or secularism forced upon them through the decay of their old religions and their manifest incompatibility for life in modern Africa.

Islam is likely to gain far more of the uncommitted than Christianity and this study has shown the reason for this forecast. Islam has had centuries to africanize and implant itself. Islam is part of the African scene, whilst Christianity still suffers from the handicap of being a Western religion, and there is even some reaction against it on this account. In many parts it is stagnant and turned in upon itself, and African Christians have shown little missionary impulse. Islam presents itself to the inhabitants of a disintegrating world as less alien, even familiar and known in the sense that it has its place in the African set-up. Although Islam is also stagnant it has the field to itself over vast areas where it spreads by natural diffusion, though it remains possible (bearing in mind the spread of the Harris movement in the Ivory Coast) for an African Christianity to awaken and spread rapidly.

Islam will progress numerically but one fact must be borne in mind which makes the situation particularly intriguing. This is the simultaneous spread of Western secularism. This means that Western civilization will have, as it is already having, a greater influence upon such neo-Muslims than Islamic culture. Africans will be gaining new modes of thought, new ideas of the function of the state, and also new ideas of religion in a secularized world. Neo-Muslims today tend to manifest a Western attitude towards religion. African governments will have to remain neutral in matters of religion. This means that the absorption of secular ideas will limit the advance of Islam primarily to its religious aspects and neo-Muslims will have more in common with their Christian neighbours than they will have with north Sudanese Muslims. As in other parts of the world Christians and Muslims in West Africa have to adjust themselves to living and letting live side by side, and allowing their encounter to be one, not of competition for adherents, but an encounter of the things that pertain to the spirit.

APPENDIX I

Ceremony of Joining Islam

THE ceremonial act of allegiance to Islam is not of great importance for there is little sense of an abrupt break with the past. Many pagans in towns just slip into Islam by calling themselves Muḥammad and imitating their fellows without any special ceremony. A rite is performed where public recognition is sought as in the case of chiefs and important men, but there is little feeling of a transitional rite. When carried out it does not differ from normal Islamic practice. The Prophet is said to have ordered those who wished to embrace Islam to perform the *ghusl* (washing of the whole body), and submit to the shaving of the head and circumcision. The Hausa term is *wankā*, 'washing', *an yi masa wankā*, 'he has been baptized', he has become a Muslim. This word has spread among Yoruba, Nupe (*wanka lisilenchi, lislámi* = Islam), Dagomba, and others influenced by Hausa. The recognized elements are: teaching, washing away the past, sacrifice with naming, and confession of faith before witnesses. Where performed the *mālam* teaches the convert the *shahāda*, ritual ablutions and prayer motions. The ceremony takes place either at the entrance hut or the mosque. The *mālam* washes him (so they said) in a rite something similar to that for the dead, the *shahāda* is recited before the assembly, and a ram is sacrificed (*yanka sadaqa*) in the courtyard or vestibule with the 'intention' of naming (say) Abū Bakr, similar to the naming of the new-born. After which all repeat the *ṣalāt ʿalā 'n-nabī* ten times and the elders give the convert their blessing.

This ceremony is performed wherever Islam is established, but newly islamized areas have local ceremonies. Among Mende of Sierra Leone the cleric places a writing tablet (*walɛi*), on which the *basmallah* has been written, on the knees of the convert (*tubimɔi*), then writes the phrase on his hands and tells him to lick it off. Next, at the cleric's house they make 'sacrifice' (dough of rice flour with which honey or sugar is mixed, topped by a kola). All place a hand upon the rice or one touching it, the cleric says an Arabic prayer and all recite the confession together. (This is the sacrifice offered at naming and death ceremonials in regions islamized through the Fulbe of Futa Jalon where it is called *tyobbal*.) After hands are removed from the rice prayer is offered in Mende asking God to accept the sacrifice and bless the convert.

Circumcision is not regarded as having anything special to do with Islam. Most Sudanese performed it before Islam came. Uncircumcised generally have it done, though clergy assert, on good textual authority, that it is not obligatory for adults. Little teaching is done since participation in the life of the community is trusted to develop in the convert the external characteristics and inward consciousness of being a Muslim.

APPENDIX II

Guṇnuṇ and Sòkó in Nupe Religion

It is impossible to gain any understanding today, not only of the displaced religion of Muslims, but also of the religion of those in process of adopting Islam. Religion in the Sudan zone was especially fluid, for a characteristic was the incorporation, but not full integration, of small groups into a dominant society. Every village had its variations. What unity religion had was largely subjective. Cosmological knowledge was the preserve of a priestly caste or circle of initiates. Consequently when Islam displaced priesthood and initiation such knowledge faded away. African religion in all regions subjected to the pressure of Islam is at an advanced stage of degeneration and fissuring into isolated cults. The difficulties may be illustrated with reference to the Nupe. Professor S. F. Nadel provides an excellent study in his *Nupe Religion* (1954). The writer worked in the region for only three weeks and was studying Nupe religion primarily with respect to the influence of Islam. The observations on Nupe religion scattered about this book are based on these restricted studies and no attempt has been made to reconcile them with those of Nadel.

The Nupe have been instanced (p. 51 above) as a people whose former earth-god has given way completely before the sky-god whose name has become a synonym for Allah. Nupe said their former creator-spirit was Guṇnuṇ, ruler of all spirits. He was in everything and could be worshipped everywhere, though special places in the bush were reserved for his worship where seven-day ceremonies were observed. Today Guṇnuṇ, as chief spirit, has died and Guṇnuṇ worship degenerated into an unrecognizable fertility cult. Pagans recognize Sòkó as chief god. Sòkó is the 'sky'.[1] Pagans when performing ritual communication (*kútiẓi*) include a prayer to Sòkó, but do not offer him *làba*, prayer with libation. They said: 'He is too far, we must use more accessible helpers to protect us and our crops.' Nor does it help when Muslims say that Sòkó hears prayers but only in Arabic. Pagans call Muslims *Sòkóbachi*, 'worshippers of Sòkó', whilst Muslims call pagans *kútibachi*, 'performers of *kúti*'. With the decline of Guṇnuṇ, therefore, Sòkó has become supreme God and

[1] Everyone had a different account of the position of Sòkó under the old régime. One old Nupe denied that he was sky-god at all. He said pagans called the sky *sàmiko*, 'the great filter', which was modified to Sòkó. Muslims adopted Sòkó, 'sky', for God. The word used today for sky is *sámà* (Ar. *samā'*). Clouds (*nanko sòkó*), he said, meant simply 'cattle of the sky', now interpreted as 'God's cattle'. Another Nupe from a different region said Sòkó was only one of the gods under Guṇnuṇ. Guṇnuṇ sent other *kútiẓi* to punish, but Sòkó was not one of them (though Sòkómaji, a lesser god, was). Sòkó was, on the contrary, the beneficent god who sent rain. They did not *làba* to Sòkó unlike Guṇnuṇ who sent good and bad and needed propitiating.

Muslims could employ the name as a synonym for Allah because no cult was associated with him. These changes had been going on for some time before the Fulbe conquest and it is impossible to know what Guṇnuṇ cult really was. Guṇnuṇ came to mean little more than 'cult', for fusion between spirit-agency and ritual is characteristic. Earth had a power of its own known as Guṇnuṇ, hence all ritual was, and still is, Guṇnuṇ.

APPENDIX III

Present-day Mahdī Expectations

BELIEF in the coming of the Mahdī is stronger in western than in central Sudan. The writer first came across it when travelling by the Fuladu on the river Gambia. This steamer was so packed with humanity that it provided a cross-section of every aspect of west Sudan Islam. There a Mandinka trader spoke of the belief of Tokolor, Fula, Soninke, and some Mandinka that al-ḥajj 'Umar was a descendant of the khalīfa 'Umar ibn al-Khaṭṭāb. Some regarded him as the khalīfa himself for they have no historical sense. Accounts were given of how he was revealed as the Mahdī in Mecca and Madina. They also asserted that the Qur'ān foretells that an 'Umar would come to restore the true religion, but since they could not read the Qur'ān they could not show me the passage. In Sierra Leone the Mahdī idea is spread by Mandinka, Susu, and Fula immigrants and traders, and in parts there was an air of expectancy. When he comes all machines will stop working and Western civilization will come to an end. The rising under Haidara in 1931 was connected with these beliefs.

Since the Mahdī myth is based on oral tradition strange ideas appear. Tokolor came nearest to Islamic tradition. They say he must be a descendant of the Prophet, and therefore white. All black mahdīs are impostors. Four cycles will bring history to an end. The first is the Nasariyanu, the dominance of Christians; the second that of the Mahdī, the third that of Masi Dajāli (al-Masīḥ ad-Dajjāl), and the last the reign of 'Īsā. Other Tokolor mentioned Jūjū and Majūjū (Gog and Magog) rampant on earth, the splitting of the moon, the sun rising in the west and setting in the east, and the ascent of the Qur'ān into the sky. Elsewhere, though the Mahdī was known, there was no expectancy. In Northern Nigeria he was formerly linked with a prophecy concerning a Fulani migration to the east, and there is still some interest in the year A.H. 1400 (A.D. 1979) associated with the second coming of the prophet 'Īsā. In general, West Africans are very apathetic about the coming of the Mahdī.

APPENDIX IV

The Aḥmadiyya: a Modern Islamic Missionary Movement

THE history, teaching, and propaganda methods of the sect known as the Aḥmadiyya is inextricably interwoven with Western influence and this movement has developed missionary activities which have carried it into British East and West Africa. The sect was founded at Qādiyān in the Punjab by Mīrzā Ghulām Aḥmad (1839–1908) who claimed to be the promised Messiah and Mahdī, and was branded as a heretic and impostor by orthodox Muslims. After the death of his successor in 1914 a group associated with Lahore broke away, asserting that Ghulām Aḥmad was only a *mujaddid* or 'reformer' and not, as he claimed, a prophet after Muḥammad, 'the Seal of the Prophets'. This dissident group, which called itself the Aḥmadiyya Anjuman-i-Ishā'at-i-Islām, or 'Society for the Propagation of Islam', claims to be orthodox and has kept out of politics. But since the formation of Pakistan the Qādiyānīs have become of considerable importance in political life. This led to a new orthodox reaction and the denial that they are Muslims. Muḥammad Iqbāl wrote: 'Qādiyāniyyat is the name of an organized effort seeking to establish a separate religious community built on a prophethood parallel to that of Muḥammad' (quoted in *Al-Furqān*, Lahore, October 1953, p. 48).

A notable feature of the Aḥmadiyya has been its missionary activity in which it has imitated Christian missionary methods, institutions, and terminology. It established itself among Indian Muslims on the east coast of Africa and was first introduced into Nigeria in 1916. The arrival in 1921 of al-ḥājj 'Abd ar-Raḥmān Nayyār, who made the Gold Coast port of Saltpond his headquarters, initiated a phase of vigorous propaganada. By 1927 the movement had formed forty branches with approximately 3,000 adherents in the Colony and Ashanti. 'Abd ar-Raḥmān also preached in the Yoruba region, where he gained followers, and even in Kano and Sokoto, where he was not well received by the *'ulamā*. In 1927 a missionary society was constituted and the movement expanded rapidly amongst Yoruba Muslims, in Gold Coast Colony and Sierra Leone.

The Aḥmadī missionaries were welcomed when they first appeared in Lagos, but after they refused to worship behind a non-Aḥmadī *imām* and clerics realized that they were regarded as heretics by orthodox Muslims, a reaction took place and bitter disputes broke out. At the same time the split in the movement in India led to divisions in West Africa. In 1939 the Khalīfat al-Masīḥ of Qādiyān announced that he disowned the Nigerian movement for its rejection of the prophethood of Ghulām Aḥmad, whereupon it altered its constitution to sever all links with Qādiyān. A section, however, refused to join this separatist movement and called themselves the Sadri Anjuman-i-Aḥmadiyya Qādiyān, and after a long litigation in the courts concerning the ownership of Aḥmadiyya mosques this party gained the suit. The split was more connected with personalities than with doctrine, and since 1947 the leaders of the two movements have been trying to reach agreement, though in fact a third group calling itself the Muslim Mission Community has split off from the dissident party. The majority seem prepared to recognize the Khalīfat al-Masīḥ of Rabwah (the headquarters since the 1947 partition) as their spiritual head, though many, and in particular the third group, do not recognize Ghulām Aḥmad as the Messiah. A new mosque was opened in 1951 by Muḥammad Zafrullah Khan, the Foreign Minister of Pakistan, who is an Aḥmadī. The effect of these sectarian movements has been to make Lagos, now the headquarters, a picture of Islamic confusion with three chief *imāms* and three Friday mosques. Branches have been established in all the important towns of south-western Nigeria, but they have had little success in the north where the *mālamai* are strongly opposed to them, and the small groups which exist in northern towns are mainly composed of southerners. The Aḥmadiyya levy the *zakāt* on their followers who include a number of wealthy merchants and in consequence have considerable funds at their disposal. They take an active part in education, maintaining primary schools in many important centres and the Tinubu High School at Lagos. Plans are being made to open schools for girls. From Nigeria Aḥmadī influence has spread into Dahomey.

The Aḥmadiyya progressed more rapidly in the Gold Coast, now Ghana (where they claimed a membership of 22,572, including children, in 1948), than in Nigeria. It is strongest in Saltpond region where a number of Fanti have been converted and individuals of the *évolué* class in the Colony have joined. In Ashanti only a few individuals and one small village claim to be Aḥmadī, but they maintain a secondary school at Kumasi with Pakistani teachers on the staff. Other schools are maintained at Saltpond, Ekrawfo, and other places. In the Northern Territories there is a centre at Wa where the chief is an Aḥmadī (see J. N. D. Anderson, *Islamic Law in Africa*, pp. 264–6). In Sierra Leone, where they are gradually gaining adherents, they maintain schools in Freetown and in the Protectorate at Bo (their headquarters), Magburaka, Rokofor, and a few smaller villages. One Sierra Leonean is at Rabwah on a six-year course of training. There are a few Aḥmadīs in the Gambia, but no missionaries since the *'ulamā*, fearing their divisive influence, prevailed upon the administration to refuse applications for their entry (1956).

The Aḥmadiyya differs from all previous Islamic action on Africa in that it was a maritime importation into the forest region, and that meant an entirely different non-African Islamic tradition. By its very nature it brought a sectarian conflict into the West African Islamic world because its whole attitude is so different from the basic assumptions and patterns of established Islamic society. One effect has been to stimulate interest in liberal Islam, particularly among the educated in British territories, and to cause controversy in Muslim circles. Many of the old school react against the liberals as strongly as against the main group holding the heresy concerning the prophetship of Aḥmad, because of practices such as permitting women to enter mosques and pray behind men and allowing the bride to be present at her wedding to give her consent. The founder and his successors have always claimed power to inaugurate new legislation, and though the Pakistani leaders who control the movement tend to follow the Ḥanafī *madhhab*, minor differences in prayer ritual and the like all cause controversy with Mālikīs. Aḥmadīs tend to form a special community, clearly differentiated from other Muslims, fully open for the reception of new members, but opposed to their daughters marrying non-Aḥmadī Muslims. Orthodox Muslims also react against its Western methods, for its African leaders are imbued with the same spirit, social welfare and educational programmes, method of propaganda and arguments as the Pakistani missionaries. Consequently the Aḥmadiyya attracts individuals of the *évolué* class, but leaves the orthodox cold. They work mainly in the British territories, as much because of language, for their medium of propaganda is English, as because the French authorities are suspicious and restrictive. Politically the Aḥmadiyya have a tradition of supporting the established authority upon whose neutrality their very existence has at times depended. In West Africa they have not allied themselves with the aims of any party and leave their members to follow their own inclinations.

APPENDIX V

Statistics of Religious Allegiance

	Animists	*Muslims*		*Christians*	*Total*
			Per cent.		
French West Africa:					
Sudan	1,509,000	1,810,000	55	17,000	3,336,000
Haute Volta	2,488,000	555,000	17	70,000	3,113,000
Guinea	728,000	1,381,000	65	22,000	2,131,000
Ivory Coast	1,642,000	324,000	15	163,000	2,129,000
Niger	320,000	1,800,000	85	4,000	2,124,000
Dahomey	1,158,000	279,000	17	143,000	1,580,000
Senegal and Mauritania	450,000	1,960,000	78	90,000	2,500,000
Total: French West Africa	8,295,000	8,109,000	48	509,000	16,913,000
French Equatorial Africa:					
Chad Territory only	630,500	1,621,500	72	..	2,252,000
Togo: French Mandate	804,000	50,000	5	166,000	1,020,000
British Mandate	330,000	30,000	7·5	40,000	400,000
Cameroons: British Mandate } French Mandate }	2,729,300	750,000	19·5	{ 113,000	1,033,000
				{ 513,000	3,072,300
British West Africa:					
Gambia	19,700	246,500	90	6,550	272,750
Sierra Leone	1,692,000	588,000	25	70,000	2,350,000
Ghana	3,498,000	300,000	6·5	750,000	4,548,000
Nigeria: Northern	4,616,000	11,661,000	69	558,000	16,835,000
Western	..	..		..	6,144,000
Eastern	..	..		..	7,229,000
Portuguese Guinea	323,230	181,280	35·6	4,410	508,920
Liberia	1,200,000	100,000	6·6	200,000	1,500,000

GLOSSARY-INDEX OF ARABIC AND AFRICAN TERMS

Abbreviations

Ar	Arabic	N	Nupe
Berb	Berber	S	Soninke
Dy	Dyula	Song	Songhay
Fr	French	Tam	Tamahaqq
Ful	Fulfulde (and Tokolor)	Te	Temne
H	Hausa	Teda	Teda
K	Kanuri	Tok	Tokolor
M	Mande (Mandinka, Bambara, and Dyula)	Y	Yoruba
Me	Mende	W	Wolof

abbāla (Ar). Camel-rearing nomadic Arab tribes, 17.

'abd mamlūka (Ar). Purchased slave, 134.

'abd qinn (Ar). Slave born in the house, 134.

Abore. Hausa term for nomadic Fulbe, 12 n.

a-boro məsar (Te). Ancestor house, 35, 104.

'āda (Ar). Customary law, 147, 148 n.

ādhān (Ar). The call to prayer, 71, 157.

afəm afi (Te). Ancestors, 181.

a-gbɔki (Te). A women's dancing society, partially secret, 109 n.

Aḥmadiyya. An Islamic messianic sect, 172 n., 210 n., 223, 230–2.

Aijɛnɛ (Me). Heaven. (Ar *al-janna*), 35 n., 58.

aiki (H). Deed; *aikin mālam*, a spell to harm, 116.

'ajamī, *'ajamiyya* (Ar). Outlandish, the term employed for vernacular texts written in Arabic characters, 84.

Ajanāsi (Y). Qur'ān reciter, co-interpreter, 72.

Ajurrūmiyya, al-. A popular manual of Arabic grammar, 82.

a-kuntha (Te). Witch's bag, 118.

alafɔshe (Y). The cleric (*alfa*) in his function as diviner, 120.

alfa (W. Sudan). A cleric, 68, 72, 73, 82, 122, 157, 163.

alifa (Ar *khalīfa*). Title of the chief of Kanem, representative of the *mai* of Bornu, 152.

Alijena (N). Heaven, 57.

alkāli (H, Song). Judge, Ar. *al-qāḍī*, 73, 148 n., 175.

alkurdu (H). Pen-case, 70.

alkyabba (H). A voluminous gown, 173.

Allāh (Ar). God, 37, 38, 51, 52, 53 n., 60, 74, 100, 227–8.

Allāh manyo (Khasonke). God's bride, marriage to a cleric by gifting the bride, 170 n.

allo (H), *alwa* (W), *walɛi* (Me), *walaṙa* (M), *wàlā̃* (Y). Writing tablet, from Ar. *al-lawḥ*, 81 n.

allowa (H, from Ar. *al-wuḍū*). Ablution, 84.

allua (W. Guinea). Writing tablet, 161 n.

almāgirī (H, Ar *al-muhājir*). An itinerant Qur'ān student, 160 n.

almāmi (Ar *al-imām*): west Sudan, (1) leader in prayer; (2) politico-religious head of a Muslim community, 69, 71, 73, 79, 121, 145, 146, 150, 156, 165 n., 207, 208.

almania (Te). A dancing society, 109 n.

amariya (H). Bride, 172.

amariyan boko (H). Mock bride, 173.

amenokāl (Tam). Chief of a Tuareg federation, 11.

amīr al-mu'minīn (Ar). Leader of the believers, 143.

amīru māgal (Ful). State herd-chief, 186.

an bese (Te). Prayer-enclosure, 35.

andi (H). Priest of a *bōri* cult, 111.

anella (Tam). Henna, 198 n.

anganchi (H). The state of being a bridegroom, 173.

ango (H). Bridegroom, 173.

anjɔnú (Y). Evil spirits (Ar *al-jinn*), 36.

aŋkaŋtha (Te). Locker; *a-kaŋtha kor*, 'to lock the farm' against marauders, 114.

aŋyesəm (Te). Life, 58 n.

'āqila (Ar). The range of kinship of those responsible for the *diya* or blood-wit, 152.

'aqīqa (Ar). Eighth-day naming ceremony characterized by the sacrifice of an expiatory offering, 154–7.

ara (Y). The physical body, 57 n.

A'rāf, al- (Ar). The partition between heaven and hell, 59.

aramat (Tam). The Great Feast, 80 n.

arbi (Teda). Clan, 130 n.

Arma (Song). Name by which the descendants of the Andalusian and Moroccan musketeers (Ar *rāmin*, pl. *rumāt*,

sharpshooter) who conquered Songhay in 1591 are called, 15–16, 136, 163 n.

arna, *asna*, *anna*, *azna* (H). Pagans = Lat. *pagani*; *chinikin azne noma*, 'farming is the pagans' occupation', 16, 39, 51.

arowāsi (Y). Megaphonist at Qur'ān interpretations, 72.

aryana (Susu and Te). Heaven; Ar *al-janna*, 58.

aserkam (Tam). Class groupings among Tuareg, 11.

'Ashūrā (Ar). The tenth day of Muḥarram, 74, 76–77, 80, 159.

askiya. Dynastic title of rulers of Songhay from 1493 to 1591, 24, 26, 28, 74 n., 116 n., 137 n., 140, 144, 151 n.

aslama (Ar). To submit to, become a Muslim, 48, (50 n.).

auran fālo (H). Veranda marriage, 169 n.

auran jin dāḍī (H). A fixed-term marriage, 168.

auran kisan wuta (H), 175 n., see *taḥlīl*.

auran kōme (H). Remarriage to a former wife after the triple divorce, 175 n.

auran kulle (H). Marriage with complete wife seclusion, 169.

auran matafi (H). Traveller's marriage, 169.

auran sadaka (H). Gift marriage to a cleric, 170 n.

auran sunna (H). Muslim consort marriage, 167.

auran zaure (H). A fixed-term marriage, 169 n.

auran zumunta (H). Kinship marriage, 165 n.

ausa, *hausa*. Left bank of Niger and country on the left bank, 16.

āwẹ (Y). Fast; *irun āwẹ* 'prayer of the fast', 79.

azalay. Saharan salt caravan. The Bilma–Air–Hausa caravan is called *taghalam*, 213.

Azawād (Fr *Azaouad*). Eastern part of the Sudanese Sahara, north of the Niger buckle, 2, 10 n., 94.

'Azrā'īl (Ar). The angel of death, 55 n., 59.

azumi (H). Fast (Ar *aṣ-ṣawm*), 78; *watan azumi*, 'the moon of the fast', Ramaḍān, 78 n.

ázuṇ (N). Fast (Ar *aṣ-ṣawm*), *etswa ázuṇ*, fast month, 78.

babaláwo (Y), 'the father who has the secret', a priest of Ifa, the Yoruba oracular deity, 120.

badolo (W). Agriculturalist class, 136 n.

bait al-māl (Ar). In Islamic states the public treasury, 175.

Bakkā'iyya Ṭarīqa, deriving from Aḥmad al-Bakkā'ī (d. 1504), 94, 97.

bàkómba (N). Twin spirit, 104; *gba bàkómba*, twin cult, 104 n., 105.

ɓalēɓe (Ful). 'Black', negroid Fulbe, 12.

bandīri (H). A basin-shaped hide drum, 96.

banya (Song). Male trade-slave, 134 n.

baŋgu (Song). Pool; *hirow baŋgu*, 'entering the pool' = circumcision; *baŋgu sola*, the collective (hut) circumcision, 163.

baqqāra (Ar). Cattle-rearing Arab tribes, 17, 185, 186.

Barābra (sing. *Barbarī*). Name applied to Nubians in Egypt, 85 n.

baraka (Ar). (1) Blessing, (2) divine power, 66, 82 n., 89, 111–12; *i-bār'ka* (M), 'thank you', 112; *omo dyogi barke* (Tok), he possesses power, 112; *o barkini* (Tok), he emanates power, 112.

bàràsa (N). Trade gin, 199.

bari (Song). Horse, mount, used of a person possessed by a spirit (*hole*), 111 n.

bari (Susu). Spirit, 183.

barzakh (Ar and Persian). In Islamic eschatology 'an intervening state (*ḥā'il*, 'barrier') between death and the Day of Judgement' (Baiḍāwī on xiii. 100), Hades, 60.

basmalla (Ar). Saying 'In the name of God' (*bismillāhi*), 226.

bāwa, pl. *bāyi* (H). Trade slaves, 133–4.

bāwa gandu (H). Tribute paid in the form of slaves, 134.

ᵐbēlu (Ful, Tok). The shadow-soul, 60–61, 118 n., 180 n.

bid'a (Ar). Innovation, new ideas and practices contrary to the *sunna* of the Prophet, 83, 90 n.

bīḍān, sing. *bīḍānī* (Ar). The Whites; in Mauritania: the Moors, 1, 10, 31.

bīḳi (H). The forty (hundred) days' seclusion of a woman after childbirth, 158.

Bilād al-Bīḍān (Ar). Land of the Whites, 1.

Bilād as-Sūdān (Ar). Land of the Blacks, 1.

biledyo, pl. *vilēɓe* (Tok, Ful). Magician, counter-witch practitioner, 119; *vinⁿdōɓe ko vileɓe*, 'those who write are magicians', 113.

Bismillāhi (Ar). 'In the name of God', uttered by Muslims before any undertaking; by pagans as an exclamation, 34.

bǒchi (N). Medicine-man, 112, 115.

bōka, pl. *bōkāyē* (H). Medicine-men, 38, 59, 115.

bōli, *bōri* (M). Material abode of a spirit, object consecrated to a spirit, symbol, altar, 37, 104, 107, 108, 112; *bōli-sōni*, 'fetish sacrifice', 75; *bōli-tigi*, guardian of a *bōli*, 107; *bōli-din'*, one allowed to sacrifice at a *bōli*, 107.

bolo-ku (M). 'Washing the hand' = circumcision, 162.

bondo or *sande* (W. Guinea). Women's mystery society, 109 and n.

bongo kyebo (Song). 'Shaving the head', name for the eighth-day naming, 157.

bõñtyẽ (Dy), *bõñdyu* (M). Amulet buried in the foundations of a house, 114.

bōri. Hausa possessive spirit cult; *ya hau bōri*, 'the spirit has mounted', *ya sauka*, 'it has dismounted, 25, 43–44, 59, 63, 92, 103, 107, 109–11, 178; *bōri jamā'a*, the *bōri* community, 111; *ḍan-* (m.), *'yar-* (f.), *'yan bōri* (pl.) initiates into the cult, 38, 39 n., 111, 115.

Bororo'en, s. *wororbe* (Ful) Nomadic cattle Fulbe of central Sudan, 12 n.

buḍar kai (H). The bride's unveiling, 173.

būdēji or *ba-budē* (H). A cleric who practises magic, 117.

būta (H). Ablution jug, 70.

būzū (H). Undressed goatskin prayer rug, 69.

byia (Song). Soul, shadow, double, of a paternal ancestor, the 'personality' which enters the body at the seventh-day naming ceremony, 51 n., 60, 154.

chasbi, *chazbi*, pl. *chazbuna* (H from Ar *tasbīḥ*). Rosary, *jā chazbi*, to tell beads; 93 n.

chigbè (N). Medicine, 112; *chigbè jinchi*, medicine-man, 115; *chigbè dèdè*, chief medicine-man, 115; *májiṇ chigbè*, bad medicine, 115.

chiyāwa (H). Grass, 59 n.

chuchenāwa, sing. *ba-chūcheni* (H). Domestic slaves (Ful *dimājo*), 133.

ḍa, pl. *ḍiya* (H). (1) Son, (2) a freeborn person, 133.

dabare (Ful, Tok). All the techniques of magic to harm, 113.

dabbāra (Ar). Magic-making, spell-binding, 113.

dagga ndangara (S). Revocable repudiation, 174.

ḍaḥīya (Ar), *layya*, *lāhiya* (H), *laiha* (Ful). Sacrifice, the Great Feast, 80 n.

ḍāki (H). A hut, house; *ḍākin tsāfi*, fetish hut, 39 n.

da-la (M). Addressing s.o.; *da-la sõnı*, addressing the ancestors with libation, 75 n.

Dalā'il al-Khairāt (Ar). 'The Proofs of the Excellences', a well-known poem in honour of the Prophet written by Abū 'Abdallāh M. b. Sulaimān al-Jazūlī (d. A.D. 1464), 53, 78.

damel. Title of the ruler of the Wolof state of Kajor, 130 n.

ḍan mai-ganyē, *ḍan māgani* (H). Seller of the materials for making medicines, 45.

Dār al-ḥarb (Ar). Land of warfare, a country where the edicts of Islam have not yet been promulgated, 33.

Dār al-Islām (Ar). Land of Islam, a country where the edicts of Islam are promulgated, 33.

dare (H). Night, 76.

da siri (M). See *siri.*

ḍauri (H). 'A tying-up', employed in names for protective charms, 115.

ḍaurin aure (H). The Islamic marriage-contract ceremony, 172.

da'wa (Ar). 'Invocation', employed generally for the lawful system of spell-binding and incantation, as opposed to *siḥr* (sorcery) and *kahāna* (divination), but in the Sudanese Sahil it is often equivalent to *da'a 'ala*, e.g. Song *addawa*, 'a curse', 116 n.

deftere fitōre koiḍi (Ful). Books of dream interpretation, 122 n.

derdɛ. Teda chief (Tibesti); *maina* among western Teda, 11.

dhikr (Ar). Remembering, technical term for the ritual 'mentioning' of the fraternities (*ṭuruq*), 92 n., 93–94, 96, 99–100, 101 n., 123.

dhikr al-awqāt (Ar). The daily office of a *ṭarīqa*, 96, 99–100.

dīmājo, pl. *rimayḅe* (Ful, Tok). Household slave, inalienable serf, 133 n., 134.

diya (Ar). Blood wit, 152.

dōki, pl. *dawāki* (H). Horse, the term used for one 'mounted' by an *iska*, 111 n.

dõ-mba (M). 'The Great Day', an earth festival = *anabī dõ*, the Prophet's birthday, 76 n., 78 n.

domi-būr (W). Noble class by the masculine filiation, 136 n.

du'ā (Ar). Invocation, prayer, 71; *ádǔwa* (N), 105, 116 n.

dūba (H). Divination; *mai-dūba*, diviner, 120.

dugu (M). Land, esp. that of a village, 106.

dugu da siri (M). Territorial spirits, 102, 103, 106.

dukhn (Ar). Sorghum, 187.

dungahi muriē (S). Divorce by mutual consent, 174.

dura (Ar). Small millet or Pennisetum, 187.

d'ya (M.) Physical life, spirit, double, 58–59.

dyabu (Song). Striking the ground with a stick on the thirteenth day of the circumcision retreat, 163.

dyāka = Ar *zakāt*, 146.

dyam-būr (W). Freemen, 136 n.

dyamgal (Ful, Tok). A head tax paid by serfs to their master, 133 n.

dyami-būr (W). Serfs, 136 n.

dyamu (M). Clan name, 130.

dyangugol (Ful). Reading, 81, 161.

dyara (M). A Mande cult, 107.

dyẽgom or *dyagobere* (Ful, Tok). Tax paid by serfs to their master, 133 n.

dyidẽ (M). Child (*dẽ*) of the water (*dyẽ*), a spirit, 110 n.

dyidẽ kuntigi (M). Chief of the cult of the water spirit, 110 n.

dyinger (Song). To pray, prayer, religious festival, *dyingerey*, mosque; *dedow dyinger*, the ʿAshūrā, 76 n.; *almudu dyinger*, Prophet's birthday, 78 n.; *koteme dyinger*, twenty-seventh night of Ramaḍān (descent of the Qur'ān), 78; *ferme dyinger*, 'festival of the open mouth', 79 n.; *tyibsi dyinger*, 'ram festival', i.e. the Great Festival, 80 n.

dyi-tigi (B), *dyi-tū* (Bozo). Master of the water, the intermediary between people and the water-spirit (*fāro*), 106.

dyo, *gyo*, *dyu* (M). Spirit of an initiatory cult, mask, altar, or other object consecrated to the spirit, 104.

dyõ, *gyõ* (M). A trade slave, 134 n.; *dyõ lāda*, law regulating slaves, 147; *dyõ-mbènde*, 'mustered slaves', the first month of the year, 76 n.

dyongolo (Song). See 178–9.

dyula (M). Trader, 14, 193.

eba (N.). Strings of shells used in divining; *ebabŏchi*, *ebasachi*, diviner; *sa 'bà*, to divine with shells (*sa*, to divine), 120.

èbalà (N). Prayer with libation (ancestral spirit cult), 105.

efo (N). Day.

efo-gò nyá yàwŏ. 'Day of the bride's reception', the first part of the marriage ceremonial, 172 n.

efo kiṇna. Day of Resurrection, 57 n.

efo kiyióma. Day of Resurrection, 57 n.

efo misun. Day of the Brink or Brim, 57 n.

efo shìriya. Day of Judgement, 57 n.

efo yàwŏ wa dzùṇ. Day of the bride's appearance, 172 n.

efo zuṇmago. The Last Day, 57 n.

èfù (N). Offering, sacrifice (yam, corn, &c.) to spirits, 105 n.

egà (N). A witch-spirit; *nya 'ga*, witchcraft; *găchi*, a witch (fem.); 56 n., 118 n.

ègbaṇgi (N). A cord used for divining, 120.

ege (N). Beer made from guinea corn, 199.

egi nuwoṇ (N). Spirit of the watering-place, 104.

èku (N). The next world, 56 n., 57, 182.

ekúṇ (N). Corpse, 57.

ẹmi (Y). Life, spirit, 57 n.

èmilo (N). 'Entering the compound', the taking of the bride to her husband's house, 172 n.

èmiṇa (N). Hell, 57.

enyawò (N). Blood sacrifice to *kútiẓi*; *enyawòbà*, place of offering, altar, 105.

èshè (N). (1) The soul, personality, of a man, 56–57, 61, 117 n., 118 n.; (2) a witch spirit, 56 n., 117 n.; *èshèchi*, one possessed of an *èshè*, 117, 118.

etsu (N). Title of the head of the Nupe state, 73 n., 77, 90.

evo balà (N). Calabash dedicated to the pouring of libations for ancestors, 105.

ewó dángiẓi (N). Kinship money, one of the marriage payments, 167 n.

ewó ejiṇdá (N). Greeting gift, sealing the betrothal, 167 n.

ewó gwada (N). Help money, a marriage payment to the bride's mother, 167 n.

ewó yàwŏ (N). The bride-price, 167 n.

fāda (H). Chief's compound or assembly-hut, 69.

Fāḍiliyya. A *ṭarīqa* in the Qādirī tradition, founded by Muḥammad al-Fāḍil (d. 1869), 90, 93, 94–95.

fafərai (K). Presents made by the bride's family to the bridegroom, 168.

fāgol or *pāgol* (Serer). Ancestral and nature spirits, 54 n.; *yal fāgol*, human intermediaries with spirits, 54 n.

falanga (Song). The elected chief of a circumcision school, 163.

fannu (Ful). Legal studies, 81–82.

faqīh, pl. *fuqahā'* (Ar). Jurisconsult, 68 n., 69, 135, 143, 148 n.

Fāro (Bamb). Self-created high-God, God of the water, organizer of the world, 58, 106, 108 n.

faskh (Ar). Annulment of a marriage or other contract, 175.

fatalwa (H). Apparition which manifests itself from the blood of one who has been killed, 59, 60.

fatauchi (H). Bull-roarer, 39.

Fātiḥa (Ar). Opening chapter of the Qur'ān, 47, 116 n., 157, 161, 172, 194.

Fātiha dõ (M). To conclude a contract by the repetition of the Fātiḥa, 194 n.

fatwā (Ar). The formal opinion of a *muftī*, 148.

fifiṇgẽ (N). The 'shadow' soul of all living things, 56–57, 118.

fineditugol (Ful). The joining of letters, 81, 161.

firugol (Ful). Qur'anic exegesis, 81–82.

fisa tyitāb (Song). Book of divination, 122 n.

fittāndu (Tok). Vital force, 60–61.

fodyo (Ful, Tok). A trained *faqīh*; *fode* (M), *ɔfode* (Te), 69, 70, 121 n., 181.

Fulānin gida (H). House (settled) Fulani,

now Hausa in culture; *Fulānin zaure* (H). Fulani ruling class, 132.

furu, futu (M). Marriage, 166; *furu-ba dō*, 'day of the great marriage', the annual festival of marriages, 171; *furu-fē*, 'marriage thing', the dowry provided by the fiancé, 166; *furu sara*, the Islamic marriage payment within the *furu sõngo*, 'marriage price', 166; *furu loro la*, to conclude the marriage contract, 166.

ga bibi (Song). 'Black body', descendant of slaves, esp. from fourth generation, 134 n., 136.

ga-korē (Song). 'White body', descendants of white Saharans and Moroccans, 136.

gǎchi (N). Witch, 118 n.

gafaka (H). Cleric's book bag, 70.

Gajērē-mai-bakā (H). 'Dwarf of the bow', a spirit of the bush, also called Kauji, Maharbin-dare, Gajērē-mai-dawa, and Sabara, 195.

gallē (Ful). Compound, 165 n.

gàmi nyá kin (N). Lit. 'The law of the land', i.e. customary law, 148 n.

gàmi nyá momodu (N). Islamic law, 148 n.

Gāna. South-Saharan Soninke state, *c.* 750–1215, 3, 14, 32, 195.

gandu (H). Capitation tax (Ar *jizya*), 134, 147.

gāni (Tam, K, Teda), *ganē* (H), *gamu* (W). The Prophet's birthday, 78.

gaŋqama-e (Susu). Men's mystery society, 109.

gāra (H). A bride's dowry, 167.

garasa (Song). Smith and shoemaker caste among the Zerma, 136.

gargassaḅe (Ful, Tok). Leather-workers, 137.

garmi (W). Ruling class by pure uterine filiation, 136 n.

gaskiya (H). Truth (Ar *ḥaqīqa*), 84.

gawlo, pl. *awlḅe* (Tok). Caste group of griots, 136 n.

gba (N). To submit; *wuṇ ágba*, he has submitted, been converted; *lǎgba*, a convert, 48.

gba bàkómba (N). Twin-cult, 104.

gbako (N). A cord used in divining, 120.

gbaŋgbani (Te). A men's society, 109 n.

gbā-sa (M). 'Horn' containing an amulet, 114.

gevel (W). Caste groups of bards, 136.

girka (H). To put a pot on the fire for cooking, to initiate into the *bōri* cult, 111.

ghafar (Maur. Ar). Tribute levied for according protection (*khufāra* is also used), 135.

Ghuḍfiyya. A small Moorish *ṭarīqa* deriving from Muḥammad al-Aghḍaf (d. 1860), 94–95.

ghusl (Ar). The complete ablution, 226.

gida (H). Compound; *gidan tsāfi*, a pagan sanctuary, 39.

godiwagi (N from H). 'Small thanks'; *godiwako*, 'great thanks', part of the marriage payments, 167 n.

gōḍiya (H). 'Mare', woman whom the spirit has 'mounted' during the *bōri* rites (*kūdiya* in Nilotic Sudan), 111 n.

goga (N). Interpreter, megaphonist (Ar *muballigh*), 72, 77.

griot (Fr. For conjectural derivation see p. 136, n. 1). Praise-singer-genealogist of caste status, 32, 102 n., 136, 137, 155, 199.

gumba (H). A porridge made of pounded millet, used at namings, funerals, and expiatory offerings, 157 n., 182.

gunki (H). Fetish, sacred tree or place; place where *bōri* performances are held, 39 n.

Guṇnuṇ (N). A Nupe ritual and cult, 51, 105, 119, 227–8.

gurma (Song). Right bank of the Niger, interior of the Niger buckle, 10.

gyesērē (Song). Caste of griots, 136.

hāḅe, sing. *kāḍo* (Ful). Name applied by Fulbe to indigenous inhabitants.

ḥaḍāna (Ar). The custody of children after divorce or death, 176.

ḥaddād (Ar). Smith-caste, 137 n.

ḥadīth (Ar). Tradition about the Prophet, 79, 82, 161.

ḥaḍra (Ar). A congregational *dhikr* gathering, 93.

Ḥāfiẓiyya. A branch of the Tijāniyya *ṭarīqa*, 90, 97.

hailala (Ar). Repetition of the phrase, 'there is no god but God', 100.

ḥalāl (Ar). Lit. 'that which is loosed', lawful (as opp. to *ḥarām*), 50, 66–67, 113.

halei, to- (Me). Medicine; *halemɔi*, medicine-man, 35, 112.

hal-pulāren (Tok). Pulār-speakers, 13 n.

Ḥamāliyya. *Ṭarīqa* founded by Ḥamāhu 'llāh b. Muḥammad (1886–1943), 94, 99.

Ḥanafiyya madhhab. The school of law deriving from Abū Ḥanīfa, 82, 232.

ḥarām (Ar). That which is sacred, that which is prohibited, 50, 66–67, 113, 174.

harbin allura (H). Invocation shooting with needles, 117.

harbin kasko (H). A form of invocation shooting, 117.

ḥarrāṭīn, sing. *ḥarṭānī* (Moorish Arabic); *ikawaren* (Tam). Free men of inferior status; in the oases it means black cultivator, 10 n., 136.

hâti (N, from Ar *khātim*). Geomancy, divination in sand (Ar *ḍarb ar-raml*), 120.

haume, *hamme* (Song). Fast month, 75 n.
Hausa (Song). Left bank of the Niger, 16 n.
Hausāwa, sing. *ba-haushe* (H). Hausa, 16.
Ḥawḍ (Fr Hodh). The western part of the Sudanese Sahara from Tagant to Timbuktu, 2, 10 n., 90, 136.
hendu, pl. *keni* (Ful). Wind, used by settled central Sudan Fulani for spirit possession, 110 n.
hew (Song). Wind, employed as synonym for the 'doubles' of possessive spirits (*holē*), 54 n.
ḥijāb (Ar). Amulet, 115.
hindē or *indē* (Ful). The personal Islamic name, 156 n.
ḥinnā' (Ar). Henna, 198 n.
hinni (Song). To have mercy on (Ar *ḥanna*), 85.
ḥirz (Ar). An amulet, 115.
ḥizb, pl. *aḥzāb* (Ar). (1) One of the 60 sections into which the Qur'ān is divided for recitation purposes, (2) a prayer or litany of a religious order, 79, 80 n., 159, 160.
holē (Song). Invisible personalized corporeal spirits, 54 n., 55, 110 n.
honamɔi (Me). Witch, 118.
honei (Me). Witch-spirit, 118.
horso (Song). Slave of first generation, 134 n.
ḥubus (Ar). North African term for religious endowments and family trusts (elsewhere *waqf*), 74.
ḥukm (Ar). A judgement given by a *qāḍī*, 148 n.
hundi (Song). Vital force, 60.
ḥurma (Ar). Dues paid by tributaries to Moorish warrior tribes, 136.

id, *ida* (Berb). Grandfather. Employed in tribal names, e.g. Ida-w-'Alī, 97, 98.
'īd (Ar). Festival day, 79, 80, 124, 180, 217 n.
'īd al-aḍḥā or *al-'īd al-kabīr* (Ar). The festival of the sacrifice, 10th Dhū 'l-ḥijja, 71, 80.
'īd al-fiṭr or *al-'īd aṣ-ṣaghīr* (Ar). The festival following the fast of Ramaḍān, 71, 72 n., 79, 146.
'idda (Ar). The period of probation incumbent upon a woman after divorce or the death of her husband during which she may not remarry, 41, 168, 174, 175, 182–3.
idyey alman (Song). Marriage (*idyey*) wealth, 168.
igīu, pl. *igāwēn*. Caste group of bards among the Moors, 136.
ijmā' (Ar). The consensus of the Islamic community, in practice the agreement of the leading jurists, 148 n.
ijtihād (Ar). Independent elucidation of some point of law based on the recognized *uṣūl al-fiqh*, 148 n.
ikhwān (Ar). 'Brethren' of a religious order, 97.
iklān, sing. *akli* (Tam). Negro serfs, former slaves of the Tuareg, 11.
'ilm (Ar). Knowledge, (*a*) occult, 113 n.; (*b*) legal, 81.
'ilm al-kalām (Ar). Scholastic theology, 49.
'ilm at-ta'bīr (Ar). Divination through dreams, 122–3.
imām (Ar). Leader of ritual prayer, political head of an Islamic community, 69, 70, 71, 73, 74 n., 77, 79, 80, 81, 121, 134, 139, 141, 143, 145, 150, 155, 179, 181, 210 n., 231.
imghad, sing. *amghid* (Tam). Vassals of a noble Tuareg tribe, 11, 168.
imoshar (Tam). Nobles, 11.
inislimen (s. *aneslem*). Clerical clans, clerics, among Tuareg, 11, 69.
Inna (H). 'Mother' of all the *iskōki* who appears as a Fulani woman, 182 n.
inuwa (H). Shadow, 59.
iska, pl. *iskōki* (H). Wind, esp. the harmattan, used for spirit influences, 54, 55, 59, 60, 63, 111, 190.
isó-yìgì (Y). The Islamic legal marriage; *isó*, state of being tied; *yìgì*, the Islamic *ṣadāq* (bride-price = *owo-idano*), 120, 168.
Isrāfīl (Ar). The angel who sounds the resurrection trumpet, 56 n.
istighfār (Ar). Repetition (*dhikr*) of the phrase *astaghfiru 'llāha*, 'I ask pardon of God', 96, 100.
istikhāra (Ar). 'Asking favour' of heaven, divination by the use of the rosary, cowries, bits of wood; divination through dreams, 123.
istisqā' (Ar). Ritual prayer for rain. It involves communal prayer on the *'īd* ground with recital of *sūras* ad-Duḥā and ash-Shams. The chief offers a sheep for sacrifice and processions of children are associated, 189 n.
itu yigi (Y). Untying the *yiji* contract, i.e. divorce, 168.

jā (Song). Title of rulers of Songhay until replaced by the *sī* in 1275, 139.
Jabarta. Ethiopian Muslims, 85 n.
jabr (Ar). The right of matrimonial restraint accorded to the father or his executor, 164–5, 171 n.
jahannam (Ar). Hell, 35 n., 58.
jāhilchi (H). The pagan way of life, 154.
jallāba (Ar cent. and east. Sudan). Merchant class, 18.

jamā'a (Ar). Council of elders, village assembly, 139.

ama'a alkādirāwa, sing. *ba-kādiri* (H). The Qādiriyya congregation, 92, 96.

jāmi' (Ar). The great mosque where the Friday prayer is celebrated, 71, 74 n., 98, 141, 143, 192, 214 n.

Jan Gari (H). 'The Red City', the abode of the spirits in *Jan Ḳasa*, 'the Red Country', 60.

jangali (Ful, H). Tax on cattle, 147.

jarirdu (Ful). Women's prayer enclosure, 74.

jāriya (Ar). Female slave, 168.

jawharat al-kamāl (Ar). 'The essence of perfection', a Tijānī prayer, 94, 99, 100.

Jibrīl, *Jabra'īl* (Ar). Gabriel, the angel of revelation, 55 n., 59.

jīgō (H). 'Pole', forked stick at entrance or sacred tree in a compound particularly associated with *kure*, 'male hyena', son of Inna, 'Mother' of all the *bōri* spirits, 39, 182 n.

jihād (Ar). Religious war to spread domain of Islam, 12, 15, 25, 26, 29, 47, 86, 92, 94, 122, 132, 141, 142, 143, 147 n., 184.

jìkànà (N). Geomancy, 120.

jinn (Ar). Terrestrial spirits formed of air and fire, 35, 51, 54–55, 78, 113, 114, 115, 123 n., 155, 159, 198; Yoruba *anjɔnu*, *alijano*, 36; Dyula *gyina*, 54 n.; Songhay *djin*, 55; Nupe *àlijènu*, 55 n., 104.

jizya (Ar). Poll-tax, 39, 147.

jūldɔ, pl. *jūlbe* (Ful). A Muslim; *jūlirde*, mosque, from *jūlde*, to perform ritual prayer, 50, 72; *jūldɔ sumaye*, the Lesser Festival, 79 n., 121 n.; *jūldɔ laiha*, the Festival of Sacrifice, 80 n.; *jūldɔ donkiri*, the Festival of Sacrifice, 80 n., 121 n.

jumbui (Me). Sin; *jumbumɔi*, sinner (Ar *dhanb*), 35 n.

jūya bai (H). 'Turning the back', last feast of the old year, 76.

kachela (K). A class of officials of servile status in the state of Bornu, 135.

kaḍaita (H). To acknowledge the divine unity, 85.

kafā'a (Ar). Marriage equality regulations, 165.

kafe, *kafi* (H). Charms buried in ground to protect compound or village, 39.

kaffāra (Ar). Expiatory sacrifice or work, 75.

kāfir (Ar). Unbeliever, infidel, 64, 142, 165 n.

kambun baka or *kandun ido* (H). Evil eye, 117.

kan gida (H). Lit. 'head of the house', the family totem, 67, 131, 132 n.

karamoko, *karamoṙo* (M). A cleric. Compound of *kara* (Ar *qara'a*, read) and M *moṙo*, 'person', 68, 78, 82, 105, 122, 156, 161, 190.

karātuṇjiṇchi (N). Qur'ān reciter (H *karātu*, reading, Ar *qirā'a*), 72.

kātimei (Me). A category of amulets, 114.

ḳawa, pl. *ḳāwāyē* (H). A woman's bond friend, 173, 183.

keme (M). A higher numeral, 197 n.; *mali-ṅkeme* = 60; *bāmana ṅ keme* = 80; *silāmi-ya-keme* or *faradye-la-keme* = 100.

kərifi (Te). Generic term for 'spirits', 106, 189; *ro-kərifi*, 'place of spirits', next world, 58; *a-bɛmpa kərifi*, sacrifice to spirits, 106 n.

khalīfa (Ar). Successor, the initiating leader of a *ṭarīqa*, 93, 97, 98, 229.

khalīfat al-masīḥ (Ar). Successor of the Messiah, 230, 231.

kharāj (Ar). Land-tax, 146–7.

khaṭīb (Ar). Preacher, 72.

khātim (Ar). Seal, signet-ring, an amulet in the form of squares; *hātumēre* (Tok, Ful), a written amulet; *hātumēre maŋkataba*, a writer of amulets, 114, 120.

khifāḍ (Ar). Excision, 162.

khiṭba (Ar). Solicitation, betrothal, 171.

khul' (Ar). Divorce by means of a compensation or indemnity paid by the wife to the husband, 175.

khuṭba (Ar). The formal homily delivered at the Friday and festival prayers, 72, 73, 77, 79, 80.

kiḍan ruwa (H). 'Beating water', performed at the time when a widow is freed from the *'idda*, 183.

kira (H). To call (to prayer); *mai-kiran-ṣalla*, muezzin, 71 n.

ḳirgi (H). Untanned ox-hide; *mālamin ḳirgi*, wandering friar, 69.

ḳofi (H). Supernatural power, weaker than *ḳwāri*, 117.

kɔfɔ (Te, Loko, Limba, &c.). A men's mystery cult, 190 n.

kōlak. Title of the rulers of Waday, 100.

komo (M). Mystery cult among Mande, 29, 35, 36 n., 103, 107–8, 109; *komo-deu*, initiates of the cult, 108; *komo-tigi*, master, priest of the cult, 108.

kongo (Song). Female trade-slave, 134 n.

kono (M). A Mande cult, 107.

kōrami (H). Pen-case, 70.

kōrāna, *kōrāni* (H). Forked stick at entrance to compound for protection, 39.

kororam (K). Asking money, the betrothal present, 167.

kpàkogi (N). A board used in divining, 120.

kpakpɛi (Me). An amulet, 114.

kpànkà (N). Lit. 'truant', water-spirits who carry away the spirits of children dying before the naming ceremony, a household cult, 104.
kpàta tsózi (N). Spirits of the watering-place, not worshipped, 104.
kpaya (Me). Power; *halei gbaya*, the power in 'medicine' (halei), 79.
kpiâkpiâ (N). Charm on a cord for divining, 120.
kuchi or *ezàtsuchi* (N). The departed spirit, disembodied soul, a new-born child before naming, 57 and n., 182; *kuchi-gangan* (N). Talking to departed spirits, 106 n.
kuḍin ada'a (H). Thanks-money, part of the bride-price, 167.
kuḍin aure (H). Marriage price, 167.
kuḍin baiwa (H). The gift signifying betrothal, 167.
kuḍin ḍaure (H). Cleric's marriage fee, 173.
kuḍin gaisuwa (H). 'Greeting money', paid by bridegroom, 167.
kuḍin kasa (H). Land tax = Ar *kharāj*, 147.
kuḍin sadāki (H). The Islamic *ṣadāq*, 167.
kuḍin sallama (H). Money for calling, the first marriage payment, 167.
kuḍin sa rana (H). Money for fixing the marriage day, 167.
kuḍin sunna (H). The Islamic *ṣadāq*, 167.
kuḥl (Ar), *kwalli* (H). Antimony, 80.
kulle (H). Wife-seclusion, 169, 176–7.
kurwā (H). Soul, double, 59–60, 112, 117, 118, 119 n.
kúti, pl. *-zi* (N). A channel of communication with divinity, a utilized divine emanation, a ritual, 53 n., 105 and n., 227.
kútigba (N). Spirit-worship, 53 n.
kútigbachi (N). Spirit-worshippers, 227.
kwanakin anganchi or *buḳin anganchi* (H). The marriage rites, 172–3.
kwanan tsīwa (H). 'Night of licence', preceding the consummation of a marriage, 173.
kwanche (H). To untie, cast off; *k. māguzanche*, he has discarded pagan rites, 39.
ḳwanḳwamai (H). Spirits associated with haunted places and the transmission of supernatural contagion, 112.
kwaraya (H). A pagan contest, 39.
ḳwāri (H). Supernatural power; *yā zuba masa ḳwāri*, he has put on him power, 112, 117.
kworē (M). A Mande cult, 107.

làba (N). To pray to ancestors with the pouring of beer libations, 105, 115, 227.
lādan (H). Muezzin, 71.
lāhira (general usage, from Ar *al-ākhira*). The next world, future life, 58, 59, 60.
laḥma (Ar). Tributaries of Arab tribes of Berber origin, 136.
lailat al-ḥinnā' al-kabīra (Ar). The night of the great henna, a feature of the Islamic marriage, 198.
Lailat al-Qadr (Ar). 'The Night of Power', 78.
lalle (H). Henna, 198 n.
lāsmɔi (Me). Small written charms, 114.
lauḅe, sing. *labbo* (Tok). Woodworker caste, 137.
lawḥ (Ar). Writing tablet, 81 n., 161 n.
lāya (H from Ar *al-āya*, verse, sign), employed in names of written amulets, 115.
lɛɛhinei (Me). Ceremony for ancestors performed only by Muslim Mende, 105.
lelú (N). Chief of the witches, 118.
Lesīdiyya (Ar). A branch of the Qādiriyya-Bakkā'iyya *ṭarīqa* founded by Sh. Sīdya 'l-Kabīr (1780–1868), 94 n.
limān (Ar *al-imām*). Central Sudan: leader of prayer, 69, 70, 141, 157.
lisimɔi (Me). A type of written charm, 114.
lislámi (N). Islam, 226.
lo-ba dõ (M). Day of final resurrection, 59.
loŋtha (Te). Spirit of interpretation whose permission has to be sought before calling up other spirits, 106 n., 122 n.
lū, *dū* (M). Family; *lū-tigi*, family head, 127, 156.
lugali (K). The bride or bridegroom's representative (Ar *walī*), 167.
lugaliram (K). Payment for fixing the date of marriage, 167.
lukɔstɔbla (Me). Muslim clergy who write charms, 114.

ma'aiki (H). Messenger; *ma'aikin Alla*, the Prophet, 53.
mābubē, sing. *mābo* (Ful, Tok). Weavers, 137.
mafoi (Te). Holy water (pagan), 115 n.
magāji (H). Official at the court of a Hausa chief, 73.
māgani (H). Medicine, supernatural power, 112, 115; *mai-māgani*, herbalist, 115.
Maghāriba, sing. *Maghribī*. North African, 85 n.
magōri (H). Seller of material for charms, 115.
Māguzāwa, s. *Ba-māguje* (H), der. from Ar *majūs*, pagan, 16, 38–39, 60, 109, 182 n.
māguzanche (H). Paganism, following local cults, 39, 154.
Mahalichchi (H). The Creator, 52 n.
al-Mahdī (Ar). 'The rightly-guided one', whose advent heralds the End, 62, 207, 229, 230.
mai. Title of the rulers of Bornu, 139, 140, 145 n.
mdjiṇ dòdǒ (N). Chief of the *ndakó gboyá* cult, 119.

Majūs, sing. *majūsī* (Ar). Magians, Zoroastrians, 39.
Makaḍaichi (H). The One (God), 52 n., 85.
makaranta (H). School, 220 n.; *makarantar allo*, Qur'ān school, 81; *makarantar ilmi*, law school, 81.
Maḳērā (H). Spirit of the smiths, 195.
malāk, pl. *malā'ika* (Ar). Angel, 55.
mālam, *mālami*, pl. *mālamai* (H) from Ar *mu'allim*. Cleric, lettered man, 43, 44, 68, 69, 70, 79, 111, 112, 117, 121, 133, 172, 226, 231.
Mālik (Ar). Guardian of the fires of hell, 56 n.
Mālikiyya madhhab (Ar). The school of law deriving from Mālik ibn Anas, 53, 82, 126, 134, 148, 152, 164, 168, 175, 177 n., 232.
Mālikiyya ṭarīqa. Order founded by Mālik Si (d. 1929), 90, 97.
māṇ, pl. *-ẓi* (N). Cleric, 70, 72, 77; *māṇko*, chief imām, 70, 77; *ènà māṇẓi*, order of clergy, 70.
ma-nasi (Te). Charmed water, 114 n., 115 n.
mānekɛ (Te). A men's mystery society (*ɔ-gbengle*, master of the society), 109 and n.
mānsa, *māsa* (M). King, 139.
marbi (K). The Islamic legal marriage payment, 167–8.
masallachi (H). (1) Mosque (Ar *muṣallā*), 71 n.; *masallachin idi*, the 'īd prayer ground, 79; (2) One who performs *salla*; *kai masallachine?* are you a Muslim?, 50.
al-Masīḥ ad-dajjāl (Ar). Anti-Christ, 229.
masihirchi (H). One who practises sorcery (*siḥr*), 117.
masjid (Ar). 'Place of prostration', mosque, 71 n., 72.
mawlid an-nabī (Ar), *mūlūd* (west Sahil region). The Prophet's birthday, 78, 223 n.
māye, f. *mayya*, pl. *māyu* (H). Wizard, witch, 59 n., 118, 119.
mayta (H). Witchcraft, 118.
mba (N). Pagan mourning feast held on the eighth day after death, 105.
mba gboli (Me). Pagan (red) rice offering, 39, 181 n.
mba jaa (Me). Muslim (white) rice offering, 39.
mba lɛwie (Me). Rice offering at mourning feasts, 181 n.
mərei (Te). Dream; *ro-mərei*, dream-world, 58 n.
miḥrāb (Ar). Niche in mosque indicating direction of prayer, 73.
minbar (Ar), *mumari* or *misiri gye kòtò* (Dy). Wooden block (in the Sudan) on right of the *miḥrāb* on which the preacher (*khaṭīb*) stands to read the homily (*khuṭba*) at Friday prayer, 71, 73, 74 n.
misidi, *misiro*, *misiri* (M, S, Bozo, &c.), Mosque, parish, 70, 71 n., 150.
mithqāl (Ar), in W. Sudan *metikale*, *mutukāle*, *minkāle*. Measure of weight utilized for gold-dust, representing ⅛th ounce or 4 to 5 grammes, 192.
modibbo (Ful, Tok). Cleric, 69.
moi. Title of the chief of the Bolewa, 145 n.
mōri, *mōru*, *mōdi*, *mōdu* (M). Muslim, sometimes 'cleric', 69; Temne *ɔ more*, pl. *a mɔre*, 35; *Mōriyu* (M), Islam.
mōriba (M). Cleric, 68.
mu'adhdhin (Ar), *almudyin* (Song). The announcer of the hours of prayer, 71 n.
mu'allim (Ar). Teacher, 68.
mu'allimīn (Ar). An occupational caste of 'skilled' workers among Moors, 136.
mubāra'a (Ar). Divorce by mutual consent, 174–5.
mudāra (Ar). Dues paid by tributaries to Arab suzerain tribes, 136.
mudd (Ar), *mūde*, *mūre*, *mule* (M). Measure of capacity, varying according to locality, 146, 147, 193.
muftī (Ar). A canon lawyer authorized to give a *fatwā* or formal legal opinion. Hausa *mufuti* is a judicial assessor appointed by the ruling authority, 148 n.
muge (N). Palm wine, 199.
Muḥarram (Ar). The first month of the Islamic year, *Herran*, *Harom* (Tok, S), 41, 76, 77, 90.
muḥtasib (Ar). Guardian of morality, 153 n.
mujaddid (Ar). A reformer, 230.
mulaththamūn. Arab term for the Saharan Berbers who wear the muffler (*lithām*), 10 n.
Munkar and *Nakīr* (Ar). Two angels who visit the dead after the funeral, 55–56 n., 57 (Walakīri).
muqaddam (Ar). A leader in a *ṭarīqa*, generally non-initiating, 93, 97, 98, 100.
murābiṭ (Ar 'member of a *ribāṭ*), Fr *marabout*, 'cleric' in general, 'devotee'; in Ḥawḍ 'link' with divinity (Lat. *re-ligare*) 69 n.
Murābiṭūn (Almoravids). Islamic movement inspired by 'Abd Allāh b. Yāsīn (d. 451/1059) among the west Saharan Ṣanhāja Berbers which led to the destruction of the town of the Gāna in 1076, though his state survived, 24.
murgu (H). Tax paid by serfs to their master, 133.
murīd (Ar). Aspirant on the Ṣūfī path, disciple of a Ṣūfī shaikh, 53, 93, 95.
Murīdiyya (Ar). *Ṭarīqa* founded by Aḥmad Bamba (d. 1927), 53, 95, 97, 188–9.

muṣallā (Ar). (1) Oratory. Small open-air plots for ritual prayer, the normal African mosque, 71 n.; (2) the praying ground for the *'īd* festivals, 72 n.
musulumchi (H). The Muslim way of life, 154, 220 n.
mut'a (Ar). Gift, pleasure. (*a*) A consolatory gift given to a wife who is repudiated or at the conclusion of a fixed-term marriage, 169, 175. (*b*) A marriage concluded for a fixed term at the conclusion of which divorce is automatic, 168–9.

na, naba (Gur language group). The political chief, 144 n.
nabī (Ar), *nabiyu* (M). Prophet, 53, 78 n.; *anabi dõ* (M), the Prophet's birthday, 78 n.
nafõre (Tok). The whole of the marriage payments whose restitution is involved if the husband is granted a divorce, 166 n.
nafs (Ar). Soul, 61 n.
nagban̩ (N). The soul of an animal, 56–57, 117 n.
nago (M). A Mande cult, 107.
nā'ib (Ar). Deputy, lieutenant, 69, 70.
na'ibi (H). An assistant *imām*, 157.
nakà (N). Body, 56.
nāma (M). Cult of a spirit represented by a hyaena mask, 29, 107, 108.
nankó Sòkó (N). 'Cattle of the sky', used of moving white clouds, 227 n.
n̩are (Song). To pray, beg, 116 n.
nasi, nɛsi (W. Guinea). Holy water, 115, 186 n.
n̩bà (n.), *yin̩bà* (vb.). Worship of spirits of ancestors (Nupe), 104–5.
ndakó (N). Spirits of the ancestors (see *n̩bà*), 104.
ndakó gboyá (N). An anti-witchcraft cult, 107 n., 119.
ndăzó (N). A chief priest of the communal *kútiẓi* cults, 105.
ndebla wovɛisia (Me). Ancestors, 181.
ndɛvui (Me). Breath, life, 58 and n.
ngafɛi (Me). Spirits of ancestors, 105.
Ngala, ṅala (M). God, sky, rain. (Ar *Allāh*), 34 and n., 52, 59.
ngauwanda (Me). Blessing, 79.
niḥla (Ar). Dowry, 166 n.
nikāḥ mut'a (Ar). Marriage for pleasure or a gift, marriage for a previously stipulated period, 168–9.
noddandu feho (Ful). Invocation-shooting = H. *harbin kasko*, 117.
noyandi (Song). Dowry, 168.
nun̩gbere (N). Gun̩nun̩ stick, placed on property as a protective charm, violation afflicts with sleeping sickness, 105.
n'ya, ni (M). Personal spirit as contrasted with *d'ya*, impersonal vitality, 58–59; *ni-mina-māsa*, chief catcher of souls, 'Azrā'īl, 59; *n'ya-kó*, cult of spirits, animism, 104; *n'ya-kó-de*, animist, 104; *n'ya-ma*, divinized spirit, a dangerous force liberated at death, 58, 112; *n'ya-tigi*, head of a spirit cult, 50; *mā-n'ya*, spirit of an ancestor; *mā-n'ya-kó*, cult of ancestors, 54 n.
nyamakhala (S). Woman of the griot caste, 155.
nyamnēdyo, pl. *nyamnēḅe* (Ful). Witch. *nyāmde*, to eat, 118 n.
nyēnybe, sing. *nyenyo* (Ful, Tok). General term for caste groups, 137.
nyiga durbe (K). Kinship, first cousin, marriage, 165 n.
nyiga maləmla (K). Gift marriage to a cleric, 170 n.

ɔba (Y). Chief, 109.
ɔfəm (Te). Person (the ordinary word is *wuni*, pl. *aŋfəm*, people), 58 n.
Ogboni (Y). The *òshugbó* mystery cult, 109.
õgùn (Y). Medicine, the power in the *tira* (amulet); *olõgun*, medicine-man, applied to Muslim *alfa* when functioning as such. Pagan medicine-man = *elegbòge*, 112.
ojiji (Y). Shadow soul, 57 n.
ɔkàn, ɔkã (Y). Corporeal 'soul', normally 'heart', 57 n.
ɔmɛn (Te). Medicine-man, destroys witches, heals and administers swear-medicine, 106 n., 115 n.
oniwāsi (Y). The preacher (*khaṭīb*) of the Friday homily; interpreter, commentator, 72.
ɔser (Te). Witch; *raser*, witchcraft, 118, 190.
ɔ-thupəs (Te). Diviner (pagan); *ɔ-thupas*, divination, 122 n.
owo-idano (Y). Bride-wealth, 168.

pɔrɔ (W. Guinea). A widespread mystery cult, 109 and n., 140.
Pulɔ, pl. *Fulḅē*. See 11 n. and Index under Fulbe.

qāḍī (Ar). Judge, 69, 137, 143, 148–53, 174, 186, 192, 194, 205, 207.
Qādiriyya. Ṣūfī order associated with the name of 'Abd al-Qādir al-Jīlānī, 90 n., 91, 92, 93, 94–96, 98, 99, 124.
qibla (Ar). The 'direction' in which prayer should be performed, 178, 179, 180.
qubba (Ar). Tomb, 90.

ra-gbenle (Te). A mystery society, 109 n.
raj'a (Ar). A revocable repudiation, 175 n.
Rajab (Ar). Seventh month of the Islamic year, 76 n., 78, 159.

rakʿa (Ar). 'A bowing', the various ritual actions and recitations constituting one act of worship, 73, 79, 123.

rakiyar wata (H). 'Escorting the moon', the ceremony for bidding the spirits good-bye before their departure into the bowels of the earth during Ramaḍān, 111 n.

Ramaḍān (Ar). The ninth month of the Islamic year, 31, 72, 74, 76, 78–79, 97, 110 n., 169, 171.

ran kiyāma (H). Day of Resurrection, 60.

ran suna (H). The eighth-day naming, 157.

rāy (H). Life, 59–60.

ráyi, láyí (N). Life, the spirit of man, 56–57, 61, 182.

ribāṭ (Ar). Frontier post manned by pious men, later equivalent to *zāwiya*, 100.

ridda (Ar). Apostasy, 48.

rijiyan rāy (H). 'The Well of Life', place of the departed spirits, 60.

riḳi (H). 'Support', charms to protect compound, 39.

rikiḍaddu (H). Men who are metamorphosed into certain animals; *ya riḳida kura*, he changed into a hyena, 117.

rindingol (Ful). Reading, 81, 161.

riwāq (Ar). A portico in a mosque set aside for groups of students, 85.

Rog (Serer). God, 54 n.

rógóngà (N). A cleric who uses a stone called *rógógi* for harmful magic, 117.

rūḥ (Ar). Vitalizing spiritual principle, 61.

ruqya (Ar). Legitimate magic, 116.

saa or *saɛi* (Me from Ar *ṣadaqa*). Offering, sacrifice, 105; *mba bɔi*, red rice sacrifice; *mba jaa*, rice sacrifice; *safanda jaa*, first sacrifice for the dead after the funeral.

sabḥala (Ar). Repetition of the phrase *subḥān Allāh*, 'Praise is due to God alone', 96.

sābon garī (H). 'New town', outside the old walled *birnis*, esp. quarters inhabited by southerners, 45, 215.

sadaka (H). Voluntary alms (Ar *ṣadaqa*), 77, 182 n.

sāḍaka (H). Slave wife (*sa*, place in, *ḍaka*, house), 168.

sadāki (H). Marriage-money, 167, 169, 175 (Ar *ṣadāq*).

ṣadāq (Ar). The Islamic marriage payment by the husband to the wife which becomes her legal property, and, in Africa, is part of the bride-price, 165–8, 170–5 *passim*.

ṣadaqa (Ar). Voluntary alms, offering, 34, 39, 44 n., 74–75, 171, 172 n., 180, 182, 184, 189, 190.

sa-d'-ya (M). 'Vivification of the dead (*sa*)', name given to one conceived or born at the time of the death of a member of the family; name given as synonym of ʿAlī because of the belief in the resurrection of ʿAlī, son-in-law of the Prophet, 157.

safanda jaa (Me). Rice-sacrifice, 181.

sāḥil (Ar). Shore, borderland between desert and sown, 2.

saʿīr (Ar). One of the seven hells, 58.

sakkēḅe, sing. *sakke* (Ful, Tok). Leather-workers, 137.

salanke (H). The *imām* who officiates at the *ʿīd* prayers in the Hausa state of Abuja, 141.

ṣalāt (Ar). Ritual prayer, 71, 72, 81, 100.

ṣalāt ʿalā 'n-nabī (Ar), 172, 226; see *taṣliya*.

ṣalāt al-ʿīd (Ar). The festival prayer, 79.

ṣalāt al-jumʿa (Ar). The prayer of assembly, the Friday prayer, 73.

sali, seli (M), *syeri* (Dy), fr. Ar *ṣallā*. Ritual prayer, religious festival, 72; *sali-bolõ*, *syeri-bolõ*, open-air prayer square, 71, 72; *sali-gyi mina*, perform the ritual ablutions; *sali-ba*, 'great prayer', 10 dhū 'l-ḥijja, 80 n.; *sali-bar̃a*, 'pray-er', i.e. Muslim, 14 n.; *sali-gyi*, ablutions; *sali-de*, 'child of prayer', i.e. newly circumcised, 162 n.

ṣallā (Ar). To accomplish the ritual prayer (*ṣalāt*), 71, 72.

salla (H). Ritual prayer, often the festival prayer, 50, 71, 79 n., 111 n.; *mai-kiran-salla*, caller-to-prayer, muezzin, 71 n.; *ḳaramar salla*, the lesser festival, 79 n.; *salla azumi*, the festival of the fast, 79 n.; *salla layya* or *lāhiya*, the Great Feast, 80 n.; *babbar salla*, the Great Feast, 80 n.

samā' (Ar). The sky, 227 n.

sàmi-ko (N). The great filter, the sky, 227 n.

sammu (H). Poison (Ar *simm*), magic to harm, 117.

sa-nan (M), a variety of tamarind tree, 49.

Ṣanhāja, Arab corruption of Berb. *azenūg*, pl. *idzāgen* (cf. *Ibn Khaldūn*, ed. de Slane, i. 194). General term for a great group of west Sahara Berbers, 10 n.

Sanūsiyya Ṭarīqa, 91, 100–1.

saraka (M), *sarakhe* (Susu), *sathka* (Te), *saa* (Me), der. from Ar *ṣadaqa*. Protective medicine placed on houses or compounds, offering, sacrifice, 105, 106 n., 156.

sarauni, sarauniya (H). Priestess of a *bōri* cult (also *sarākī* and *uwar girka*), 111.

sarki, pl. *sarākuna* (H). Chief, headman, 73, 144 n.; *sarkin tsāfi*, *sarkin arna*, priest of the pagan rites, 38; *sarkin musulmi* = Ar *amīr al-mu'minīn*, 98; *sarkin māyū*, chief of the witches, 119; *sarkin bōri*, chief of the cult, 144 n.

sauka (H). To dismount (of a *bōri* spirit), 111.

ṣawm (Ar). Fast, 78.

sebe, sewe, sefe (M). The general term in western Sudan and Guinea for a written charm, 114, 115.

sebe-tu-la (M). Cleric who ingurgitates holy water and spits on the patient, 115.
seli (Me). To pray (Ar *sallā*), 35 n.
səm (Te). Sacred; *ra-səm*, holiness, *mə-səm*, taboo; *dɛr-ɔ-məsəm*, sacred place; *ŋləsər mə-səm*, to violate ceremonial law, 67.
seriñ (W). Cleric; *seriñ-dāra*, schoolmaster, 70, 130 n., 136 n.
Sha'bān (Ar). Eighth month of the Islamic year, 76 n., 78.
shābūr, *shābīr* (N. Afr. Ar). Spur, 84.
Shādhiliyya ṭarīqa, 91, 96–97, 98.
shahāda (Ar). The confession of faith, 42, 49, 53, 146, 178, 226.
shaikh (Ar). Elder, head of tribe, religious leader, &c. In Sudanese languages *shīhu*, *sēku*, *sēhu*. In Mauritania (with pl. *ash-yākh*) 'religious leader', whilst *shīkh*, pl. *shyūkh*, 'political leader', 84, 93, 98, 188.
Shēhu (Ar *shaikh*). Title of the ruler of Bornu, Masina, &c., 145 n.
Shaiṭān. Chief of the evil spirits, 53 n.
shanchi (H). A contest of the Māguzāwa, 39 n.
shan kabēwa (H). 'Pumpkin festival', a rite of *bōri* devotees before the pumpkin harvest (*sha*, to partake of fruit), 111.
sharī'a (Ar). The canon law of Islam, 125, 146, 147 n., 148–9, 182, 205, 207, 220. In African languages it generally means 'judgement', Hausa *ya yanke sharī'a*, 'he passed sentence'.
sharīf, pl. *shurafā'* (Ar). One who claims descent from the Prophet, 131 n., 136.
shibr (Ar). Span, 193 n.
shika (H). Annul (a marriage), 175; *skikan batta*, the triple repudiation, 175 n.; *shikan sunna* or *s. raja'i*, revocable repudiation, 175 n.
Shinqīṭ, Fr. *Chinguetti*, Azer *Si-n-gede*. A *zāwiya* centre (founded A.D. 1262) in the Sāqiyat al-Ḥamrā' region of Mauritania. The name was extended by the Arab world to the whole of western Moorish Sahara, 85 n., 97.
Shinqīṭī, pl. *Shanāqṭā*, an inhabitant of Shinqīṭ, a Moor of Mauritania, 85 n.
sī (*sonni* in *T. as-Sūdān* and Leo Africanus). Dynastic title of rulers of Songhay from 1275 to 1493; 139.
sibḥa (Ar). Rosary, 121 n.
sigi (Ful). Pronunciation and spelling, 81.
siḥr (Ar). Sorcery, 116.
silāmi (M). Islam; *silāmi ya kó*, the Islamic cult, 104; *silāmi ya kó de*, a Muslim, 104; *silāmi ya keme*, a hundred, 197 n.; *silāmi ya lāda*, Islamic law, 147.
sī-ra-lāda (M). 'Custom of the family', customary law as regulating free men, 147.
ṣirāṭ (Ar). In Islamic tradition a bridge across the eternal fire, 57, 80.
siri (M). Tie, link, 53 n., 114; *lā siri*, *da siri*, link with spirits, ritual, cult, offering, 53 n.; *lā* (*da*) *siri dugu*, genii loci, 102, 103, 106; *lā siri folo*, fourth month of solar year, Rabī' II of Islamic year, 76 n.; *lā siri lā ba*, sixth month of solar year; Jumādā II of Islamic year, 76 n.; *lā siri tigi*, religious chief of a village, master of the land.
sirruyaŋke, pl. *sirruyaŋkoɓe* (Tok). Magician-diviner, versed in occult sciences who writes *hātumēre sirru*, secret amulets, 121.
siyāsa (Ar). Policy. Justice rendered at his own discretion by a Muslim ruler, parallel to customary and Islamic law, a recognized restriction of the competence of the *qāḍīs* by those who appoint them to their office, 147.
So. Mythical name for the former inhabitants of the Chad region, 16, 190 n., 145 n., 199 n.
so, *su* (M). Family (total); *so-tigi*, family-head, 127, 130.
sodāḍo, pl. *sodāɓe* (Ful). Trade-slaves, 134 n.
soggē (Ful). Dowry, 166 n.
Sòkó (N). Sky, undifferentiated spirit, God, 51, 227–8.
Sòkóbachi (N). Worshippers of *Sòkó*, 227.
so-ni (M). Sacrifice, libation, 75; *sonoŋke*, sacrificer, a Muslim by name only, which in the Gambia has been confused with *Sōniŋke*, the Sarakole.
soṙo, *soġo* (M). Sacrifice (bloody), 74–75.
sōssē (S). A porridge of ground millet and milk prepared for the mourning feast as alms, 181.
sū or *sō* (M). Offering, sacrifice, libation, 74–75; *sū-ni-ke-baġa*, *sōro-ŋge*, *sōno-ŋke*, a sacrificer, 75.
sū-baṙa (M). Witch, 118.
subalɓe, sing. *tyubballo* (Ful). A free group of fishers assimilated among the Fulbe as members of the upper class (*rimɓe*) but inferior to Fulɓe proper, 15.
sūdān, s. *sūdānī* (Ar). Blacks, 1, 10, 31, 85 n.
sukunya, pl. *-ābe* (S, Tok). Witch, 61, 118.
sule (Song). Slave of second generation, 134 n.
sule-hule (Song). Slave of third generation, 134 n.
sulmiya (H). To fall off, apostatize, 85.
sumburuku (Song), Ar *baraka*, pronouncing formula of blessing with spitting, 157.
sūna (H). A name; *sūnan fito*, the real name of a person, 157 n.; *sūnan wāsā*, the known or nick-name, 157 n.; *ran sūna*, naming day, 157.

suṅkālo (M). 'Moon of deprivation', ninth month of the solar year = Ramaḍān, 75, 76 n., 78 n.

sunna (Ar). The model behaviour of the Prophet, one of the foundations of Islamic jurisprudence, hence employed for 'the custom of Muslims', 154, 162.

sunna hindē (Ful). The animal sacrifice (*'aqīqa*) at the naming ceremony, 156 n.

sunnigol or *sugol* (Ful). Circumcision, 162.

sūq (Ar). Market, 195.

sūra (Ar). Chapter of the Qur'ān, 81, 123, 151, 158, 161.

surkullē (H). Spell-casting by means of incantation, 55.

tabaskē, *tafaskē*, *afisko* (W. Sudan), *aid-n-tfaska* (south Moroccan Berber); Muslim Great Festival (*al-'īd al-kabīr*); *Tifeski* (Mauritania) 'spring' (*πάσχα*), 76, 80 n., 110 n.

tafsīr (Ar). Explanation, commentary, 70, 81–82.

Tafsīr al-Jalālain (Ar). The commentary of the two Jalāls, al-Maḥallī and as-Suyūṭī, 78, 79 n.

tāggalt (Tam). Bride-price, 168.

taghelmūzt (Tam). Mouth-muffler, 69.

taḥlīl (Ar). 'Legalization', the arranged temporary marriage of a woman triply-divorced to enable her to remarry her former husband, 175 n.

tahlīl (Ar). Repetition (*dhikr*) of the phrase, *lā ilāha illā 'llāh*, 'there is no god but God', 96, 100.

takaba (H). Widow's mourning period, 183.

takarda (H), *takàda* (N). Paper; *būḍe takarda* (H), opening of the book (of the year), 77 n.; *takàda eyaẓe* (N), 'the Book of the Years', 77; *maga takarda* (H), a chief's scribe, 77 n., 141.

takbīr (Ar). The expression *Allāhu akbar*, 'God is most great', 179.

takhmīs (Ar). An expansion of a poem by adding three couplets to the original two, 78.

Takrūr. Arab form for Tokolor state on the Senegal, 13 n.

Takrūrī, pl. *Takārīr* (Ar). West Sudan Negro, 13 n., 85 n.

talaka, pl. *talakāwa* (H), *latqa*, *taleqqi* (Tam.). Poor, the free peasant class, 110, 132–3, 168.

ṭalāq (Ar). Repudiation of the wife by the husband, 174.

ṭālib, pl. *ṭalaba* (Ar). Student, disciple, 93.

Tamāhaqq. Language spoken by the Tuareg, 10.

tamma, *tāmba* (Sudan region). A standard length of cloth = 10 cubits, 192.

tamsīr (Wo, Ful). One learned in Islamic law; Ar *tafsīr* = *mufassir*, commentator, 70, 148 n.

tana, *ntana*, *tne* (M). Taboo, sacred thing, 53 n., 130, 131 n.

tarancis (Te). A dancing society, 109 n.

ta'rīkh (Ar). Chronicle, tribal genealogy, inventory of a *qāḍī*'s clerk, 74 n., 119.

Ta'rīkh al-Fattāsh, 74 n., 88 n., 90 n., 116 n., 119 n., 137 n.

Ta'rīkh as-Sūdān, 90 n., 116 n., 151 n.

Ta'rikh Sokoto, 119, 143 n., 147 n., *see* Index under alḥājj Sa'īd.

ṭarīqa (Ar). A mystical path, Ṣūfī brotherhood, 45, 46, 53, 82, 88–101, 188.

tāriyan wata (H). 'Gathering of the moon', the ceremony of welcoming back the spirits after the Ramaḍān fast, 111 n.

tàsàbi, *tasba* (N). Rosary, divination by the rosary, 120.

tasbīḥ, *tasbiḥa* (Ar). Rosary, 93 n., 120.

tashi (H). Courting, betrothal, 167.

taṣliya (Ar). Calling down blessing on the Prophet with the phrase *ṣallā 'llāh 'alaihi wa sallam*, 96, 100.

taṭlīq (Ar). Judicial divorce, 175.

tawba (Ar). Repentance, 48.

tawḥīd (Ar). Doctrine of the divine unity, 81, 82.

ta'zīr (Ar). A discretionary punishment imposed by a *sharī'a* court, 152.

təmər kabo (Te). Ceremony of rice flour bread on the fortieth day after a death, 181 n.

temezzid (Tam). Mosque, 71 n.

ten'dana or *tegatu* (N.T. of Ghana). The indigenous priest-chief authority, 144 n.

tenga naba (Mole). Village chief, 144 n.

tenga soba (Mole). Master of the land, 144 n.

teŋe (Ful, Tok). Bride-price, 166 n.

tere (M). The nature or character of a person, 58.

tewenjamɛi (M). 'Crossing the water-place', pagan ceremonies on the third or fourth days after death, 57.

thamdɔgɔ (Susu). Sacrifice at the mourning feasts, 181 n.

Tifīnagh. The Libyco-Berber characters employed for writing the Tuareg language, 10, 84.

Tijāniyya. Ṣūfī order founded by Aḥmad b. M. at-Tijānī (1737–1815), 83, 85, 91, 92, 93, 95, 96, 97–100, 124.

Tijānī sīra (M). The Tijānī way, 92 n.

tiku (Ful). Assembly of elders, 150.

tīmōwo (Tok), diviner, pl. *tīmōɓe*; *tīmgal*, divination, 120.

tira (Song, Y). Writing, amulet (*oni tira*, a charm-writing cleric); *tira ferey* (Song). 'Opening the book' (Berb *terē*); Islamic

wońki (Ful). Vital force, 60–61.
wōriwò (N), *wowo, wauwau* (H). The festival on the eve of New Year, 77; *etswa wōriwò*, the first month of the year, 77.
woro-so (M). 'Born in the house', household slaves, 134 n.
wuḍū (Ar). Ritual ablutions, 84.

yanka (H). To cut the throat, to sacrifice, 226.
'yan tashe (H). Freedman, 133.
Yā Sīn (Ar). A *sūra* of the Qur'ān especially efficacious in incantation, 116, 117, 178.
yàwǒ (N). Bride; *yàwǒjin*, marriage ceremonies, 167 n., 172 n.
Yer-koy, Iri-koy (Song). 'Our Lord', God, 51.
yesi (Song). The coming year, 77.
yettōdē (Ful). The clan name, also taken by the *rimayḇe* or household slaves, 156 n.
yiji yàwǒ (N). The bride's dowry (*yi*, our; *egi*, child), 167 n.
yiji (Y). The Islamic *ṣadāq*, 168.
yisabi (N from Ar *ḥisāb*). Divination by numbers, 120.
yońki (S). Vital force, 60.

zakāt (Ar). Legal alms, 74, 77, 133, 146–7, 184, 231.
Zanāgā, Znāga, Idnāgen (Berb). Tributaries of Berber origin among Moors, 136.
zār. A possession cult in Nilotic Sudan, Egypt, and Abyssinia, 110 n.
zaure (H). Entrance-hut to a compound, 39, 132, 157, 169.
zawāl (Ar). Declension of the sun, 73 n.
zāwī, plur. *zwāyā* (Moorish Ar), cleric, 10, 69, 135.
zāwiya, pl. *zawāya* (Ar). Cell, retreat, multi-function convent, 93, 94, 95, 96, 97, 100, 101.
zwāyat ash-shams, independent Moorish tribes, 135.
zwāyat aẓ-ẓull, tribes needing shade or protection, 135.
ẓè (N). To change, metamorphose, 117 n.; *a ẓe Nupe*, people assimilated into the Nupe, 119; *bàẓè*, conversion; *ebàẓè*, a convert; *màkuṇduṇnu ẓèchi*, people who change into hyaenas, 117 n.
ẓigi (N). A priest, 105, 189 n.
ẓihār (Ar). A form of wife repudiation (= *ḥarām*), 174.
ziyāra (Ar). Visitation rites at tombs of saints, 89.

INDEX